2004

Regionalism, Multilateralism and Economic Integration

The value of the studies and analysis in this book is that it moves the debate forward into new territory: on the basis of specific case studies of six regional agreements, it examines how they each deal with a range of regulatory issues and how this relates to WTO rules. A thought provoking read for anyone with an interest in the subject of regionalism and its relationship to multilateralism.

Roderick Abbott, *Deputy Director General, World Trade Organization*

Sampson and Woolcock provide one of the most comprehensive and accurate reviews of regulatory policy in the Regional Trade Agreements completed to date. Their book is clear, concise and thought provoking, reflecting both high academic standards as well as concrete practitioner insight.

Pierre Defraigne, *Deputy Director General, DG Trade, European Commission.*

Regional and bilateral trade agreements are an increasingly important feature of international trading arrangements. This book makes a valuable contribution to the study of the deeper integration embodied in such agreements, and of the challenges and opportunities arising for the multilateral trading system.

Ken Heydon, *Deputy Director, Trade Directorate, OECD*

Free Trade Agreements may carry similar titles but they are not all alike. Indeed, particularly when they deal with behind-the-border policies, "the devil", as the saying goes, "lies in the details". The authors of this well-integrated study advance our appreciation of these details by presenting a meticulous and comprehensive analysis of recent Regional Trade Agreements. The volume will be valuable for all who are interested in the trading system.

Professor Robert Z Lawrence. *Albert L William Professor of International Trade and Investment, Harvard University and Senior Fellow, Institute for International Economics.*

Regionalism, multilateralism and economic integration: The recent experience

Edited by Gary P. Sampson and Stephen Woolcock

United Nations University Press

TOKYO · NEW YORK · PARIS

United Nations University Press
The United Nations University, 53-70, Jingumae 5-chome,
Shibuya-ku, Tokyo 150-8925, Japan
Tel: +81-3-3499-2811   Fax: +81-3-3406-7345
E-mail: sales@hq.unu.edu   (general enquiries): press@hq.unu.edu
http://www.unu.edu

United Nations University Office in North America
2 United Nations Plaza, Room DC2-2062, New York, NY 10017, USA
Tel: +1-212-963-6387   Fax: +1-212-371-9454
E-mail: unuona@ony.unu.edu

United Nations University Press is the publishing division of the United Nations University.

Cover design by Joyce C. Weston
Photograph by Pacific Press Service

Printed in Hong Kong

UNUP-1083
ISBN 92-808-1083-9

Library of Congress Cataloging-in-Publication Data

Regionalism, multilateralism, and economic integration : the recent experience / edited by Gary P. Sampson and Stephen Woolcock.
    p.   cm.
Includes bibliographical references and index.
   ISBN 92-808-1083-9
   1. International economic integration. 2. Regionalism. 3. Free trade.
4. Foreign trade regulation. 5. Commercial treaties. 6. International economic relations. I. Sampson, Gary P. II. Woolcock, Stephen.
HF1418.5 .R4438 2003
382'.9—dc21   2003010733

Contents

Part III Horizontal case studies

Part IV Conclusions

Figures

Tables

Abbreviations

AFTA	ASEAN Free Trade Area
APC	Asia, Pacific, Caribbean
APEC	Asia-Pacific Economic Cooperation
ASEAN	Association of South East Asian Nations
BITs	bilateral investment treaties
CCAEC	Chile–Canada Agreement on Environmental Cooperation
CCALC	Chile–Canada Agreement on Labour Cooperation
CCFTA	Chile–Canada Free Trade Agreement
CEECs	Central and East European countries
CEFTA	Central European Free Trade Agreement
CEP	Closer Economic Partnership
CER	Australia–New Zealand Closer Economic Relations Agreement
CGE	computable general equilibrium
COFEMER	Comisión Federal de Mejora Regulatoria [Federal Regulatory Improvement Commission]
Comecon	Council for Mutual Economic Assistance
CUSFTA	Canada–US Free Trade Area
DSM	dispute settlement mechanism
DSU	Dispute Settlement Understanding
EA	Europe Agreement
EC	European Communities
EEA	European Economic Area

EEC	European Economic Community
EFTA	European Free Trade Association
EMA	Euro-Mediterranean Association Agreement
EMP	Euro-Mediterranean Partnership
EMU	European monetary union
EU	European Union
FAO	Food and Agriculture Organization of the United Nations
FDI	foreign direct investment
FSA	Financial Services Agreement
FTA	free trade agreement/area
FTAA	Free Trade Area of the Americas
GATS	General Agreement on Trade in Services
GATT	General Agreement on Tariffs and Trade
GDP	gross domestic product
GM	genetically modified
GPA	Government Procurement Agreement
GSP	Generalized System of Preferences
ILO	International Labour Organization
IMF	International Monetary Fund
MAI	Multilateral Agreement on Investment
MENA	Middle Eastern and North African
Mercosur	Southern Common Market
MFN	most favoured nation
MNC	multinational corporation
MNE	multinational enterprise
MPC	Mediterranean Partner Country
MRA	mutual recognition agreement
MTA	multilateral trade agreement
NAAEC	North American Agreement on Environmental Cooperation
NAFTA	North American Free Trade Agreement/New Zealand Australia Free Trade Agreement
NEPAD	New Economic Partnership for Development in Africa
NGO	non-governmental organization
NT	national treatment
ODA	overseas development aid
OECD	Organisation for Economic Co-operation and Development
PPMs	process and production methods
PTA	preferential trade agreement
RTA	regional trade agreement
SPS	sanitary and phytosanitary measures
TBTs	technical barriers to trade

TEC	Trade and Economic Cooperation (Canada–New Zealand)
TPRM	Trade Policy Review Mechanism
TRIMs	Trade-Related Investment Measures
TRIPS	Trade-Related Aspects of Intellectual Property Rights
TTMRA	Trans-Tasman Mutual Recognition Arrangement
UNCTAD	United Nations Conference on Trade and Development
USTR	United States Trade Representative
WHO	World Health Organization
WTO	World Trade Organization

Foreword

In the early 1990s, the world witnessed a growth in regional trade agreements unprecedented in history. This proliferation was rationalized at the time in terms of widespread concern relating to the potential failure of the Uruguay Round of multilateral trade negotiations and the ensuing weakness – if not collapse – of the rules-based multilateral trading system. Countries were installing their own safety nets on a regional basis should the multilateral system disintegrate.

One decade on – and notwithstanding both the success of the Uruguay Round and the launching of the Doha Development Round of multilateral negotiations – the exponential growth of regional trading arrangements continues. This new burst of growth is characterized by a number of peculiarities that set it apart from traditional agreements based on the agreed reduction of border restrictions for states located in the same part of the world. Many agreements now reach deep into the regulatory structures of the parties concerned, addressing, *inter alia*, regulations relating to competition policy, investment, harmonization of standards, the environment and labour standards. In addition, some agreements are no longer regional in character and span continents to build new agreements or create fusions between existing ones.

These and other peculiarities of the recently negotiated regional trade agreements raise crucial questions with respect to current and future international economic relations. What motivations lie behind the negotiation of these agreements, and is a pattern emerging in their nature and content? Do they have implications for the multilateral treading system and, if so, are these positive or negative? What do the new agreements mean for developing countries looking to expanded trade as a vehicle to promote sustainable growth? Are there best practices for parties to follow in negotiating such agreements?

All these questions can be addressed only by looking at the characteristics of recent regional agreements and examining the motivation for creating them. This is the goal of this Institute of Advanced Studies (IAS) publication – *Regionalism, Multilateralism and Economic Integration: The Recent Experience* – edited by Gary P. Sampson and Stephen Woolcock. It is part of the ongoing research at the IAS enquiring into key issues relating to international economic governance and multilateral diplomacy. My expectation is that this publication will usefully add to our understanding of what is a critical phenomenon from an international economic governance perspective.

A.H. Zakri,
Director,
Institute of Advanced Studies,
United Nations University,
Tokyo

Part I

Setting the scene

1

Introduction

Gary P. Sampson

From the perspective of international economic relations, the years spanning the end of the second millennium and the start of the third are characterized by two developments of major importance. In the space of one decade, the world has witnessed both the successful conclusion of the most ambitious round of multilateral trade negotiations in the history of humankind and the launching of another. At the same time, the world has seen a proliferation of regional trading arrangements unprecedented at any period in history. To say the least, these parallel developments appear to be paradoxical: on the one hand, non-discrimination is the pillar of the multilateral trading system;[1] on the other, all but 2 of the 140-plus members of the World Trade Organization (WTO) are parties to at least one – and some as many as 26 – preferential trading arrangements.[2] By definition, the cornerstone of these regional trading arrangements is preferential treatment for some members of the multilateral trading system, and discrimination for others. Given this apparent anomaly, it is not surprising that the question has been posed of whether regional trading arrangements hinder or contribute to the good functioning of the multilateral trading system.

This question clearly emerged with the surge in the number of regional trading agreements (RTAs) during the Uruguay Round. The phenomenon was rationalized in some quarters on the grounds that there were doubts about whether the negotiations would succeed. In that environment, it was not surprising for countries to create what were perceived as safety nets by forming or joining regional trading groupings. In other words, it could well be that membership in these trading blocs was seen as an insurance against the possible collapse of the Round and the fore-runner of the adoption of inward-looking trade policies in the event of a failed Round. The alternative view was that the growth in regional trad-ing arrangements was taking place for good economic and political rea-sons, which owed much to the past successes of the multilateral system embodied in the General Agreement on Tariffs and Trade (GATT). Parties to the agreements were not only firmly committed to multilateral trade liberalization but prepared to liberalize faster on a regional basis than multilaterally.

Irrespective of the rationalization of the rapid increase in RTAs, the expectation of many was that there would be abatement in the growth in numbers of these arrangements in the event of a successful conclusion to the Uruguay Round.[3] Recent history makes clear that this has certainly not been the case. In fact, regional trade agreements have proliferated at an accelerating pace, launching again the debate about their motivation and effect on the multilateral trading system.

The complexity of this debate has increased as a concomitant devel-opment has been a change in the nature of these trade agreements. In conventional terms, the analysis of the effects of preferential regional trade agreements has been couched in terms of the net trade and welfare effects of the removal of border protection.[4] On this front, empirical studies conducted by the WTO, the World Bank, the Organisation for Economic Co-operation and Development (OECD) and other bodies have all concluded that regionalism has supported the multilateral trad-ing system in the past, and has not in general undermined its influence (WTO Secretariat, 1995).

However, with the progressive liberalization of border protection world-wide, regional trading arrangements have now come to be charac-terized by RTAs that at times extend deep into the regulatory struc-ture of the parties to the agreement. This deepening is considered to occur when these agreements go beyond addressing traditional border measures affecting trade, and extend their reach to the liberalization, elimination and harmonization of trade-impeding regulatory policies. Although the concept of deeper integration is imprecise, it does imply a degree of uniformity in a new approach to regional trade agreements. This has sparked a new interest in not only the motivation for the con-tinuing proliferation of RTAs but also the extent to which they promote deeper integration in the regulatory structures of the countries con-cerned. This interest is further heightened because there may well be profound implications for the multilateral trading system that extend far beyond those of more conventional RTAs.

The intention of this book is to evaluate the impact of a selection of regional agreements on the regulatory structure of the parties to the agreement. It also addresses whether or not recent RTAs have led to increased cooperation and coordination of domestic regulatory policies on a regional basis. More specifically, three central questions are addressed.

1. What is the impact of regional agreements in those non-border areas of regulation that have most recently become the subject of trade agreements?
2. How do the approaches to regulatory barriers differ between regions and, in particular, is there a form of "regulatory regionalism" where different approaches compete (such as those of the European Union and the United States).
3. Are regional trade agreements competing with or complementing multilateral attempts to remove regulatory barriers to trade?

To address these questions, the following chapters analyse six regional trade agreements that are very different in their coverage and objectives. These agreements are the Association Agreement between the European Union (EU) and Poland, the Euro-Mediterranean Association Agreement between the European Union and Tunisia, the North American Free Trade Agreement, the European Union–Mexico Agreement, the Chile–Canada Free Trade Agreement and the Closer Economic Relations (CER) Agreement between Australia and New Zealand. In these case studies, special attention has been paid to six areas in which regulatory measures may have an important impact on trade flows: technical barriers to trade, food safety, environmental labelling, public procurement, services and investment. Two chapters also present the results of case studies conducted across different regional trade agreements to determine similarities and differences in the areas of trade in services and of food and environmental standards and labelling.

The proliferation of regional trade agreements

Because the objective of granting preferences to other trading partners is a clear violation of the non-discrimination principle of the multilateral trading system, all regional trade agreements involving WTO members are to be notified to the WTO and examined. The key GATT 1994 Article establishing the rules and procedures for the examination of regional preferential trading arrangements is Article XXIV, entitled "Territorial Application – Frontier Traffic – Customs Unions and Free Trade Areas". The WTO rules on regional agreements are designed to minimize the possibility that non-parties are adversely affected by the creation of the regional arrangement and that the arrangements themselves do not become narrow and discriminatory trading entities. Article XXIV of GATT 1994 spells out the guiding principles for RTAs, both customs unions and free trade areas for trade in goods. Free trade areas are to facilitate trade between the parties and not to "raise barriers to the trade" of other WTO members. Further, customs duties and other restrictive regulations of commerce are to be eliminated with respect to "substantially" all trade between parties to the agreement. The obligations for a free trade area and for a customs union are basically the same, except that for the latter "substantially the same duties and other regulations of commerce" must be applied by each member of the union.

As far as developing countries are concerned, the relevant provision emerged from the Tokyo Round and is commonly referred to as the Enabling Clause. This includes a number of provisions permitting WTO members to grant differential and more favourable treatment to developing countries (such as preferences under the Generalized System of Preferences). The Enabling Clause also creates the possibility for developing countries to enter into regional or global arrangements *amongst* less developed members of the WTO for the mutual reduction or elimination of tariffs. They are not subject to the "substantially-all-the-trade requirement" of Article XXIV, but they must "not raise barriers to trade" for WTO members.

The General Agreement on Trade in Services (GATS) includes an Article on Economic Integration (Article V), which establishes rules that broadly parallel those in the GATT 1994 for goods. However, the negotiators saw no need to provide a GATS equivalent to the distinction between customs unions and free trade areas found in Article XXIV; the relevant Article refers only to economic integration agreements for services, rather than customs unions and free trade areas.

Information on these notifications provides a particularly valuable source of information on the incidence of RTAs involving the 140 WTO members.[5] The analysis of these notifications reveals that, compared with previous decades, the proliferation of RTAs during the past 10 years has taken place at an unprecedented rate. Since the conclusion of the Uruguay Round and the establishment of the WTO in January 1995, 125 new RTAs have been notified to the WTO, with an average of 15 notifications per year. During the four and a half decades of the GATT, the annual average was less than 3.

As of March 2002, a total of 172 RTAs actively in force had been notified to the GATT or the WTO. This falls short of the total number of RTAs in existence, because not all WTO members fulfil their WTO obligations by notifying agreements to which they are a party. If RTAs not (or not yet) notified are also taken into account, the total number in force rises to 243.[6] According to the WTO Secretariat, even taking into account the increase in notifications as a result of increased WTO membership, the break-up of the Soviet Union, European integration initiatives and new notification obligations,[7] "it is obvious that the rate of growth of RTAs is continuing unabated" (WTO Secretariat, 2002).

The notifications to the WTO reveal that free trade agreements (FTAs) are the most common form of RTAs: they account for 72 per cent of the total number, while customs unions account for 9 per cent; RTAs with only a partial sectoral coverage account for the remaining 19 per cent. The configuration of RTAs is diverse and becoming increasingly more complex, with overlapping RTAs and networks of RTAs spanning within and across continents at the regional and subregional levels. The simplest configuration is a bilateral agreement between two parties. These account for more than half of all RTAs in force and for almost 60 per cent of those under negotiation. More complex are plurilateral RTAs and agreements in which one of the parties is itself a regional trade agreement; the latter account for 25 per cent of the RTAs currently in force.

It is clear that there now exists a plethora of regional trade agreements in all hemispheres of the world. Although a comprehensive coverage of all recent agreements is not possible, some prominent examples include the following.

The Free-Trade Area of the Americas (FTAA) involves 34 countries and has set a deadline of January 2005 to conclude negotiations to establish a free trade area. Canada concluded a bilateral agreement with Chile in 1997 (see chapter 7) and with Costa Rica in April 2001, and appears to be preparing for a series of FTAs with other countries in Central America. The United States is now negotiating with Chile and Singapore and has concluded an agreement with Jordan. Mercosur (Argentina, Brazil, Paraguay and Uruguay) is engaged in regional trade negotiations with Mexico and neighbouring countries as well as with the European Union. Mexico has concluded its agreement with the European Union (see chapter 4) and along with Chile is considering arrangements with countries in East Asia and South-East Asia.

The European Union is negotiating with the former centrally planned economies of Europe with a view to their acceding to the Union (see chapter 3). It is also conducting negotiations with a number of countries within the context of the European Mediterranean Agreements (see chapter 5). The European Union also has bilateral agreements with Mexico (see chapter 4) and South Africa and less formal links with the Association of South East Asian Nations (ASEAN), and is negotiating with Mercosur as well as engaging in talks on trade agreements with Russia.[8] The Central European countries, the Baltic states and Turkey are also engaged in a number of RTAs. This process has recently also extended to south-eastern Europe, in particular the countries of the former Yugoslavia.

A relatively recent development is the activity that is taking place in the Asian region. The ASEAN Free Trade Area has added four more to its six members, with the inclusion of the transition economies Cambodia, Lao PDR, Myanmar and Vietnam. Regular consultations between ASEAN and the three East Asian countries (ASEAN plus three) may well evolve into some form of regional arrangement in the future. The members of ASEAN have recently agreed to initiate RTA negotiations with China and are exploring the possibility of negotiations with Japan and the Republic of Korea. Australia and New Zealand have been exploring the possibility of an agreement with ASEAN (chapter 8), and have recently ratified a free trade agreement with six Pacific Island countries *en route* to a Pacific free trade area involving 16 counties. Japan has recently initialled an agreement with Singapore, and Australia has been discussing a free trade agreement with Singapore for the past two years. The Asia-Pacific Economic Cooperation (APEC) involves 21 economies from four continents: Asia, Oceania, North and South Americas. Other RTAs have recently been completed within the Asian region (Singapore–New Zealand), as well as between individual countries from across continents (Chile–South Korea). Discussions are also taking place on the possibility of a free trade area between Japan and South Korea (and perhaps China). Australia has been exploring for some time the possibility of a free trade area with the United States, and a new impetus appears to have been given to this initiative. Australia has also recently opened discussions with Thailand with the possibility of an agreement between the two countries in view. There are proposals for a Closer Economic Partnership between New Zealand and Hong Kong, China, and Sri Lanka and Pakistan are discussing the possibility of a free trade agreement.

A number of North African and Middle Eastern countries are involved in the Euro-Mediterranean Partnership. This involves individual (Euro-Med) agreements between the European Union and individual countries (chapter 5), as well as the objective of a free trade area involving a number of countries by 2010.[9] There have been recent efforts to create an Arab Free Trade Area by 2007.[10] The Gulf Cooperation Council countries are working towards the establishment of a common external tariff by 2005, and are engaged in discussions with the European Union on the negotiation of a possible RTA.

There have been some advances by the 20 members of the Common Market for Eastern and Southern Africa (COMESA) to reduce border protection, and the parties to the South African Development Community (SADC) have set an objective of concluding a free trade area by

2004. South Africa has negotiated a free trade area with the European Union, and is exploring the possibility of similar RTAs with a number of other countries. The African Economic Community is an initiative that will group SADC, COMESA, the Economic Community of West African States, the Economic Community of Central African States and the Arab Maghreb Union in an effort to achieve Africa-wide economic integration.

The regional structures pertaining to the Soviet era have been replaced by RTAs among the countries of the former USSR, as well as with their neighbours. In addition to the CIS (Community of Independent States) free trade agreement and a customs union agreement (between the Kyrgyz Republic, the Russian Federation, Belarus, Kazakhstan and Tajikistan), a large number of bilateral agreements have also been concluded. In 2001, Georgia alone notified RTAs with Armenia, Azerbaijan, Kazakhstan, Turkmenistan, Ukraine and the Russian Federation to the WTO.

Characteristics of regional trade agreements

In the academic debate on RTAs in the early 1990s, a popular contention arose that three major trade blocs were emerging and the death of the GATT was nigh. Theories emerged to support the notion that RTAs were obstacles to the multilateral trading order (Bhagwati and Krueger, 1995). Others stressed that the RTAs of the 1990s had different starting points and that the objectives of integration today are fundamentally different from those that were driving the "old" regionalism. It was argued that recent RTAs represent efforts to facilitate their members' participation in the world economy rather than their withdrawal from it. This was thought to differentiate the recent integration initiatives from those among developing countries in the 1950s and 1960s, which extended national import-substituting policies to the regional level. Among other factors, the increasingly dominant view that openness to world trade and investment plays a vital role in a country's development and economic growth contributed to the reorientation of recent regional initiatives (Sachs and Warner, 1995). Furthermore, the setting of regionalism changed as the world moved to freer trade with the commitments undertaken during the Uruguay Round. RTAs potentially complemented rather than competed with the multilateral trading system.

The current situation is that some RTAs are now characterized by deeper integration, where the arrangements between parties go beyond the traditional reduction of tariffs and other border measures to include the liberalization, elimination and harmonization of trade-impeding regulatory policies. Through cooperation and coordination of domestic regulatory policies, regional trade agreements are considered to address what is regarded as one of the most important remaining categories of barriers to trade. Deeper integration agreements shift the focus from liberalizing barriers that lie at the border to the liberalization or harmonization of barriers and policies that exist "within" or "beyond" the border. In this regard, an attractive regulatory environment can be conducive to private sector investment. If RTAs promote domestic regulatory reform, they may well contribute to the creation of such regulatory best practice and thus ease barriers to market access. It is argued that, as countries integrate more deeply on a regional basis, welfare gains may be higher and may exceed the gains from the reduction of tariffs.[11] The elimination of regulatory barriers to trade may also have the potential to produce dynamic welfare effects.[12] Even though authoritative and conclusive results are lacking, the case for the dynamic gains of economic integration has been made by some.

Although the notion of deeper integration is often applied as a generic term to the current phase of regionalism, the studies carried out for the current project reveal that it is an oversimplification to group recent agreements under the same heading in this manner. One reason is that regional trade agreements differ considerably with respect to their objectives, country composition and scope. As far as country composition is concerned, the simplest configuration is a bilateral agreement formed between two parties; a plurilateral agreement engages three or more. There are also agreements in which one (or more) of the parties to an agreement is an RTA itself. Regional agreements composed of two parties account for 98 of the 172 RTAs in force, and for half of all RTAs under negotiation. Plurilateral RTAs account for 16 per cent of all RTAs currently in force, but make up less than 10 per cent of RTAs under negotiation. The percentage of RTAs where at least one party is an RTA itself is about 30 per cent of both the RTAs under negotiation and those in force.[13] According to the WTO Secretariat, the most noteworthy development expected in the next five years is the emergence of a new category, namely RTAs where each party is a distinct RTA itself.[14] None are in force at present, but they account for 9 of the 68 RTAs under negotiation and are composed of both regional and cross-regional initiatives. This new trend reflects the growing consolidation of established regional trading arrangements.

As far as the objectives of the RTAs are concerned, the case studies reveal that the depth and nature of the integration sought are inextricably linked with the motivation for negotiating the agreement in the first place. Depending on the motivation, the desire for and extent of genuinely deeper integration may be of more or less importance. This is in line with the existing literature on regional agreements, which has discussed the various motivations behind the efforts to create regional agreements from the commercial, economic, strategic and political economy perspectives.

For example, the original literature on European integration as well as more recent international relations writers have pointed to the strategic motivations behind regional agreements. Regional free trade agreements have, for example, been motivated by a desire to reconcile previous enemies or to promote economic and political stability in a neighbouring country. Guaranteed market access has clearly also been an important motivation when there has been some uncertainty about the progress in multilateral negotiations in the WTO, or when access to a major market is threatened by domestic regulation. For example, Canada pressed for an FTA with the United States in an effort to reduce the impact of administrative protection on the part of the United States. The threat of trade diversion has also been a factor in the EU–Mexico FTA following the conclusion of NAFTA. Domestic sector interests have been seen as another major driving force behind the negotiation of RTAs when these offer enhanced market access. It has been argued that groups representing sectors with increasing returns to scale will tend to argue in favour of RTAs. Examples include the telecommunications and financial services sectors in the United States in their support for NAFTA. Finally there is also the objective of consolidating reforms or liberalization by ensuring that a government binds its successors. This was the case with Mexico after the shift to liberal policies in the mid-1980s (see chapter 4), and with Poland and other transition economies in more recent times (see chapter 3).

The various motivations behind the formation of the RTAs will certainly shape negotiations. For this reason, the judgement of whether an RTA is "effective" in meeting its objectives will vary. For example, to argue that the Euro-Mediterranean Agreements are not effective in opening markets in non-traditional areas such as services does not necessarily mean that the agreements are not fulfilling important objectives. What emerges from the case study of the Euro-Med Agreements is that, although it would be reasonable for the European Union to introduce harmonization and liberalization provisions similar to those adopted in the process of European integration, this has not been the case. The Euro-Med Agreements are characterized by a gradual and limited coverage of regulatory matters and are much weaker in terms of obligations and slower in terms of implementation than the EU–Poland Agreement, for example. A crucial difference between both sets of agreements is that the Central and East European countries have the incentive of EU membership, which is not the case for the Euro-Med Agreements.

The case study of the EU–Mexico agreement in chapter 4 shows how the European Union was motivated in part by geo-political considerations in response to the apparent success of NAFTA. Market access was also an issue because the establishment of a network of regional trade agreements by Mexico meant that it could potentially function as a stepping-stone into a number of markets in the hemisphere. Another motivation was the European Union's desire to defend long-established economic ties with Mexico, especially at a time when regulatory reform in Mexico promised to make it a more attractive market. Given that the EU share of total Mexican trade shrunk from 10.6 per cent in 1991 to 6.5 in 1999, and given the considerable gap between Mexico's average applied most favoured nation tariff (8.7 per cent) and the preferential NAFTA tariff (less than 2 per cent), there was also a clear concern about trade diversion.

Because NAFTA covered the regulatory issues of services, investment, competition, procurement, technical barriers to trade and sanitary and phytosanitary measures, the European Union also sought to include these in the EU–Mexico FTA. These motivations, along with a desire to deal with long-standing irritants in EU–Mexican trade relations, such as Mexico's labelling schemes, resulted in the EU–Mexico FTA covering an unprecedented 95 per cent of total current trade, and even 62 per cent of agricultural products. But the EU–Mexico FTA also reveals a number of important shortcomings, especially in the areas of regulatory policies.

In many important aspects, the EU–Mercosur and EU–Chile negotiations bear resemblance to the trade negotiations with Mexico (see chapter 4). Besides the political rhetoric and the aim of strengthening the political ties between the two regions, the driving force in the negotiations has been to solidify and expand the existing economic relationships. As in the case of Mexico, the initiative to establish agreements with Mercosur and Chile was, at least in part, a reaction to negotiations in the Western hemisphere – namely, to compete with the United States given the prospective commitments under the FTAA.

In the case of the EU–Poland Agreement, chapter 3 reveals that the intention was to prepare the way for Polish membership of the European Union by deepening cooperation between the European Union and Poland. For Poland, accession to the Union locked Poland into the reforms required for a successful transition from central planning characterized by positive economic, political and security externalities. There was no viable set of national regulatory norms undertaken by Poland and no competing set of regional norms (as with NAFTA in the case of EU–Mexico). Although the WTO offered a potential set of multilateral norms, these were not sufficient to consolidate the initial trade liberalization initiated in Poland in 1990. A political backlash against liberalization led to increases in tariffs and other measures in 1991. Thus, although extensive efforts are needed for Poland to implement the *acquis communautaire*, the benefits of doing so are clear-cut. The possible disadvantages of the *acquis* are real in that the standards it contains may not be appropriate for Poland at the moment and it may not have broad public support on all counts. The institutional reforms required for transition, however, entail putting in place not just laws and regulations but also mechanisms for ensuring effective implementation and the training of officials to carry out these functions in the intended way. In this respect, the EU–Poland Agreement (and other European Agreements) includes procedural mechanisms that go beyond existing trade regimes and have probably contributed significantly to both regulatory reform in Poland and market opening.

As far as NAFTA is concerned, it is noted in chapter 6 that the US perspective was basically driven by three considerations, apart from what could be called the "geo-strategic" aims. First, Mexico, with a market of 90 million consumers, was of commercial interest to some leading US sectors. Second, Mexican poverty levels created problems of immigration for the United States. Third, if the United States did support economic and other reforms in Mexico, the embrace had to be so tight that these reforms would be permanently "locked in". For Mexico, as for Canada, guaranteed access to the US market and a desire to "lock in" regulatory reforms, or at least provide an ultimate set of objectives for reform, were the key motivations.

In the case of the Closer Economic Relations Agreement between Australia and New Zealand, the objectives were to strengthen the broader relationship between the two countries. One of the tools for doing so was developing closer economic relations through the progressive elimination of trade barriers under an agreed timetable (see chapter 9). At the time of signing, the two countries had the highest average tariff protection of all OECD countries. Thus, a motivating force was the prospect of expanded trade in an area of the world where both countries had much in common in terms of culture and history, and where significant gains were to be had through expanded trade. Although the first years of the agreement saw the emphasis being placed on reductions in border protection, since each country was pursuing a policy of unilateral trade liberalization, tariffs and quantitative restrictions on goods were quickly eliminated. Thus, the depth of integration was accelerated to include trade in both goods and services, and a process of harmonizing a range of non-tariff measures on trade in goods and services was commenced.

In the ensuing years, a process of deeper integration was pursued through the adoption of the Uruguay Round agreements and the creation of a number of additional arrangements in the areas of technical barriers to trade, food standards, sanitary and phyto-sanitary measures, customs harmonization and mutual recognition. Although the objective of closer economic relations between the two countries was the driving force, a reduction of trade barriers and a rationalization of industry were commonsense goals to pursue, especially between two countries with a common cultural heritage and history and geographical location.

Policy conclusions

The case studies reveal that the agreements under review differ considerably in scope and level of ambition, with the differences being clearly apparent in the nature of the rights, obligations and processes that they establish. The result is that any assessment of their success or otherwise should be made in the light of the objectives of the agreement concerned. To facilitate this task, a common yardstick has been developed in chapter 2 to assist in reviewing the agreements – namely, whether the commitments undertaken at the regional level go beyond those in the WTO agreements. In so doing, the concept of WTO-plus is developed to indicate whether the individual agreements under review add to or detract from WTO rights and obligations. In fact, as the motivation behind the agreements differs widely, so does the extent to which they result in deeper integration. The answer to the question of whether the "new" regional agreements lead to deeper integration is: it depends.

The concluding chapter (chapter 12) spells out in detail the extent to which the various agreements are WTO-plus or not, but a number of general conclusions can be drawn here. In particular, the case studies reveal that the impact of regional agreements in the new regulatory issues has been broadly consistent with the substantive multilateral principles governing regulatory barriers in the WTO. Indeed, most agreements restate the parties' obligations contained in the various WTO agreements. In this sense, the WTO rules constitute a floor that underpins additional commitments in the regional agreements.

Another conclusion is that there is a more pronounced WTO-plus result in the procedural provisions of agreements than in the extension of substantive obligations. The regional agreements under review generally prove to be effective in improving transparency helping the development of the institutional and regulatory infrastructure; and through cooperation and technical assistance among regulatory authorities. This combination of procedural provisions and reviews contributes to trade facilitation, and thus market opening, in some sectors characterized by regulatory barriers to trade.

It is clear that divergent approaches to dealing with more recent regulatory policy issues have the potential to result in competing spheres of regulatory influence. However, the broad conclusion of the ensuing chapters is in line with earlier studies by the WTO Secretariat, OECO and others: that the RTAs under review have proven to be complementary arrangements when it comes to promoting more open markets in sectors characterized by barriers to trade.

Regional trade agreements are a fact of life: given their characteristics and the number of RTAs currently under negotiation, it is clear that their incidence will grow and their nature will evolve over time. When asking whether regional agreements are building or stumbling blocks, it is timely to ask what role regional agreements can play in this multi-level process and how the international community can ensure that the measures taken on the respective levels are consistent and mutually reinforcing. These detailed case studies of very different regional trade agreements have as their objective taken a step in the direction of answering this important policy question.

Notes

1. Non-discrimination was the pillar of the General Agreement on Tariffs and Trade (GATT) and is now the pillar of the World Trade Organization (WTO). Members of the WTO are obliged to grant unconditionally to each other any benefit, favour, privilege or immunity affecting customs duties, charges, rules and procedures that they give to products originating in or destined for any other country.
2. There are presently 144 governments that constitute the membership of the WTO. In what follows, these will be referred to as the WTO members. Although the 15 countries of the European Union are individual members of the WTO, they are represented at WTO meetings (with the exception of the Budget Committee) by the European Commission, which speaks on behalf of the 15 member states.
3. John Jackson predicted 30 years ago that "as the general incidence of all tariff and other trade barriers declined world wide, assuming the trend of the past twenty years continues, the problem of preferential arrangements may fade away" (Jackson, 1969, p. 623).
4. Customs unions are considered to raise welfare to the extent that they create trade by diverting demand from higher-cost domestic to lower-cost partner products, and to reduce welfare through the diversion of trade from lower-cost foreign to higher-cost partner sources.
5. The WTO Secretariat has usefully analysed these notifications, and in the following paragraphs the figures relating to the number and type of RTAs are drawn from either WTO Secretariat (2002) or WTO Secretariat (1998).

6. Information on notified and non-notified agreements has been gathered by the WTO Secretariat from notifications to the WTO, reports on the operation of agreements and standard formats on information of RTAs submitted to the WTO Committee on Regional Trade Agreements, WTO accession documents, Trade Policy Reviews, and other public sources such as press clippings, websites and publications of other organizations.

7. Prior to the establishment of the WTO, members were not required to notify economic integration areas in services. Of the RTAs identified, 18 (17 free trade areas and 1 customs union) contain commitments on trade in services in addition to tariff concessions on goods.

8. The European Union also has a comprehensive agreement with Norway (and Iceland and Liechtenstein) in the shape of the European Economic Area, which provides an interesting model in deep integration with efforts to retain political autonomy. The European Union has also recently concluded a series of sectoral FTAs with Switzerland and is negotiating a further group.

9. Algeria, Tunisia, Morocco, Egypt, Israel, Jordan, Lebanon, the Palestinian Authority and Syria have negotiated bilateral RTAs based on reciprocal exchange of preferences.

10. Gulf Cooperation Council members (Bahrain, Kuwait, Oman, Qatar, Saudi Arabia and United Arab Emirates) plus Jordan, Tunisia, Egypt, Sudan, Syria, Somalia, Iraq, Palestine, Lebanon, Libya, Morocco and Yemen.

11. The Euro-Med Agreements provide examples of this. See Hoekman and Konan (2000).

12. Most of the quantitative work on FTAs and customs unions has been based on the impact of tariff reductions on trade diversion and trade creation. But tariffs are now of less and less importance, especially with regard to the third phase of regionalism. Quantitative measures based on dynamic growth effects and imperfect competition have also been limited (mainly to work on the European Union) and have not been very conclusive either. Wider survey work on the impact of regional agreements, such as that carried out in the early 1990s by the WTO and OECD, found that regional agreements were not, in general, inimical to multilateralism. But in all this work there was little focus on the impact of regional agreements on the new issues of regulatory barriers to trade.

13. Examples include the RTAs signed between the European Communities and the European Free Trade Area, as well as those signed by the Caribbean Community and Common Market and the Central American Common Market with third parties.

14. Examples include EU–Mercosur and Closer Economic Relations–ASEAN.

REFERENCES

Bhagwati, Jagdish, and Anne O. Krueger (1995), *The Dangerous Drift to Preferential Trade Agreements*, Washington DC: American Enterprise Institute for Public Policy Research.

Hoekman, Bernard, and Denise Konan (2000), "Rents, Red Tape, and Regionalism: Economic Effects of Deeper Integration", in Bernard Hoekman and Jamel Zarrouk (eds.), *Catching up with the Competition: Trade Opportunities and Challenges for Arab Countries*, Ann Arbor: Michigan University Press.

Jackson, John (1969), *World Trade and the Law of GATT*, New York: Bobbs-Merrill.

Sachs, Jeffrey, and Andrew Warner (1995), *Economic Reform and the Process of Global Integration*, Brookings Papers on Economic Activities, Washington DC: Brookings Institution.

WTO Secretariat (1995), *Regionalism and the Multilateral Trading System*, Geneva: WTO, April.

——— (1998), *Inventory of Non-Tariff Provisions in Regional Trade Agreements*, Background Note by the Secretariat, WT/REG/26, 5 May.

——— (2002), *Regional Trade Integration under Transformation*, document presented at a WTO seminar on 26 April 2002, and available at http://www.wto.org.

2

A framework for assessing regional trade agreements: WTO-plus

Stephen Woolcock

Introduction

As the motivation behind the various agreements differs considerably, so does their content in terms of the tools adopted to achieve the objectives. In order to compare the various regional agreements and comment on the depth of trade liberalization involved, as well as the extent to which regional agreements covering regulatory policy areas establish new regional preferences, it is necessary to have some yardstick. In this study we have taken the existing provisions of the World Trade Organization (WTO) as the yardstick in assessing the regional trade agreements (RTAs), and considered whether they are WTO-plus and, if so, in what respects. In order to do this effectively it is also necessary to be aware of the various elements of each agreement. This chapter sets out an analytical framework for a qualitative assessment of regional agreements. In so doing it distinguishes between four broad (and sometimes interdependent) elements of any trade/integration agreement, namely: coverage, procedural and substantive provisions, and implementation and enforcement (see table 2.1).[1]

The analytical framework

Coverage

The RTAs under review could be considered WTO-plus in the application of non-discrimination if their reach extends beyond the obligations undertaken in the WTO. In going beyond the existing multilateral rules, RTAs may create regional preferences if they do not extend non-discrimination (most favoured nation and national treatment) to third countries. Because of the different nature of the agreements under review and the provisions they contain, such assessments must be made on a case-by-case basis.

In the case of services, for example, the General Agreement on Trade in Services (GATS) requires non-discrimination for a number of its obligations (e.g. those relating to transparency) for all services sectors. In the case of others (e.g. market access and national treatment), they are negotiable and applied only (sometimes with extensive reservations) to the sectors that are positively listed in the schedules attached to the agreement. With respect to most favoured nation (MFN) treatment, this is a general obligation from which limited exceptions have been taken. In the case of GATS, a hybrid approach has therefore been adopted with respect to scheduling liberalization commitments. In the schedules, there is a positive listing (or bottom–up approach) for the sectors for which liberalization commitments have been undertaken, and a top–down approach for the reservations applied in the schedule sectors.

With respect to services, the approaches adopted in the regional agreements under review vary quite considerably. Some have a negative-list approach whereas others use a positive-list approach. In the case of the Closer Economic Relations (CER) Agreement between Australia and New Zealand and the North American Free Trade Agreement (NAFTA), for example, the parties have opted for a negative-list approach. The services component of both these agreements pre-dates the completion of GATS, where commitments by the countries concerned are with respect to a positive listing of sectors. Any assessment of whether an RTA is WTO-plus or not in the area of services will therefore require consideration of whether the regional obligations extend beyond those undertaken at the multilateral level.

In the case of investment, WTO provisions are fairly modest with regard to goods, although the provisions on establishment in GATS go some way to including investment under multilateral rules. It is not difficult therefore for regional agreements to be WTO-plus in investment. Perhaps the clearest example of this is NAFTA, which has extensive

Table 2.1. Analytical framework for assessing the impact of regional trade agreements in the field of regulatory policy

Area of potential impact of RTAs	Type of measure	Effect on market opening	Nature of potential regional preference
Coverage			
Non-discrimination: most favoured nation (MFN) and national treatment (NT)	RTAs extend non-discrimination to signatories beyond levels provided for in WTO schedules; for example, wider coverage of the service sector or investment	National treatment means that companies from the region are treated (on the face of it) the same as domestic companies	Third countries do not benefit from the extended NT and MFN
Procedural provisions			
Transparency	Improved notification of regulatory acts or norms/standards through legal requirements in the RTA or closer and more intense regional consultation and peer review	Better information on regulatory norms and their application enables regional suppliers to comply sooner or more easily	Non-regional suppliers will generally benefit from improved information, but third-party authorities/governments will not be involved in consultation
Due process or open decision-making	Provisions requiring the national authorities to give (possibly prior) notification of decisions implementing regulations, and/or provision for representation of interested parties	Promotes the use of best regulatory practice, which will tend to make regulation more predictable and help reduce regulatory capture	Non-regional suppliers benefit from improved regulatory practices, but are not allowed to make representations
Promotion of institutional infrastructure	RTAs provide for technical/financial assistance, cooperation or twinning between regulatory authorities	Improved regulatory capabilities and better-trained staff facilitate better, more rapid regulatory decisions	Non-regional suppliers will tend to benefit from improved regulation, but third-party authorities do not benefit from cooperation

Substantive provisions

Approximation or compatibility	RTAs require regulatory policies or norms to be compatible or they require their approximation/even harmonization	Reduced costs of different standards and conformance assessment	Regional norms may not be based on international norms
Mutual recognition or equivalence	RTAs may provide for full mutual recognition or the recognition of conformance testing and accreditation	With full mutual recognition, goods or services sold in one market can circulate in the others; recognition of conformance testing reduces costs for third-party supplies	Third-party suppliers do not benefit from mutual recognition or reduced costs of conformance assessment
Containing regulatory discretion	Substantive provisions in RTAs such as requiring or interpreting "least trade restrictive measures" that limit the discretionary powers of regulators	Regional suppliers are less likely to face de facto discrimination in the application of regulations	Discretion and thus scope for de facto discrimination retained with regard to third-country suppliers

Implementation and enforcement

Effective reviews and remedies	Provision of more effective and immediate dispute settlement, reviews and remedies	More effective implementation of liberalization or non-discriminatory measures	Reviews and remedies not extended to third parties
Promotion of competitive markets	Provision of "flanking measures" in RTAs that help maintain competitive markets, i.e. competition policies	Controls on abuse of market power by national companies that might otherwise prevent effective market access; for example, after privatization/deregulation or the removal of public protection	Criteria other than competition criteria applied to third-country firms

provisions on investment, including a negative-list basis for coverage that probably exceeds the plurilateral OECD codes in some respects.

Because the WTO Technical Barriers to Trade (TBT) and Sanitary and Phytosanitary (SPS) Agreements require non-discrimination in all sectors, coverage of these agreements is not determined by sector schedules. The WTO agreements do not, however, cover all levels of government in the same fashion. The TBT Agreement, for example, requires central governments only to make "best endeavours" to ensure that sub-federal governments comply with the provisions. So, in assessing the extent to which RTAs are WTO-plus, it will be important to bear in mind their coverage of different levels of government and these different elements of the TBT Agreement. In addition, the TBT Agreement encourages a number of procedures to facilitate trade (e.g. the adoption of international standards). Measures such as these are discussed below.

There is no multilateral WTO agreement on public procurement, although the plurilateral Government Procurement Agreement (GPA) was negotiated under the auspices of the General Agreement on Tariffs and Trade (GATT) and the WTO. The GPA does, however, provide a reference point for assessing the various provisions on public procurement in the RTAs. As with the GATS, the GPA consists of a framework agreement and schedules determining coverage. So it is important to consider these schedules when assessing the degree to which RTAs are more or less extensive than the GPA. Some regional agreements, such as the Europe Agreement between the EU and Poland and other Central and East European countries, include central as well as local or provisional government; others, such as the EU–Mexico RTA, do not. Some RTAs include privatized utilities in the scope of procurement rules, whereas other do not. In public procurement, coverage is also determined by thresholds that seek to restrict coverage to larger, more economically significant public contracts. An RTA may therefore be GPA-plus if it sets lower thresholds and thus covers more public procurement contracts than the GPA does. Also, the GPA being plurilateral in nature, not all members of the WTO have undertaken obligations at the multilateral level. WTO-plus can mean undertaking commitments at the regional level that were not undertaken at the multilateral level.

In addition to assessing whether an RTA is WTO-plus or not, it is helpful to know whether regional preference can result from RTA provisions covering regulatory policies, and if so what kind. This is unlikely to be as straightforward as a preferential tariff. The final column of table 2.1 therefore seeks to identify the nature of a potential regional preference resulting from measures in regulatory policy. In the case of coverage, this regional preference is reasonably straightforward. If regional partners benefit from greater sector or other coverage of national treatment or other substantive provisions, there is a regional preference.

Procedural provisions

In additional to assessing whether RTAs are WTO-plus with regard to extending non-discrimination, it is important to consider the procedural provisions in RTAs. As the following case studies will show, the procedural elements of RTAs are frequently WTO-plus. This model includes three elements of procedural rules: transparency, openness of decision-making, and what has been called the promotion of institutional infrastructure. These are described below and illustrated by examples from the case studies.

Transparency

Transparency in national policy measures has long been recognized as an important first step in any efforts to make markets more open. As a result, all the main WTO agreements dealing with regulatory policy include transparency requirements. Likewise, all regional agreements include transparency measures.[2]

Transparency provisions require, at a minimum, that all statutory measures affecting the relevant sectors of the economy are notified. It is standard practice to include a requirement on notification of statutory measures in trade agreements, but some provide for notification when the legislation is adopted (such as GATS) and some require prior notification of any legislation (such as in the TBT Agreement, NAFTA or the EU provisions on services). Prior notification provides an opportunity for the responsible authorities in a trading partner to make representations on the proposed measure. In some instances this may trigger efforts to adopt a joint approach. This is, for example, the case with notifications of technical regulations in the CER and in the European Union itself. In other words, if notification results in regional partners disputing the need for regulation or regulation in the form proposed, it may lead to common regulatory norms being developed. As far as the market impact of prior notification is concerned, it provides advance warning to foreign suppliers to modify their product or service in order to conform with the new provision. The absence of prior notification can provide domestic suppliers with an advantage because foreign suppliers may not be able to comply with the new provisions from day one. Most WTO agreements require the notification of new statutes, but these have seldom been very effective, at least to date. For example, the TBT Agreement requires notification to the WTO Secretariat of new mandatory regulations, but not all WTO members have complied with this.

Although statutory instruments generally set out the objectives of regulatory policy, much of the day-to-day implementation of policy takes the form of decrees, executive orders or guidelines from regulatory agencies, administrative guidance from ministries, or judicial or arbitral decisions. For effective transparency in regulatory policies it is therefore necessary to include these subsidiary instruments. Often a precedent set in arbitration or in the form of guidelines from a regulatory agency will shape market access. The specific conditions concerning market access will often be decided by regulatory agencies or individual departments. For example, the conditions for interconnection to telecommunications networks are laid down by the relevant regulatory agencies. The GATS agreement on basic telecommunications therefore requires notification of such conditions.

In public procurement, agreements aimed at liberalization of procurement place great store by transparency measures. Indeed, current discussions on a wider multilateral version of the plurilateral GPA are centred on enhancing the transparency of public procurement. Calls for tender for public contracts are issued by a range of public bodies, with literally thousands of calls for tender being issued every day. For foreign tenderers to have any chance of competing, it is therefore essential to have transparency with respect to individual contracts. Further, close links between domestic suppliers and regulators can result in the exclusion of foreign suppliers from markets. Generally speaking, one would expect that the more immediate nature of RTAs would make them more effective than the more remote WTO in enhancing transparency with regard to such subsidiary instruments.

Another area in which subsidiary bodies play an important role in the case studies considered in this volume is that of technical standards. These are generally developed and promulgated by private standards-making bodies. The WTO Agreement on TBTs does not cover such bodies, except in the form of a voluntary Code of Conduct, which standards-making bodies are signing on to, albeit rather slowly. This Code includes provisions on transparency or notification of standards developed by national standards-making bodies, but it does not benefit from the force of a binding agreement. Some regional agreements include more effective notification provisions in their systems of dealing with technical standards.

Regional preferences in the provision of information are unusual. In almost all cases information provided by national or regional bodies is made generally available to third parties. This is especially the case for statutory measures when it comes to the day-to-day activities of regulatory agencies or procurement entities, information flows may well be more effective in the smaller regional setting. The introduction of electronic means of disseminating information has, however, facilitated more or less immediate dissemination of information around the world. This is actively promoted for applications such as calls for tender for public contracts. Regional preference is unlikely in this field but, if it occurred, it would arise when information supplied to regional suppliers is not provided to third-country suppliers.

Openness in decision-making

Openness in decision-making is a further important aspect of transparency because it provides an opportunity for all those affected by regulatory policy to comment on the decision of a regulatory agency. This clearly requires prior notification. Openness in decision-making may also require that the regulatory agency give consideration to the views of market participants (including foreign suppliers, consumers and other civil society non-governmental organizations). Procedures on consultation within trade or integration agreements may involve a number of stages: for example, prior consultation with recognized associations in sectors likely to be affected, circulation of information to a broader set of constituencies, followed by invitations to file claims or objections to what is going on. Such structured procedures are quasi-judicial in nature. Procedural transparency can promote best practice by ensuring that the experience of all market participants is included in any decision. Information from foreign suppliers may also help correct the usual information bias in favour of domestic suppliers and hence improve decision-making (OECD, 1998, p. 315). Open decision-making can also help shine the light of scrutiny into those corners in which regulatory capture might otherwise go unnoticed.

Open decision-making and/or due process can therefore help to ensure regulatory best practice, which is likely to facilitate trade and investment, but not at the expense of legitimate domestic policy objectives. It can contribute to a more predictable regulatory environment, because decisions of regulators are based on clear criteria and precedent. Predictability for investors is essential, especially given the long-term nature of many investment decisions, and so open decision-making can promote investment and trade.

As with the provision of information, regional preferences are unusual in this area. Some countries or regions may have different practices with regard to access to decision-making. For example, the practice in the United States tends to be to provide for access for all interests to regulators, including foreign companies. This is not generally the practice in Europe, however; at least there are no statutory or other guidelines requiring such consultation. Provision within a regional agreement that grants the right to make submissions to national regulators to regional suppliers but not to third-country interests might be seen as a form of preference. Such preferences are likely to be of considerable significance in certain clearly limited cases, such as important decisions on network technology that affect market access, but do not emerge as general problems in the case studies.

Institutional infrastructure

All countries need to have adequate institutional infrastructure (e.g. competent and perhaps independent regulatory agencies) if regulatory reform and thus regulatory barriers are to be tackled effectively. Effective transparency and implementation are unlikely to be achieved unless there is an adequate institutional framework. One example of how institutions are needed to facilitate market opening can be found in conformance assessment in the area of TBTs and SPS. If there is no effective institutional infrastructure in conformance assessment, it is unlikely that regulators in importing countries will recognize test results carried out in the exporting country. Confidence in the standards of testing laboratories is especially important when the aim is to introduce mutual recognition of conformance assessment.

As the case of Poland illustrates in this volume, best practice in public procurement policies cannot occur unless the staff responsible for making decisions are adequately trained. Institutional infrastructure is also important in the sense that independent regulatory agencies can facilitate best practice in regulatory policy and reduce the risk of regulatory capture. Without such institutions, regulatory decisions will be taken by sponsoring ministries of specific industries, which increases the likelihood that regulatory policies will de facto favour local suppliers. But professional staff and resources are needed for independent regulatory agencies to function effectively. If RTAs contribute to promoting the establishment of suitable domestic institutional infrastructure, they could be said to be going beyond the provisions of the WTO in a procedural sense, since the WTO, given the number of members, cannot do much in this regard. Most regional agreements include some form of cooperation or assistance and many have extensive networks of committees and other links. RTAs may promote institutional infrastructure in lesser developed members through financial assistance, cooperation between regulatory agencies in the signatory countries, or twinning of regulatory agencies.

As with the other procedural topics in this framework, such cooperation seldom creates a regional preference of any significance. If better resourced, more professional regulatory agencies result from regional cooperation, this is likely to benefit third-country producers as much as regional suppliers. One way in which regional cooperation may have an impact on third parties is that it may consolidate regional regulatory norms or practices. In terms of market access, this is not necessarily an issue, since the beneficial effects discussed above could well exceed any disadvantage of having a regional norm that is distinct from that of an exporting country. Indeed, replacing a set of national regulatory norms with a regional norm is likely to facilitate market access for third-country suppliers. However, cooperation might contribute to regulatory regionalism, in which different regions develop distinct regulatory norms. The case in point is food safety, which is discussed in chapter 9.

Substantive provisions

Compatibility/approximation

Regional agreements can enhance market access by promoting approximation or compatibility of national regulations, standards or conformance assessment provisions. Different national regulations, standards and conformance assessment result in increased costs for foreign suppliers. Approximation reduces these costs and thus enhances market access. This is the case when, for example, a number of national regulatory norms or standards are replaced by one regional standard. OECD governments accept the use of internationally harmonized standards as an important way to overcome national regulatory barriers. Both TBT and SPS Agreements under the WTO support the use of common international standards. GATS also includes important elements of harmonization, such as in the sector agreements on basic telecommunications and financial services. This reflects a widely held view that some degree of harmonization is needed to facilitate market access for service providers. All RTAs include some element of harmonization, even if the less pejorative terms of policy approximation and compatibility are used, for example in the European Union and NAFTA. In assessing the impact of RTAs it will therefore be necessary to determine the degree to which the RTAs go further than the WTO or other international bodies in promoting policy approximation or compatibility within the region. If regional standards diverge from international standards, a form of regional preference may emerge.

Unlike in procedural measures, where preferences are seldom used or even possible, this is clearly not the case with harmonization or policy approximation. Regional regulatory norms or standards, whether mandatory or even voluntary, can constitute a form of preference in the sense that they diverge from the standards that prevail in the exporter's domestic market. Harmonization can still result in better market access than occurs when each national norm or standard has to be complied with. But suppliers from outside the region may still have additional costs in complying with the regional norms or standard. This will be the case whenever there is no agreed international standard that is accepted and applied by all.

Regional harmonization or approximation can also have the effect of "obliging" other countries to fall into line with the dominant regional standard. This is, for example, the case in Europe where the EU *acquis* is a prerequisite for guaranteed access to the EU market, whether the home country is negotiating accession to the European Union or not. A similar situation probably exists in North America, with all in fact being obliged to use US standards and norms even if there is no legal requirement to do so.

Mutual recognition

RTAs may also promote mutual recognition or equivalence. Full (mutual) recognition means that the performance standards or legitimate policy objectives in the exporting country are considered equivalent to those in the importing country, so that no further testing or certification is required. Recognition of test results means that laboratories in the exporting country test products for conformity with the standards of the importing country, so the product does not need to be tested twice. Mutual recognition or equivalence can be applied in any field of regulatory policy, although not in the case of public procurement considered here.

The TBT Agreement of the WTO encourages the use of mutual recognition and GATS provides for (mutual) recognition in its further commitments section. The question to be addressed in this study is whether RTAs go beyond the WTO in applying mutual recognition. Although mutual recognition is generally considered to be a "good thing" in that it facilitates more open markets and reduces costs, there is some concern that not all countries will be able to satisfy the expectations of regulators in some of the core developed economies. If third countries satisfy the conditions of equivalence in regulatory policies within the RTA, but are not allowed to negotiate mutual recognition agreements, this could be seen as a form of regional preference. More generally, of course, mutual recognition is a derogation from MFN because only those countries or suppliers that meet the criteria for equivalence are granted access to the target market without any further need for conformance testing.

Regulatory discretion

Another important area in which regional agreements can be WTO-plus in either a substantive or a procedural sense is that of reducing regulatory discretion. It is not just the substance of rules that is important but also how these rules are applied. Generally, all rules are open to various interpretations, which provides scope for discretion on the part of regulators. Abuse of such regulatory discretion can then represent an important barrier to market access. As noted above, the scope for the abuse of regulatory discretion may be checked by the use of transparency in decision-making procedures. But it is also possible to limit the scope for discretion in agreements or through judicial or arbitral decisions on the interpretation of provisions. An important example of where regulatory discretion may be abused as a means of restricting market access is in the application of exceptions to the non-discrimination requirements of multilateral and regional agreements. The TBT, SPS and GATS agreements all provide for exceptions to non-discrimination on the grounds of human health or animal or plant health and safety. There are also general exceptions within the GATT (1994) under Article XX. RTAs also have equivalent exceptions.

RTAs could be said to be WTO-plus if they interpret these general exceptions more restrictively than the multilateral rules. This may involve substantive provisions implementing the provisions of multilateral rules that call for the application of criteria such as "least trade restrictive measures" or no "unnecessary trade restrictions" unless regulatory policies pursue "legitimate policy objectives". Alternatively, RTAs may result in the interpretation of such criteria in judicial or quasi-judicial procedures. The European Court of Justice decisions over the years, such as *Dassonville* and *Cassis de Dijon*, are examples of the use of such a juridical approach.

If regulators are allowed to retain more discretionary power when dealing with third-country suppliers or companies, then one could say that a preference existed in this area.

Implementation and enforcement

Effective implementation/reviews

Efforts to reduce or remove regulatory barriers to trade will have an impact only if there are means of ensuring that they are implemented. Regional agreements may offer more immediate remedies and thus facilitate effective enforcement of rules, even when WTO dispute settlement remains an alternative. Given the number of potential disputes concerning the application of regulatory policy, some form of decentralized means of promoting implementation and enforcement is needed. This has to date taken the form of some recourse to action by the aggrieved parties, i.e. companies or other legal persons. The GATS agreement on basic telecommunications provides that suppliers, both domestic and foreign, should have recourse to a review of decisions concerning interconnection to the network. The GPA provides aggrieved parties that believe they have been unfairly treated in the granting of a public contract with the option of mounting a "bid challenge". In measuring the RTAs against the WTO standard of provision, it would therefore be necessary to assess whether the RTA offers more effective or more immediate remedies than the WTO. NAFTA, for example, offers investor–state dispute settlement under national law in addition to redress via the tripartite NAFTA dispute settlement. A regional preference in these areas would arise if companies from third countries were not granted equal rights to remedies.

In practice, the remedies available for aggrieved parties are likely to be limited under the WTO. Not all countries are ready to accept investor–state procedures or "direct effect" in regional agreements. The current WTO dispute settlement mechanism, although effective in ensuring that national governments implement WTO rules, is probably too remote to have much impact on how national laws and guidelines are implemented by regulatory agencies, where many of the regulatory barriers to trade have their origin. RTAs can therefore be WTO-plus in the sense that they provide reviews and ultimately remedies for market participants with regard to the application of regulatory policies.

Anti-competitive practices

Finally, regional agreements can help market access by ensuring that anti-competitive practices do not limit trade. As public regulatory barriers to trade are removed, less transparent private barriers may develop to replace them, especially if the market structure following deregulation is characterized by increased concentration. Regulated sectors are generally exempt from the provisions of competition (anti-trust) legislation. This means that when these sectors are deregulated there is often little knowledge or experience of the sector in competition authorities, and little information on market behaviour. Monopoly providers in one market may also seek to enter foreign markets as these are liberalized, thus introducing competitive distortions. This is important with regard to, for example, network standards in such sectors as (tele)communications or energy, where publicly owned operators can abuse monopoly positions. Thus GATS Article VIII:2 includes specific provision for such cases. The same holds for privately owned operators that benefit from exclusive rights to provide network services. Market closure can also occur as a result of the abuse of market power by private companies, such as in the use of de facto or industry-led standards (i.e. software standards for computers). In short, "it is important that competition principles be implemented as a key component of regulatory reform" (OECD, 1998, p. 316). In measuring the impact of RTAs, it will therefore be necessary to see if the RTAs go beyond the limited competition provisions included in GATS or other international agreements such as those in the OECD. Regional preference in the application of competition principles would occur if regional competition authorities or principles discriminated against third countries by not extending the application of competition principles to companies from these countries.

Applying the framework

This chapter has sought to provide an analytical framework for the case studies that follow. The emphasis is very much on how to assess the impact of regional agreements in the field of regulatory policy. As set out in the introduction, an important criterion for such a qualitative assessment is the degree to which regional agreements are WTO-plus. This chapter has sought to provide a breakdown of the components that are likely to be included in regional agreements. In the "vertical" case studies on recent RTAs in part II and the two "horizontal" case studies in part III, the authors have made use of the framework in looking at the particular elements of RTAs on regulatory policy. In each case the authors have, to a greater or lesser degree, felt it necessary to go beyond the confines of the framework in explaining the dynamics and issues in each of the RTAs or horizontal cases. This chapter nevertheless provides a common point of reference and thus facilitates the drawing of conclusions in part IV of the book.

Notes

1. For a similar discussion of the impact of regulation and regulatory reform on trade, see OECD (2000a).
2. For a recent discussion of transparency measures in national rules, see OECD (2000b).

REFERENCES

OECD (Organisation for Economic Co-operation and Development) (1998), *Regulatory Reform. Volume II: Thematic Studies*, Paris: OECD Secretariat.
——— (2000a), *Trade and Regulatory Reform: Insights from the OECD Country Reviews and Other Analysis*, Working Party of the Trade Committee, TD/TC/WP (2000)21 FINAL, 3 November.
——— (2000b), *Strengthening Regulatory Transparency: Insights from the GATS from Regulatory Reform Country Reviews*, Working Party of the Trade Committee, TD/TC/WP (2000)21 FINAL, 3 November.

Part II

Case studies in regional agreements

3

The Association Agreement between the European Union and Poland

Magnus Feldmann

Introduction

The collapse of communism in Eastern Europe marked the beginning of a complex set of political and economic processes that are generally referred to as transition. Transition in the East European context means the transformation of a one-party command economy into a democratic market-based economy including the creation of supporting institutions. Agh (1998) defines this transformation as a triple transition, comprising an economic, a political and a social part. Some observers (Mayhew, 1998) would argue that another integral part of transition for historical reasons is the reintegration with Western Europe, especially for many Central and East European countries (CEECs). The perceived end-point of this process is EU membership, which would also mean full integration into the European market and adoption of EU policies and regulations. The interaction of these two processes – transition and EU integration – creates both opportunities and tensions for the countries in transition.

This chapter focuses on one CEEC – Poland – and assesses the impact of regional integration in some new issue areas of international trade policy in the transition context. The "new issues" examined are technical barriers to trade (TBTs), food safety, public procurement, services and investment.

The focus of the chapter is on the Association Agreement (also known as the Europe Agreement) between the European Union and Poland.

The Europe Agreements (EAs), which the European Union has concluded with Bulgaria, the Czech Republic, Estonia, Hungary, Latvia, Lithuania, Poland, Romania, Slovakia and Slovenia, form the legal basis of the ex-communist countries' regional integration with the European Union.[1] By examining one Europe Agreement in particular, the chapter will try to assess the effectiveness of regional integration in these new issue areas in terms of market opening and in terms of its likely effect on the multilateral system. The theoretical framework set out in chapter 2 of this book is used to consider whether the Europe Agreement is "WTO-plus", i.e. whether it goes beyond the provisions of the World Trade Organization (WTO). In this context it is important to distinguish between the Europe Agreement per se and the integration dynamic in general, since it is clear that full EU membership is WTO-plus. Finally, the chapter considers whether any general lessons for other trade agreements emerge from this analysis.

The main argument of this chapter is that regional integration on balance strengthens Polish reform in the policy areas considered and facilitates the adoption of international standards. The ultimate aim of EU accession and harmonization with the *acquis communautaire* provides a role model and an incentive for regulatory reform, which has facilitated market opening and which should in most cases have beneficial effects on the multilateral level. The EA is WTO-plus in most regulatory issue areas, especially if enforcement and provisions for institution-building are considered. The general implication of the Polish case is that "deep integration" and what could be called "multidimensional interaction" (i.e. political, economic, legal and institutional cooperation between Poland and the European Union) are conducive to regulatory harmonization. It should be noted that some of these reforms impose significant costs on Poland, especially in the short run. The wholesale adoption of another regulatory system may require introducing regulation that is not optimal for Polish conditions. The extent to which the Polish experience and the findings of this chapter can be generalized remains unclear, especially given the uniqueness of the current EU enlargement.

The structure of the chapter is as follows. It begins by giving an introduction to Polish economic reforms and Polish trade policy in the 1990s. This is followed by an analysis of the Europe Agreement and a discussion of both its general rationale and its impact on Polish trade policy in transition. The next section discusses the new regulatory issues of international trade policy examined in this volume: technical barriers to trade, food safety, public procurement, investment and services. The final section considers what general conclusions might be drawn from the case study.

Poland in the 1990s

From plan to (common) market

What distinguishes Poland and the other CEECs from most other countries entering regional trade agreements is that the adoption and implementation of the Europe Agreements coincided with a period of profound change and reform of the economy. At the outset of the 1990s, Poland was a command economy characterized by high levels of centralization, state ownership and bureaucratic coordination.[2] Companies operated under soft budget constraints and there was widespread use of barter. At the beginning of transition there were significant shortages, a monetary overhang and then also hyperinflation. Moreover, the supporting institutions of a capitalist economy – bankruptcy laws, competition policy, contract enforcement, a legal system, and so on – were either absent or highly politicized.[3]

By the end of the decade Poland could be characterized as a market economy. Many changes had been carried out relatively swiftly – stabilization, liberalization and some privatization – whereas other aspects of reform, such as large-scale privatization, the introduction of effective corporate governance and legal and institutional reform, inevitably have taken much longer.[4] Indeed, some of these reform processes have not yet been completed.

Institutional reforms do not just require the putting in place of laws and regulations; there is also a need for mechanisms to ensure effective implementation and for training officials to carry out these functions in the intended way. This chapter argues that the process of European integration has a big role to play in this respect, which can be viewed on balance (despite some qualifications) as positive. It gives the reform programme a clear aim and anchor, which adds to the overall credibility of the policies. In this respect there are also clear parallels with the new issues in trade policy, which are the main topic of this chapter.

Polish trade policy and performance in the 1990s

Prior to transition, foreign trade was subordinated to the broad strategy of economic coordination in a command economy, i.e. central planning. This meant that the economic rationale for many transactions was very weak. Centralization of international transactions was essential in order to ensure that foreign trade flows did not impinge on plan targets, which were supposed to reflect a social optimum.

It bears noting that, although Poland predominantly traded with other countries of the Council for Mutual Economic Assistance, trade with the

West had started growing in the 1970s as part of the so-called import-led growth strategy. The idea was to combat the problem of sluggish technological innovation by importing high-quality capital goods from the West (Gomułka, 1978). As a result of this, trade with the West was a relatively important aspect of economic policy even before transition, at least by command economy standards.[5] Poland has also been a member of the General Agreement on Tariffs and Trade (GATT) since 1967, which has in practice imposed only very limited obligations on Poland. Since conventional measures of protection such as tariffs were meaningless in a command economy, a special arrangement was made when Poland acceded to GATT. In exchange for most favoured nation (MFN) treatment, Poland agreed to increase its imports by 7 per cent on an annual basis, which turned out to be unrealistic even in the 1970s. Poland's official status was changed only in 1994 along with the creation of the WTO.[6] The impact of this was that GATT membership had given Polish officials some experience of international trade negotiations before transition, but conventional international constraints through GATT bindings, for example, became operational only during transition.

In 1990, foreign trade was rapidly liberalized as part of Finance Minister Leszek Balcerowicz's "big-bang" reform programme.[7] Quantitative restrictions and state trading were removed and low tariffs were implemented across the board. Reforms were so far-reaching that Poland, along with the Czechoslovakia, arguably had the most liberal trade regime in Europe at the end of 1990 (Messerlin, 1994). Trade liberalization was inextricably linked to the broader objectives of the reform programme. It was seen as a means of removing shortages, introducing hard budget constraints, creating a market economy where prices reflect relative scarcities and are close to world market prices, as well as providing a means of creating a competitive market environment to counteract monopolistic behaviour.

However, in the second half of 1991 a backlash against liberal foreign trade occurred and tariff rates were raised to higher levels. Many politicians had viewed the dramatic liberalization as part of a short-term policy package, which applied only during a period of sharp real devaluation. Interest group activity – especially by the strong and influential agricultural lobby and the steel and ship-building industries – in response to the strains of economic restructuring was also instrumental here (Wellisz, 1995). Moreover, unlike in Estonia where the free trade consensus was much stronger (see Feldmann and Sally, 2002), no effective lock-in strategy to maintain free trade was in place.

Subsequently tariffs have gradually been reduced again, partly as a result of domestic reforms and partly as a result of multilateral and regional commitments. Multilaterally, Poland became a founding member of the

WTO in 1995 after participating in the Uruguay Round as the only "developed" country without any bound rates of tariffs. The main Polish commitments for trade in goods in the WTO were to bind about 94 per cent of all tariffs, to reduce tariffs on industrial products by 38 per cent and on agricultural products by 36 per cent over six years, and to reduce domestic support for agriculture (Michalek, 2000). A key consideration during the Uruguay Round was to avoid bound rates below current EU bindings in order to avoid compensation to trading partners after accession to the European Union.

In addition to the WTO commitments and the Europe Agreement, Poland has concluded a wide range of preferential trade agreements (PTAs).[8] These are mostly modelled on the Europe Agreement and guarantee free trade in manufactured goods as well as more limited liberalization of trade in agriculture. These trade agreements were also a way of harmonizing the preferences with other applicant countries and with the European Union itself in order to prepare for accession and to avoid complexities relating to Rules of Origin regulations. Table 3.1 lists Poland's PTAs and table 3.2 illustrates the evolution of Polish tariff schedules.

As a result of this extensive web of preferential trade agreements, about 77 per cent of Polish imports of industrial goods are not subject to tariffs. Under the Generalized System of Preferences (GSP) Poland

Table 3.1. Preferential trade agreements concluded by Poland

Country	Concluded	Came into force
European Union	16 December 1991	1 March 1992 (trade part); 1 February 1994 (whole EA)
Central European Free Trade Agreement (CEFTA): Czech Republic, Hungary, Slovakia	21 December 1992	1 March 1993
European Free Trade Association	10 December 1992	15 November 1993
Slovenia (accession to CEFTA)	25 November 1995	1 January 1996
Lithuania	27 June 1996	1 January 1997
Romania (accession to CEFTA)	12 April 1997	1 July 1997
Bulgaria (accession to CEFTA)	17 July 1998	1 January 1999
Latvia	28 April 1997	1 June 1999
Estonia	5 November 1998	Provisionally applied since 1 January 1999
Israel	21 July 1997	1 June 1999
Faroe Islands	3 November 1998	1 June 1999
Turkey	4 October 1999	1 May 2000

Source: Kawecka-Wyrzykowska (2000).

Table 3.2. Poland: Evolution of customs tariff structure, 1989–97 (percentage rates)

Harmonized commodity description and coding system	January 1989	August 1990 to August 1991	August 1991	December 1993	June 1995	December 1996	January 1997
All commodities	18.3	5.5	18.4	19.0	9.4	8.0	6.3
Agriculture products	17.2	4.0	26.2	26.2	19.5	18.3	17.3
Industrial products	18.7	—	16.3	17.0	8.0	6.8	5.1
Mineral products	7.8	3.4	8.9	8.9	2.3	3.1	2.1
Chemical products	13.5	3.9	14.1	13.7	6.8	6.6	3.4
Plastics	19.9	5.5	15.0	14.9	9.5	9.1	3.9
Fur and leather products	17.2	5.1	25.7	23.5	10.3	6.6	7.9
Wood and paper products	18.7	7.4	13.4	13.4	5.3	4.6	3.6
Textiles, footwear, clothing	22.2	9.7	20.6	21.4	12.4	8.2	6.9
Industrial mineral and metal products	15.4	4.2	14.7	17.6	10.1	8.9	6.7
Machinery, transport equipment, precision instruments	21.9	3.9	16.1	16.6	16.3	12.7	9.1
Jewellery, arms, art objects, miscellaneous manufactured products	19.9	11.6	19.1	17.0	13.2	9.8	6.9

Source: IMF (1998).

offered preferences to 45 developing countries with a lower GDP per capita than itself, and to 49 countries considered as least developed. Tariff rates on imports from developing countries were 80 per cent of the MFN level and imports were duty free from least developed countries (WTO, 2000a). As a result of the EA, free trade in industrial goods has applied with the European Union since 1 January 1999 (with the exception of cars, for which customs duties were phased out gradually by the beginning of 2002). By contrast, agricultural protection, especially on specific products such as rape seed, sugar and butter, has been increased over recent years (Kawecka-Wyrzykowska, 2000). The average weighted tariff in 1999 for all goods was 3.3 per cent; the corresponding figures for agricultural and non-agricultural goods are respectively 15.8 per cent and 2.2 per cent (Michalek, 2000). Poland has also used safeguards and other types of non-tariff protection, also against the European Union, but these means of protection will not be analysed in this chapter.[9]

For the purposes of this chapter, two important conclusions follow from the discussion above. First, there was progressive liberalization of trade in the 1990s, but also strong domestic resistance in sensitive sectors. EU integration has been one of the driving factors for resisting protectionism in conventional trade policy and, as will be argued here, the same is largely true of non-tariff barriers as well. The exception to this rule is agriculture, where the European Union itself does not practise liberal trade. Therefore the EA provisions with respect to agriculture are not stringent and it is unclear to what extent the accession process will lead to further liberalization.[10]

Second, as trade has become progressively more liberal, the relative importance of non-tariff protection as a proportion of total protection has risen. Therefore attention is shifting from tariffs to non-border or "new" issues. Anti-dumping measures, regulatory barriers and other new issues have to be addressed to ensure that one means of protection is not substituted for another.

The Europe Agreement

This section briefly outlines some general provisions of the Association Agreements between the European Union and the CEECs,[11] which are important for an understanding of the institutional framework for deep integration and the incorporation of the new issues into this relationship.[12]

Transition countries have largely viewed EU accession as the endpoint of their transformation process, or as a seal of approval on their reforms, which are seen as generating various economic, political and security externalities (especially for countries closer to Russia). Despite growing concerns about the loss of sovereignty and the potential costs of accession among the populations, this policy remains fixed.

The European Communities and Poland signed the Europe Agreement on 16 December 1991. At the same time, similar EAs were concluded with Czechoslovakia and Hungary. This agreement superseded the Trade and Cooperation Agreement that was signed in 1989. The EA came into force on 1 February 1994, although the trade provision took effect as part of an interim agreement on 1 March 1992.

The Europe Agreements (EAs) formalize the relationship between the European Union on the one hand and the CEECs applying for membership of the Union on the other. The aim of the Agreements is to deepen cooperation between the European Union and CEECs in many policy areas. Although the European Union did not make any commitment on EU enlargement in the EAs, it was acknowledged that this was the ultimate aim of the CEECs. In other words, the EAs provide a legal framework for the accession countries' relations with the European Union and for their preparations for accession (see table 3.3).

Table 3.3. Structure of the EU–Poland Association Agreement

Preamble
Objectives of the Agreement
Title I: General principles of the agreement
Title II: Political dialogue
Title III: Free movement of goods
  Chapter 1: Industrial products
  Chapter 2: Agriculture
  Chapter 3: Fisheries
  Chapter 4: Common provisions
Title IV: Movement of workers, establishment, supply of services
  Chapter 1: Movement of workers
  Chapter 2: Establishment
  Chapter 3: Supply of services
  Chapter 4: General provisions
Title V: Payments, capital, competition and other economic provisions, approximation of laws
  Chapter 1: Current payments and movement of capital
  Chapter 2: Competition and other economic provisions
  Chapter 3: Approximation of laws
Title VI: Economic co-operation
Title VII: Cultural co-operation[a]
Title VIII: Financial co-operation
Title IX: Institutional, general and final provisions

a. Agreements concluded after 1995 also include an article about prevention of illegal activities (see Mayhew, 1998, p. 44ff.).

The preferential trade agreements are arguably the most important aspect of the EAs, especially in the short run, since they have an immediate and direct economic impact. The EAs require both the CEECs and the European Union gradually to liberalize trade in industrial goods over a transition period. However, with one exception this liberalization is to occur asymmetrically in favour of the CEECs; in other words, the European Union, as the stronger party, had to liberalize trade with the CEECs more rapidly than its counterparts in the EAs. The exception is Estonia, which operated a unilateral free trade regime in the 1990s. This means that the EU–Estonian EA was asymmetric in favour of the European Union because the Union maintained, for example, various quotas with respect to agricultural imports (see Feldmann and Sally, 2002).

One of the most important aspects of the EA is the requirement that the CEECs adopt and implement the *acquis communautaire*, the European Union's corpus of legislation and regulation (this relates to Articles 68 and 69 of the EA; see the next section). This is an example of deep integration. Implementing the *acquis* is a crucial precondition for EU membership, which requires extensive efforts in order to harmonize legislation and regulation in many areas of economic activity. Some of this relates to the new issues, which will be discussed below. Progress in implementing the *acquis* is monitored by the European Union in annual reports, and accession is to be conditional on advances made in adopting the *acquis*. EU membership is a top priority for Polish policy makers, and this creates an incentive structure promoting reforms.

Another important dimension of the EAs is *institutional cooperation*. This includes meetings at the ministerial level, observer status of the CEECs at several EU summits and the creation of an Association Council and Association Committees (see Mayhew, 1998, p. 15ff). Since the key challenges in many cases relate to institution-building and establishment of good procedures, technical assistance and twinning are important components of institutional cooperation. The twinning projects are defined more narrowly and are aimed to facilitate the adoption of the *acquis* (European Commission, 2001b). Finally there is substantial financial assistance to the CEECs as part of Phare, SAPARD, ISPA and other programmes. Phare, in particular, is an important instrument, which is used to prepare the countries for accession by promoting institution-building and facilitating the adoption of the *acquis* (European Commission, 2002).[13] This creates what might be called a pattern of *multidimensional interaction*, including economic, political, institutional and financial dimensions.[14] Such multidimensional interaction is likely to be particularly important when the aim is regulatory harmonization. Without financial support and institution-building, formal goals are unlikely to be realized in practice.

The key issue to note for the purpose of this study is that this set of regional trade agreements has made use of an existing regulatory template – the *acquis*. Although it may be resisted in part, it has to be implemented by the CEECs. It is obviously not clear whether all aspects of EU regulation are appropriate for the accession countries. Nevertheless, there is a process of regulatory harmonization, which is driven by the issue-linkage to the CEECs' overarching aim of EU accession and which is monitored in regular progress reports by the European Commission. Therefore there is both an incentive structure and an indirect enforcement mechanism in place for deep integration in the regulatory field.

This process is also facilitated by the multidimensional interaction referred to above, which is part of deep integration. It is the goal of future accession to the European Union that makes the EA stand out from an ordinary free trade agreement. This combination is especially conducive to integration in the new issue areas of trade policy. EU integration provides a role model and rationale for reform in these areas and also helps to anchor it. This may be one of the main benefits of the integration process and one of the reasons why there have not been any major backlashes against transition in the countries aiming to join the European Union (compared with the rather unsuccessful reforms further East).[15]

New issues

This section focuses on a number of new issues in international trade policy and on how they are addressed in the Europe Agreement. The analysis focuses not only on the actual text of the agreement, but also on the impact of Poland's EU accession requirements and related domestic reforms.

Technical barriers to trade

Technical barriers to trade (TBTs) have received increased attention in recent years, because they may have a significant impact on trade flows. As pointed out before, their relative importance as a proportion of total protection is rising, other things being equal, as tariff rates have been coming down. Technical barriers to trade can be divided into three components: regulation, standards and performance assessment (Hoekman and Kostecki, 1995).

The challenges in this area can be expected to be significant for transition countries, given the significant institutional deficits and lack of experience of market regulation. The challenge is two-fold: first, the ap-

propriate regulation needs to be adopted, and, second, impartial implementation needs to be ensured. Incorporating TBTs into regional
agreements with transition countries may be a way of promoting reform
in this sphere, but there are also potential costs and risks associated with
premature harmonization of regulations with developed country or West
European standards. The main advantage of adopting EU regulation and
standards is that there is a clear role model. No effort needs to be ex-
pended to devise a complex set of rules and practices from scratch. The
possible disadvantage may be that not all these regulations and standards
are appropriate for Poland. It will also involve significant short-run costs,
which may translate into popular resistance against regulatory harmonization.[16]

Some (primarily export-oriented) sectors may benefit from the new
regulation more quickly. There is some evidence to suggest that some
Polish industries covered by EU "new approach" directives have a comparative advantage in trade with the European Union (as well as a
smaller number of "old approach" industries),[17] and the adoption of the
relevant regulation may well facilitate their market access (Brenton et al.,
2001).

The EA states that "the major precondition for Poland's integration
with the Community" is that Polish legislation approximates and is made
compatible with EU legislation (Art. 68). Given the difficulty of harmonizing all legislation at once, Article 69 defines a number of priority
areas, where approximation of laws is deemed to be particularly urgent.
These areas are customs law, company law, banking law, company accounts and taxes, intellectual property, protection of workers at the
workplace, financial services, rules on competition, protection of health
and life of humans, animals and plants, consumer protection, indirect
taxation, technical rules and standards, transport and the environment. It
should be noted that the EA per se does not define any precise timetable
for when this harmonization ought to be completed or when specific
areas of legislation should be approximated. This is where it is important
once again to emphasize the importance of the integration dynamic, and
especially Poland's desire to join the European Union as quickly as possible, in motivating Poland to carry out this approximation.

At present Poland's system of regulation is not fully approximated with
that of the European Union. Regulation in Poland is based on a law
passed in 1993, which came into force in early 1994. This is when the
process of regulatory harmonization with the European Union started.
Until then, existing norms dated from the communist period and were
neither adjusted to a market economy nor compatible with West European norms (Kundera, 2000, p. 94). The key difference between Polish
and West European regulatory practice is that in Poland there exist

compulsory standards that can be unilaterally defined by ministries. These standards are often not compatible with Western standards, and there have been significant efforts recently to stop the issuance of such standards.[18] The Polish Committee for European Integration has stipulated that all standards will become voluntary by June 2002 (European Commission, 2001a, p. 38).

In June 2000 Poland had adopted 30 per cent of the total number of European standards. By June 2001 this had risen to 45 per cent, which still falls short of the 80 per cent required if Poland is to join the European Standardization Committee (CEN) and the European Electrotechnical Standardization Committee (CENELEC) (European Commission, 2001a, p. 38). By 2002 Poland intends have at least 80 per cent of standards harmonized with EU standards and to introduce EU norms wherever they differ from international norms (WTO, 2000a). Poland has compulsory health and safety standards (B certificate) on many products to protect consumer interests. The B certificate is required for about one-third of products sold in Poland, down from about two-thirds in 1997. Many of these standards do not conform to international norms. Information about new regulations and norms tends to be hard to get, and Polish firms are often unaware of them (Kundera, 2000, p. 95). Moreover, relevant documentation may not be available in any foreign language, which has also proved to be a barrier to trade. Progress in adopting "old approach" regulation, "new approach" regulation and mutual recognition has been made, although much work remains, especially on "old approach" regulation (European Commission, 2000, 2001a).

Certification of foreign goods has been restricted and complicated, although a lot of progress was made in 2000. Poland needs to implement the Agreement on the Protocol on European Conformity Assessment (PECAA), which would imply automatic granting of certification for products that have already received certification in the European Union (European Commission, 2000, p. 8). Before 2000, the accreditation, standardization and certification of goods were handled by the same authority. This made conformity assessment more difficult. The Law on Conformity Assessment adopted in April 2000 has separated accreditation by creating the independent Polish Accreditation Centre, which began its operations in January 2001 (European Commission, 2001a, p. 40). This contrasts with the Polish Committee for Standardization, which remains a government-controlled agency whose members are appointed and dismissed by the prime minister. Steps have been taken to increase its independence, and a legislative amendment passed in January 2003 has addressed most of these issues (European Commission, 2001a, p. 40).[19] Conformity assessment has also been problematic in practice given various institutional deficits, such as poorly trained officials. Such problems are exacerbated by low civil service pay and organizational problems, another issue addressed in the EU Progress Report (European Commission, 2000). The European Union provides some material support for remedying the matter. The 2000 Phare programme for Poland consists of €428 million and, of this, €21 million is allocated for improving the internal market – on customs, certifications and standards, competition and consumer protection, intellectual property rights and telecommunications (European Commission, 2000, p. 10).

To conclude, the adoption of the EU standards and regulations and improvements in conformity assessment are likely to lead to greater market opening, especially with respect to EU imports. The continuous monitoring of progress in harmonization and implementation by the European Commission also adds pressure on the Polish authorities to proceed with reform. Exporters from non-European countries may in some cases face new regulatory barriers, although this effect is likely to be outweighed by the existence of a clearer framework and better conformity assessment. The latter two problems have been mentioned as the major problems by, for example, US exporters to Poland (US Department of Commerce, 2000). It is likely that big exporters from developed countries that probably also sell goods to West European countries will benefit, whereas the impact on developing countries may be less clear.

The EA and the accession process are clearly WTO-plus in the case of TBTs. Not only is full harmonization required – which is not a general requirement in the WTO TBT agreement – but there has also been an emphasis on institution-building. This should promote openness and institutional best practice, which should benefit third countries as well. The inclusion of TBTs in the EA has meant that regulatory harmonization is indeed continuing apace and likely to be completed either by the time of accession or shortly thereafter. Multidimensional interaction incorporating legal, political, economic and aid-related links is particularly conducive to this kind of complex process. But the general lessons remain ambiguous for two reasons. First, the EA provisions are rather vague and therefore unlikely to be a sufficient driving force for regulatory harmonization without the imperative of accession. Second, since EU enlargement to the ex-socialist countries can be viewed as a one-off event, it is unclear whether this is a model that can be adopted in the future, so the EA provides a model only for RTAs with countries likely to become future members of or at least very closely integrated with the European Union.

Food safety

The area of food safety bears a lot of resemblance to the TBT and general regulatory issues outlined in the previous section. Here alignment with the *acquis* is also required, as stated in Articles 68 and 69 of the EA. According to Commission assessments, there has not been much progress as yet, although new Polish legislation on food safety will help to harmonize laws and regulations with EU standards (European Commission, 2000, p. 35). Phare 2000 has allotted €42 million for projects aiming at institution-building in agriculture, and a part of this is to be used to enhance food safety (European Commission, 2000, p. 10).[20]

Food safety is also an area where Poland has requested a large number of transition periods. Four key examples are:

- temporary permission to sell Polish raw milk not fulfilling Community requirements relating to micro-organisms and somatic cells and selling such products to markets outside the European Union for two to three years after accession;
- temporary permission to produce consumption milk of a different fat content than stipulated by Community regulations for the home market and exports for two years after accession;
- permanent derogation from EU regulations for the production and sale on the domestic market of some specific regional products such as cheese made from sheep's milk (*bryndza* and *oscypek*);
- temporary permission to produce meat and meat products for the home market and exports to third countries in establishments (exceeding EU ceiling for small-capacity undertakings) that do not meet all the EU veterinary requirements for four years after accession (Kawecka-Kyrzykowska and Synowiec, 2000).

About a quarter of the Polish labour force is employed in agriculture and many of the farms are very small. Therefore the cost of adjusting to EU food safety standards is likely to be a big challenge in the short run, although it may yield benefits (such as improved export opportunities and marketability in Western Europe) in the longer run. This is again an area where there is a potential tension between the costs of transition and the imperatives of EU integration.

Compulsory standards have been the norm for foodstuffs; i.e. prior approval has been required before goods can be marketed. Polish standards (including the B certificate) have sometimes placed quite high demands on goods and the licensing procedure can be complex. These procedures will be phased out gradually and the administration will be changed to take into account the new system. The adoption of the standard West European model is likely to improve market access by providing a clearer legal framework, but it is possible that some producers exporting to Poland may find it costly to adjust to the new standards.[21]

Poland has also taken active measures, including import controls, to contain the spread of BSE and foot and mouth disease. Non-harmonized Polish norms are very restrictive about genetically modified organisms and beef hormones and Poland has blocked such imports from the United States. Some Polish civil servants argue that unharmonized Polish standards are already closer to EU standards than to the North American model, at least in this respect, which might imply that there is little scope for trade diversion here.[22]

As pointed out at the beginning of this section, food safety issues bear a lot of resemblance to the general regulatory issues discussed in the section about TBTs. The general conclusion is also the same: EU integration is WTO-plus in terms of harmonization of standards and procedures and in terms of institution-building. Eastern enlargement, at least as far as Poland is concerned, therefore seems to be consolidating the European approach to the regulation of risk and food safety (see chapter 9).

Public procurement

Public procurement constitutes a very significant part of total expenditure in most countries. In the European Union, for example, public procurement made up approximately 14 per cent of GDP in 1998, which was equivalent to about half of Germany's GDP or the total GDP of Belgium, Denmark and Spain (Kundera, 2000). Nevertheless, the multilateral regime regulating public procurement is weak; it has been labelled the last remaining hole of the multilateral trading order (Hoekman and Mavroidis, 1995). Public procurement is explicitly excluded from the scope of GATT and the General Agreement on Trade in Services (GATS), as spelt out in GATT Articles III (8a) and XVII (2) and GATS Article XIII:1. Instead, government procurement is regulated as part of the WTO's plurilateral Government Procurement Agreement (GPA). The first GPA was signed in 1979 and came into force in 1981; the current GPA was negotiated during the Uruguay Round and came into force at the beginning of 1996. The GPA currently has 28 members, if (as on the WTO website) all the EU members are counted separately; if not, the number falls to 13.[23] Most CEECs, including Poland, are observers of the GPA, and Bulgaria, Estonia and Latvia are currently engaged in accession negotiations. Membership of the GPA is a prerequisite of EU accession.

The new GPA is expected to have increased the amount of public procurement subject to competition by a factor of 10. The scope of the agreement is limited by the positive-list approach, provisions for limited and selective tenders and thresholds levels, below which the GPA rules do not apply (WTO, n.d.). Hence there is significant scope for going beyond the WTO provisions on public procurement at the regional level.

Article 67 of the EU–Poland Association Agreement (in Title V, Chapter 2) is the key article defining the provisions with respect to public procurement. The first part is very general and only highlights that the contracting parties view liberalization of public procurement on the basis of non-discrimination and reciprocity to be a "desirable objective". The second section spells out the specific provisions, where again the principle of asymmetric liberalization applies. Polish firms were granted national treatment ("a treatment no less favourable than that accorded to Community companies") in bidding for public procurement contracts in the European Union as soon as the Association Agreement came into force. By contrast, Poland committed itself to the same degree of liberalization by the end of a 10-year transition period. EU firms established in Poland were granted national treatment as soon as the agreement came into force. The agreement also stipulates that the Association Council should regularly review whether Poland might be able to liberalize the procurement regime more quickly. The third and final section of Article 67 confirms that the general provisions regarding establishment, operations, supply of services and movement of labour of Articles 37 to 58 are relevant in the area of procurement as well.

Public procurement is known to be a difficult area to reform in any country. Even in the case of the European Union, progress in introducing competition in procurement has not been altogether satisfactory (WTO, 2000b). Moreover, knowledge in EU member states about the public procurement provisions of the Europe Agreement and about their precedence over national law has at times been limited. For example, Polish firms have on some occasions been denied the right to bid for tenders in Greece.

On the Polish side, the Europe Agreement has been an engine for progressive liberalization and legal reform in the area of public procurement, but more challenges remain before Polish law and practice can be said to conform fully to EU standards. Although the Polish law on procurement incorporates the international norms of competition, transparency and public calls for tender, it does not yet cover most purchases by state organizations and firms. Domestic firms bidding for contracts get a 20 per cent price preference, and the domestic performance section in the law requires 50 per cent domestic content (US Department of Commerce, 2000). The threshold level above which open tenders are compulsory is €20,000.

There is an appeals process for allegedly unfairly awarded tenders, which goes some way towards improving the procedural aspects of procurement. The Central Policy Office of Public Procurement lists all tenders valued at €30,000 or more.

Harmonization of the public procurement regime with that of the European Union has been required by the European Union, especially in terms of specifying the coverage of the legislation, the elimination of the clause giving Polish firms preferences and the specification of Polish national standards (European Commission, 2000, p. 36). Two amendments to the Public Procurement Law were passed in June and July 2001 and will come into force gradually and move Polish legislation closer to the norms of the *acquis* (European Commission, 2001a, p. 41). The European Union has also identified the urgency of training Polish officials at all levels in public contracting (European Commission, 2001a). Anecdotal evidence suggests that implementation is still problematic, and complaints have been made in both Poland and the Czech Republic of split tenders, to ensure that the value is below stated threshold levels in order to avoid compliance with the law.[24] It seems that the system operates better and more transparently on the national than on the local and regional levels. There are bid challenge procedures in place. A large number of complaints (1,565) were launched in 2000, which led to the initiation of 460 investigations by the Public Procurement Office. Out of the 340 investigations that were completed, 28 concluded that breaches of the law had occurred (European Commission, 2001a, p. 41). A new and improved review system was introduced in early 2002.

EU accession basically means taking over EU procurement rules. In terms of coverage, the EU rules are extensive and there are only very limited sectoral exceptions, although this obviously does not extend to third parties. However, Poland is an observer to the WTO Government Procurement Agreement and will need to become a signatory prior to EU accession.

In the case of government procurement, EU pressure has been a very important engine for reform. It is very unlikely that the reforms in public procurement would have occurred "bottom–up" or that Poland would, for example, have allocated the resources unilaterally to train government officials at all levels in public procurement principles. The promotion of transparency and open calls for tender should benefit all non-Polish bidders. Polish public procurement has been rather restrictive and the adoption of EU standards should lead to a net fall in protection. Since EU accession also presupposes membership of the WTO GPA, the regional and multilateral tracks also seem to be moving in tandem. Given the weakness of the plurilateral procurement regime, the EAs are all WTO-plus. In this area, much like in the previous two, it seems clear that the imperatives of EU accession and the conditionality this imposes have been the main engine of reform, rather than the EA provisions per se.

Investment

The establishment of multilateral rules on foreign investment has proved to be a complex and tortuous process, as evidenced by the failure of the

Multilateral Agreement on Investment and the extremely limited coverage of investment by the WTO. Given the interdependence of foreign direct investment (FDI) and trade and the importance of investment both to transition and to growth in general, it is important to assess the impact of the Europe Agreement on investment and to see whether it provides a model for other free trade agreements. There is considerable overlap between this section and the following one, which deals with services.

First and foremost, the EA locks in the status quo in Poland, which means that no new permanent restrictions on investment as a result of regulation can be introduced after the Agreement comes into force (Art. 44.2). Second, as with conventional tariff-based trade policy, the principle of asymmetry applies. The European Union immediately offered national treatment with respect to establishment of Polish firms on its territory, whereas Poland agreed to liberalize establishment gradually according to the timetable described in table 3.4 (Arts. 44.1 and 44.3).

The Association Council is given the task of monitoring the Polish investment regime and of examining whether it is possible to shorten the transition periods (Art. 44.5). Another key clause, which is also related to the principle of asymmetry, is Article 50. This states that temporary restrictions on foreign investment, including derogations from national treatment, are permissible during the first five years for sectors in XIIa and XIIb, and for the whole 10-year transition period for sectors in XIIc and XIId. This clause is comparable to the restructuring clause of the trade in goods part of the EA (Art. 28). The possible restrictions apply to firms undergoing restructuring, infant industries or other firms experiencing difficulties. The safeguard measures should be temporary; that is, they must cease two years after the transition period for the industry in question ends (or at the latest by the end of the general transition period) and they must be reported to the Association Council. Such restrictions should also be "reasonable and necessary in order to remedy the situation" and apply only to firms established after the measures come into force. An element of preference for EU companies should be retained. This clause is an acknowledgement of the tensions arising during the transition process in the form of dislocations.

Regulation of foreign investors established in Poland and the European Union should be non-discriminatory. The only major exception applies to financial services, where some derogations are possible if the soundness of the financial system is at stake. Essentially this relates to prudential regulation of the financial sector (Art. 45). EU companies are given the right to buy property and lease land when necessary for the conduct of business, which basically means that a foreign firm may get permission to buy the land on which its factory is located (Art. 44.7). Land and property purchases have proved to be a very delicate matter in

Table 3.4. Liberalization of investment and services in Poland: Timetable for introducing national treatment

Immediate liberalization

Annex XIIa:
1. Manufacturing industry including fuel and power industry, metallurgical industry, electro-engineering industry, transport equipment industry, chemical industry, construction materials industry, wood and paper industry, textile, leather and apparel industry, food processing industry, but excluding mining, processing of precious metals and stones, production of explosives, ammunition and weaponry, pharmaceutical industry, production of poisonous substances, production of distilled alcohols, high voltage power lines, pipe-line transportation.
2. Construction.
Also for any other industry not mentioned in Annexes XIIb, c, d, and e.

Liberalization by the end of the 10-year transition period

Annex XIIb: gradually, and no later than at the end of transition period
1. Mining, processing of precious metals and stones, production of explosives, ammunition and weaponry, pharmaceutical industry, production of poisonous substances, production of distilled alcohols.
2. Services excluding:
– financial services as defined in Annex XIIc,
– dealing and agency services in real estate and natural resources,
– legal services not including legal advice in business-related matters and international law.

Annex XIIc:
All financial services, including insurance and banking (detailed definition spelt out in the text).

Annex XIId:
1. Acquisition of state-owned assets under privatization process.
2. Ownership, use, sale and rent of real estate.
3. Dealing and agency activities in real estate property and natural resources.
4. Legal services which are excluded in Annex XIIb.
5. High voltage power lines.
6. Pipe-line transportation.

No national treatment (permanent exclusion)

Annex XIIe:
1. Acquisition and sale of natural resources.
2. Acquisition and sale of agricultural land and forests.

the integration process. Both Poland and other Central European states fear a large influx of Germans, who might reclaim or wish to buy large sections of (by West European standards) cheap land that belonged to their families prior to the Second World War.

The current foreign investment regime in Poland can on the whole be characterized as rather liberal. National treatment applies for most industries. Exceptions are similar to those in other OECD countries and include radio and television broadcasting and selected fields of communications, where the upper thresholds for foreign ownership are 33 and 49 per cent, respectively. Gambling and betting activities can be carried out only by wholly owned Polish companies (Papliński, 2000). Limitations apply to both domestic and foreign companies with respect to privatized entities; here the maximum stake a strategic investor may hold is 80 per cent. Most of the sectors to which transition periods apply have now been liberalized, including insurance and banking services (liberalized in 1999).

In practice, FDI is welcomed in Poland in many sectors, most notably in many manufacturing industries and in the shape of strategic bidders in the privatization of state firms. After slowing down in the mid-1990s, privatization accelerated again from 1998 after the election of a more liberal government. In some cases this has had negative repercussions on trade liberalization, as the foreign investors (such as Volkswagen) bargained for tariffs (or, more generally, guaranteed market share provisions) in exchange for the investment (Mayhew, 1998).

To give a comprehensive assessment of the investment climate, we also need to consider supporting arrangements, most notably current account, capital account and labour mobility. Current account mobility already applies, and Poland is in the process of moving towards capital account mobility as a result of both EU and OECD commitments. There are, however, significant limitations to labour mobility, because only key personnel are allowed to relocate for fixed contracts. There have in some cases been problems on both sides, such as when Poles working for foreign subsidiaries of Polish companies have sometimes had difficulty getting work permits (Mayhew, 1998, p. 130, mentions the case of a Pole who was supposed to work for the Polish flag carrier LOT in Austria). Currently it seems that there is likely to be a seven-year transition period during which there will be controls on the free movement of labour between current and new EU members.

The impact of the EA on market opening in the field of investment remains unclear. Much of the liberalization would be likely to have occurred anyway, especially that of strategic investment in privatized companies. Market opening in sensitive sectors may have been accelerated by the EA and the integration process more generally. It is also not possible to comment on the multilateral effects with any precision at this point, since it is not yet clear what restrictions Poland will retain vis-à-vis third countries after accession. EU member states have individual bilateral investment treaties. On the whole, it is unlikely that significant new barriers will be erected.

This discussion of investment in the EU–Poland EA suggests the following conclusions. Unlike the provisions on regulatory harmonization or food safety, the section on establishment contains a precise listing of sectors and a timetable for liberalization. This means that progress in liberalization can be gauged against a clear benchmark, although the politically expedient restructuring clause has given Poland some flexibility during the transition phase (it might also not have been possible to reach such an agreement otherwise). Moreover, the dynamic of the integration process improves the prospects of enforcing the agreement, which many would view as much better than, for example, in the OECD.[25] The EA, and EU integration more generally, go beyond any multilateral or plurilateral agreements, like the modest Trade-related Investment Measures in GATT, the OECD codes or relevant GATS provisions (e.g. transport services, movement of personnel). Remaining constraints on establishment include limited labour mobility and land purchasing rights, which are very sensitive issues for the European Union and Poland, respectively.

Services

This section will briefly address some additional aspects of the EA pertaining to services. Much of what was covered in the previous section on investment applies to services as well. There is, however, a separate section on services in the EA and some other considerations are also relevant here.

The EA provisions on services cannot be described as far-reaching. There is a general commitment to taking the necessary steps in order progressively to liberalize the supply of services (Art. 55.1). The temporary movement of labour – but key personnel only! – is liberalized to support the provision of services (Art. 55.2). Article 56 spells out the specific provisions pertaining to the usually protected transport services, which include a lock-in of the status quo at the time of signing the agreement. In other words, no new restrictions are allowed. Moreover, free access to the market of international maritime transport and national treatment of the other party's ships regarding access to infrastructure, ports, etc. are established, and there is a general statement about future negotiations to bring about further liberalization of transport services.

Poland is also bound by its multilateral GATS commitments and by the EU accession requirements more generally. The GATS bindings mainly act as a lock-in, whereas EU accession will require removing a few remaining barriers (for example, bodyguard services, gambling, translation and tourism services) and implementing EU-style regulation, such as in financial services. On the whole, Poland has already achieved a high degree of alignment with respect to the *acquis* provisions on the free movement of services (European Commission, 2000, p. 37ff).

The EA service provisions are somewhat vague and unlikely to contribute significantly to market opening. However, more specific provisions are contained in the articles on investment and establishment discussed in the previous section, which are more effective than most of the service provisions. As in other areas, the integration process is likely to have accelerated liberalization of sensitive sectors and led to the removal of remaining Polish barriers vis-à-vis EU countries and vice versa. The impact of the EA provisions on the multilateral rules is unclear. It again seems unlikely that any significant new barriers will be erected against third countries. The EA could also be said to be weakly GATS-plus, since it goes beyond locking in existing liberalization by including some additional sectors, such as tourism.

Conclusion

This chapter has examined some "new issues" in trade policy and how such regulatory barriers are dealt with in the Poland–EU Europe Agreement. More generally, the aim has been to make an assessment of whether this regional agreement promotes market opening and is WTO-plus in the sense of going beyond WTO provisions. Multilateral effects and implications for other trade agreements have also been addressed.

On balance it would appear that integration with the European Union has promoted market opening in Poland. This applies to conventional trade policy measures (except agricultural protection), because Polish tariffs on manufacturing goods have been higher than the European Union's common external tariff although they are coming down gradually. Although it must be acknowledged that new barriers may potentially be erected vis-à-vis the rest of the world in some areas (possibly in food safety), other countries are likely to benefit in a number of ways from EU integration. Reforms in Poland should, for example, yield benefits to all of Poland's trading partners and lead to market opening.

First, adoption of EU regulation and in some cases defining clear regulation where the previous regime was ambiguous promote transparency and predictability. This is perhaps especially important for public procurement, but also for TBTs and to some extent for food safety. In other words, the European Union offers a role model for regulatory reform, and the imperatives of EU integration provide both a purpose and an anchor for locking in such reforms. The main caveat here is whether all aspects of EU regulation are appropriate for Poland at its current level of development and whether some sectors of the economy will face severe adjustment costs, especially in the short run.

Second, as has already been emphasized, institutional deficits are likely to be a particularly big problem for transition countries. Financial assistance and training of officials should make for better and less erratic implementation of regulations. Again, the effect of taking over EU-style institutions and norms may go some way towards promoting institutional best practice.

Third, the European Union's annual Progress Reports and dispute settlement mechanisms in the Association Council put pressure on Poland actually to implement its commitments (this pressure is obviously asymmetric in favour of the European Union). The linkage between regulatory reform and prospective EU accession gives Poland the incentive actually to implement these regulatory changes and to contain regulatory discretion. All of these factors should contribute to market opening and a more predictable business climate for exporters both within and outside the European Union.

It should be noted that the EA provisions per se are rather vague in most of the issue areas considered, in that they require harmonization or liberalization without defining clear timetables. The relative success achieved in Poland is probably attributable to the dynamic of EU accession itself – and the conditionality imposed by the need to meet the accession criteria – rather than to the EA. This linkage seems to have been crucial. However, the section on investment and establishment contains more specific and far-reaching provisions and may serve as a role model for other agreements.

The EA can be viewed as WTO-plus on several counts. First, the substantive provisions in the issue areas discussed in this chapter and the rest of the book go beyond WTO provisions in their scope. The adoption of the *acquis* is an example of very ambitious "deep integration". Second, what makes the EA stand out from virtually all other multilateral and plurilateral agreements is that the procedural and institutional underpinnings are much stronger. For regulatory issues, unbiased and competent implementation and credible enforcement may well be much more important than the actual substance of the agreement. The multidimensional interaction between the European Union and Poland, which addresses both institution-building (through financial aid, twinning and other exchanges) and enforcement, is probably the most important sense in which the EA is WTO-plus.

It may be impossible or undesirable to repeat such a large-scale enlargement project, but there may be substantial benefits from applying such a multidimensional approach if indeed deep integration is desired.

The reason is that removing trade barriers in the regulatory domain is much more complex than, for example, simply removing tariffs. Adjusting to a regional hegemon (even a benign one) is politically controversial and may impose significant economic costs in the short run, especially if the countries are at different levels of development and the anchor country's regulation is viewed as too advanced for the other countries. Such adjustment costs may warrant aid (especially when the counterpart is a poorer country), and institutional exchanges can help create the skills and institutional infrastructure needed for harmonization of regulation and its implementation. Finally, the political interaction and continuous control can help to improve enforcement. It seems unlikely that deep integration is feasible without such underpinnings.

Notes

1. These agreements could be most readily compared to the Association Agreements concluded with Malta, Cyprus and Turkey in the 1960s.
2. It bears noting that some reforms had occurred already in the 1980s. Moreover, agriculture had always been in private hands (see Wellisz, 1995).
3. On all this, see Kornai (1992).
4. For overviews of Poland's economic reforms, see EBRD (various years) and IMF (1999, 2000).
5. Trade with Western Europe accounted for about 20 per cent of total trade in 1985 (see Varblane, 2000).
6. On all this see Michalek (2000).
7. For surveys of these reforms, see Sachs (1991) and Balcerowicz (1995).
8. I avoid the phrase free trade agreement, since none of them remove all barriers to trade.
9. For an overview of anti-dumping, safeguards, voluntary export restraints, etc., see Kaliszuk (2000a, 2000b).
10. Estimates by Urmas Varblane (2000) suggest that support for agriculture in Poland is well below the EU level, which means that net protection may in fact go up after accession.
11. The EAs were signed between the European Communities and Poland, but I often refer to the European Union in the text for ease of exposition. I therefore use the two terms interchangeably.
12. The term "deep integration", denoting wide-ranging liberalization and harmonization of many policy areas, is borrowed from Lawrence (1995).
13. See also Jahns (2000) and Mayhew (1998, p. 135ff.) for a general discussion of financial aid to transition countries.
14. In reality there are even more dimensions, for example cultural cooperation, which are not considered in this chapter.
15. A similar argument is made in Lainela (2000).
16. Compliance with the *acquis* applies to mandatory technical regulations and regulatory norms concerning conformance assessment. The standards-making process in the European Union is in the hands of non-governmental standards institutions and the standards are generally voluntary.

17. The EU new approach directives are based on limited harmonization of minimum essential (safety) requirements and then the operation of mutual recognition. The old approach was essentially harmonization of everything through EU directives and regulations.
18. Interviews with Polish civil servants. The Committee for European Integration is now supposed to check the conformity of any standards and laws with the *acquis* before these are passed.
19. The Polish Committee for Standardization is also the national enquiry point for the implementation of the TBT commitments in the WTO.
20. Other areas of institution-building in agriculture include rural development, agri-environment and afforestation, early retirement, veterinary and phytosanitary administration and preparation for CAP instruments and common market organizations.
21. Interviews with Polish civil servants and business people.
22. Interviews.
23. The members of the current committee on government procurement are: Aruba, Austria, Belgium, Canada, Denmark, European Communities, Finland, France, Germany, Greece, Hong Kong, Iceland, Ireland, Israel, Italy, Japan, Korea, Liechtenstein, Luxembourg, Netherlands, Norway, Portugal, Singapore, Spain, Sweden, Switzerland, United Kingdom and United States.
24. Interviews.
25. Interviews at European Commission.

REFERENCES

Agh, Attila (1998), *The Politics of Central Europe*, London: Sage Publications.

Balcerowicz, Leszek (1995), *Socialism, Capitalism, Transformation*, Budapest: Central European University Press.

Brenton, Paul, John Sheehy and Marc Vancauteren (2001), "Technical Barriers to Trade in the European Union: Importance for Accession Countries", CEPS Working Paper 144, Brussels: CEPS.

EBRD (European Bank for Reconstruction and Development) (various years), *Transition Report*, London: EBRD.

European Commission (2000), "Regular Report on Poland's Progress towards Accession 2000", at http://www.europa.eu.int/comm/enlargement/dwn/report_11_00/pdf/en/pl_en.pdf.

——— (2001a), "Regular Report on Poland's Progress towards Accession", at http://europa.eu.int/comm/enlargement/report2001/index.htm#Regular_Reports.

——— (2001b), *Twinning in Action*, Brussels: European Commission – Enlargement Directorate General, October.

——— (2002), *The Enlargement Process and the Three Pre-accession Instruments: Phare, ISPA, Sapard*, Brussels: European Commission – Enlargement Directorate General, February.

Feldmann, Magnus, and Razeen Sally (2002), "From the Soviet Union to the European Union: Estonian Trade Policy, 1991–2000", *The World Economy* 25 (1), pp. 79–106.

Gomułka, Stanisław (1978), "Growth and Import of Technology: Poland 1971–80", *Cambridge Journal of Economics* 2, pp. 1–16.

Hoekman, Bernard, and Michel Kostecki (1995), *The Political Economy of the World Trading System: From GATT to WTO*, Oxford: Oxford University Press.

Hoekman, Bernard, and Petros C. Mavroidis (1995), "The WTO's Agreement on Government Procurement: Expanding Disciplines, Declining Membership?", CEPR Discussion Paper No. 1112, London: CEPR.

IMF (International Monetary Fund) (1998), *Republic of Poland – Selected Issues and Statistical Appendix*, IMF Staff Country Reports No. 98/51, 22 June, available at http://www.imf.org/external/pubs/.

—— (1999), *Republic of Poland – Selected Issues*, IMF Staff Country Reports No. 99/32, 5 May, available at http://www.imf.org/external/pubs/.

—— (2000), *Republic of Poland: Selected Issues*, IMF Staff Country Reports No. 00/60, 11 May, available at http://www.imf.org/external/pubs/.

Jahns, Hanna (2000), "EU Aid Fund for Poland 1997–2000: Methods and Chances of Their Effective Utilisation", in Foreign Trade Research Institute, *Poland's Foreign Trade and Economic Policy*, Warsaw: Foreign Trade Research Institute.

Kaliszuk, Ewa (2000a), "Non-Tariff Restrictions on Polish Imports and Exports", in Foreign Trade Research Institute, *Poland's Foreign Trade and Economic Policy*, Warsaw: Foreign Trade Research Institute.

—— (2000b), "Zastąpenie przepisów antydumpingowych przepisami o knkurencji", in Instytut Koniunktur i Cen Handlu Zagranicznego, *Korzyści i Koszty Członkowstwa Polski w Unii Europejskiej*, Warsaw: Foreign Trade Research Institute.

Kawecka-Wyrzykowska, Elzbieta (2000), "Tariff Policy and Charges on Imports in 1999–2000 in the Context of Poland's Preparations for Accession to the European Union", in Foreign Trade Research Institute, *Poland's Foreign Trade and Economic Policy*, Warsaw: Foreign Trade Research Institute.

Kawecka-Wyrzykowska, Elzbieta, and Ewa Synowiec (2000), "The Process of Negotiations and Poland's Adjustment to the Requirements of EU Membership", in Foreign Trade Research Institute, *Poland's Foreign Trade and Economic Policy*, Warsaw: Foreign Trade Research Institute.

Kornai, János (1992), *The Socialist System: The Political Economy of Communism*, Oxford: Oxford University Press.

Kundera, Jaroslaw (2000), "Certyfikacja i zakupy publiczne", in Instytut Koniunktur i Cen Handlu Zagranicznego, *Korzyści i Koszty Członkowstwa Polski w Unii Europejskiej*, Warsaw: Foreign Trade Research Institute.

Lainela, Seija (2000), "Lamasta kasvuun – Baltia vuosituhannen vaihteessa", BOFIT Online Working Paper No. 6/2000, Helsinki: Bank of Finland, at http://www.bof.fi/bofit.

Lawrence, Robert Z. (1995), *Regionalism, Multilateralism, and Deeper Integration*, Washington DC: Brookings Institution.

Mayhew, Alan (1998), *Recreating Europe: The European Union's Policy towards Central and Eastern Europe*, Cambridge: Cambridge University Press.

Messerlin, Patrick (1994), "Central European Countries' Trade Laws in the Light of International Experience", CEPR Discussion Paper No. 1044, London: CEPR.

Michalek, Jan Jakub (2000), "The Europe Agreement and the Evolution of Polish Trade Policy", *Yearbook of Polish European Studies* 4, pp. 99–124.

Papliński, Andrzej (2000), "Legal Conditions of Investment in Poland", in Foreign Trade Research Institute, *Foreign Investments in Poland: Jubilee Report*, Warsaw: Foreign Trade Research Institute.

Sachs, Jeffrey D. (1991), *Poland's Jump to the Market Economy*, Cambridge, MA: MIT Press.

US Department of Commerce (2000), *Review of Poland*, available at http://www.usatrade.gov/website/ccg.nsf/CCGurl/CCG-POLAND2002-CH-6:-00507DAB.

Varblane, Urmas (2000), "The Trade Policy Implications of Joining the EU: Poland and Estonia Compared", in Marzenna Waresa (ed.), *Foreign Direct Investment in a Transition Economy: The Case of Poland*, London: SSEES.

Wellisz, Stanislaw (1995), "Poland", in Padma Desai (ed.), *Going Global: Transition in the World Economy*, Cambridge, MA: MIT Press.

WTO (World Trade Organization) (2000a), "Trade Policy Review Poland: Minutes of Meeting", WTO Document WT/TPR/M/71, at http://www.wto.org.

——— (2000b), "Government Procurement Review of the European Union", Document WT/TPR/S/72, at http://www.wto.org.

——— (n.d.), *Overview on Government Procurement*, available at http://www.wto.org/english/tratop_e/gproc_e/gp_gpa_e.htm.

4

The EU–Mexico Free Trade Agreement: Assessing the EU approach to regulatory issues

Joakim Reiter

Introduction

Many modern regional trade agreements (RTAs) go beyond traditional trade issues, such as the liberalization of tariffs and quotas, and thereby represent examples of what has been coined "deep integration". These RTAs include trade issues that were incorporated in the multilateral trading system at the Tokyo and Uruguay Rounds, such as services, government procurement, intellectual property rights, sanitary and phytosanitary measures (SPS), and technical barriers to trade (TBTs). But some more recent agreements also extend to cover new trade-related policy areas that are, at least in part, on the Doha Development Agenda established at the Ministerial Meeting of the World Trade Organization (WTO) in Qatar in November 2001. In the WTO context, these policy areas are often referred to as the Singapore issues, because they were discussed at the 1996 WTO Ministerial in Singapore, and include transparency in government procurement, trade facilitation, investment and competition. Some modern RTAs go one step further and include other important and potentially even more controversial policy issues, such as environmental regulation and labour standards.

Although regulatory and other "behind the border" issues are key elements of many modern regional trade agreements, the WTO provides little guidance on what types of commitments in RTAs will be compatible with WTO obligations. This is in contrast to the area of trade in goods and services, where a number of WTO provisions – under Article XXIV of the General Agreement on Tariffs and Trade (GATT), Article V of the General Agreement on Trade in Services (GATS) and the Enabling Clause – spell out what is expected in terms of liberalization both between the parties of the agreement and between the signatories and third parties. These WTO provisions establish a minimum level of commitment necessary in order to enter into an RTA. Moreover, they serve to safeguard the integrity of the multilateral system by prohibiting the parties to an agreement shifting the burden of adjustment onto third parties. For many of the regulatory trade issues and trade-related policy areas there is either a lack of clarity concerning the coverage of regulatory issues or, as in the case of intellectual property rights and government procurement, no WTO provisions governing RTAs. As a consequence, the parties to RTAs have substantial room for manoeuvre to pursue agendas and adopt commitments based on highly distinct models and with very different levels of ambition.

Furthermore, the economic impact and the type of challenges that these "deep" regional agreements pose for the multilateral system are highly complex and largely unknown. There exists a longstanding and inconclusive debate over whether RTAs are stumbling or building blocks for the multilateral trading system. The debate has to date mostly focused on the trade creation and diversion caused by RTAs. However, "deep integration" adds a new, and somewhat different, dimension to the debate about regionalism versus multilateralism. In addition to the economic impact, there is also the question of the compatibility of different regulatory frameworks, or what the WTO (1995) has called institutional complementarity. Regional trade agreements could consolidate regulatory rules and practices that might either facilitate or hinder the establishment of new WTO provisions. For example, if different RTAs create divergent regulatory rules in new policy areas, this could obstruct the development of new disciplines at the multilateral level. In such cases RTAs might be seen as a stumbling block, and vice versa.

This chapter addresses the question of the importance and the complex implications of "deep" regional trade agreements, as outlined above, by conducting a case study of the free trade agreement (FTA) between the European Union and Mexico. Three interrelated issues are covered. First, the chapter describes the European Union's approach to regulatory issues in the agreement with Mexico – more specifically TBTs, SPS, public procurement, services and investment. Second, the chapter discusses the economic impact of the EU approach and the final EU–Mexico FTA in the area of regulatory policies. Third, the chapter considers the interaction between the EU–Mexico FTA and other agreements, in particular the North American Free Trade Agreement (NAFTA) and multilateral trade rules.

The primary purpose, and hence focus, of the chapter is the analysis of the EU approach to dealing with regulatory policies. There are a number of reasons for this. The approach adopted determines the agreement's potential economic impact in terms of market opening. The approach is also decisive for the agreement's complementarity, or lack of complementarity, with the approach to these new regulatory policy issues employed in other FTAs and in the WTO. Moreover, given the fact that the EU–Mexico FTA entered into force only in July 2000 (and for some sections of the agreement, March 2001), it is not possible to make more than tentative conclusions concerning the economic impact of the agreement. Few economic assessments have so far been made of the agreement, and its effectiveness in addressing existing trade barriers, and in particular regulatory barriers, can be evaluated only once the agreement has been in effect for some time.

The EU–Mexico FTA represents a particularly suitable and illustrative case study. Mexico is a contracting party of NAFTA, which constitutes one, if not the foremost, example of the existing US approach to regulatory barriers. The analysis of the EU–Mexico FTA should thus provide a good indication of the interaction between the two trading powers' approaches. The potential economic effects of NAFTA also meant that commercial motives played a bigger role in the driving forces behind the European Union's desire to negotiate with Mexico than has been the case with previous EU FTAs or Association Agreements. These commercial motives, to level the playing field with the United States, may have led the European Union to explore and adopt new policy positions in relation to different regulatory areas.

The aim of this chapter is first and foremost therefore to describe the "regional approach" to regulatory issues that was established in the EU–Mexico FTA. The chapter also includes some general conclusions concerning the agreement's economic impact, on the one hand, and the interaction between the agreement and the WTO, on the other. Finally, I look at the recently concluded free trade agreement with Chile in order to facilitate an assessment of whether the European Union's approach to regional trade is developing over time. First of all, however, I describe the background and motives for the EU–Mexico negotiations.

Driving forces behind the EU–Mexico FTA

The political and economic relationships between the European Union (formerly the European Communities) and Mexico were formalized in the 1991 Framework Agreement for Cooperation. However, with Mexico becoming more open and active in regional trade negotiations, as well as undergoing substantial domestic liberalization and deregulation, there was an increasing need for the European Union to reach a new agreement with Mexico that would safeguard its interests in that market. These driving forces, or motives, culminated with the launch of the negotiations for a free trade agreement in the second half of 1998.

"Stop and go" in the preparations of the EU–Mexico FTA

In the early 1990s Mexico engaged in the negotiations that ultimately led to the creation of NAFTA on 1 January 1994. That same year, Mexico negotiated no fewer than four other FTAs, with Venezuela, Bolivia, Colombia – under the framework of the Latin America Integration Agreement (LAIA) – and Costa Rica. Mexico had also already signed an FTA with Chile 1991.

Spurred by the immediate competitive disadvantage that these developments, particularly NAFTA, represented for EU exporters and investors, the European Union began exploring ways to strengthen its political and economic relations with Mexico. At Essen in December 1994, the European Council called upon the Council and the European Commission to "put forward ideas on the future forms of relations with Mexico". The Commission's response was a Communication to the Council and the European Parliament in February 1995. The Commission proposal, "Towards Closer Relations between the European Union and Mexico", constituted a strategy to strengthen political dialogue, increase cooperation between the two parties and gradually liberalize trade. On the basis of this strategy, in April 1995 the General Affairs Council requested the Commission to prepare draft negotiating directives.

The Commission presented its draft negotiating directives to the Council in the second half of 1995. The proposals consisted of three main pillars:
- political dialogue in the shape of a regular high-level dialogue;
- cooperation in further areas than those covered by the 1991 Framework Agreement;
- trade in the form of the gradual establishment of a framework to encourage the development of trade in goods, services and investment *inter alia* through progressive and reciprocal liberalization.

In the discussions over the months that followed, however, the Council failed to reach an agreement on a number of aspects of the draft directives. Most contentious was the issue of progressive and reciprocal liberalization. Despite these difficulties, the Madrid Summit in December 1995 saw agreement in the European Council that negotiations with Mexico should begin as soon as possible on "a new agreement covering political, economic and commercial aspects, including progressive and reciprocal trade liberalization". The problems that remained unsolved related to the *form* of liberalization that should be pursued in negotiations with Mexico. On the one side, a group of member states wanted to create an FTA and grant preferential treatment to Mexico. On the other side were some member states calling for liberalization on a multilateral most favoured nation (MFN) basis and/or expressing reservations regarding an FTA.

On two occasions in late 1995 and early 1996 the Mexican government conveyed to the European Union its objective of establishing an FTA. Mexico rejected liberalization on an MFN basis as lacking commercial incentives. In the EU Council of Ministers, however, the issue remained unsolved. So the Commission was asked to conduct an impact assessment of the WTO compatibility of an agreement. The Commission study, finalized in the summer of 1996, set out the economic costs and benefits of an agreement, as well as the implications of an FTA for EU common policies and EU relations with its main trading partners (EC Commission, 1996). Shortly thereafter, a consensus on the negotiating directives was reached in May 1996 (EC Council, 1996).

Finally, in June 1997, almost two years after the Commission tabled its draft negotiating directives, the European Union and Mexico concluded new framework agreements that provided a starting point for the subsequent negotiations on an FTA between the European Union and Mexico. There were three legal texts:

- a Global Economic Partnership, Political Coordination and Cooperation Agreement (also called Global Agreement), which covered objectives for "progressive and reciprocal liberalization" of trade in goods, services, for public procurement, competition, intellectual property, capital movements and payments;
- an Interim Agreement on trade and trade-related matters, which implemented the aims of the Global Agreement with the exception of services, capital movements and payments, as well as aspects of intellectual property;
- a Joint Declaration providing for parallel negotiations of those aspects covered by the Global Agreement but not included in the Interim Agreement (services, etc.).[1]

In early 1998 the European Union discussed new directives for the trade negotiations. However, since some member states did not approve of the Commission proposal on "guidelines" for the negotiations, a more elaborated and detailed mandate was tabled by the UK presidency. The Council adopted the negotiating directives, or mandate, in May 1998. The objectives of establishing a free trade area in goods and an economic integration agreement in services were explicitly stipulated in the mandate, as was the requirement that national treatment should be extended to all areas covered by the agreement. So the negotiating mandate covered a number of "new" trade policy issues, such as capital movements and payments, public procurement, competition and intellectual property.

Securing a market and levelling the playing field

The European Union had a number of motives for attempting to solidify its relations with Mexico. Mexico had, after a "lost" decade in the 1980s, embarked on a domestic reform process of deregulation, privatization and general market opening to foreign goods and investors. A central element of this reform process was Mexico's accession to the international economic institutions. In 1986, Mexico became a Contracting Party of the GATT. Less than a decade later, in 1994, Mexico acceded to the Organisation for Economic Co-operation and Development (OECD).

Of potentially more importance for Mexico's liberalization process, however, was the country's parallel regional trade strategy, which dominated Mexico's policy in the 1990s. Starting with the agreement with Chile in 1991, Mexico established a web of preferential trade agreements with its neighbours in the Western hemisphere, such as the United States and Canada (1994), Colombia (1995), Venezuela (1995), Bolivia (1995), Costa Rica (1995), Nicaragua (1998) and Uruguay (1999) – not to mention Mexico's joining of Asia-Pacific Economic Cooperation (APEC) in 1993.

The European Union in general, and some of its member states in particular, had long-established and prosperous economic ties with Mexico. The reforms of the Mexican economy increased the perception of Mexico as a promising market and an attractive destination for foreign investments and exports. Furthermore, European investors saw the network of agreements between Mexico and its neighbours as granting Mexico the potential function of a stepping-stone for trade and investment into many of the other important markets in the Western hemisphere.

Simultaneously the European Union was experiencing a sharp and continuing decline in its market share in Mexico (see figure 4.1). The European Union's share of total Mexican trade shrunk from 10.6 per cent in 1991 to 6.5 per cent in 1999. Between 1991 and 1995 EU–Mexico trade hardly grew at all in *absolute* terms. Although the growth in EU trade with Mexico picked up between 1995 and 1999 in *relative* terms, EU–Mexico trade was still outperformed by overall trade, thus resulting in a continued reduction in market shares for the European Union. These developments were in contrast to trade between Mexico and its FTA partners in the region. During the same period, these countries benefited from very positive growth in trade in absolute terms and improved mar-

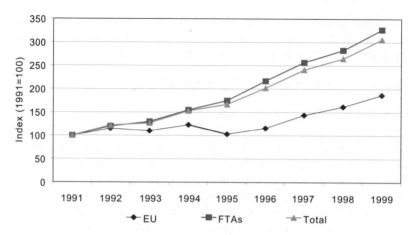

Figure 4.1 Evolution in Mexico's trade, 1991–9 (index 1991 = 100)
Source: SECOFI, Mexico.

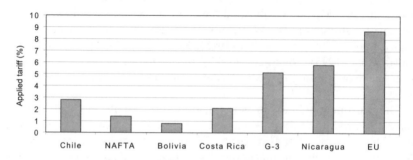

Figure 4.2 Mexico's weighted average applied tariffs, 1999
Source: SECOFI, Mexico.

ket shares in Mexico. Many EU member states therefore feared trade diversion was occurring, not least from the establishment of NAFTA.[2]

The gap between bilateral EU–Mexico and overall trade growth can be traced, to some extent, to the lack of equivalent market opportunities, or "a level playing field", for EU exporters and investors (see figure 4.2). This should not be confused with situations in which trade with partners occurs *at the expense* of trade with third countries. At the same time, however, the favourable treatment granted to, for example, US firms under NAFTA is hardly the only explanation, since the decline in EU exports started in 1991 when NAFTA was only an idea.[3] Nevertheless, the issue of a level playing field certainly had some relevance, not the least in the eyes of EU decision makers.

The gap between Mexico's applied MFN tariff rates and the preferential rates was, and remains, considerable. In 1999, EU exports faced an average applied duty of 8.7 per cent to enter the Mexican market, compared with an average preferential duty of less than 2 per cent for the parties of NAFTA. US exporters were thereby given an average preference margin of approximately 7 per cent. For many important products, such as automobiles, automotive parts and telecommunications equipment, Mexico's MFN applied rates were considerably higher, often around 15–20 per cent.

Moreover, in view of the trade deficit with the European Union and partly as a result of the financial crisis at the end of 1994 and onwards, the Mexican authorities took measures – stricter rules on certificates of origin and higher customs duties for example – in order to reduce imports from the European Union in certain sensitive sectors. For some products, tariff peaks were as high as 35 per cent, which was the general bound rate for tariffs on non-agricultural products in the WTO. These high bound rates for tariffs left the Mexican authorities considerable room for manoeuvre to increase rates on imports from countries with which Mexico was not bound by RTAs. In contrast, the tariffs paid by Mexico's FTA partners were approaching zero as tariff phase-out periods came to an end. A strong motive for the European Union to establish an FTA with Mexico was thus to balance the potential trade diversion effects of NAFTA, to level the playing field with US operators and to safeguard EU interests, in a wider sense (including in public procurement, services and direct investment markets), in this important market.

Market access and regulatory barriers

Another motive for the European Union to launch negotiations with Mexico was to address a number of trade irritants related to Mexican regulatory policy. Although the FTA negotiations never aimed to address individual market access barriers, the European Union had identified a number of important barriers for EU companies in the preparations of the negotiations.[4] Most of these barriers were not a result of non-compliance by Mexico with its current obligations, for example under the WTO. In other words, the FTA negotiations offered an opportunity of dealing with a number of pervasive regulatory barriers to market access in Mexico.

Non-tariff measures

A number of complaints were raised against Mexico's customs procedures. EU exporters considered Mexican customs procedures to be plagued by a lack of transparency, incoherent and inconsistent treatment of importers, long clearance times and a high frequency of random checks. Customs authorities were also known to reject import documentation on the basis of minor administrative shortcomings (spelling errors, etc.). Since 1994, products originating in NAFTA had benefited from a customs valuation system based on f.o.b. (free on board) prices, whereas imports from all other third countries, including the European Union, are subject to a system based on c.i.f. (cost, insurance, freight), which results in higher duties. The EU mandate therefore sought an agreement that would provide for the harmonization of both parties' customs valuation systems.

In the area of standards and other technical requirements (TBT), the European Union was concerned with a significant increase in the number of mandatory technical standards in Mexico. Of particular concern were the Mexican labelling requirements, on which there was insufficient transparency. For EU exporters, Mexican labelling regulations also requested excessive commercial information. Furthermore, all products, including intermediate products, were affected by the labelling regulations despite the fact that Mexico had notified its labelling regime as a consumer protection measure. Finally, verification procedures took place in the customs authority and not, as for domestic products, at the point of sales. All in all, on a number of accounts, the European Union felt that the Mexican labelling regime was more trade restrictive than needed to fulfil Mexico's legitimate objectives (as defined in the WTO Technical Barriers to Trade Agreement). The mandate therefore called on the European Union to include provisions in the final agreement, such as regulatory cooperation, that could lead "to harmonization of regulatory requirements on the basis of international standards and to the mutual recognition of conformity assessment".[5]

Investment

Although the Mexican investment regime had undergone substantial unilateral liberalization, many restrictions – ranging from outright prohibitions to ceilings on equity participation – remained in a number of sectors. In 16 sectors there were complete prohibitions on foreign investment. Ceilings for foreign ownership (variously 10, 25 or 49 per cent) existed in an additional 35 sectors. Finally, in 37 sectors, full foreign ownership was allowed only with prior permission by the Committee of Foreign Investment. Surprisingly, given these clear market restrictions, the mandate contained no references to investment and investment promotion, besides that covered by the provisions on trade in services. The mandate merely sought liberalization of capital movements. In trade in services, however, the mandate clearly stipulated that MFN and national treatment should be guaranteed for the right of establishment.[6]

Services

Many of the restrictions on investment were also related to trade in services (see above). The most common restriction was a 49 per cent ceiling on equity participation for foreign owners in service sectors such as telecommunications and many financial services. The issue of establishment of subsidiaries in financial services was particularly important for the European Union. The only foreign financial companies allowed to be established in Mexico were subsidiaries (not branches) of institutions based in a country with which Mexico had an agreement on free trade in financial services, for example NAFTA. Although the GATS negotiations on financial services, which were concluded in 1997, resulted in an increase of Mexican ceilings on aggregate and individual foreign holdings of voting share, EU institutions still faced important restrictions. These concerns were therefore reflected in the mandate, which sought the right for EU providers of financial services to establish wholly owned subsidiaries in Mexico and thus parity with NAFTA.

Public procurement

EU companies were generally excluded from Mexico's international tendering procedures, which guarantee participation of foreign bidders only from those countries, such as the United States and Canada, with which Mexico has signed FTAs (NAFTA) covering government procurement. The purchasing entity in Mexico could choose to open tendering to bidders from other countries, but this was discretionary. The EU mandate therefore stated that the Commission should negotiate "the maximum possible opening of the Mexican public procurement market".

The EU approach in the FTA with Mexico

The negotiations between Mexico and the European Union began in the latter part of 1998. The parties met for the first negotiating round in Mexico City, on 9–13 November. In all, the negotiators conducted nine negotiating rounds in little more than a year and the negotiations were concluded by the end of 1999. The agreement, which was signed with the Lisbon Declaration in March 2000, entered into force for trade in goods on 1 July 2000.[7] The Free Trade Agreement for services, as well as investment, intellectual property and government procurement, came into effect on 1 March 2001.[8]

General features of the agreement

The EU–Mexico FTA represented a unique phenomenon in EU trade policy in at least three regards:
- the agreement was claimed to cover an unprecedented broad spectrum of economic activities, and it was also the first transatlantic agreement for the European Union;
- it was the European Union's first post-GATS regional agreement in services, notified under Article V of GATS and based on GATS concepts and *acquis*;
- it was the fastest regional trade negotiation concluded by the European Union with a third party.[9]

In many ways, therefore, the EU–Mexico FTA was a major achievement for the European Union's trade policy in general and its approach to regional trade relations in particular. There are five main benefits of the agreement:[10]

1. *Coverage of goods, services and other regulatory issues.* Apart from trade in goods and services, the EU–Mexico FTA also covered regulatory issues such as government procurement, intellectual property rights, competition, and investments and related payments.
2. *High coverage in terms of trade volume and sectors.* Compared with the European Union's previous association and free trade agreements, the EU–Mexico FTA had a very substantial coverage, amounting to 95 per cent of current total trade. The parties agreed to abolish their tariffs on all industrial products, and 62 per cent of agricultural trade would be fully liberalized. In services, the FTA substantially eliminated all discrimination, covering both all modes of supply (as defined in GATS) and almost all sectors.[11]
3. *Short transition periods.* An important achievement of the EU–Mexico FTA was the relatively short transition periods for industrial products, whereby both parties refrained from making full use of the transition periods permitted under GATT Article XXIV (a maximum of 10 years). All industrial goods originating in Mexico were to be duty free within less than three years, by 1 January 2003 (82 per cent from the entry into force of the agreement). In exchange, Mexico will liberalize all industrial products by 2007 (almost half from the entry into force of the agreement), with a maximum tariff of 5 per cent from as early as 2003. The transition periods for agricultural products, on the other hand, are up to 10 years.
4. *NAFTA parity for the most part.* The value of the Mexican concessions in the EU–Mexico FTA was almost at the level of those in NAFTA. The transition periods naturally extended the time during which US (and Canadian) companies would benefit from the NAFTA prefer-

ence, but the fact that the agreement's transition periods are quite short, especially in a number of EU target sectors, reduced the impact of such preferences. In many respects, however, the EU–Mexico FTA successfully established parity with NAFTA in terms of both sector coverage and the coverage of tariff and regulatory barriers to trade and investment.

5. *Institutional mechanisms in terms of the dispute settlement mechanism and frameworks for further negotiations.* The EU–Mexico FTA fostered a rules-based framework by setting up special committees and establishing an ambitious dispute settlement mechanism. The European Union's previous regional trade agreements had not tended to opt for a fully fledged system for bilateral dispute settlement. The agreement provides for no fewer than seven special working committees on: rules of origin and customs cooperation; technical standards; sanitary and phytosanitary measures; government procurement; financial services; intellectual property; and competition policies.

The negotiation of the EU–Mexico FTA therefore represented a success for the EU approach to regional trade. In many respects, the FTA with Mexico went further than the European Union's previous regional integration agreements. The coverage of the agreement, amounting to 95 per cent of total current trade, was more or less unprecedented. Even on agricultural products, the coverage of 62 per cent had to be considered very ambitious from the EU point of view. Moreover, the European Union was *demandeur* on many of the regulatory policy issues in trade, such as government procurement, services and competition. In each of these issues, the FTA established high levels of commitment. At the same time, however, as we shall see below, the EU–Mexico FTA reveals a number of important shortcomings, especially in the areas of regulatory policies.

The EU approach to regulatory issues in the EU–Mexico FTA

At the outset of the negotiations with Mexico, the European Union had already identified a number of trade irritants, often related to regulatory policies in Mexico, that the agreement should help to remove. Based on the progress of the negotiations and final text of the EU–Mexico FTA, the scorecard of the EU approach to regulatory policies in regional trade negotiations gives a somewhat contradictory picture.

Technical barriers to trade (regulation, standards and conformance assessment)

The EU–Mexico FTA includes both substantive and procedural provisions in the area of TBTs (Art. 19 of the agreement). The substantive parts of the FTA confirm the parties' rights and obligations under the WTO TBT Agreement (Art. 19.2) (i.e. MFN, national treatment and transparency obligations). The FTA does not contain any WTO-plus commitments or even clarifications or elaborations of existing WTO provisions.

The procedural provisions, on the other hand, are more ambitious. These encompass, among other things, the establishment of a Special Committee (Art. 19.6) to act as a forum for consultations and to "work towards the *approximation* and *simplification* of labelling requirements, including voluntary schemes" (Art. 19.7(c)). However, given the serious problems facing EU companies as a result of excessive labelling requirements in Mexico, these procedural commitments appear surprisingly vague and non-binding. The European Union had raised the issue of labelling on various occasions, both in the regional negotiating rounds and in the WTO (the TBT Committee and the Trade Policy Review Mechanism). So one would have expected a concerted effort to incorporate substantive provisions in the FTA, or at least to make more binding procedural commitments that could help solve the issue.

The initial draft negotiating directives of the European Commission had proposed mutual recognition agreements (MRAs) and the promotion of harmonization (EC Commission, 1998). During the negotiations, however, the European Union was hesitant on MRAs. This was possibly because MRAs require, *ex ante*, broad equivalence between, and high levels of confidence in, the parties' different regulatory systems, including regulatory norms, standards and conformance assessment. When these conditions are not satisfied, there is the option of agreeing on procedural commitments, including a framework for consultations, bilateral cooperation, measures to promote international standards and technical assistance. The European Union opted for such procedural commitments in the FTA with Mexico. The Mexican authorities later claimed that they were prepared to engage in negotiations on MRAs. The reluctance on the part of the European Union to engage in MRA negotiations with Mexico probably stemmed in part from the lack of equivalence between the EU and Mexican regulatory norms and systems and in part from the highly burdensome nature of MRA negotiations.

Sanitary and phytosanitary measures

The provisions in the EU–Mexico FTA relating to sanitary and phytosanitary measures (Art. 20 of the FTA) resemble the structure of the article on TBT, but they are arguably even less elaborate. Accordingly the substantive provisions are merely a reaffirmation of the parties' existing WTO commitments (Art. 20.1). As with TBTs, the EU–Mexico FTA establishes a Special Committee (Art. 20.2) to "provide a forum to identify and address problems that may arise from the application of specific sanitary and phytosanitary measures" and "to consider, as necessary, the development of specific provisions for the application of *regionalisation*, or for the assessment of *equivalence*" (Art. 20.3).[12] Although this procedural commitment allows for the future incorporation of more extensive provisions, it provides little legal certainty. The impact of the EU–Mexico FTA in this area can therefore be established only in due course, once one can see what emerges from the largely ad hoc future consultations and deliberations of the Committee.

One important difference between the SPS and TBT sections is the lack of reference to technical assistance (under TBT, Art. 19.5) or to the importance of increasing mutual understanding (Art. 19.3). Conversely, it is underlined that "[e]ach party shall contribute to the work of the Special Committee, and consider the outcome of its work in accordance with its own internal procedures" (Art. 20.5). These provisions must be seen in the context of the potential divergence between North America (and thus NAFTA?) and the European Union over food safety and related issues (see chapter 9).

Services

All four modes of supply and all sectors are included in the EU–Mexico FTA (Title II, trade in services), except for the usual exclusions for audio-visual services, air transport and maritime cabotage. From the entry into force of the EU–Mexico FTA, the agreement establishes substantive bilateral rights and obligations, in terms of a standstill clause (for all sectors except financial services) and the exchange of lists of commitments (financial services).

Mexico transposes its commitments under international agreements into its national legislation. As a consequence, some of Mexico's commitments under, for example, the NAFTA have been more or less autonomously extended to the rest of the world. The main caveat to this is that the status of operators from third countries can be altered. In other words, the Mexican authorities have discretionary powers with regard to third-country suppliers that they do not have vis-à-vis NAFTA suppliers. The standstill clause in the EU–Mexico FTA provides a remedy for the potential problems caused by the exercise of such discretion by "locking in" the existing access that has in practice already been granted to EU companies. In so far as domestic liberalization is more comprehensive than the country's commitments under the WTO (GATS) or NAFTA, which tends to be the case, the standstill clause therefore provides even more favourable treatment (de jure not de facto) for EU services operators.

In financial services, on the other hand, both parties agreed to adopt a negative-list approach.[13] In these negotiations the European Union accomplished one particular objective specified in the mandate, namely that EU banks and insurance companies would be allowed to establish and operate on Mexican territory.

The services chapter of the EU–Mexico FTA also contains comprehensive procedural commitments. Recall that the standstill clause does not entail commitments on further liberalization. It is therefore important that the FTA provides for measures to be undertaken, within three years from the entry into force of the agreement, with a view to additional liberalization (Art. 7). This clause foresees the "elimination of substantially all remaining discrimination" (Art. 7.3), with maximum transition periods of 10 years, through the adoption of lists of reservations and calendars for further liberalization. Furthermore, in contrast to the provisions on TBT/SPS, the services FTA also calls on the initiation of negotiations on MRAs, particularly for the movement of natural persons, no later than three years following its entry into force (Art. 9). Finally, the FTA establishes a Special Committee on Financial Services that, among other things, has the competence to review the FTA in case Mexico or the European Union grants more favourable access to their markets to a third party pursuant to the conclusion of another (future) regional trade agreement (Art. 23).

The real impact of many of these procedural commitments remains to be seen, but they constitute an important complement to the substantive provisions of the FTA. All in all, despite the fact that the negotiations on liberalization for most sectors need to be resolved in the future, the EU–Mexico services FTA must be considered very ambitious. It should also be recognized that the negotiations were complicated by the fact that the European Union applied a "post-GATS model" whereas Mexico was familiar with a NAFTA type of structure. For example, in NAFTA, commitments relating to commercial presence in services are treated under the chapter on investment. The European Union, on the other hand, completely separates the services chapter from the investment chapter, so that the latter deals only with investments in production of goods. The final EU–Mexico agreement (in financial services) was structured in line with this so-called post-GATS approach.

Investment

In the area of investment, Title III of the EU–Mexico FTA does not add much to the OECD Code of Liberalization of Capital Movements and/or to the bilateral agreements on the protection of investments, the so-called BITs (bilateral investment treaties) that member states have signed with Mexico. Paradoxically, the FTA contains a definition of investment in Article 28.1 that is also equivalent to the OECD Code,

Annex 1, list A:I–IV, but there are no substantive liberalization commitments for these categories of investments. In fact, the only substantive provision seems to be the commitment progressively to eliminate restrictions on payments related to investment and a standstill. Apart from these provisions the parties merely agree to "recall their international commitments with regard to investment" (Art. 34). Moreover, the FTA includes a highly vague "declaration of intention" by the parties to promote investment through, for example, the conclusion of BITs and double taxation agreements by the EU member states and Mexico (Art. 33).

The limited nature of the provisions on investment reflects the great difficulty of the negotiations and the fact that they were plagued by internal EU problems related to, among other things, the issue of competence between the member states and the Commission. Member states have occasionally resisted competence passing to the European Communities on topics covered by trade negotiations. The Commission initially tabled a very ambitious proposal with even more far-reaching commitments than in NAFTA. Mexico did not reject the proposal but responded with a list of proposed exceptions. Opposition from a majority of EU member states based on the competence issue, however, led to the Commission withdrawing its proposal on investment in the latter part of the negotiations. In its place, the Finnish presidency of the Council tabled the very watered-down text that later became the FTA's provisions on investment.

There were two main problems with the Commission proposal. First, the proposal was perceived as sidestepping and having negative implications for member state competence and the authority of member states to negotiate BITs. Second, some member states were hesitant to engage in comprehensive investment negotiations in advance of the Seattle Ministerial Meeting, at which the European Union was seeking to include investment on the WTO agenda. The latter concern resulted in a compromise in terms of a review clause, whereby the parties agree to review the legal framework of the FTA within three years, "with the view of the objective of progressive liberalization of investment" (Art. 35). The final result, however, was that the EU–Mexico FTA is left without any real substantive or procedural commitments on investment.

Government procurement

The EU–Mexico FTA is very ambitious in the area of public procurement (Title III). The substantive provisions of the agreement are comprehensive and, in many respects, match the European Union's commitments under the plurilateral Government Procurement Agreement (GPA) in the WTO and Mexico's commitments under NAFTA. Mexico is not a member of the WTO GPA. Consequently, the agreement covers central purchasing entities and utilities, but provincial/sub-federal levels are excluded. In contrast to the TBT and SPS provisions, the FTA spells out the relevant obligations contained in the agreement rather than just referring to the parties' commitments under other agreements. The FTA explicitly provides for national treatment and non-discrimination (Art. 26) and includes provisions specifying procurement procedures (Art. 29), detailed commitments on bid challenge (which grants companies rights to challenge contract award procedures) (Art. 30) and provisions on information/transparency (Art. 31).

As in the case of services, it was recognized from the outset that the EU–Mexico FTA had to accommodate the fact the parties had different traditions and regulatory systems in the area of public procurement. Mexico was a contracting party of NAFTA and naturally predisposed to the rules and procedures of that agreement. The final text of the FTA therefore provides for what are in effect parallel provisions on procurement procedures and thresholds. The opening of the respective procurement markets is based on NAFTA provisions on the Mexican side and on the WTO GPA on the EU side.

With regard to procedural commitments, the FTA stipulates that the parties shall renegotiate the title on government procurement in the event of Mexico or the European Union granting more favourable access to their procurement markets to a NAFTA or GPA party in the future (Art. 37). A Special Committee on Government Procurement is established and mandated to "make recommendations for the improvement and amendment" of the scope of the FTA (Art. 32). Finally, the procedural provisions include a commitment to cooperate to further the use of information technology in procurement practice to facilitate the timely and effective flow of information (Art. 33).

The chapter on government procurement in the EU–Mexico FTA entered into force on 1 March 2001, after certain statistical information had been exchanged between the parties.

Impacts and institutional complementarity on regulatory issues

The rise in "deep" regional trade agreements such as the EU–Mexico FTA that cover a number of "behind the border" issues poses new questions about the relationship between regional trade agreements and the multilateral rules-based system. Provisions in regional agreements that are deeper and wider (broader) than the existing levels of commitments under the WTO are referred to as WTO-plus rules.[14]

WTO-plus commitments can take various forms. They can be broader in sector coverage than equivalent WTO agreements, contain more substantive commitments than the WTO or establish more extensive procedural obligations than in the WTO. Examples of broader coverage would be granting national treatment or MFN to a broader range of service sectors than in the GATS. Substantive commitments deepen the existing obligations under the WTO agreements by, for example, providing for mutual recognition, policy approximation or harmonization. Procedural commitments, on the other hand, include measures to increase transparency, enhance cooperation – so as to address specific market access issues (including dispute settlement procedures) – and review existing agreements with a view to strengthening them.

Substantive provisions will generally be more ambitious and provide greater market opening than procedural commitments. However, the two forms of commitment can serve as substitutes. For example, in order properly to resolve regulatory barriers to another party's market, a regional agreement can either (1) establish substantive WTO-plus commitments that clarify the existing rules of the WTO and perhaps also establish new rules that target these specific problems; or (2) reconfirm existing WTO rules and place a greater emphasis on their effective implementation (i.e. procedural WTO-plus commitments such as a bilateral dispute settlement procedure). Procedural commitments can therefore have important implications for the long-term effectiveness of RTAs.

In so far as the parties of regional trade agreements establish WTO-plus provisions, this can raise important concerns over the institutional complementarity between regional and multilateral agreements. The concept of institutional complementarity describes the compatibility (the synergies and potential contradictions) between the political/legal frameworks that are embedded in different trade agreements on the regional and multilateral levels.[15] Institutional complementarity is more of an issue in the case of substantive WTO-plus commitments in RTAs or when there are important, or controversial, differences between the regulatory regimes in the policy area concerned between major trading partners. More extensive sector coverage of WTO conform agreements may create regional preferences but does not raise issues of institutional complementarity. Procedural commitments also, almost by definition, rarely pose any threat to multilateralism.

The nature of WTO-plus commitments in regulatory policy areas, as well as the large variations in the scope of the various RTA commitments in this area, makes it difficult to conduct economic assessments of "deep" FTAs. It is very hard, if not impossible, therefore to quantify *in absolute terms* the economic impact of the EU–Mexico FTA in the area of regulatory policies. For example, how would one value the economic benefits of procedural WTO-plus commitments, such as information exchange, in the area of standards? Such economic impact assessments would instead need to focus more on the capacity of the FTA to resolve general market access issues and to "level the playing field" with third countries.

The analysis of the effects of the EU–Mexico FTA can therefore be seen as consisting of three elements:

- the economic impact of the agreement, in terms of resolving market access barriers and establishing NAFTA parity;
- the extent of WTO-plus (substantive) rules and potential contradictions between the EU–Mexico FTA and WTO agreements; and
- the existence of procedural commitments and their potential long-term impact as complements to other provisions of the FTA and substitutes for weak substantive rules.

Market opening, economic impact and NAFTA parity

The general economic importance of the agreement is underscored by its substantial coverage, amounting to 95 per cent of total trade in goods. The value of the total trade in goods in 1999 between the European Union and Mexico was US$18 billion (SECOFI, 2000, 2001). In the same year, trade in services amounted to €3.1 billion. So one can say that the FTA has an important economic impact. By and large, the value of the Mexican concessions to the European Union in the FTA equals that to the United States and Canada in NAFTA. Therefore, in terms of coverage, the EU–Mexico FTA generally succeeds in establishing parity with NAFTA.

Recent developments in bilateral trade seem to underscore the importance of the EU–Mexico FTA and have produced concrete results. During the first 18 months of the FTA, trade grew by 28.6 per cent. Mexican exports to the European Union appear to have benefited primarily from the agreement (exports increased by 44.1 per cent), but EU sales to the Mexican market also grew at an impressive rate (23.1 per cent). As a result, the European Union's share of total Mexican trade increased by 20 per cent.[16]

However, the economic impact on trade in goods must also be reviewed in light of how well the agreement provides for measures to address existing market access restrictions. As discussed above, the European Union identified a number of serious impediments to market access in Mexico, such as in TBT and SPS measures, even though there were no clear-cut cases of non-compliance with Mexico's obligations under the WTO in these areas. Moreover, the EU–Mexico FTA largely fails to address these regulatory barriers. The European Union refrained from pressing for MRAs because of the burdensome negotiations that this would have involved. Neither the SPS nor the TBT sections of the FTA contain any substantive provisions of importance. Therefore, the commitments fall short of the aims of the negotiating mandate, which were harmonization and mutual recognition. The agreement contains a rather weak best endeavours provision on the use of international standards. In short, the agreement contains no WTO-plus commitments in these areas.

Concerning procedural commitments, the agreement establishes Special Committees that will work towards the approximation and simplification of labelling requirements (in the TBT area) and the development of provisions on "regionalization" and equivalence (in the SPS area). There must be considerable doubt that these committees will make more than marginal contributions to improving market access in sectors where TBT and SPS measures are important. The committees may, however, help to improve the transparency of regulatory policies in Mexico and initiate cooperation and dialogue on existing trade irritants.

The TBT and SPS provisions of the EU–Mexico FTA are also much less elaborate than those in NAFTA. The TBT chapter of NAFTA both reiterates many of the provisions under the TBT and SPS agreements in the WTO and provides additional clarifications of some concepts (it is important to recall that NAFTA was concluded before the Uruguay Round). Key issues such as "compatibility and equivalence", "assessment of risk" and "legitimate objectives" are more clearly defined in NAFTA. In other words, the degree of discretion that national authorities have in implementing and interpreting NAFTA is less than in the case of the EU–Mexico FTA. The scope of the NAFTA TBT chapter is also broader than the equivalent article in the EU–Mexico agreement. For one thing, the NAFTA TBT chapter also covers trade in services. The provisions under NAFTA should thus be regarded as both deeper and wider than those under the EU–Mexico FTA.

In the same way, in the area of investment, the FTA with Mexico does not provide any legal certainty for EU investors. In the period between 1992 and 1998, EU investment in Mexico ranged from approximately €0.8 to €3.1 billion annually (Swedish National Board of Trade, 2001). As with TBT and SPS, the EU–Mexico FTA provisions on investment in manufacturing fall far short of the commitments on investment in NAFTA. In fact, NAFTA is potentially one of the most ambitious investment agreements in the world. NAFTA's investment chapter includes a large number of substantive provisions, covering national treatment and most favoured nation treatment for both pre- and post-establishment, as well as dispute settlement. Moreover, given the often complementary relationship between trade in services and trade in goods, there is a risk that the weak investment provisions of the EU–Mexico FTA may hamper liberalization in the considerably more ambitious area of commercial presence (under mode 3) in the services part of the agreement.

In contrast, the chapter on public procurement of the FTA grants access for EU companies bidding for contracts in the Mexican procurement market that is in line with the coverage of NAFTA. The coverage of the EU–Mexico FTA in terms of market value does not reach the level of the European Union's commitment under the GPA. This is mainly owing to the fact that the GPA covers regional and local government, which the FTA does not. Nevertheless, the European Union has been granted access that more or less matches Mexico's commitments under NAFTA.[17]

In some respects the EU–Mexico FTA does include "NAFTA-plus" commitments in the area of public procurement. The provisions on bid challenge are copied from the GPA and represent a more elaborate text than that in NAFTA. Additionally, the commitments relating to information and cooperation in the use of information technology should be considered NAFTA-plus as well as GPA-plus.

Another success story for the EU–Mexico FTA is provisions on services. The EU–Mexico services FTA has many benefits. For most sectors, the agreement establishes NAFTA parity. In some instances, the standstill clause even locks in reforms at a NAFTA-plus level because Mexico's liberalization has progressed since the entry into force of NAFTA. The parties have also agreed to initiate further talks to go beyond the already ambitious level of liberalization within a maximum time-frame of 10 years.

A further and more immediate benefit of the agreement is the liberalization commitments accomplished in financial services. The agreement makes it possible for EU financial services providers to establish and operate on Mexican territory on the same conditions as any competitors from NAFTA. But here the real economic impact of the EU–Mexico services FTA must be qualified. First, large EU financial services providers have often successfully circumvented the previous restrictions in Mexico by investing through their subsidiaries in the United States (hence free-riding on NAFTA). Second, the standstill clause of the services FTA has resulted in only limited de facto enhancement of market access in Mexico, because Mexico usually transposes most of its international commitments into national legislation anyway. As stated above, the standstill clause primarily serves to reduce the scope for discretion on the part of Mexican regulators and thus enhances legal security and predictability for EU services operators.

Interestingly, a closer look at the lists of commitments on financial services shows that these largely coincide with the parties' bindings under the WTO and/or in NAFTA. Very few alterations have been made. Despite the clear objective of increased liberalization, this confirms the view that services negotiations largely tend to lock in reforms that have already been achieved either through unilateral domestic decisions or through bindings in other agreements with third parties.

In sum, despite the comprehensiveness of the EU–Mexico FTA, in many regards the agreement fails properly to address some regulatory issues, such as investment, the environment, and TBT and SPS measures. In these areas the FTA is WTO compatible but fails to produce WTO-plus commitments for the parties. The agreement therefore reveals some serious shortcomings from an EU point of view in terms of establishing WTO-plus commitments and addressing regulatory policies that constitute market access barriers for EU companies. Although the European Union succeeded in establishing extensive coverage of substantive commitments on trade in services and government procurement, in most other areas the EU–Mexico FTA was limited to WTO-plus provisions of a procedural character. It is too early to make any definitive comments on the effectiveness of these procedural commitments. Nevertheless, these procedural provisions will probably prove all too vague to perform the function of solving regulatory barriers to the Mexican market.

Institutional complementarity: WTO-plus and multilateralism

Owing to the general lack of WTO-plus commitments in the EU–Mexico FTA, the agreement poses no or very few challenges, in terms of institutional complementarity, to the WTO rules-based system and multilateralism.

Rather than establishing new preferential rules and procedures, the EU–Mexico FTA appears to lock in reforms on regulatory issues such as government procurement and services. This is particularly relevant in the case of EU–Mexico, owing to the fact that Mexico often transposes its international commitments into domestic legislation and hence extends the treatment to all trade partners more or less automatically (see services above). Once reforms are locked in there is generally a strong resistance to changing the established domestic regimes. It is often neither feasible nor advisable to offer preferential treatment to trading partners in terms of the treatment of exports or investors by regulatory authorities, unless there is scope for regulatory discretion. Put simply, in contrast to preferences in the coverage of agreements, it is difficult to single out individual trading partners to which general regulatory norms, standards or labelling requirements should not apply. On the other hand, regional agreements could primarily be used to foster common understandings, including equivalence, or even regional standards, for example through harmonization. This would then constitute a form of preference. However, these forms of preferential regulatory treatment are much more difficult to achieve than regional preferences in traditional trade policy, such as tariffs.

These findings largely confirm previous analyses. In a report by the WTO Secretariat in 1995, it was stressed that "[m]embers of most regional agreements have continued to apply non-tariff barriers on imports from *all* trading partners" (WTO, 1995, p. 62). The report showed that non-tariff measures are usually not administered preferentially and domestic regulatory policies often cannot be administered preferentially.

At the same time, however, there are a few examples where substantive and procedural measures in the EU–Mexico FTA that are WTO-plus could illustrate a degree of divergence between the different FTAs. As we have seen in the case of the EU–Mexico FTA, the negotiations on services and public procurement were complicated by the differences between the US and EU approaches.[18] In this respect, the EU–Mexico FTA is a good illustration of the challenges for the multilateral system posed by divergent regional approaches.

In services, the problem was primarily due to the fact that NAFTA was established before GATS and, consequently, the structure of the NAFTA approach differs in important respects from that of the EU post-GATS approach. The solution in the EU–Mexico FTA was to merge the respective approaches in the negotiations, which required substantial effort and time. Ultimately, however, it is the EU approach to services that is applied in the EU–Mexico FTA (for now in financial services).

In the case of public procurement, the problem was, once more, that NAFTA was negotiated before the GPA. Also, Mexico was not a signatory of the GPA. The solution in the EU–Mexico FTA was to use parallel provisions; that is, the opening of the respective markets is based on NAFTA provisions on the Mexican side and the WTO GPA on the EU side.

Based on the experiences of the EU–Mexico FTA, we can conclude that differences in regulatory approaches generally increase the transaction costs of trade negotiations. The existence of separate EU and NAFTA approaches to services and government procurement was a complicating factor in the negotiations. But the transatlantic, cross-regional differences were certainly not insurmountable. The EU–Mexico agreement is one case where the NAFTA and EU approaches came together. In other words, cross-regional agreements do not seem to present major problems because of the general similarities between the NAFTA and EU approaches and the fact that, where differences exist, they appear to be manageable.

Of course, in theory, it would seem that the establishment of regional agreements that consolidate divergent approaches to new trade-related policies that are only in part, or not at all, covered by existing multilateral rules could run the risk of obstructing or at least complicating trade negotiations in the WTO. However, it remains to be seen how much of a problem this will be in practice in future multilateral negotiations such as the Doha Development Agenda. Just as in the case of services in the EU–Mexico FTA, it is not clear, for example, why and in what way the NAFTA investment chapter would slow down progress in preparing the investment negotiations in the WTO (such as on the issue of whether the approach to liberalization should be based on negative or positive listing).

Transparency, compliance and the diffusion of regulatory policies

It should be recognized that most of the WTO-plus commitments on regulatory issues in the EU–Mexico FTA take the form of procedural provisions. This minimizes concerns about potential incompatibilities between regionalism and multilateralism. But it also creates uncertainty about the future shape of the agreement.

As we have seen above, the EU–Mexico FTA includes a number of comprehensive procedural commitments relating to, among other things, future reviews of the agreement, information exchange between the parties and the establishment of various Special Committees to promote cooperation and consultation. Therefore, despite the often weak substantive provisions on regulatory issues, it may be too early to make any definitive judgement on the final effectiveness of the agreement in establishing WTO-plus commitments and in resolving market access issues such as regulatory barriers.

Through the deliberations in the large number of committees, transparency of the respective parties' regulatory systems should be enhanced. The transparency and consultation exercises of the Special Committees provide additional frameworks for discussing specific market access barriers, thereby complementing mechanisms such as the WTO Trade Policy Review Mechanism and notifications to the WTO. At the same time, however, owing to the lack of more substantive provisions in the FTA, there are no guarantees as to the result of such consultations.

Unfortunately, the lack of substantive provision does also have important repercussions on the issues of enforcement and compliance in some areas. The bilateral dispute settlement mechanism (DSM) enshrined in the FTA is very ambitious. But the lack of substantive rules on regulatory issues – even when these are exact copies of the existing WTO commitments – impedes the use of bilateral dispute settlement. For example, in the area of SPS and TBT, by merely referring to the commitments under the WTO, the European Union de facto precludes the opportunity of having recourse to bilateral dispute settlement in these two areas, since the bilateral DSM may not be applied to issues relating to the interpretation of WTO rules. The bilateral dispute settlement can thus not be used to solve bilateral trade irritants in the area of TBT and SPS. In these cases, there is no substitute for addressing the problems head on by establishing bilateral rules that are WTO-plus commitments, which is exactly what the EU–Mexico FTA fails to do.

A more positive example is the provisions on government procurement. Although many of the provisions largely echo those under the GPA (on the EU side) or NAFTA (on the Mexican side), the EU–Mexico FTA nevertheless specifies in detail all relevant commitments. That ensures a high level of legal security for EU operators in terms of both clarity of the rights and obligations under the agreement and recourse to bilateral dispute settlement.

It would also be premature to write off the long-term potential benefits of consultations and increased transparency, even where these occur on a voluntary basis. Transparency helps to promote understanding and confidence, two necessary – but not sufficient – conditions for any future negotiation of mutual recognition agreements. Moreover, by diffusing certain regulatory practices – for example through the promotion of international regulatory norms or standards – these mechanisms have the potential of facilitating regulatory best practice and/or approximation between the regulatory systems of the parties.

Such long-term benefits may result from the EU–Mexico FTA. As shown above, in the domain of non-tariff barriers and regulatory issues on trade in goods, the provisions of the FTA are mainly non-compulsory means of promoting regulatory cooperation. In any event, the implementation of the relevant provisions is still in its initial phase. The technical bodies have only just begun their respective activities. At the same time, at only the second meeting of the Joint Council in Brussels in May 2002, the parties agreed to accelerate the tariff phase-out for a group of products with a total estimated value of €1.7 billion.[19] Even taking into account these and future potential positive outcomes of the procedural commitments under the agreement, the EU approach to regulatory barriers reveals serious shortcomings.

The future of the EU regulatory approach: Path-dependency or filling the gaps?

In many respects the EU–Mexico FTA should probably be regarded as a major achievement for the European Union and, in particular, for the Union's approach to regional trade. The agreement was driven by strong economic incentives, it is ambitious in its scope and level of liberalization and, in some respects, it includes important commitments on non-tariff issues. In addition, the EU regional approach in the EU–Mexico FTA seems to pose few, or no, threats to the multilateral system. What is more, despite some differences between the EU and NAFTA approaches, the EU–Mexico FTA illustrates the general compatibility of the approaches of the two dominant actors in the international trading system.

However, in a number of areas the European Union failed to make full use of the regional negotiation with Mexico as a laboratory for elaborating on substantive rules for dealing with "new" trade issues, such as regulatory measures. Of the six specific trade policy areas that have been analysed and highlighted in this chapter – TBTs (including environmental labelling), SPS, services, investment and government procurement – in only two cases (government procurement and services) did the EU approach to regulatory trade issues somewhat match, or go beyond, Mexico's existing substantive commitments in the WTO (or NAFTA). In the other areas the agreement contained no commitments, or merely procedural commitments, of a WTO-plus nature. Investment remains the biggest disappointment in the EU approach to regional trade negotiations, which is partly owing to the issue of competence between the Commission and the member states within the European Union. The area of investment strikingly illustrates the problems for the European Union in taking more active positions when it is plagued by internal divisions. Particularly appalling is the fact that there simply does not exist an EU approach to environment in regional trade negotiations, as illustrated by the EU–Mexico FTA. It remains to be seen if some more recent developments, particularly the discussions on an EU strategy on sustainable development and how that strategy should relate to the EU position in the WTO, spill over to the European Union's regional trade policy strategy. In that case, it could potentially provide a starting point for a more proactive position on environmental issues. Finally, there is a strong need to establish substantive bilateral rules in the area of TBTs and SPS – not merely to include references to the obligations under the relevant WTO agreements – if the European Union seriously intends to address market access issues. Although there were some indications of a nascent interest in WTO-plus rules in the EU–Mexico FTA, the present levels of commitment virtually preclude recourse to any bilateral dispute settlement.

Therefore, the key question is to what extent the FTA with Mexico represents a first step in the evolution of a new comprehensive EU approach to regulatory issues in regional trade agreements. It remains to be seen whether the European Union is prepared to "fill the gaps" in the EU–Mexico FTA and explore further the possibilities of making WTO-plus commitments on regulatory issues in up-coming regional trade negotiations with non-applicant countries outside the Union. Presently, the European Union is engaged in, or is planning to initiate, regional trade negotiations with a large number of countries.[20]

Among the most important negotiations in recent years have been those with Mercosur[21] and Chile. These were launched almost back to back with the finalization of the EU–Mexico FTA. The two negotiations – aiming to establish Association Agreements covering political dialogue, cooperation and trade – were parallel but not formally linked. As it turned out, however, the pace and progress were very different with Chile than with Mercosur. After two years of negotiations, on 26 April 2002, the European Union and Chile publicly announced that the parties had successfully concluded an Association Agreement. The Association Agreement incorporates a free trade area, a political dialogue and extensive cooperation aspects. The negotiations with Mercosur, on the other hand, are still inconclusive and seem set to continue for quite some time. Nevertheless, in May 2002 in conjunction with the EU–Latin America Summit in Madrid, the European Union and Mercosur agreed on an Action Plan on Business Facilitation, covering SPS measures, standards, technical regulations and conformity assessment, customs and electronic commerce.[22]

Therefore, the EU–Chile Association Agreement (and to a lesser extent the EU–Mercosur Action Plan on Business Facilitation) provide a good point of reference to evaluate the changes and learning curve, over time, in the EU regulatory approach to regional agreements.

The launch of the negotiations with Chile

The preparations for the negotiations with Chile followed as a natural consequence from the preparations with Mercosur. Chile was interesting from an EU point of view primarily because of its assumed integration with Mercosur: in 1996 Chile had signed an association agreement with Mercosur. The market of Mercosur was the obvious driving force. In the period 1992–8, EU export growth to that region exceeded that to the Mediterranean or to South-East Asia.[23]

Partly as a means to support and reinforce the regional integration process within Mercosur – with the ultimate aim of completing a customs union and establishing a common market by 1 January 2006 – the European Union signed an Interregional Framework Co-operation Agreement with Mercosur in December 1995. Six months later, the European Union signed a similar agreement with Chile, the Framework Co-operation Agreement (Official Journal, 1999). These agreements laid down the objective of strengthening economic relations through the progressive and reciprocal liberalization of trade, in order to lead to the establishment, in the long term, of a political and economic association between the European Union and Chile and Mercosur respectively. As in the case of Mexico, however, the preparations for the negotiations became both long and, on many occasions, contentious, as was reflected in the preparatory work and in the internal EU discussions on the negotiating directives. Nevertheless, the European Union, Mercosur and Chile were able agree on the launch of negotiations on a future EU–Chile Association Agreement and an Interregional Association Agreement between the EU and Mercosur at the EU–Latin America Summit on 28 June 1999. The formal negotiations on the establishment of a political and economic association were then launched in November 1999.

In many important aspects, the driving forces behind the negotiations with Mercosur and Chile resemble those behind trade negotiations with Mexico. Besides the political rhetoric and the desire to strengthen political ties between the two regions, the aim of the negotiations was largely to solidify, and expand, existing economic relationships. As in the case of Mexico, the initiative to establish Association Agreements with Mercosur and Chile represented, in part, a reaction to the launch of trade negotiations in the Western hemisphere, the purpose being to level the playing field with the United States and the prospective commitments under the Free Trade Area of the Americas.

Additionally, a number of "behind the border" measures, including the area of investments, trade in services and government procurement, as well as competition policy and intellectual property rights, were of high priority for the European Union, and a comprehensive agreement could serve important and strategic economic interests. Particularly in relations with Mercosur, EU exporters and investors experienced many of the same types of market access barrier related to regulatory issues as in Mexico. For example, there were various problems with customs procedures, excessive labelling requirements and control measures. Even though the negotiations were not aimed at solving individual market access problems, providing a framework for dealing with such issues was obviously one motive.

The EU–Chile Association Agreement and WTO-plus commitments

The negotiations on an EU–Chile Association Agreement were concluded at the end of April 2002. The agreement was initialled on 10 June 2002 in Brussels and was signed in the autumn of 2002, when the ratification processes of the parties began. The Association Agreement comprises three main chapters: political dialogue, cooperation and trade. In total, it required 10 rounds of negotiations before the agreement could be concluded.[24]

The trade chapter is highly ambitious. Immediately after the conclusion of the agreement, Commissioner Pascal Lamy stated: "Our negotiation has delivered the most ambitious and innovative results ever for a bilateral agreement by the EU. This is a 'fourth generation plus' agreement."[25] The trade chapter establishes a free trade agreement in goods covering all sectors, with a high level of liberalization and, in most cases, short transition periods.[26] It also includes a comprehensive free trade agreement in services, as well as in investment and government procurement. Moreover, the trade chapter covers all the areas of EU–Chile trade relations, including competition policy and intellectual property rights, and provides for recourse to a bilateral dispute settlement mechanism.

Although it is premature to evaluate its potential impact in the field of regulatory policy, the agreement is important in terms of both economic implications and the EU approach to regulatory policy issues in regional trade agreements. The EU–Chile Association Agreement seems to have filled the gaps in, or progressed from, the EU–Mexico FTA in a number of notable areas and done so thoroughly. The main gaps filled are on SPS measures, trade facilitation and investment, and substantial progress was also made in services and government procurement. It is safe to say that, in almost all of these areas, the agreement goes well beyond the parties' respective commitments under the WTO.

Investment is probably the most notable achievement of the negotiations. The EU–Chile Association Agreement represents the first time that the European Union, and its member states, have agreed to commitments on establishment (of investments) in a bilateral agreement with another party.[27] As noted above, there have been considerable internal difficulties within the European Union when dealing with investment in RTAs. The chapter on establishment provides for national treatment for the establishment and operation of EU companies in Chile, and vice versa. Chile had initially proposed an investment chapter in line with that of NAFTA, which covers both pre- and post-establishment and investment in services and manufactures. However, the final agreement followed the EU proposal, which covers only non-service sectors and focuses on the establishment of investments rather than the protection of investments once established. This more limited approach was necessary if the Commission was to get sufficient support among the member states for the inclusion of investment. The EU–Chile agreement therefore provides a new EU model for the coverage of direct investment.

In trade in goods, the EU–Chile agreement also includes substantial commitments on cooperation and information exchange among customs authorities. Under the article on customs and related trade matters (section 3 under Chapter II on non-tariff measures), an ambitious trade facilitation agenda is established. In contrast, no reference is made in the EU–Mexico FTA to trade facilitation. The EU–Chile agreement underscores the importance of transparency and efficiency in customs operations and outlines a long list of actions in order to achieve these two goals (Art. 79). It targets burdensome legislation as well as discretionary practices, and provides for consultations to solve such problems. Moreover, the EU–Chile agreement includes an article on the enforcement of preferential treatment (Art. 82), in which administrative cooperation is called upon so as to avoid de facto impairment of the benefits accruing from the preferences under the agreement. It also gives the parties the right to retaliate, through temporary suspension of the preferences, in the event of systematic failure to provide administrative cooperation or of fraud.

In the area of SPS (section 5 in Chapter II), the agreement includes a comprehensive annex that aims to facilitate trade in animal and animal products and plants, while safeguarding public, animal and plant health. The EU–Mexico FTA has no equivalent agreement, but merely reiterates the obligations under the WTO SPS Agreement. Chile had initially favoured something along similar lines, but the European Union pushed for more substantive bilateral commitments. The final agreement therefore goes far beyond the EU–Mexico FTA.

The chapter on government procurement has also been hailed as a success. This is the first time that the European Union has devoted a separate chapter to government procurement in an agreement with a party that is not a signatory of the GPA (in EU–Mexico FTA it constituted part of the chapter on goods) (Swedish National Board of Trade, 2002). The text of the agreement is directly inspired by the provisions in the GPA. Moreover, the coverage of the agreement seems to go well beyond the EU–Mexico FTA. For example, the chapter covers not only the central government but also sub-federal levels.

The free trade agreement in services represents the first fully fledged agreement based on the GATS model. In the case of the EU–Mexico FTA, the parties agreed only to lists of commitments on financial services. The agreement with Chile follows the GATS model in all sectors.[28] Initially, the Chilean negotiating team tabled a proposal in line with the NAFTA model. In the end, however, Chile agreed to apply the EU post-GATS model in the agreement. Apart from the overall architecture of the services chapter, the chapter also introduces some novelties compared with the EU–Mexico services FTA by including an article on domestic regulation in relation to licensing and certifications and an article on electronic commerce. The article on mutual recognition is also more elaborate than the one in the agreement with Mexico.

In some areas, however, the EU–Chile Association Agreement failed to produce any important substantive commitments that are WTO-plus in character. Environment and, more specifically, environmental labelling are once again excluded from the final agreement (as they were from the negotiating mandate).

The TBT section on standards, technical regulation and conformity assessment procedures (section 4) also mainly follows the path laid down in the EU–Mexico FTA; that is, it establishes WTO-plus commitments of a more procedural than substantive character. However, the specific actions listed in the section reflect a level of ambition that exceeds that of the EU–Mexico FTA. The EU–Chile agreement is more open-ended: it identifies a number of mechanisms that could be pursued in bilateral cooperation, ranging from regulatory cooperation to, *inter alia*, convergence, equivalence and even mutual recognition agreements. It calls upon the Special Committee that will be established for this purpose to "explore any means aiming at improving access to the Parties' respective markets and enhancing the functioning of this section" (Art. 88.e).

Political analysis: Does the EU–Chile Association Agreement represent a new context?

The EU–Chile Association Agreement seems to represent a unique illustration, or even a model, of a new EU approach to regulatory issues. It has certainly filled the gaps in the EU–Mexico FTA. To understand this important achievement, and the possibility for the agreement to serve as a model in future negotiations, we must first understand what political factors within the European Union played a role in moving the Union's negotiating positions in comparison with the EU–Mexico FTA. Of course, there were a number of issue-specific reasons why the European Union tended to refrain from pushing for WTO-plus commitments in the FTA with Mexico. However, based on the presentation above, three aspects seem to have been particularly relevant:

- divergent views and attitudes within the European Union on the principle of the so-called regional track (especially in relation to WTO);
- tensions arising from the distribution of competence within the European Union (between the Commission and the member states) and the resultant complex procedures for trade policy-making;
- shortage of time in the critical periods of the negotiations.

Divergent views on regionalism

First, the member states of the European Union have diverging views on and attitudes to regionalism as well as the relationship between regionalism and multilateralism. In the negotiations with Mexico, these different attitudes to regionalism created an internal deadlock in 1995–6, and the pattern repeated itself many times in course of the preparations for the negotiations. This issue resurfaced in the preparations for the EU–Mercosur/Chile negotiations. The attitudes to regional trade negotiations and their relation to a future WTO round represented one, but arguably not the most difficult, stumbling block in the internal EU negotiations over the EU mandate. But internal discussions resulted, among other things, in the inclusion of a reference in the mandate that the EU–Mercosur and EU–Chile negotiations could not be finalized before the conclusion of the new round in the WTO. This decision was taken in view of the expected success of the Seattle Ministerial Meeting in December 1999, which aimed to launch a ninth round of trade negotiations under the auspices of the WTO.

Also, in the preparations for the negotiations, a number of southern EU member states demanded that the European Union should link an agreement with Chile with the successful conclusion of an agreement with Mercosur. They were afraid that an early agreement with Chile would pave the way for more extensive demands on agricultural liberalization from Mercosur. In contrast, both the Commission and the northern group of member states, as well as Spain, pushed hard for the principle that each negotiation should be judged on its own merits. These internal discussions arose on many occasions during the negotiations and especially during the Swedish presidency, when the issue of the relationship between the negotiations with Chile and those with Mercosur was at a critical juncture.

As the negotiations with Chile progressed, however, the reference to the WTO and the demand to link Chile with Mercosur became increasingly unsustainable, not least from a political point of view. The negotiations with Mercosur showed little progress. In the end, therefore, the case for a link between the two negotiating processes was unrealistic. Moreover, the decision to forgo the reference to the WTO in the case of Chile was easily adopted because the conclusion of an agreement was already in sight at the launch of the Doha Development Agenda.

Distribution of competence

The issue of competence within the European Union and its implications for decision-making/consultative structures probably reduce the general flexibility of the Union in trade negotiations. When there are sensitive issues of substance, differences over competence can result in virtual deadlock in internal decision-making procedures in the European Union.

This was particularly apparent in the negotiations on an investment chapter in the EU–Mexico agreement. Investment is a mixed-competence issue in which the member states share competence with the Commission. In addition, a number of member states have signed bilateral investment treaties with countries outside the Union, with the aim of providing protection for investments. Moreover, the legacy of the negotiations over the Multilateral Agreement on Investment (MAI) still has important knock-on effects in the sense that it has sensitized a number of member states to the issue. There has been a general reluctance to push for investment treaties that could appear, in the eyes of the public, remotely similar to the MAI.

The area of investment continued to be very sensitive in the initial rounds of the EU–Chile negotiations. As a consequence, the Commission was not able to table any proposal until the very end of the negotiations. At this time the internal EU deadlock on competence could be effectively solved only through the involvement of member states. Hence, under the Swedish presidency of the Council in spring 2001, Sweden took the initiative to bridge the division among the member states. Only after lengthy discussions with France (but also with Germany, Denmark and the United Kingdom) were France and Sweden able to agree to table a joint investment proposal as a basis for further discussions. The Commission thereafter skilfully exploited the "truce" among member states to push for a more comprehensive compromise.

Shortage of time

A final reason for the European Union's tending not to adopt WTO-plus commitments in the FTA with Mexico was the shortage of time. Urgency is often a necessary ingredient of any successful negotiation. In such circumstances, however, the ability of the trade negotiators to adopt new positions is limited, especially considering the complex consultative and decision-making procedures within the European Union. This problem is particularly acute in areas of regulatory policy. Consequently, when time is tight in any negotiation, there is a tendency to make use of previous positions and agreements and merely adopt incremental changes.

The negotiations between the European Union and Mexico were influenced by such a time constraint. The European Union wanted to conclude the negotiations before the expected launch of a new trade round in the WTO. More generally, the gradual phasing out of the transition periods under NAFTA put pressure on the European Union to conclude an agreement with Mexico as soon as possible. All in all, the agreement was concluded in little more than a year and after merely nine negotiating rounds.

The time factor was not so important in the negotiations with Chile (or Mercosur), or at least not on the EU side of the negotiating table. Chile, however, was anxious to bring the negotiations to a conclusion by the Madrid Summit in May 2002. This allowed the European Union to press even more aggressively for its positions in the negotiations.

The negotiations with Chile are in sharp contrast to those with Mercosur. In the EU–Mercosur case, the issue is the absence of a common position among the countries of Mercosur and the lack of a common secretariat/commission. In fact, apart from the common external tariff, there are no common policies or internal cohesion in Mercosur on most of the issues covered by the negotiations. The European Union has so far completely rejected the idea of negotiating with the Mercosur countries on a bilateral basis. The negotiations with Mercosur are thus not expected to be concluded for at least two years.

Notes

1. The Global Agreement was signed in Brussels on 8 December 1997 but it entered into force on 1 October 2000 when the FTA had been established (Official Journal, 2000d). The Interim Agreement entered into force on 1 July 1998 (Official Journal, 1998).
2. However, in reality, the development of EU–Mexico trade was not necessarily an effect of trade diversion from NAFTA. NAFTA has been thoroughly examined to establish if the agreement gave rise to an increase in regional concentration of trade. It appears that the importance of the region's intraregional trade has increased, while there has been a drop in the importance of external trade. Theoretically, this provides compelling evidence of trade diversion, i.e. that intraregional trade has occurred at the expense of trade with third countries, such as the European Union. Nevertheless, in the case of NAFTA, the diversion effects that are likely to have taken place are judged to have been very limited indeed. See, among others, Report of the Study Group on International Trade (1997).
3. See, however, chapter 6 on NAFTA, which shows that the growth in US trade with and investment in Mexico was as much due to the confidence provided by the idea of NAFTA as to the agreement itself.
4. The Commission's Market Access Database (http://mkaccdb.cec.eu.int) contains a good and comprehensive list of regulatory barriers.
5. Concerning sanitary and phytosanitary measures, however, the negotiating directives merely stipulated that such legislation should be covered by the agreement.
6. The EU approach, in contrast to the US/NAFTA approach, differentiates between the right to establishment under the chapter on trade in services and the investment chapter of an agreement. Therefore, EU services investors are accorded a different, and often better, treatment than other types of EU investors since the commitments in the overall services chapter tend to be more profound than those under the investment section.
7. Decision 2/2000 was adopted on 23 March 2000 by the EU–Mexico Joint Council (Official Journal, 2000a, 2000b, as well as, in the case of the annexes, Official Journal, 2000c). This Decision lays down the necessary arrangements for the implementation of: (a) the progressive and reciprocal liberalization of trade in goods, in conformity with Article XXIV of GATT 1994; (b) opening the agreed government procurement markets of the Parties; (c) establishing a cooperation mechanism in the field of competition; (d) setting up a consultation mechanism in respect of intellectual property matters; and (e) establishing a dispute settlement mechanism.

8. Decision 2/2001 of the EU–Mexico Joint Council was adopted on 27 February 2001 (Official Journal, 2001). This Decision lays down the necessary arrangements for the implementation of: (a) the progressive and reciprocal liberalization of trade in services, in conformity with Article V of GATT; (b) the progressive liberalization of investment and related payments; (c) ensuring an adequate and effective protection of intellectual property rights, in accordance with the highest international standards; and (d) establishing a dispute settlement mechanism.

9. See, among other sources, the European Commission web page: http://europa.eu.int/comm/external_relations/mexico/intro/index.htm and http://www.europa.eu.int/comm/trade/bilateral/mex.htm.

10. This section is primarily based on the Communication from the Commission to the Council and the European Parliament (EC Commission, 2000), as well as two reports by the Swedish National Board of Trade (2000, 2001).

11. Three sectors were excluded from the scope of the agreement: audio-visual services, maritime cabotage and air transport.

12. Regionalization refers to Article 6 of the WTO SPS Agreement concerning regional conditions and pest- or disease-free areas.

13. In a negative-list approach, everything but the sectors or activities listed is liberalized. This is generally more liberal than the positive-list approach, in which only those areas listed are liberalized.

14. The primary reasons for establishing WTO-plus rules in FTAs are probably two-fold: (1) WTO-plus commitments help to promote better market opening; (2) WTO-plus provisions help to create a precedent and could thus promote strategic "principal" positions.

15. The concept of "institutional complementarity" is described in greater detail in the report by the WTO (1995), p. 2.

16. Press release, 13 May 2002, second meeting of the EU–Mexico Joint Council, EC Commission web page at http://www.europa.eu.int/rapid/.

17. However, although the chapter on public procurement largely levels the playing field with the United States, the de facto economic impact of the FTA should not be exaggerated. Many multinational corporations originating in the European Union have already been able to participate in public tenders through their subsidiaries in Mexico. These subsidiaries are considered to be legal persons in Mexico and hence evade potential discrimination. The largest economic benefits of the FTA thus accrue to small and medium enterprises, but these firms face additional problems because of their lack of proximity to the market.

18. Another case in point not covered by this study concerns rules of origin, where the negotiations of the EU–Mexico FTA revealed the same problems in terms of merging the NAFTA and EU approaches.

19. The products that were decided upon at the Joint Council were in the automotive and pharmaceutical sectors, batteries, bicycles and mechanical equipment. The first meeting of the Joint Council took place on 27 February 2001. In October 2001, the Joint Committee also held its first meeting.

20. For example, the Cotonou Agreement foresees negotiations of Economic Partnership Agreements, starting in September 2002, with the former colonies of the EU member states (the African, Caribbean and Pacific countries). The European Union is also involved in negotiations with neighbouring countries around the Mediterranean Sea in the Barcelona Process, as discussed elsewhere in this book.

21. Mercosur (Mercado Comun del Cono Sur) is a customs union between Argentina, Brazil, Paraguay and Uruguay.

22. The negotiations between the European Union and Mercosur have been obstructed by

internal coordination problems within Mercosur (for example, the lack of common positions on a number of issues) and the specific circumstances related to the financial crises that have plagued the region (Brazil in January 1999 and Argentina from December 2001). The Action Plan is published on the Directorate-General for Trade (DG Trade) web page at http://europa.eu.int/comm/trade/bilateral/mercosur/mercosur.htm.

23. This and similar arguments were made in a number of impact assessment studies, such as in the 1999 Report on EU interests in Mercosur and Chile, or the 1998 Commission Staff Working Paper concerning the establishment of an interregional association between the European Union and Mercosur. Both are published on the Directorate-General of External Relations (DG RELEX) web page at http://europa.eu.int/comm/external_relations/mercosur/intro/index.htm.

24. In line with the modalities and schedule established at the launch of negotiations in November 1999, the different trade issues were divided into three categories, or sets of issues, for which separate technical groups were created to handle the negotiations at the expert level. For competence reasons, member states participated only in the technical group that covered all issues of mixed competence (services, intellectual property and investment).

25. Press release, Brussels, 26 April 2002: Statement of Commissioner Lamy announcing agreement on the EU–Chile free trade negotiation within the Association Agreement (DG Trade web page at http://europa.eu.int/comm/trade/bilateral/chl.htm).

26. Because the agreement was published only on 10 June 2002, it has not been possible to evaluate the total coverage of the agreement. However, in the final round negotiations, the European Union offered to liberalize 99.8 per cent of EU imports of industrial products immediately (and the rest after three years), to liberalize 75 per cent of imports of fish and fishery products within four years, and ultimately to liberalize 90 per cent of the Union's existing imports of agricultural products. In the case of Chile's imports, the Chilean offer was to liberalize 91.7 per cent of EU exports in industrial products and 98 per cent of fisheries exports immediately. The transition periods comply with GATT Article XXIV and, in the case of industrial products primarily but also in some other sectors, are much shorter than the maximum 10-year period.

27. The EU member states have signed a number of bilateral investment treaties with third parties. These, however, cover only post-establishment – i.e. the protection of investments – not the establishment of investments as such.

28. This is not to say, however, that the level of commitment (liberalization) is higher in the EU–Chile Association Agreement than in the EU–Mexico FTA. In fact, the EU–Mexico FTA may very well prove more ambitious in the long run, depending on the envisaged future expansion of the EU–Mexico Agreement.

REFERENCES

EC Commission (1996), "A Free Trade Area between the EU and Mexico", Brussels, staff working paper, SEC (96) 843.

――― (1998), "Negotiating Guidelines for Trade Liberalization between the European Community and Its Member States and the United Mexican States", Communication from the Commission to the Council, Commission document SEC (1998) 350 Final, Brussels, 4 March 1998.

――― (2000), "Proposal for a Council Decision on the Community Position within the EU–Mexico Joint Council on the Implementation of Articles 3, 4, 5,

6 and 12 of the Interim Agreement", Communication from the Commission to the Council and the European Parliament accompanying the final text of the draft decision by the EC–Mexico Joint Council, Brussels.

EC Council (1996), "Relations with Mexico: Negotiating Directives for a New Agreement and Joint Declaration on Political Dialogue between EU and Mexico", Document 7592/96, 23 May.

Official Journal (1998), "Interim Agreement on Trade and Trade-Related Matters between the European Community, of the One Part, and the United Mexican States, of the Other Part", 1998/504/EC, *OJ* L226, 13 August, pp. 25–48.

—— (1999), "Council Decision of 25 January 1999 Concerning the Framework Cooperation Agreement Leading Ultimately to the Establishment of a Political and Economic Association between the European Community and its Member States, of the One Part, and the Republic of Chile, of the Other Part", 1999/127/EC, *OJ* L42, 16 February, p. 46; also published on the DG RELEX web page at http://europa.eu.int/comm/external_relations/chile/intro/index.htm.

—— (2000a), "Decision No 2/2000 of the EC–Mexico Joint Council of March 2000", 2000/415/EC, *OJ* L157, 30 June, pp. 10–29.

—— (2000b), "Council Regulation (EC) No 1362/2000 of 29 June 2000 Implementing for the Community the Tariff Provisions of Decision No 2/2000 of the Joint Council under the Interim Agreement on Trade and Trade-related Matters between the European Community and the United Mexican States", *OJ* L157, 30 June, pp. 1–5.

—— (2000c), "Decision No 2/2000 of the EC–Mexico Joint Council of March 2000", *OJ* L245, 29 September, pp. 1–1168.

—— (2000d), "Council Decision of 28 September 2000 Concerning the Conclusion of the Economic Partnership, Political Coordination and Cooperation Agreement between the European Community and its Member States, of the One Part, and the United Mexican States, of the Other Part", 2000/658/EC, *OJ* L276, 28 October, pp. 44–79.

—— (2001), "Decision No 2/2001 of EC–Mexico Joint Council of February 2001 Implementing Articles 6, 9, 12 (2)(b) and 50 of the Economic Partnership, Political Coordination and Cooperation Agreement", 2001/153/EC, *OJ* L70, 12 March, pp. 7–50.

Report of the Study Group on International Trade (1997), *Reflections on Regionalism*, Carnegie Endowment for International Peace, Washington DC: Brookings Institution Press.

SECOFI (Mexican government, Secretaría de Economía) (2000), *The EU–Mexico Free Trade Agreement: Building Bridges across the Atlantic*, Brussels: Mission of Mexico to the EU.

—— (2001), *The EU–Mexico FTA: One Year after*, Brussels: Mission of Mexico to the EU.

Swedish National Board of Trade (2000), *Frihandelsavtal EU–Mexico*, Document No. 1230-243-2000, Stockholm, February.

—— (2001), *Analys av FTA EU–Mexico avseende investeringar, SPS, TBT, tjänster och offentlig upphandling*, Document No. 110-806-01, Stockholm, April.

—— (2002), "Frihandelsavtal EU–Chile: Preliminär analys", working paper, Stockholm, May.

WTO (World Trade Organization) (1995), *Regionalism and the World Trading System*, Geneva: WTO.

Internet sources

Directorate-General for Trade (DG Trade)
http://europa.eu.int/comm/trade/bilateral/index_en.htm
http://europa.eu.int/comm/trade/bilateral/mex.htm
http://europa.eu.int/comm/trade/bilateral/chl.htm
http://europa.eu.int/comm/trade/bilateral/mercosur/mercosur.htm

Directorate-General for External Relations (DG RELEX)
http://europa.eu.int/comm/external_relations/mexico/intro/index.htm
http://europa.eu.int/comm/external_relations/mercosur/intro/index.htm
http://europa.eu.int/comm/external_relations/chile/intro/index.htm

The Commission's Market Access Database
http://mkaccdb.cec.eu.int

5

The Euro-Mediterranean Agreements

Tomas Baert

Introduction

In the 1990s, the European Union decided to renew relations with 12 of its partners in the southern and eastern Mediterranean. Until this time there had been individual Cooperation Agreements, created in the 1970s, that provided for (largely asymmetrical) duty-free access of non-agricultural goods to the European single market. In Barcelona in 1995, EU member states and 12 Mediterranean Partner Countries (MPCs) decided to turn these Cooperation Agreements into the Euro-Mediterranean Partnership (EMP). The Barcelona Summit initiated a process, commonly referred to as the "Barcelona process", that led to the conclusion of Euro-Mediterranean Association Agreements (EMAs) covering a wide range of issues under three pillars: political and security, economic and financial, and social, cultural and human. As far as the economic pillar was concerned, it was clear at the outset that negotiations would not be confined to market access and "tariff issues". Rather, the progressive establishment of a free trade area by 2012 would be accompanied by cooperation on a range of trade-related regulatory policy issues. There have, however, been relatively few studies of the regulatory dimension of the partnership.

In addressing the three questions posed in this volume, the EMAs are of interest for a number of reasons. First, EMAs provide an example of how the European Union approaches regulatory barriers and harmonization of policies with neighbouring countries, in the absence of the accession imperative. The EMAs differ in some important respects from the Europe Agreements (EAs) with the European Union's Central and East European neighbours (see chapter 3), even though both types of agreement are called Association Agreements. It is no great surprise that the EAs go beyond the provisions of the World Trade Organization (WTO-plus) in many areas, since compliance with the *acquis communautaire* constitutes a *conditio sine qua non* for acceding to the European Union (see chapter 3). As a result, it is also inevitable that the European Union exports its "regulatory model" and that the impact of this on the Central and East European partner countries is considerable. For the MPCs, there is, for the moment, no prospect of EU membership (except for Cyprus, Malta and ultimately Turkey).

Second, the EMAs offer an opportunity of considering whether there is a pattern of "imperial" or "hegemonic" harmonization of regulatory policies (Baldwin, 2000; Lawrence, 1995) emanating from the European Union, and, if so, what are its effects. Even without the imperative of accession there are reasons to expect the European Union to employ an approach similar to that used with the Central and East European countries. The EMAs are an example of North–South integration. In the full or partial absence of a strong regulatory framework, Southern countries can be inclined to adapt rules and policies of Northern partners, particularly when the former depend on trade with the latter. In this respect, the success and learning experience of the European single market comprise an obvious "model" that is supposedly "exported" in full or in part to the South. The EMP therefore provides a means of assessing the extent to which Northern approaches are adopted, whether these represent a form of hegemonic harmonization, and whether it is benign or malign.

The economic welfare impact of North–South integration on Southern partners can be substantial. There appears to be a growing consensus in the academic literature that substantial (dynamic) welfare gains can be achieved through "deep" integration, which exceed the limited Vinerian gains associated with "shallow" integration (see chapter 1). The experiences of other North–South agreements, such as Mexico's participation in the North American Free Trade Agreement (NAFTA; see chapter 6) and, probably more important in this context, the EU membership of Mediterranean countries such as Portugal, Spain and Greece, suggest that regional integration leads to increased competition, efficiency and investment. In other words, the qualitative and quantitative welfare impact of agreements like the EMAs is potentially very high. Such gains are all the more likely with the EMAs, because administrative and regulatory barriers are prevalent in Middle Eastern and North African (MENA) countries. The current system of standards in countries such as Egypt, for example, shows signs of former inward-oriented policies.

Third, the EMAs are interesting in the sense that they provide an opportunity of comparing the EU approach with the US approach, in North–South regional trade agreements (RTAs) in general (see discussion of NAFTA in chapter 6), but also, to some extent, in the MENA region. The United States has recently shown interest in concluding free trade agreements with MENA countries. It has a preferential agreement with Israel (since 1985), and has a number of trade- and investment-related cooperation agreements with, *inter alia*, Algeria and Egypt. In 1999 the Clinton administration signed a free trade agreement (FTA) with Jordan and, in April 2002, President Bush announced plans to embark on bilateral trade negotiations with Morocco, with the ultimate aim of concluding an FTA that builds on the agreement with Jordan. In sum, the United States is expanding its preferential relations with MENA countries and in so doing may develop its own "approach" to regulatory barriers. This chapter will therefore briefly consider the US motives in and approach to agreements on regulatory issues in the MENA region.

The chapter is structured as follows. First, there is an introductory overview of the Euro-Med Partnership and the evolution of the negotiations with specific reference to the *why* and *how* of regulatory liberalization in the Euro-Med context. The three subsequent sections each address one of the three central questions of this volume. Section two assesses the impact of the EMAs on regulatory policies and regulatory barriers to market access, in qualitative as well as quantitative terms. On the latter, an overview of existing research on deep integration suggests that, on balance, the aggregate welfare losses associated with regulatory barriers in the MPCs are high. Hence the potential benefits of deeper integration are likely also to be high. A qualitative analysis assesses to what extent this welfare potential linked to deeper integration is achieved by regulatory liberalization in the EMAs. This qualitative analysis uses the "WTO-plus" concept as a yardstick to measure the potential impact of the EMAs that have been signed (are still being signed) after the Barcelona Declaration of 1995. The Agreement with Tunisia, which was the first to be signed, will be used as the basis of the analysis because subsequent Association Agreements have used it as a model. Other agreements, such as those with Turkey and Israel, are used to provide some guidance on the possible course and direction of the "standard" Association Agreement in the region. Section three looks at the evidence of a distinct "European approach" to regulatory liberalization. It then briefly reviews the US–Jordan Free Trade Agreement to see if this suggests a substantive divergence between the EU and the US approaches on regulatory issues, which could potentially complicate multilateral liberalization. Section four deals with the final question raised in the book, namely whether the regulatory provisions of the EMAs detract from or contribute to multilateral liberalization. In other words, are the EMAs "building blocks" or "stumbling blocks" on regulatory issues?

The Euro-Med Agreements: An introduction

The Barcelona process

The Mediterranean has always been a region of importance to the European Union, for strategic, historical, cultural and economic reasons. In March 1957, when the Treaty of Rome establishing the European Economic Community (EEC) was signed, France was still active as a colonial power in Algeria and retained considerable influence in already independent Tunisia and Morocco. France therefore advocated a special relationship between the newly created EEC and these countries and was supported in this endeavour by Italy and the United Kingdom (once it became a member of the European Communities in 1973), which sought to retain preferential policies towards Libya and Egypt, respectively. As a result, bilateral agreements were concluded between the European Communities (EC) and Israel, Morocco, Tunisia, Spain, Portugal, Malta, Lebanon, Cyprus and Egypt, which provided duty-free access to the European market for non-agricultural products originating in these countries. In addition to these (post) colonial ties, the Cold War gave the Mediterranean region a geo-strategic importance, which contributed to the fact that EC Association Agreements were signed with Greece and Turkey.

There was, however, no coherent policy towards agreements with the Mediterranean countries, and fierce criticism of the lack of consistency in the European Communities' approach led to the creation of a "Global Mediterranean policy" adopted at an EC summit in Paris in 1975. This policy provided for the conclusion of asymmetrical Cooperation Agreements, guaranteeing duty-free access for Mediterranean partner countries to the European Communities for goods and preferential access for agricultural products. The agreements were supplemented by Financial Protocols, which were renewed every five years.

In the 1990s, relations between the Mediterranean countries and the European Union were put under strain as a result of the increasing number of migrants leaving North Africa for Western Europe. Fundamentalism and the crisis in Algeria had also made stability of the southern and eastern Mediterranean one of Europe's vital interests. Spain, Portugal, France and Italy became the "sponsors" of renewed efforts to

strengthen relations with the Mediterranean, advocating the establishment of a zone of "peace and prosperity" on the southern flank of
Europe. The Mediterranean countries' interest in deepening relations
with Europe also increased when Germany's campaign for a common
and comprehensive EU policy vis-à-vis the Central and East European
countries (CEECs) resulted in the conclusion of the Europe Agreements
and the CEECs' coming higher up the European "preferential pyramid".[1]
Furthermore, the tariff preferences enjoyed by the Mediterranean countries under the Cooperation Agreements were being eroded as a result of
the tariff reductions in the Uruguay Round of the General Agreement on
Tariffs and Trade (GATT).

These factors led to the agreement on the Euro-Med Partnership at the
Euro-Mediterranean Conference in Barcelona in November 1995. The
partnership consists of three pillars: political and security, economic and
financial, and social, cultural and human. The basic economic objective of
the EMP is to achieve bilateral reciprocal free trade by 2010. In this
respect, Association Agreements are to be concluded to progressively
establish free trade, with the exception of some specific arrangements in
sensitive sectors including agriculture. Negotiations have, however, pro-
ceeded slowly. Between November 1995 and 2000, only five agreements
were signed and ratification by all 15 EU member states has further delayed the entry into force of these agreements. The negotiations with
Jordan, for example, were concluded in April 1997 and the agreement
signed in November 1997, but it did not enter into force until 1 May
2002. An overview of all negotiations and their status is presented in
table 5.1.

The slow progress in the negotiations, along with political factors and
the low levels of intraregional "South–South" trade, led the European
Commission to produce a Communication entitled "Reinvigorating the
Barcelona Process" (European Commission, 2000). The Commission
Communication would form the basis for the fourth Euro-Med Conference, held in Marseilles five years after the inaugural Barcelona meeting.
In Marseilles, foreign ministers of all Euro-Med partners decided that the
negotiation, signature and ratification of the Association Agreements
should be speeded up. They also recommended closer links among the
MPCs, which it was hoped would attract increased inflows of foreign
direct investment (FDI), and agreed guidelines for the adoption of harmonization measures in certain priority sectors, such as customs, norms
and standards.

Despite the resounding declarations in Marseilles, little changed with
regard to the speed at which agreements were signed. Results from the
economic and financial pillar also remained meagre. Levels of trade be-

Table 5.1. The Euro-Mediterranean Association Agreements: Overview of the partners and the status of the negotiations

	Status of Association Agreement	Interim agreement[a]	WTO status	Application for EU membership	Agadir process
Algeria	Signed	No	Accession talks started	–	–
Cyprus	Signed Ratified In Force	NA	Member since July 1995	Yes	–
Egypt	Signed Ratified In Force	NA	Member since June 1995	–	Yes
Israel	Signed	Yes	Member since November 1995	–	–
Jordan	Signed Ratified	NA	Member since November 1997	–	Yes
Lebanon	Signed	Yes	Accession talks started	–	–
Malta	Signed Ratified In Force	NA	Member since January 1995	Yes	–
Morocco	Signed Ratified In Force	NA	Member since January 1995	–	Yes
Syria	Under negotiation	–	–	–	–
Palestinian Authority	Interim agreement	Yes	–	–	–
Tunisia	Signed Ratified In Force	NA	Member since March 1995	–	Yes
Turkey	Customs union Signed In Force	NA	Member since March 1995	Yes	–

a. NA = not applicable.

tween the MPCs and FDI inflows into the region failed to match expectations. But in 2001 political events in the shape of the September 11 attacks on the United States and the turmoil in the Middle East again underlined the importance of a peaceful and prosperous southern flank for the European Union's security. In response, European leaders made another attempt at revitalizing the Barcelona process, this time under the Spanish presidency of the European Union. Spain could be said to be a "sponsor" for Mediterranean countries seeking preferential agreements with the European Union – just as Germany is a sponsor for the Central and East Europeans and France perhaps for the Asia, Caribbean and Pacific (ACP) countries. The second Euro-Med Ministerial Meeting on Trade in Toledo (March 2002) and the fifth Euro-Med Conference of Foreign Ministers in Valencia (April 2002) launched an Action Plan on the further development of the partnership. As far as the regulatory dimension is concerned, ministers decided that regional integration among the MPCs should be strengthened and further developed, particularly in the light of the small share of FDI the region is able to attract. This took the form of a harmonization of the origin rules, which would enable the MPCs to participate in the pan-European system of origin rules through the cumulation of origin throughout the region. This would stimulate intraregional trade and make investment in the region more attractive. The European Union also decided strongly to encourage sub-regional integration initiatives such as the Agadir process between Egypt, Jordan, Morocco and Tunisia. The EU trade ministers created a Working Group on trade measures relevant to integration in the region, with instructions to look at the harmonization, simplification and automation of customs procedures and other measures such as services (see below).

The regulatory dimension

In view of the above, it should not surprise that regulatory liberalization is not the driving force of the Euro-Med Partnership. The Barcelona Declaration said little about harmonizing or liberalizing regulatory barriers to trade, although the establishment of a Euro-Mediterranean free trade area is the centrepiece of the economic and financial pillar of the Euro-Med Partnership. The Barcelona Declaration calls for "the adoption of suitable measures as regard rules of origin, certification, protection of intellectual and industrial property rights and competition" in order to facilitate the progressive establishment of this free trade area. The Declaration repeatedly stresses the need to "establish an appropriate institutional and regulatory framework for a market economy". EU–MPC cooperation in improving the institutional infrastructure is seen as an important means of enhancing the competitive position and thus im-

Table 5.2. Share of the European Union in the external trade of the Mediterranean Partner Countries in 2000 (per cent)

	Imports	Exports	Total
Tunisia	71.6	80.0	75.0
Morocco	57.9	74.7	64.5
Algeria	58.0	62.7	61.2
Turkey	48.9	52.5	50.1
Malta	60.0	33.4	48.8
Cyprus	51.6	36.5	48.6
Syria	29.6	65.0	48.6
Lebanon[a]	45.9	24.1	43.8
Israel	43.3	27.2	35.8
Egypt	34.1	40.0	35.6
Jordan	33.0	3.3	25.6
Palestinian Authority[a]	15.4	0.4	13.5
MPCs	47.5	48.4	47.8

a. 1999 data.
Source: Eurostat (2002).

proving the poor performance of the region in attracting FDI. In this way regional agreement(s) could give national regulatory reform in the MPCs greater permanence and thus enhance their attractiveness to FDI.

During the individual negotiations, the requests to include regulatory policy issues came mostly from the European Union. The European Commission argued that compliance with European standards, norms and customs procedures would facilitate access to the European market and increase export opportunities. As a large share of Mediterranean exports goes to the European Union (see table 5.2), such cooperation made sense to MPCs. The MPCs saw commitments in the regulatory field mainly as a means of creating the kind of environment conducive to investment discussed above. But there were fears that commitments on regulatory issues would also necessitate restructuring and result in high implementation costs. Financial support and technical assistance were initially offered by the European Union to compensate the MPCs for lost tariff revenue. Reciprocal market access concessions offered nothing for the MPCs because access for Mediterranean exports to the European market was largely free under the Cooperation Agreements. In later stages, however, financial support measures were seen as compensating for the costs of complying with trade-related regulatory measures, especially when these appeared to offer little immediate benefit for the MPCs, as in the case of competition policy. Whenever commitments in the regulatory field were deepened or broadened, Euro-Med ministers ensured increased and targeted financial transfers and technical assistance. In short, financial support became a "carrot" for increased regulatory reform under the Euro-Med Partnership.

The regulatory impact

This section assesses the regulatory impact of the EMAs. First, the potential quantitative impact of the agreements is outlined, focusing on existing studies that project the net welfare impact of deeper integration. In the second part, the question is raised of whether and to what extent this potential is realized through effectively addressing regulatory issues.

Quantitative assessment

Substantial research, largely pertaining to Tunisia, Morocco and Egypt, has been conducted on the potential economic impact of the EMAs on the Mediterranean countries. Most analyses focus exclusively on the static effects of reductions in tariffs and non-tariff barriers (NTBs) – trade creation and trade diversion – which result from the reallocation of labour and capital along the lines of respective comparative advantage. Rutherford et al. (1993), for example, use a computable general equilibrium (CGE) model of 39 sectors to estimate the economic effects on Morocco of an FTA with the European Union. The net welfare benefits of an FTA are estimated to amount to 1.5 per cent of GDP, and the benefits from non-discriminatory liberalization, in which trade-diverting effects are absent, would be around 2.5 per cent of GDP. A similar study on Tunisia has similar results, estimating allocative efficiency gains around 1.7 per cent of GDP (Rutherford et al., 1995).

Employing a different computable general equilibrium model, Brown et al. (1997) estimate the net welfare effects of the EMA with Tunisia to be slightly negative in the short run. To a large extent, this negative short-run result can be attributed to the adjustment costs associated with the degree of inter-sector capital and labour immobility. In the long run, however, Tunisian aggregate welfare is likely to be raised by an FTA with the European Union because no allowance is made for dynamic efficiency gains and productivity growth.

A recent study on the effects of an FTA between the European Union and a "representative Mediterranean country", that is, a small and open economy, has confirmed the results above (Rutherford et al., 2000). This study went one step further, however, by analysing the impact of the various separate elements of an agreement in terms of aggregate welfare gains. The study therefore goes beyond tariff measures undertaken in the Mediterranean model country to consider regulatory policies as well as the importance of the liberalization and harmonization of such policies. The authors conclude that, for the representative Mediterranean country, it is not tariff reductions or the removal of NTBs but less traditional improvements in market access via harmonization and mutual recognition of standards that generate the most welfare gains. Earlier results from a study of Egypt (Konan and Maskus, 1997) also suggest that large welfare gains from an FTA with the European Union would result only from the elimination of regulatory barriers and "red tape" measures, and a "shallow" agreement would be "merely diversionary and lead to a small decline in welfare" (see also Hoekman and Konan, 1999, 2000).

Even though the databases and CGE techniques employed in most of this research have their limitations and result in large differences in the estimated gains of integration, some general conclusions emerge:

- The different static efficiency analyses of the welfare gains of the EMAs point in the same direction: net welfare effects are expected to be small but positive. Especially in the short run, no substantial gains will occur. The analysis of different scenarios of trade liberalization suggest that most of the welfare gains are associated with a reduction in administrative "red tape" barriers and the harmonization of regulatory regimes. This is consistent with the theory of deeper integration, which predicts the aggregate welfare gains to be substantially higher if one goes beyond traditional tariff and NTB measures.

- The question of whether gains will be higher once one takes dynamic and longer-run growth effects into account remains largely unanswered. Even though the case for dynamic gains seems theoretically plausible, there is no empirical evidence on how large these gains could be, in particular with respect to the Euro-Med Agreements.

- Economic effects are expected to be optimal if deeper non-discriminatory trade liberalization is pursued vis-à-vis the rest of the world and if the Euro-Med Agreements include the liberalization of agricultural trade and petrochemicals.

- In addition to the elements mentioned, the main reason for the relatively small static gains is the loss of tariff revenues on imports of EU origin. As nearly half of the trade of most MPCs is conducted with the European Union, this revenue loss is substantial (see above).

It is difficult to draw conclusions on dynamic welfare effects from the Euro-Med Agreements because the limited quantitative estimates available are also of limited usefulness. Although there are expectations of potential gains, it is important to mention a few reservations with respect to the possible dynamic gains (Tovias, 1997; Hoekman and Djankov, 1997; United Nations Economic and Social Commission for Western Asia, 1999). First, the existing tariff-free access to the EU market for MPC producers of manufactured goods means that Mediterranean exporters will not benefit from any scale economies. The situation would change, however, if the cumulation of rules of origin were to be implemented effectively (see below).

A second qualification of the case for dynamic gains is that increased inflow of FDI into the Mediterranean countries is likely to be small because investors are more likely to be attracted to the "hub" of the agreements, namely the European Union (Baldwin, 1994; Hoekman and Djankov, 1997). Improved market access to the Mediterranean countries encourages companies to invest in the European Union and export to the Mediterranean. Furthermore, commercial presence in a Mediterranean country is discouraged because there is no preferential access to the other (non-EU) markets of the neighbouring (Mediterranean) countries. In short, the Euro-Med Agreements create a "hub and spoke" relationship in which the European Union is the hub and the Mediterranean countries are disadvantaged in terms of attracting FDI because they are the "spokes". There may even be de-localization effects, in which firms settled in Morocco, for example, move to Spain or Italy to avoid tariffs against exports to other MPCs. Thus, whereas MPC-based firms were, under the Cooperation Agreements, in a privileged position to supply the EU market, this will no longer be the case under the Euro-Med Agreements in their present form.

This situation can be rectified, however, if market access among the Mediterranean partners is improved through the cumulation of rules of origin or the creation of a free trade area among the MPCs.[2] The Central European Free Trade Agreement (CEFTA) among the Visegrád countries was partly signed for these reasons (Balázs, 1997). The European Commission has proposed the "diagonal cumulation" of origin rules for the MPCs through their participation in the pan-European system of origin rules. The proposal, which received political support at the Toledo and Valencia ministerial conferences in March and April 2002, will allow exporters based in the MPCs to import intermediate products from other partner countries and still enjoy duty-free access to the EU market. Cumulation of origin rules would therefore improve both access to the EU market and sourcing possibilities and thus intraregional trade among the MPCs, which currently accounts for only 5 per cent of their total trade. A precondition for cumulation is to have identical systems of rules of origin in the agreements and here a lack of institutional complementarity in origin determination is a main cause of the delay.

A third dynamic effect likely to result from the EMAs concerns the gains from increased competition. It is argued that integration and thus competition in the MPCs will threaten public enterprises and national or local monopolies and oligopolies (United Nations Economic and Social Commission for Western Asia, 1999). However, in view of the lack of competition in many MENA countries, characterized by high levels of state subsidies, the EMAs are likely to generate dynamic gains from competition, especially if they include competition provisions (UNCTAD, 1998a, 1998b).

A final, more general, remark on the nature of dynamic effects is that the progressive nature of liberalization in the EMAs (a 12-year transitional period) necessarily means that, *if* dynamic gains occur, these will accrue incrementally and their impact is likely to vary across countries. Again, this necessitates some qualification of the case for dynamic gains from the EMAs. None the less, on balance the arguments and evidence discussed here suggest that deep integration agreements between the European Union and the MENA countries could lead to substantial overall welfare gains. But can these potential gains be realized?

Euro-Med Agreements and regulatory issues

It is not possible to assess whether the potential welfare gains of the EMAs have been realized until they are fully implemented. To make some assessment of the likely realization of welfare gains, we must assess the substance of the agreements themselves, particularly the "new" regulatory policy areas.

Technical barriers to trade

A first observation that can be made with respect to technical barriers to trade (TBTs) in the EMAs is that the European Union extends its "new approach" philosophy in dealing with technical standards and regulations to the MENA region. The objective of mutual recognition (of conformance assessment) is present in the body of the agreement, even though the language remains very vague, especially with regard to the objective of concluding agreements on the mutual recognition of certification "when the circumstances are right" (Art. 40, section 2). There are no further specifications on the conditions or criteria that would determine when the circumstances might be right. The agreement with Tunisia does, however, provide for the updating of Tunisian laboratories in order to help facilitate the conclusion of mutual recognition agreements for conformity assessment (Art. 51 (b)). It remains to be seen whether these vague commitments will ultimately result in the conclusion of mutual recognition agreements. But it seems unlikely that full mutual recognition of regulatory policies will be feasible in the short to medium term given that the "new approach" assumes an equivalence of national regulatory policies. For most MPCs, such equivalence of regulatory systems is some way off. Mutual recognition of test results may be a less distant prospect. In this regard, the European Union has indicated a possible approach in its agreement with Israel on the mutual recognition of the

Organisation for Economic Co-operation and Development's principles of "good laboratory practices" and conformance assessment programmes (Official Journal, 1999). Under this agreement the European Union will recognize any test facility found in conformity with the OECD's "good laboratory practices" requirements (OECD, 1981).

In the case of Turkey, which forms a customs union with the European Union, the EU model for dealing with TBTs has been applied.[3] In other words, the *acquis communautaire* is to be applied by Turkey. In this case, the mutual recognition of, for example, conformity assessment procedures becomes a more likely if not imminent prospect. It is unlikely that the MPCs that do not have the motivation of EU accession and do not adopt the full *acquis* will be able to enjoy such treatment.

Mutual recognition is only one facet of the agreements. There is also the objective of bringing Tunisian procedures and practices in line with European ones, through encouraging the use of EU rules and standards by Tunisia for industrial and agri-food products (Art. 40, section 1, and Art. 51 (a)). Approximation or standardization with European standards generally also means conformity with international standards. Tunisia has, for example, made efforts in recent years, and 80 per cent of the national standards are believed to be in conformity with international equivalents (Handoussa and Reiffers, 2002). As a means of promoting harmonization or regulatory norms and standards there are also general procedural provisions in Article 52 (entitled "The approximation of legislation") that provide for cooperation "aimed at helping [Tunisia] to bring its legislation closer to that of the Community in the areas covered by the agreement".

The issue of approximation is also reflected in Article 59 on closer cooperation on customs matters. This introduces the use of the "Single Administrative Document" and creates a link between the EU and Tunisian transit systems and seeks to simplify customs checks and procedures. Progress in such trade facilitation issues can be expected to be rather more straightforward than dealing with TBTs because of the lower demands in terms of institutional capabilities.

If the Euro-Mediterranean Partnership is to function effectively, some lessons will have to be drawn from the EU experience with the internal market. The need to promote policy approximation/harmonization is likely to be one of them. A first step in this direction has been made with the creation of the programme on Euro-Mediterranean Market Mechanisms, dubbed "Euro-Med Market". This programme is intended to identify areas where harmonization with EU rules would be particularly useful and then address them as a matter of priority.[4]

The trade dependence of the MPCs makes a de facto approximation desirable because this would result in lower transaction costs and higher revenues. The business community has identified the simplification and harmonization of customs procedures and other technical barriers as being a priority.[5] In sum, the Euro-Med Partnership is likely to progress in the field of technical barriers because they are relatively uncontroversial, have visible benefits and are strongly supported by business.

Services

The EU current account balance with the MPCs (excluding Cyprus, Malta and Israel) has traditionally been in surplus for the past 10 years. Whereas trade in goods systematically showed a surplus, trade in services has mostly been in deficit. Services trade between the European Union and the Mediterranean shows little diversification: tourism and transport together represent more than two-thirds of total trade in services (see figure 5.1). The EU services balance has generally been in deficit in these sectors, whereas other services (communication, construction, information technology and financial services) have been in surplus.

The transport sector in the Mediterranean (especially maritime and port facility services) is characterized by substantial regulatory barriers – these services typically belong to the public sector, which retains a de facto monopoly. Because transport and tourism represent most of the trade and because transport has, in particular, been systematically excluded from the General Agreement on Trade in Services (GATS) schedules by MPCs, inclusion of these sectors in the EMAs would clearly be WTO-plus, but this has not occurred.

The EMAs reaffirm the parties' obligations under GATS, "particularly the obligation to grant reciprocal most-favoured-nation [MFN] treatment in the service sectors covered by that obligation" (Art. 32, section 1). But the EMAs do not go beyond GATS commitments. Each party's exemp-

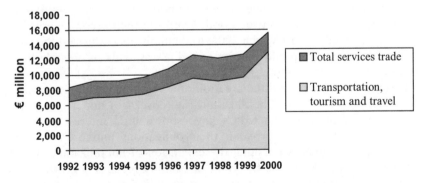

Figure 5.1 Share of transport, tourism and travel services in total services trade from the Mediterranean to the European Union, 1992–2000 (€ million)
Source: Eurostat (2001).

tions from MFN commitments under GATS are carried over into the EMAs. MPC commitments under GATS are at best modest. Of the 161 sectors of Central Product Classification nomenclature of the WTO, Tunisia is committed to only 11.0 per cent, Egypt to 26.7 per cent, Morocco to 21.1 per cent and Israel to 29.8 per cent.[6] Thus the scope for regional preferences in services through the EMAs has not yet been exploited. So the Article V provisions of GATS for regional trade agreements in services have not really been applied.

For agreements with countries that are not members of the WTO and thus not signatories to GATS, a framework agreement similar to GATS is included. At the time of the EMA negotiations, Jordan was, for example, not a member of the WTO, so the EU–Jordan EMA provides for best endeavours in progressively open services markets and for a review after five years of the possibility of negotiating an agreement under GATS Article V. The EU–Jordan EMA also provides for MFN on the establishment of firms in sectors other than maritime, air and inland waterways transport. Jordan accepted commitments for over 68.9 per cent of the services listed by the WTO.[7]

The EMAs also include provisions on procedural measures to help further the scope of the liberalization of trade in services, with a view to creating full rights of establishment (Art. 31, section 1). The implementation of these objectives is in the hands of the Association Council, which is to take account of past experiences and the obligations under GATS when making the necessary recommendations (Art. 31, section 2). At the first Euro-Mediterranean Ministerial Meeting on Trade of 29 May 2001 in Brussels, trade ministers established a Working Group on services and charged it with the task of exchanging information and sharing experience in services trade with a view to ultimate further liberalization.[8] The Working Group is not part of any mandated negotiation. Its task is confined to the preparation of negotiations, at both bilateral and multilateral levels, and coordination between both levels. At their second ministerial meeting in Toledo on 19 March 2002, trade ministers reaffirmed the work of the Working Group and recommended assessments of possible liberalization in a number of sectors.

Despite the rhetoric and the creation of a Working Group on services, the widening of services liberalization (i.e. coverage) under the EMAs has remained limited. The MPCs have shown little interest in taking initiatives to deepen or broaden their obligations under GATS, and the European Union is pursuing the expansion of liberalization in non-sensitive sectors. As far as the right of establishment is concerned, the European sensitivities associated with immigration and the movement of labour from the periphery are likely to produce few concessions on "mode 4" services, which involve the movement of natural persons to perform services in importing countries. Given that a new round of multilateral negotiations – the Doha Development Agenda – has been launched, it remains to be seen whether the parties will expand the coverage and schedules at the bilateral, rather than the multilateral, level.

Public procurement

In Article 41 of the EMAs the liberalization of public procurement is set out as an objective for the Association Council to implement.[9] So far, only a few implementing initiatives have been taken. Some indication of the European Union's possible future approach might be provided by two agreements that have been signed within the framework of the interim EMA with Israel. The first agreement aims to "complement and broaden" the scope of either party's commitments under the plurilateral Government Procurement Agreement (GPA) of the WTO, which both the European Union and Israel have signed. Additional reciprocal concessions have already been made for urban transport vis-à-vis the other signatories of the GPA. The European Union included opening up the procurement of bus services vis-à-vis Israel; the latter will "use its best endeavours" to further market opening on bus services and medical equipment (Official Journal, 1997b). The second agreement is a purely bilateral deal, establishing the mutual opening of procurement by providers of public telecommunication services and operators of public telecom networks through the mutual introduction of national treatment (Official Journal, 1997b). The agreement reflects the European Union's interest in and strong position on telecommunications, which was also evident in the GPA negotiations during the Uruguay Round.

The European Union's agreement with Turkey establishing a customs union, Decision 1/95, contains a similar objective to that of the EMAs: the mutual opening up of government procurement markets (Art. 48). The wording is more concrete with regard to implementation: "as soon as possible after the date of entry into force ... the Association Council will set a date for the initiation of the negotiations." These negotiations were initiated by Decision 2/2000 of the EU–Turkey Association Council (Official Journal, 2000).

The impact of the provisions on public procurement in the agreement with Tunisia (and other partners) is likely to be minimal and, at best, will lead to incremental opening. This is mainly owing to the presence of persistent political, institutional and ideological obstacles and the fact that the public sector is and remains strongly embedded in the MENA societies. Decades of state domination and "big spending" cannot be changed in a fortnight. Public procurement is gradually being opened up and made more transparent as part of a larger tendency to reduce the direct involvement of the state in the economy. Against this background, sector-by-sector agreements similar to the one struck with Israel may offer a way forward, with general measures being promoted by, for example, more MENA countries signing up to the WTO Government Procurement Agreement.

Investment

As discussed above, the creation of an environment conducive to investment was a key driver of economic cooperation in the Euro-Med Partnership. But provisions in the EMAs on investment are limited. There is general hortatory language on the "promotion and protection" of investment by harmonizing and simplifying procedures and through the conclusion of investment protection agreements and agreements preventing double taxation (Art. 50). This absence of concrete provisions is, in part, owing to the political debate within the European Union on the question of competence, which has influenced the Union's lack of position in multilateral as well as regional investment agreements.

The EU member states show great keenness to retain national control over investment rather than see it move into EU competence.[10] *Inter alia*, this was showcased at the Nice Summit (2000), where EU member states agreed to amend Article 133 of the Treaty of Rome (which governs the Union's common commercial policy) by extending EU competence to a number of "new" areas. In a few sensitive sectors such as audio-visual services (e.g. "l'exception culturelle") and investment, EU member states did not agree on handing over "shared" or "mixed" competence to the European Union (strictly speaking to the European Communities). With the ratification of the Treaty of Nice, investment will therefore be one of a few most sensitive issues that remain subject to the rules and procedures of intergovernmentalism, as opposed to the "community approach". One of the consequences of this is that investment is covered by a plethora of bilateral investment treaties (BITs) between individual EU member states and MPCs. BITs are considered to be the single most important tool in investment relations between countries. Figure 5.2

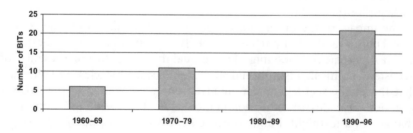

Figure 5.2 The number of bilateral investment treaties between the EU member states and Mediterranean Partner Countries, 1960–96
Source: International Centre for the Settlement of Investment Disputes.

shows the rising trend with which BITs have been concluded between EU member states and MPCs, between 1960 and 1996. This trend has continued since 1996.

Competition

As it became clear that the new relations between the European Union and the Mediterranean would take the form of a "Partnership" and thus encompass more than just market access commitments, competition policy became a desired domain of cooperation for the European Commission. The Commission's desire to include competition flows from experience with the European internal market, for which competition policy has long constituted one of the main foundations. The Commission sought the inclusion in the EMAs of principles similar to those embodied in EU primary (and secondary) legislation. The inclusion of competition provisions was envisaged as a means of injecting much-needed dynamism into the Mediterranean economies and locking in ongoing reform (Pons, 2002). Some MPCs lacked effective competition laws and several sectors of the economy in many MPCs were dominated by the public sector. The Commission was also concerned about anti-competitive practices in MPCs that could discriminate against EU firms in the Mediterranean.

For the MPCs, the advantages of concluding an agreement including rules on competition were far from obvious. No laws of this kind have ever been adopted in Lebanon and Syria, and Egypt and Jordan have only recently embarked on the process of creating competition law. Moreover, the whole region is characterized by a lack of a competition culture, which is arguably a far more important ingredient in making competition work than the mere adoption of a formal legal framework. The MPCs therefore saw it as essential to limit the scope and defer the implementation of the commitments on competition, even though most realized that competition policy is beneficial in bolstering the national economy. The issue then became one of the European Union granting temporary derogations and providing technical assistance, administrative cooperation and financial support in return for the inclusion of competition provisions in the EMAs.

The European Union model for competition was clearly present in the form of the EU primary legislation, and particularly Articles 85 to 94 of the Treaty of Rome (now Articles 81 to 89 of the Treaty on European Union) addressing anti-competitive practices such as cartels, monopolies and market-distorting state aid. These "ingredients" had been used before in the negotiations with the CEECs and provided an obvious basis for the EMAs. In effect, the EMAs incorporate the basic philosophy of eradicating collusive behaviour (Art. 36, section 1(a)), the abuse of a dominant market position (section 1(b)) and competition-distorting state aid (section 1(c)). Even though the wording of Article 36 is more general than the elaborate description of what is considered to be anti-competitive in the relevant articles of the Treaty of Rome, de facto differences remained limited. Article 36, paragraph 2, states: "any practices ... shall be assessed on the basis of the criteria arising from the application of the articles 85, 86 and 92 [*sic*] of the Treaty establishing the European Community." In short, a wider interpretation of the articles is necessary because reference is made to EU law, i.e. secondary legislation (Hakura, 1999).

In addition to Article 36 on cartels, monopolies and state aid, the EMAs also require adjustment of state-owned monopolies engaged in commercial activities (Art. 37), public enterprises and enterprises that are granted special or exclusive rights in order to fulfil their socio-economic functions (Art. 38). Article 37 specifies that "any state monopolies of a commercial character" will be progressively adjusted "so as to ensure that by the end of the fifth year of the agreement no discrimination regarding the conditions under which goods are procured and marketed exists". Article 38, with respect to public enterprises, has a similar objective, ensuring that no measures that disturb trade or run counter to the interests of the parties can be adopted from the fifth year following the entry into force, while safeguarding the specific functions assigned to those enterprises.

The implementation of paragraphs 1 and 2 of Article 36 is in hands of the Association Council, which will adopt the necessary rules within five years of the entry into force of the agreement. So far, no rules have been adopted. The first decisions are not expected until 2003. The Europe Agreements, in which implementation rules had to be taken within three years after entry into force, are indicative of the way the Euro-Mediterranean Association Councils can be expected to implement the competition provisions in the EMAs. Here the European Union law (Community *acquis*) is preponderant.

In addition to the back-loaded implementation agenda, some temporary derogations were allowed. For example, for five years after the entry into force of the agreement, Tunisia will be regarded as a disadvantaged region under Article 88, section 3(a) of the Treaty establishing the European Community, which means that state aid can continue to be granted. During the same period, Tunisia may grant state aid for restructuring purposes to the sectors that fall under the European Coal and Steel Community, in accordance with the conditions of Article 36, section 4(a). Until the rules for the implementation of Article 36, section 1(c) on state aid are adopted, GATT rules on anti-dumping, countervailing duties and subsidies (GATT Articles VI, XVI and XXIII) apply.

Environment

The proximity of the partners and the commonality of environmental problems made environmental cooperation an important issue on the agenda of the Euro-Med Partnership. Article 48 of the Agreement with Tunisia has the aim of "co-operation to prevent deterioration of the environment, to improve the quality of the environment, to protect human health and to achieve rational use of natural resources for sustainable development". Furthermore, the parties undertake to cooperate in the following areas: soil and water quality; the consequences of development, particularly industrial development (especially safety of installations and waste); monitoring and preventing pollution of the sea.

These provisions resemble the Preamble to the Agreement Establishing the WTO, which states that the members seek to "protect and preserve" the environment and strive for an "optimal use of the world's resources in accordance with the objective of sustainable development" (WTO, 1995, p. 4). The EMAs go one step further than the WTO by aiming to "improve the quality" of the environment. Even though specific areas of cooperation are listed, these are only indicative. The general lines of policy are set out by the short- and medium-term priority action programme for the environment (SMAP), created in 1997. The SMAP provides for capacity-building, training and the use of environmental impact assessments. Even though on substance the parties go further than what is agreed upon in the WTO, the EMAs contain no trade-related procedural provisions that balance environmental protection and trade liberalization.

Overview

The above summaries of the regulatory commitments of the EMAs do not suggest much in the way of deeper integration in either substantive or procedural commitments. In summing up, I translate these into the different dimensions of the concept of WTO-plus set out in chapter 2.

Coverage

Cooperation on regulatory issues in the EMAs is limited. In the area of services and government procurement, coverage does not qualify as WTO-plus. Investment provisions do not attain the (minimal) level of protection of the WTO and are therefore WTO-minus. Competition is WTO-plus in the sense that there are no multilateral rules on competition. On substance, the environmental provisions go further than the WTO in that they seek to improve the quality of the environment (rather than just "preserve and protect" it). Finally, on technical barriers the agreements appear to aim for WTO-plus outcomes but, as elsewhere, much will depend on the implementation of the provisions.

Procedural elements

The EMAs attempt to promote transparency and predictability through the simplification of administrative procedures and through the greater predictability resulting from the introduction of competition rules that will restrain anti-competitive practices such as state subsidization, cartelization and monopolization. The approximation of legislation and the use of common rules and procedures (i.e. the Single Administrative Document) will also help to promote transparency and predictability in customs procedures. Transparency through open decision-making remains limited, in contrast to the American focus on "due process" in the US–Jordan FTA. In some areas, procedural provisions aim to strengthen existing national institutions through collaboration. This is particularly the case in the areas of customs cooperation, the making of technical standards and conformity assessment. Article 51 (c) specifies that the parties will cooperate in "developing bodies responsible for intellectual, industrial and commercial property and for standardisation and quality in [Tunisia]". In the same vein, the objective of concluding mutual recognition agreements entails the strengthening of Tunisian laboratories. The extensive provisions on competition will also require the development and expansion of national competition authorities, and cooperation and technical assistance is envisaged to help facilitate this expansion.

Policy approximation

In the agreements, the approximation of legislation and regulatory policies is set out as an objective as far as technical barriers (regulations, standards and conformity assessment procedures) are concerned, but approximation is not foreseen and is unlikely to take place in any other area, except for competition policy. On technical barriers, a process is set in place to identify priority areas where simplification through harmonization is necessary (Euro-Med Market). Substantive progress will mostly occur upon creation of the Euro-Mediterranean Free Trade Area. The case of Tunisia shows that there is high convergence, of about 80 per cent, between Tunisian and international standards.

Mutual recognition

The EMAs aim to conclude mutual recognition agreements (MRAs) on conformance assessment and certification procedures. However, the language on mutual recognition is rather hortatory. When and how MRAs will be signed is everything but clear. Moreover, the lack of institutional conformity and equivalence leaves doubt about swift progress towards mutual recognition. The asymmetry between the partners makes the unilateral adoption of European rules and procedures (i.e. approximation) a more realistic option. Only when substantive progress in this direction is made will mutual recognition or equivalence be realistic. In the meantime, technical cooperation and assistance will gear up the MPCs for mutual recognition.

Regulatory discretion

The nature and the number of possible exceptions or exclusions from the obligations of the parties will determine the degree of policy discretion. When looking at the "loopholes" and the conditions attached to the use of these loopholes in the EMAs, one can conclude that the EMA with Tunisia is equivalent to the WTO. Whereas GATT Article XXV provides for the option of waivers or general exceptions to GATT rules, the EMAs do not include such a provision. For almost every other loophole of the GATT (anti-dumping and countervailing duties, restrictions to safeguard the balance of payments, safeguard clause, general and security exceptions, governmental assistance for economic development), there is an identical provision in the EMA. So the EMAs appear to take the WTO model for norms on discretion.

Effective reviews and remedies

To the extent that regional dispute settlement procedures are faster, wider or more efficient than multilateral mechanisms, one can argue that compliance is more effective when they exist. In the EMAs, dispute settlement procedures are covered by Article 86 and are largely similar to the dispute settlement process in the WTO. There is one important difference: the wording of Article 86 is less automatic than the rule-oriented consultation and adjudication procedures in the WTO. Whereas disputes in the WTO are constrained by time limits and stricter procedural requirements, the EMAs are "looser". Either party "may" refer any dispute to the Association Council (section 1), which the Council may settle by means of a decision (section 2) and if this is not sufficient either party "may" notify the other of the appointment of an arbitrator (section 4). In sum, the EMAs provide no strong (or no stronger) framework for the settlement of disputes and, as a consequence of the emphasis on political consultation rather than judicial adjudication, the arbitration procedures are likely to be used sparingly (Hakura, 1999).

Promotion of competitive markets

The EMAs include the basic European philosophy in dealing with anti-competitive practices, such as cartelization, monopolization and state aid. The competition commitments are devised as a trade-related instrument, in that they envisage the promotion of trade and transparency. The extent to which this will in effect happen depends largely on the implementation of the provisions. The lack of a "competition culture" in the MPCs has been identified as an obstacle to implementation.

Regulatory regionalism: Approaches

The European approach

In some areas the EMAs resemble what could be called a European approach to regulatory issues. On technical barriers, policy and approximation and mutual recognition are provided for even though there must remain some doubt as to whether, and if so when, mutual recognition of, for example, conformity assessment will be achieved. The de facto approximation of MPCs' policies and practices to the European regulatory standards is a more likely outcome. This will help to reduce transaction costs and will be driven by the pattern of trade. The approach to competition policy is also very "European", with the basic set of EU definitions and rules to eradicate anti-competitive practices being transposed in full. Here again the implementation phase is still to come. In some areas there will clearly be a convergence between European and Mediterranean policies and practices. But EU policy will not change; it will be Mediterranean policies that will have to change.

To what degree will this "hegemonic harmonisation" (as Baldwin calls it) take place? Experience suggests that the full adoption of the *acquis communautaire* occurs only when countries are seeking accession, or when countries are at a similar level of development to the European Union but reject EU membership, as in the cases of Switzerland and the members of the European Economic Area (EEA). Even though the adoption of the *acquis* is seemingly the direction in which the Euro-Med Partnership is moving, it is doubtful that a pan-European economic area *à la* EEA, including Central and East European and North African and Middle Eastern countries, will ever be created. The efforts to harmonize rules of origin on a pan-European level have illustrated the difficulties associated with divergent levels of development and limited institutional complementarity. The end-state and end-date of the Euro-Med project are hard to predict in view of the multitude of factors shaping the process. At this stage, the political incentives or imperatives are not as great as has been the case in EU negotiations with the CEECs.

In order to better understand the distinctive elements of this EU approach, it might be worthwhile to draw some comparisons with the US approach in the Mediterranean Basin. This also touches upon the issue of regulatory regionalism or competitive (hegemonic) harmonization.

The US approach

Are there competing European and American models of regulatory liberalization? Recent declarations by United States Trade Representative (USTR) Zoellick suggest some concern that there are: "There are over 130 free trade agreements in the world; the United States is party to two. The issue extends beyond market access because each of these agreements is setting the rules for the future ... The rules others are making without us will determine the future" (2001, p. 5). Zoellick quotes as an example Brazil a century ago: "when electricity was just being introduced into Brazilian society, the Brazilians looked to Europe as a model, not to the United States.... The example is being repeated again and again in the world." Zoellick continues: "The US can also establish models of success and precedents that we can apply elsewhere" (2001, p. 5). In outlining the costs of the US non-participation in regional trade agreements to the Senate Finance Committee, Jeffrey Schott makes a similar case. Non-participation in RTAs "will increase transaction costs and establish precedents that differ from US practices and proposals that the signatory might wish to extend to other regional and WTO accords" (Schott, 2001).

These statements presume that there exists *a priori* something like a European and an American model. What evidence do the regulatory provisions in the trade agreements that both the European Union and the United States concluded with Mediterranean partners provide to support this hypothesis? Answering this question requires us first to look in more detail at the US-centred agreements with Mediterranean countries. The free trade agreement between the United States and Jordan is used here as the basis for tracking the US approach.

The United States and Jordan signed a free trade agreement on 24 October 2000 that provides for the progressive establishment of an FTA and closer cooperation on a range of trade-related issues. From a US perspective the motivation for the agreement was to support reforms under way in Jordan that had, among other things, facilitated Jordan's accession to the WTO. The United States also wished to send a broader political signal in the Middle East. In a letter to President Clinton, then House majority leader Richard Gephardt urged the President to expand the FTA between the United States and Israel to include countries "that sign comprehensive peace agreements with Israel" (Gephardt, 1994).

The ratification of the agreement with what was considered to be an "uncomplicated" trade partner turned out to be more difficult than anticipated. Despite the strong political incentives to adopt the agreement in the aftermath of 11 September 2001, the US Senate foundered over the inclusion of labour and environmental provisions in the text of the agreement. Republican senators expressed the fear that the agreement would have an impact on issues of national sovereignty: the enforcement of national environmental and labour legislation could become binding, possibly trigger trade disputes and potentially lead to sanctions (on either side). A second concern expressed in the US Senate was that the US–Jordan FTA would serve as a "template" for subsequent trade agreements. This was a view the Clinton administration appeared to hint at and one that was later confirmed by USTR Zoellick. In his speech to the Senate Finance Committee setting out the Bush administration's trade objectives in 2002, Zoellick stated that "[in 2001] we charted progress on incorporating labor and environmental concerns in US trade policy. The US–Jordan Free Trade Agreement is the first US free trade accord to include enforceable environmental and labor obligations in the body of the agreement", topics that "we are pursuing ... in our current FTA negotiations" (Zoellick, 2002). So the treatment of labour and environment, as well as other measures in the US–Jordan agreement, could provide a precedent for other agreements. First some highlights from the US–Jordan FTA.

- **Trade in goods and services**. The FTA foresees a gradual reduction in duties over a transitional period of 10 years. Tariff reductions take place in four stages and follow a so-called "band-approach", in that all tariffs within a certain range are brought down to a single tariff. The FTA provides national treatment: "Each Party shall accord to services and service suppliers of the other Party, in respect of all measures affecting the supply of services, treatment no less favorable than that it accords to its own like services and service suppliers" (Art. 3.2(b)). Jordan agreed to open up its services market to US providers.
- **Environment**. Environment is included in the text of the US–Jordan agreement for the first time ever, rather than in a side agreement (as in NAFTA). The agreement states that it is "inappropriate to encourage trade by relaxing domestic environmental laws. Accordingly, each Party shall strive to ensure that it does not waive or otherwise derogate from, or offer to waive or otherwise derogate from, such laws as an encouragement for trade with the other Party" (Art. 5.1). Although striving to maintain a high level of environmental protection, the agreement recognizes the right of each country to establish its own levels of domestic environmental policies and priorities.[11] Furthermore, it is stated that "a Party shall not fail to effectively enforce its environmental laws, through a sustained or recurring course of action or inaction, in a manner affecting trade between the Parties" (Art. 5.3(a)).

On procedural matters, the United States and Jordan created a Joint

Forum on Environmental Technical Cooperation, which has the task of working to "advance environmental protection in Jordan by developing environmental technical cooperation initiatives, which take into account environmental priorities, and which are agreed to by the two governments".

- **Labour**. With the FTA, the United States and Jordan "reaffirm their obligations as members of the International Labor Organization (ILO) and their commitments under the ILO Declaration on Fundamental Principles and Rights at Work and its follow-up" (Art. 6.1). Parallel to the provision on environmental standards, "the Parties recognize that it is inappropriate to encourage trade by relaxing domestic labor laws. Accordingly, each Party shall strive to ensure that it does not waive or otherwise derogate from, or offer to waive or otherwise derogate from, such laws as an encouragement for trade with the other Party" (Art. 6.2). Although recognizing the right of each partner to establish its own domestic labour standards, laws and regulations, the parties will strive to ensure that these are consistent with the internationally recognized labour rights. The FTA states that "a Party shall not fail to effectively enforce its labor laws, through a sustained or recurring course of action or inaction, in a manner affecting trade between the Parties" (Art. 6.4(a)).

- **Intellectual property**. Most international standards for the protection of intellectual property rights (IPRs) have been incorporated in the US–Jordan agreement. In the first place, the agreement requires Jordan (and the United States) to give effect to various World Intellectual Property Organization agreements, including those covering trademarks, geographical indications, copyrights and patents. Enforcement of IPRs is a clear priority and Article 4.24 sets out the requirement that each country "shall ensure that its statutory maximum fines are sufficiently high to deter future acts of infringement". Most provisions come into effect between six months and three years from the date of entry, whereas some will take effect upon entry.

- **Procedural provisions**. The FTA establishes a dispute settlement body, and an associated Memorandum of Understanding on Transparency in Dispute Settlement has been signed. The Memorandum obligates the parties to "solicit and consider the views of members and their respective publics in order to draw upon a broad range of perspectives. Any submission made to a dispute panel once established, will be made available to the public; oral presentations before the panel shall be open to members of the public; the panel shall 'accept and consider' *amicus curiae* submissions by individuals, legal persons, and NGOs; and the panel shall release its report to the public."

Although the US–Jordan FTA is innovative and expands the horizon on certain issues, little is said on technical barriers and sanitary and phytosanitary (SPS) measures. On TBTs, technical assistance and mutual customs cooperation are established. On SPS measures, the parties envisage "bilateral ... consultations on recognition of equivalence".[12] In addition, GATT Article XX is incorporated into the agreement in order not to reduce the level of protection of human, animal or plant life. On government procurement, the parties agree to enter into negotiations upon Jordan's accession to the WTO Government Procurement Agreement (Art. 9).

The procedural provisions of the FTA reflect the US approach in ensuring due process and transparency and contrast somewhat with the EU approach. On the whole, however, the main conclusion that can be drawn from a brief comparison between the regulatory approaches of the European Union and the United States in the MENA region is that there is not a great divergence between the respective approaches to *how* things are done. There is, rather, a difference in *what* is done, i.e. the coverage of areas where cooperation is established. The European Union shows an interest in the approximation of laws and standards and is keen on introducing competition policy in the EMAs, whereas the United States introduces environmental and labour issues in the body of a trade agreement. The United States also indicates its interest in strengthening the framework of cooperation on intellectual property rights. Both the European Union and the United States refrain from commitments on investment in the respective agreements and aim to bolster investment mainly through bilateral investment treaties.

Hence, rather than representing a model or template of regulatory liberalization, the agreements disclose the European and American interest in introducing (new) areas of cooperation. In a speech on a possible conclusion of an FTA with Singapore, EU Trade Commissioner Pascal Lamy made the concept of WTO-plus understood as "enhancing the EU's multilateral ambitions" (*Business Times*, 2002). This definition seems to apply to a considerable extent in the MENA region. Intellectual property rights, labour and environmental issues are part of the United States' multilateral ambitions, whereas a multilateral framework on competition is among other issues favoured by the European Union. These preferences were reflected in their respective agendas for the third and fourth WTO Ministerial Conferences in Seattle (1999) and Doha (2001). This observation also supports the thesis that large industrialized trading partners such as the European Union and the United States seek to advance issues at a regional level when a consensus is much harder at the multilateral level.

Even though the United States and the European Union both show an eagerness to introduce different areas of cooperation with the MPCs, there is – for the time being – little reason to worry about institutional incompatibility in their respective approaches. Neither the European initiatives on, for instance, technical barriers or competition nor the US initiatives on the environment and labour standards are "deep" or far-reaching commitments. Thus, even though cooperation is established in some areas for which no extensive framework has been set in the WTO, the respective commitments do not take things much further than what has been agreed upon at the multilateral level. In other words, the agreements are not WTO-plus. Moreover, both the European Union and the United States show great interest in guaranteeing conformity to WTO disciplines, which also reduces the risk of regulatory regionalism. This brings us to the final question on regionalism and multilateralism.

The Euro-Med Agreements and the multilateral system

As noted above, the EMAs are not "deep" and are generally not WTO-plus. This implies that they cannot significantly deviate from the WTO path and philosophy or unduly add obscurity and complexity to the world trading system. The liberalization of services, for instance, makes full reference to the parties' schedules and exceptions under GATS and provides for extensions in line with GATS commitments. On government procurement, the EU agreement with Israel was within the framework of the plurilateral GPA. Even on environmental policy the philosophy of the EMAs and the WTO appear to be similar. In short, wherever possible, the parties to the EMAs have made reference to the relevant WTO agreements. On balance, then, one can conclude that the substance of the EMAs on regulatory issues is WTO compatible and is unlikely to detract from multilateral liberalization.

The European Union has also become much more sensitive to the compatibility of its RTAs with WTO rules since the Uruguay Round, and the EMAs and the Barcelona process date from this post–Uruguay Round period. The European Union was not always so concerned about the compatibility of its RTAs. The North American Free Trade Agreement (NAFTA) was concluded during the Uruguay Round. Until this time the United States had been a staunch supporter of multilateral trade liberalization and had not engaged in regional trade pacts – the only exceptions being the FTAs with Canada and Israel. During the Uruguay Round, however, the United States shifted to embrace regionalism when multilateral negotiations were proceeding slowly, and others followed suit as part of what was perceived as an "insurance policy" against a lack of results in the GATT/WTO. When the European Union maintained a quasi-monopoly over the conclusion of RTAs, it was less concerned about compatibility, but when more countries started using the provisions of GATT Article XXIV governing FTAs and customs unions the EU position shifted.

On the one hand, the European Union was concerned about the potential trade-diverting effects of other agreements, such as the effects of NAFTA on EU trade and investment in Mexico (see chapter 4). On the other hand, although the European Union wanted a clarification of Article XXIV, which was generally considered to be ambiguous, the European Union itself might be in trouble, in view of the plethora of (often asymmetrical) trade agreements it signed over the years, if Article XXIV were to be applied stringently. The strengthened dispute settlement procedures of the WTO even raised the possibility of a case being brought on the compatibility of an RTA with WTO Article XXIV.

These EU concerns were reflected in a later 1997 Commission Communication:

[T]he EU ... has an interest in further reinforcing the position of its own agreements in the WTO. There is an unwelcome level of uncertainty in GATT rules, which do not mesh with the binding nature of the Dispute Settlement System. Therefore, while we need to be aware of the need to avoid putting at risk our own free trade agreements, clearer GATT rules would help both the EU's market access interests and its interest in greater certainty for its own agreements ... The fact that a number of our trading partners are themselves likely to put preferential agreements in place is a cause of concern, given the uncertainties identified in respect of Art. XXIV. (European Commission, 1997)

EU concerns over the conformity of regional trade agreements with GATT rules remained, despite the creation at the end of the Uruguay Round of the Committee on Regional Trade Agreements and the Understanding on the Interpretation of Article XXIV. As a result, the June 1996 European Council in Florence mandated the European Commission to investigate the evolution and the WTO conformity of EU-centred preferential trade agreements. From this time the Commission made it clear that the issue of WTO compatibility would have to be addressed before signing any new RTA. The agreements with South Africa, Mexico and Chile, the negotiations with Mercosur and even ACP relations testify to this trend.

These concerns are also mirrored in the Barcelona process, where extensive reference is made to guaranteeing the conformity of the EMAs to world trade rules. In the Commission's view, in order to be WTO compatible, reciprocity had to be introduced in Euro-Mediterranean trade relations. The Cooperation Agreements were largely asymmetrical, with the European Union according mostly unilateral preferences. Moreover, there was no full coverage of all sectors under the Cooperation Agreements, so concessions needed to be extended on the sensitive area of agriculture if the "substantially all trade" condition of Article XXIV, section 8, was to be met. It was in this atmosphere of WTO compatibility that the commitments in the new regulatory policy areas were agreed upon.

In short, there is little to indicate that the EMAs are detracting from multilateral liberalization, adding complexity to global trade or resulting in the preferential administration of regulatory policies against the interests of third countries. In the first place, this relates to the nature of the regulatory provisions: no substantive "deep" or WTO-plus commitments have been undertaken. Most of these substantive commitments have in any case not been implemented. Second, the political context in which the EMAs are signed is one of heightened awareness and concern over WTO compatibility.

Conclusion

The Euro-Med Partnership is a process that is very much driven by factors other than economic or commercial interest. There is more behind Euro-Med integration than the economic rationale. This can to a certain extent be attributed to the lack of an effective European Common Foreign and Security Policy. Europe, often said to be an economic giant but a political dwarf on the international scene, employs its economic muscle also for non-economic purposes. Free trade agreements and unilateral trade preferences have become key ingredients of European political relations. Consequently, when political relations are troubled, this can easily affect the economic and regulatory dimension of the agreement. A spiral of violence in the Middle East, for instance, has occasionally led to demands in Europe to suspend economic concessions in the Euro-Israeli Association Agreement.

The regulatory dimension of the Euro-Med Partnership has to be evaluated against these other factors. The prevalence of political and geo-strategic motives in the Barcelona process makes the economic and regulatory dimension of the Barcelona process rather unpredictable. In addition, the lack of a prospect of accession for the countries concerned makes it difficult to predict where the process will end up and when.

The discussion of existing studies of the quantitative impact of "deep" agreements between the European Union and countries of the southern and eastern Mediterranean suggests that regulatory elements of the agreements could contribute a good deal to overall welfare. But some caution is called for in accepting the case for the dynamic gains hinted at by many authors. The qualitative analysis of the current Euro-Med

Agreements suggests that the potential gains from the EMAs are unlikely to be fully realized owing to the limited effectiveness of the agreements.

The Euro-Med Agreements are characterized by a gradual and limited coverage of regulatory issues. Even though I have not undertaken a comparison between the Europe Agreements and the Euro-Med Agreements here, there seems to be little doubt that the latter are a "weaker and slower" version of the former. A crucial difference between the two sets of agreements is that the Central and East European countries have the prospect of EU membership, which is not the case for the Middle Eastern and North African countries (except for Cyprus, Malta and ultimately Turkey).

This chapter has argued that the hortatory language in most provisions of the Euro-Med Agreements makes them ineffective in addressing regulatory barriers to trade. Moreover, there are few procedural mechanisms for ensuring compliance. In terms of substance there are, as yet, no substantive commitments in public procurement, services or the right of establishment/investment. However, it is necessary to point out that the Euro-Mediterranean Partnership is a long-term process. The basic framework of Euro-Med relations has been set out with the Barcelona Declaration and this framework is likely to grow. One promising prospect for the Euro-Med Partnership is to turn the network of bilateral Association Agreements into a single Euro-Mediterranean economic space. This would clearly be a form of deeper integration and would require a strengthening of subregional integration in the Mediterranean, which could, in part, be achieved by the diagonal cumulation of origin rules.

The potential of the Euro-Med Partnership will be fully realized only once all partners have signed a Partnership Agreement with the European Union and these agreements have been ratified. To date, only four of the agreements signed since the Barcelona Declaration have been ratified (the agreements with Tunisia, Morocco, Egypt and Jordan). Moreover, the ratification of the EU–Jordan EMA showed how slow ratification can be even for an "uncomplicated" dossier.

In two areas (competition and technical barriers) the Euro-Med Agreements show signs of being WTO-plus. But the degree to which these areas are really WTO-plus will depend on whether and how they are implemented. Greater progress in technical standards, regulations and conformance assessment has probably been made because the benefits are more visible here than in other areas. Trade patterns between the European Union and the MPCs also illustrate the potential impact of such closer cooperation. The picture is less clear with respect to competition policy, which was presented by the European Commission as part of the "Partnership package". The European competition philosophy has been successfully introduced in the EMAs, but the impact of the competition provisions will also depend on how they are implemented.

The developments in TBTs and competition provide some support for the view that the European Union is transposing its regulatory "model" into the Euro-Med Agreements and thereby acting as a "regional regulatory hegemon" vis-à-vis the MPCs. However, regulatory regionalism in the Mediterranean Basin is benign rather than malign. The shallow nature of the agreements that both the European Union and the United States have signed also means there is likely to be only a limited divergence of the respective approaches. Furthermore, the EMAs appear to be signed in a context of a heightened awareness about the possible threat of regional trade agreements to the multilateral trading system.

Notes

1. The relationship between the Europe Agreements and the demands for a new Euro-Med relation parallels Richard Baldwin's "Domino Theory" (1995): a change in the preferential status of one country will alter the position of everyone else in the hierarchy, resulting in demands for a deepening of the preferential status from those affected by the change.
2. Full multilateral liberalization is another, less realistic option.
3. Article 8, Council Decision 1/95, and implemented by Decision 2/97 of the Association Council (Official Journal, 1996, 1997a).
4. Fourth Euro-Mediterranean Conference of Ministers for Industry, "Conclusions", Malaga, 9–10 April 2002.
5. Fifth Euro-Mediterranean Business Summit, "Mediterranean Region and the Global Economy. Final Declaration of the Summit", Istanbul, 1–2 March 2002.
6. Ibid., p. 10.
7. Ibid., p. 10.
8. First Euro-Mediterranean Ministerial Meeting on Trade, "Conclusions of the Presidency", May 2001.
9. The article states that "the parties shall set as their objective a reciprocal and gradual liberalisation of public procurement contracts and the Association Council shall take the steps necessary to implement paragraph 1".
10. See also chapter 4 on how this shaped policy on investment in the negotiations with Mexico.
11. These provisions are in line with the NAFTA provisions on environment.
12. "Joint Statement on WTO Issues", Annex to the US–Jordan Free Trade Agreement; see also http://www.ustr.gov/regions/eu-med/middleeast/US-JordanFTA.shtml.

REFERENCES

Balázs, Péter (1997), "Subregional Cooperation in Central and Eastern Europe, the Visegrád Declaration and the Central European Free Trade Agreement", in Paul Demaret (ed.), *Regionalism and Multilateralism after the Uruguay Round: Convergence, Divergence and Interaction*, Brussels: European Inter-University Press.

Baldwin, Richard E. (1994), *Towards an Integrated Europe*, London: CEPR.

—— (1995), "A Domino Theory of Regionalism", in R. Baldwin, P. Haaparanta and J. Kiander (eds.), *Expanding Membership of the European Union*, Cambridge: Cambridge University Press, pp. 25–53.

—— (2000), "Regulatory Protectionism, Developing Nations, and a Two-Tier World Trade System", in *Brookings Trade Forum*, pp. 237–93.

Brown, Drusilla K., Alan V. Deardorff and Robert M. Stern (1997), "Some Economic Effects of the Free Trade Agreement between Tunisia and the European Union", in Ahmed Galal and Bernard Hoekman (eds.), *Regional Partners in Global Markets: Limits and Possibilities of the Euro-Med Agreements*, London: CEPR.

Business Times (2002), "EU Studying Free Trade Pact with Singapore: Lamy Strong Case Made, but Some Conditions Must Be Met First", 16 February.

European Commission (1997), *WTO Aspects of EU Preferential Trade Agreements with Third Countries*, SEC (95) 2168, 16 January.

—— (2000), *Reinvigorating the Barcelona Process*, COM (2000) 497, 6 September.

Eurostat (2001), *External and Intra-European Union Trade – Statistical Yearbook*, Luxembourg.

—— (2002), *External and Intra-European Union Trade – Statistical Yearbook*, Luxembourg.

Gephardt, Richard (1994), "House Letter on Middle East Trade", *Inside U.S. Trade*, 29 July, pp. 30–1.

Hakura, Fadi S. (1999), *EU–Mediterranean and Gulf Trade Agreements*, Isle of Wight: Palladian Law Publishing.

Handoussa, Heba, and Jean-Louis Reiffers (2002), *The FEMISE Report on the Evolution of the Structure of Trade and Investments between the European Union and Its Mediterranean Partners*, The Euro-Mediterranean Forum of Economic Institutes, at http://www.femise.org/acceuil3en.html.

Hoekman, Bernard, and Simeon Djankov (1997), "Free Trade Agreements in the Mediterranean: A Regional Path to Liberalization?", World Bank, mimeo.

Hoekman, Bernard, and Denise Eby Konan (1999), "Deep Integration, Non-discrimination and Euro-Mediterranean Free Trade", Policy Research Working Paper WPS 2130, Washington DC: World Bank.

—— (2000), "Rents, Red Tape, and Regionalism: Economic Effects of Deeper Integration", in Bernard Hoekman and Jamel Zarrouk (eds.), *Catching up with the Competition: Trade Opportunities and Challenges for Arab Countries*, Ann Arbor: Michigan University Press.

Konan, Denise Eby, and Keith E. Maskus (1997), "A Computable General Equilibrium Analysis of Egyptian Trade Liberalization Scenarios", in Ahmed Galal and Bernard Hoekman (eds.), *Regional Partners in Global Markets: Limits and Possibilities of the Euro-Med Agreements*, London: CEPR.

Lawrence, Robert Z. (1995), *Regionalism, Multilateralism, and Deeper Integration*, Washington DC: Brookings Institution.

OECD (Organisation for Economic Co-operation and Development) (1981), Council Decision C(81)30 Final Concerning the Mutual Acceptance of Data in the Assessment of Chemicals, 12 May.

Official Journal (1996), "Decision No 1/95 of the EC–Turkey Association Council of 22 December 1995 on Implementing the Final Phase of the Customs Union", *OJ*, L035, 13 February, pp. 1–47.

—— (1997a), "Decision No 2/97 of the EC–Turkey Association Council of 4 June 1997 Establishing the List of Community Instruments Relating to the Removal of Technical Barriers to Trade and the Conditions and Arrangements Governing Their Implementation by Turkey", *OJ*, L191, 21 July, pp. 1–67.

—— (1997b), "Council Decision No 97/474/EC of 24 February 1997 Concerning the Conclusion of Two Agreements between the European Community and the State of Israel on, Respectively, Procurement by Telecommunications Operators and Government Procurement", *OJ*, L202, 30 July, p. 72.

—— (1999), "Agreement on Mutual Recognition of OECD Principles of Good Laboratory Practice (GLP) and Compliance Monitoring Programmes between the European Community and the State of Israel – Agreed Minutes", *OJ*, L263, 9 October, pp. 7–18.

—— (2000), "Decision No 2/2000 of the EC–Turkey Association Council of 11 April 2000 on the Opening of Negotiations Aimed at the Liberalization of Services and the Mutual Opening of Procurement Markets between the Community and Turkey", *OJ*, L138, 9 June, p. 27.

Pons, Jean-François (2002), "Le Rôle accru de la politique de la concurrence dans la relance du partneriat euro-méditerranéen", speech at the Séminaire régional sur la politique de concurrence et les négociations multilatérales, Tunis, March, unpublished.

Rutherford, Thomas F., E. E. Rutström and David Tarr (1993), "Morocco's Free Trade Agreement with the European Community: A Quantitative Assessment", Policy Research Working Paper WPS 1173, Washington DC: World Bank.

—— (1995), "The Free Trade Agreement between Tunisia and the European Union", World Bank, unpublished mimeo.

—— (2000), "A Free Trade Agreement between the European Union and a Representative Arab Mediterranean Country: A Quantitative Assessment", in Bernard Hoekman and Jamel Zarrouk (eds.), *Catching up with the Competition: Trade Opportunities and Challenges for Arab Countries*, Ann Arbor: Michigan University Press.

Schott, Jeffrey J. (2001), Testimony Before the Subcommittee on Trade of the House Committee on Ways and Means, "Hearing on Free Trade Deals: Is the United States Losing Ground as Its Trading Partners Move Ahead?", 29 March.

Tovias, Alfred (1997), "The Economic Impact of the Euro-Mediterranean Free Trade Area in Mediterranean Non-Member Countries", *Mediterranean Politics* 2(1).

UNCTAD (United Nations Conference on Trade and Development) (1998a), *Empirical Evidence of the Benefits from Applying Competition Law and Policy Principles to Economic Development in Order to Attain Greater Efficiency in International Trade and Development*, Geneva: UNCTAD.

────── (1998b), *Experiences Gained so far with International Cooperation on Competition Policy Issues and the Mechanisms Used*, Geneva: UNCTAD.

United Nations Economic and Social Commission for Western Asia (1999), *Euro-Mediterranean Partnership Agreements: A Critical Assessment*, New York: United Nations.

WTO (World Trade Organization) (1995), *The Results of the Uruguay Round Negotiations: The Legal Texts*, Geneva: WTO.

Zoellick, Robert B. (2001), "American Trade Leadership: What Is at stake?", speech at the Institute for International Economics, Washington DC, 24 September.

────── (2002), "USTR Zoellick Outlines Trade Objectives for 2002", at http://www.useu.be, February.

6

The North American Free Trade Agreement

Julius Sen

Introduction

This chapter explores whether policy reforms and their implementation in the "new" regulatory areas of the North American Free Trade Agreement (NAFTA) serve to support or impede the multilateral process. In other words, do NAFTA's provisions in the "new" regulatory areas go beyond those of the World Trade Organization (are they WTO-plus or not) and, if so, how and to what extent? The chapter endeavours to reach a determination on this point and to assess some of the broader implications of NAFTA for regulatory approaches at the multilateral level.

NAFTA is a good case to study for several reasons. In the first place it is a powerful new regional trade agreement (RTA) with the United States at its centre. It is therefore capable of developing regulatory systems of its own that could genuinely threaten the principles promoted at the multilateral level. Secondly, it links a developing country (Mexico) with two highly developed economies (the United States and Canada) within a single RTA. This poses a significant challenge to the regulatory systems of all the parties involved and could provide some valuable insights into whether developing and developed countries can co-exist within a single multilateral arrangement, and, if so, how. Thirdly, NAFTA as an agreement, together with its two side agreements on labour and the environment, is structured differently from the single undertaking that emerged from the Uruguay Round. Does this matter and could it influence the way in which the multilateral process develops? Finally, NAFTA does not replicate the institutional arrangements of the WTO, but opts for a more flexible and diffuse structure. Could there be lessons and indicators here for the multilateral process?

Although some of these issues are obviously beyond the scope of this chapter, they are nevertheless of linked significance, and thus need to be borne in mind when considering the broader implications of NAFTA's regulatory systems for the multilateral process.

Scope of the chapter

Both NAFTA and GATT/WTO seek to promote improvements in the way that trade policy and trade regulations are made, applied and adjudicated. Improvements in the transparency of trade policy-making and regulatory intervention, the use of clear and fair rules, the creation of institutions that act in support of these systems, improved levels of compliance with commitments, and effective redressal procedures are just some of the features of the domestic policy environment that are thought to be essential to the process of building a rules-based system, whether at the regional or multilateral level.

The question this chapter addresses is whether NAFTA's regulatory systems, in certain select areas, are compatible with the multilateral process and work to further its principles or not. In other words, is NAFTA "institutionally compatible" with the WTO?[1] To assess whether this is the case, NAFTA's policies and practices with respect to some of the more important "new" regulatory areas will be explored: technical barriers to trade; food safety; public procurement; services; investment. Other regulatory issues, including those concerning the side agreements on labour and the environment, though important and interconnected with some of these issue areas mentioned above, have not been included because this would make the study unwieldy. There are, however, references to these issues in the chapter. A wider coverage would not in any case significantly change some of the essential lessons and conclusions. The issue areas proposed for this analysis are therefore selective rather than exhaustive but are no less representative of NAFTA's regulatory regime for that.

Methodology

The impact of regulatory measures in the issue areas mentioned above will be assessed in accordance with the analytical framework developed by Woolcock and Sampson, which employs a yardstick that evaluates the impact of regulatory regimes in RTAs largely on the basis of their substantive, institutional and procedural implications. To provide a fuller picture of what is happening in the NAFTA context, this chapter will also briefly explore the contribution of the political process that underpins the agreement to NAFTA's regulatory regime, because this appears to be decisively important in certain circumstances.

Measuring whether NAFTA's regulatory systems are WTO-consistent or WTO-plus is less subjective than would at first seem to be the case. This is for three reasons. First, the coverage and scope of the agreement itself indicate whether an RTA goes beyond the commitments required at the multilateral level – as with the coverage of investment, services and government procurement in NAFTA. In these areas NAFTA is clearly WTO-plus to a significant degree by virtue of coverage alone. Secondly, the question of whether other features of the agreement could actually represent impediments to developing multilateral regulatory disciplines (through regulatory regionalism for instance) is possible to determine fairly objectively by looking in some detail at procedure and practice within NAFTA. And, thirdly, the way the system actually operates (taking political and institutional features into account) gives a fairly clear reading of the direction of events – in this case its capacity to solve problems. Here again it is possible to assess quickly whether NAFTA systems undermine or support the application of multilateral principles from a reading of how the system is working.

In the conclusion an attempt is made to represent the findings of this chapter in schematic form, based upon the analytical framework developed by Woolcock and Sampson. This is obviously a simplification of essentially complex issues, and is thus supplemented with a narrative summation of some of the findings that will perhaps give a more qualitative feel to the conclusions drawn.

This chapter is divided into three sections. The first will look at the larger picture regarding the NAFTA agreement and recount its political and negotiating context. It will also look in broad terms at the impact of the agreement on the three economies and on systems and procedures. The second section will attempt to evaluate the policy impact of NAFTA provisions in the identified "new" regulatory areas and to determine where and how they could be problematic in so far as the furtherance of multilateral principles is concerned. This section will also attempt to discern how these regulatory policies may affect external trading interests. The third section will draw some conclusions from the findings and endeavour to give a specific answer to the question of whether regulatory reforms within NAFTA promote or hinder the multilateral process. This part of the chapter will also attempt to see why this may be so.

General characteristics of NAFTA and its members

The general context

Even without going into detail it is obvious that NAFTA is an agreement between three very different partners – countries with significant, even profound, differences in the size and structures of their economies, their histories and culture, their political traditions, their levels of economic development and their expectations. Yet all three members consider the agreement to be of fundamental importance to their national interests, and they have all sought and found domestic and international compromises that have tended to lessen the points of friction between them. At the same time, all of them have reservations about its consequences (foreseen and unforeseen) and are fundamentally cautious in making long-term commitments.

Whereas Canada and the United States can at least point to almost two centuries of reasonably amicable relations,[2] and some deeply shared cultural, social and political traditions, the same cannot be said of Mexico's position in this unusual *ménage à trois*. Mexico is, or rather was, an underdeveloped country sitting just south of one of the most developed and powerful economies in the world, and with a gross domestic product (GDP) of less than 4 per cent of that of the United States. At the same time, Mexico does not share the political and legal systems and structures of either of its two northern neighbours, and of course it is divided even further by its language, culture and religion. Mexico also has deep internal social and political divisions, which obviously affect its internal political processes and priorities.

In terms of the three countries' experience with international economic institutions, the differences between them are again striking. Whereas the United States can be said to be the architect of the post-war international system, and Canada one of its most ardent supporters, the same cannot be said of Mexico. Its retreat into isolation from the early part of the twentieth century, in large part because of its fear of US dominance (which Canada shared but for which it adopted a different response), only really began to change in the 1980s. Similarly, Mexico's economic policies were based on models of autonomy and self-sufficiency that were the virtual opposite of those of its northern neighbours, which was again a product, to a large extent, of its fear of the United States.

Canada for its part, though sharing much of the economic ideology of the United States in general terms, was equally apprehensive of domination by its southern neighbour. From the late 1960s to the early 1980s Canada had constructed a number of policies to "regain" control of its economy from US interests and to isolate itself from US cultural influence, which was thought to threaten its "independence". This, however, changed in the mid to late 1980s and Canada, along with the United States, adopted a number of policy reforms in the macroeconomic management of the economy that included a more open trade regime.

The only thing that the three countries had in common, therefore, was that they were all located in North America (sort of), they were all federal entities (sort of) and they were all democracies (sort of).

From the 1980s onwards, and in part as a consequence of the catastrophic effects of the debt crisis, Mexico's leadership started to rethink its domestic and international policies. The conversion, when it took place, in effect entailed the reversal of decades of policies, strategies and attitudes. The process was obviously painful and complex, and many of the shocks were sudden and socially and economically severe. Political opposition was always strong – even within the ruling party, which in effect had a stranglehold on the Mexican political system – and it remains a feature of the Mexican political landscape despite the fact that federal power has now been transferred to an opposition party.

Mexico's leadership attempted to systematically redesign many features of its internal financial and economic system to create a policy environment that was basically neo-liberal. This proved far more complex than anyone had anticipated and successes were inevitably accompanied by massive set-backs, which threatened economic collapse and reopened many of the ideological issues that had dogged the early part of the reform process. Even with the support of Structural Adjustment Programmes, Mexico's entry into the General Agreement on Tariffs and Trade (GATT) in 1986 and its active efforts to participate constructively in the Uruguay Round were of little use in attracting foreign investment, promoting economic growth or resolving the debt crisis. The economy seemed to lurch from one economic crisis to another, interspersed with political crises of almost similar magnitude. The process of internal economic reform, because it did not really enjoy popular support, was very top–down – a fact that becomes important when considering the difficulties Mexico had and still has with regulatory reform.

Given this context, and given all the differences between Mexico and its northern neighbours, its interest in joining the Canada–US Free Trade Area (CUSFTA) is nothing short of astonishing. Yet, to make it happen, the United States and Canada had to commit to support the process, notwithstanding the very long distance that the Mexican economy had to travel and the enormous reforms that it had to make.

The US perspective on all this was basically driven by three considerations: that an outward-looking Mexico was a good potential market with 90 million consumers; that Mexican poverty levels created problems of migration, which were becoming politically problematic in an already sensitive area; and that, if the United States did get involved in helping Mexico, the embrace had to be so tight that Mexico's reforms would be permanently "locked in", as it is politely expressed in United States Trade Representative (USTR) documents. At the same time, the United States was a little frustrated at the slow pace of progress in the Uruguay Round negotiations and wanted to demonstrate that its ideas could work just as well in a regional setting.

So, starting in 1991, the improbable process of creating a CUSFTA-plus-Mexico started. Though starting considerably later than the Uruguay Round (which began in 1986), NAFTA was negotiated in parallel with it, and concluded a year earlier. It entered into force on 1 January 1994, exactly a year before the WTO came into existence and the provisions of the Uruguay Round entered into force.

The negotiating context of NAFTA

Negotiations for NAFTA (1990–2) and its predecessor the CUSFTA (1986–8) ran substantially in parallel with those of the Uruguay Round, concluded earlier, and indeed influenced the multilateral process in a number of significant ways. The reverse, however, was not apparently the case, largely because the initiative for many important aspects of the multilateral process came from the United States and were therefore pursued, quite logically, in parallel at the regional and multilateral levels. In fact the NAFTA process is even referred to in USTR documents as the template for US strategy in the Uruguay Round.

From a US perspective, NAFTA was in many ways a better agreement than the Uruguay Round. The United States got more of what it wanted in areas of importance to it (especially services and investment) and for major trading partners, without having to accept a supranational regional trade authority, and it was able to deal simultaneously with troublesome side issues through the device of separate environmental and labour agreements. The political package that NAFTA represented – though opposed by many in Congress – was more acceptable to the United States than the Uruguay Round perhaps because the pre-eminence of the United States within this arrangement was clear to everybody.

In the Uruguay Round, the United States achieved less with more ambiguity in the language, and it had to make concessions to the Europeans in important areas such as agriculture and to developing countries in a number of other areas. It also had to accept the establishment of a new international institution – the World Trade Organization – at a time when the whole idea of such supranational bodies was a growing anathema to politicians in Congress. Moreover, the whole idea of a rules-based system with independent arbitration under the authority of the WTO gave the impression to many members of the US Congress that the United States was going to lose control over one of its most important and strategic assets. Indeed, this sense of apprehension was reflected in the final enabling legislation approved by the US Congress, which provided for a review after a five-year implementation period. Side agreements of the sort seen in NAFTA would have been impossible at the multilateral level, given the number of countries involved, the complexity of the issues and the suspicion of developing countries in particular about negotiating such agreements as part of the multilateral trade liberalization process. The multilateral process was just too large and unwieldy to accommodate something of this sort.

The NAFTA agreement thus gave the United States, Mexico and Canada the chance to push further and faster in a number of areas than was possible at the multilateral level, even if the agenda was largely driven by the United States. This was done by building essentially upon the Canada–US Free Trade Agreement and extending its operation to include Mexico.

The pace of events within the Uruguay Round process was also "forced", to an extent, by the United States moving quickly within NAFTA and, in late 1993, towards a regional agreement for the Asia-Pacific (Asia-Pacific Economic Cooperation, APEC). These two regional agreements (NAFTA and APEC) would encompass the most dynamic economic regions in the world and, more importantly, isolate Europe from the process that regional liberalization entailed. The prospect of two new and mightily powerful trading blocs, with the United States at the centre of each, was meant to daunt the Europeans and bring them to a compromise over agriculture.[3] The use of regional agreements as a tactic to force the pace at the multilateral level would suggest that the principles and objectives of the two processes were broadly in harmony and that the issue was really one of tactics and strategy and finding the right (and acceptable) level for this integrative process to stabilize at.

This brings us to really the most significant point about the parallel negotiations at the regional and multilateral level. They were both founded upon similar if not identical economic assumptions and objectives, and they espoused the same principles and methods to achieve them. The issue that has excited debate and generated controversy relates largely to operational differences and how these would play out through the international trading system, particularly with reference to third-party interests. But this argument has been vastly overstated: if the underlying philosophy is the same; if the definitional work is founded on the same systems of classification and categorization; if the principles sought to be applied are the same or substantially similar; and if many of the approaches and methods are the same – then any combination of implementational and operational factors that *apparently* detract from this process can at the most have only a marginal effect.

Experience with implementation

NAFTA is perceived to be a success by all three member states.[4] Intra-regional trade has grown faster than global trends, and Canada and Mexico have become the largest trading partners of the United States, and vice versa. Investment is generally booming, which reflects long-term confidence about the future. Mexico in particular has benefited, demonstrating that a trading relationship has to be supported politically, particularly in an unequal situation.

Some of the broader findings of a review of NAFTA after eight years of implementation bring this out strongly (NAFTA Free Trade Commission, 2002):

Export performance:
- Canada's merchandise trade within NAFTA, between 1993 and 2001, increased by 95 per cent, compared with a 5 per cent increase with respect to trade with the rest of the world for this period.
- Mexico's exports to its NAFTA partners increased by 225 per cent between 1993 and 2001, whereas its international exports increased by 93 per cent.
- US exports to NAFTA partners increased by almost 100 per cent between 1993 and 2001, against an increase of 44 per cent in exports to the rest of the world.

Investment performance:
- Foreign direct investment (FDI) inflows into the NAFTA region as a whole between 1994 and 2000 reached US$1.3 trillion, or 28 per cent of the global total.
- The United States continued to be the highest recipient of FDI in the world, with an inflow of about US$110.2 billion per year during 1994–2000.
- Canada registered a massive increase in inward investment between 1994 and 2000 that was four times the average registered over the previous seven years, and now stands at US$21.4 billion.
- Mexico's increase in inward investment in the same period was three times the average of the previous seven years, and in 2000 stood at US$11.7 billion.

Curiously enough, the report is silent on services sector performance and is selective about what it says are the domestic effects on the three economies. It does suggest that export-dependent jobs in the three NAFTA economies pay higher rates than other jobs, and that the bulk of job creation is because of exports, but this is not really NAFTA specific.

It also suggests that half of Mexico's GDP growth can be accounted for by the export sector, but again is not necessarily NAFTA specific.

USTR-based reports are far more cautious about the domestic effects of NAFTA for member economies; they suggest for example that "NAFTA had a modest positive effect on U.S. net exports, income, investment and jobs supported by exports" (USTR, n.d., p. 2). This report further asserts that NAFTA's trade openness helped the Mexican economy recover rapidly from the peso crisis and recession of 1994–5 (pp. 2–3).

National Trade Estimates by the USTR for Mexico and Canada give firm figures for the services sector (USTR, 2002a, 2002b). These show that intra-NAFTA services trade is only about 10 per cent of total trade (estimated at US$622 billion), which is surprising. World figures for trade in services constitute about 20 per cent of global trade.

Taken together, these figures suggest that NAFTA has made a decisive difference in merchandise trade and investment but has yet to yield strong results in services. They also tend to confirm that some trade diversion in merchandise trade must have resulted from the agreement, because of the abnormal surge in NAFTA's internal trade figures but not (yet) in the services sector. It is however difficult, if not impossible, to ascribe cause and effect to NAFTA alone. It could very well have been a host of other factors (high US demand, political factors, etc.) that played a role in this process.

But within this larger picture is the issue of actual implementation, measured not in terms of trade outcomes but in terms of the codification of rules and procedures and the creation of systems and institutions that will administer, monitor and review them, along with procedures to attend to complaints, challenges and grievances. Furthermore, the requirements also relate to the creation of technical and scientific facilities and their integration into the process.

In the context of NAFTA generally, it is really only Mexico that has a mountain to climb in this regard. Canada and the United States have the legal and organizational infrastructure to comply (generally) with whatever is agreed, although they both have constitutional limitations on how far they can enforce compliance below the national level. Mexico has to build and create the systems, draft the laws and codes across a wide range of commercial and investment policy areas, and then bring the provisions into compliance. Of course, the process of rule-making and institution-building started before Mexico's accession to NAFTA, and was also shaped by its obligations to the Organisation for Economic Co-operation and Development (OECD; which it qualified to join only in 1994), but the Mexican government has found it far harder than initially thought.

Although Mexico has been quite successful at things such as reducing tariffs and passing laws (the Mexican government lists 15 *major* enactments between 1995 and 2000) (COFEMER, 2001), there are still huge problems with policy coordination and implementation, which are reflected in the tetchy tone adopted year after year in the USTR's National Trade Estimates for Mexico (USTR, 1995–2001).

To convey an idea of the complexity of this exercise, one need only visit the Mexican government's website for the Comisión Federal de Mejora Regulatoria (COFEMER). The government of Mexico has established a Federal Regulatory Improvement Programme charged with coordinating "the programme [for the consolidation of a system of regulatory management] ... to ensure transparency in the drafting of federal regulations, and to promote the development of cost effective regulations that produce the greatest net benefit for society" (COFEMER, 2001). This is obviously a massive task, complicated by the multiplicity of objectives and general confusion about who does what in Mexico's federal system.

The Mexican government has also, by presidential decree, withdrawn the application of 181 regulations (*reglamentos*) and reviewed and amended 500 legislative and administrative provisions. It also mentions that by the end of the year 2000 nearly 50 per cent of the formalities of 11 different ministries had been eliminated and 90 per cent of the remaining ones simplified. By 2003 it is hoping to move to a system of positive listing for applicable regulations: regulations not listed will no longer apply. This is obviously an idea borrowed from trade negotiations, although it is of doubtful constitutional validity, as explained below.

At the state level, of which Mexico has 31, the government has attempted to resolve this tangle by getting state governments to sign agreements accepting the federal regulatory reform programme, which means that Mexican states have transferred their constitutional authority in a range of sensitive areas relating to trade and regulatory management to the federal government. The issue of whether this is constitutionally sustainable is unclear, and it could become problematic should a state government challenge the commitments made by the federal authorities or should state authorities challenge the authority of the federal government to implement policies on their behalf. It is therefore a political move of huge significance considering the adverse social consequences of economic liberalization, and it is not clear how this arrangement will translate into consistent regulatory policies consistently applied. It is also not clear how the Mexican judiciary will respond over time.

By any standard, creating a regulatory system and reforming the investment codes and procedures of a federal structure is a massive task and it is not surprising that confusion abounds. In effect the Mexican government is trying to create an entirely new system of jurisprudence for commercial activities, within a complex federal system that had previously been governed by government directives, presidential decrees and administrative regulation. At the same time, it is trying to create the consultative and procedural requirements of an open and transparent policy-making process, within strict time schedules. It is interesting to note that the COFEMER committee does not mention issues pertaining to judicial reform at all, yet these are really integral and fundamental to this reform process.

Perhaps in recognition of the extraordinary complexity of this undertaking, both Canada and the United States give considerable latitude to their Mexican counterparts. By adopting a non-confrontational approach, NAFTA (that is the United States and Canada) is again conveying a very important political message to Mexico, and to investors, which perhaps accounts for the rapid growth in confidence in the Mexican economy reflected in sharply increasing investment figures and trade flows. Success in this case has less to do with actual progress in regulatory reform within Mexico than with a sense of political certainty about Mexico's long-term intentions.

The other distinct feature about this process of regulatory reform has been the way in which American concepts of jurisprudence and due process have intruded, which, when considered with reference to the effect of NAFTA-level regulatory reform on the multilateral process, is very significant. There can be little doubt that this approach serves to improve all the standards identified (transparency, rule-making, institution-building, etc.). Hence, adopting US standards regarding due process and judicial review in the design of a regulatory framework serves both multilateral and regional objectives simultaneously.

Linked to this is the issue of redress or compliance. NAFTA has provided private interests with several options to choose from in pursuit of dispute resolution or to enforce compliance, whereas the multilateral process really has only one. Under NAFTA, an aggrieved party can:

- use the dispute settlement procedures of NAFTA *or* the WTO;[5]
- use the trilateral intergovernmental committees, of which there are dozens covering various sectors, to try to resolve systemic or generic problems that may be specific to a particular industry or activity; or
- use local courts to challenge regulatory findings that are arbitrary, capricious or vague. (This will depend on the legal presence of a party within the local jurisdiction, which is more likely under NAFTA because the investment agreement creates a right of establishment.)

Apart from these formalized systems, informal points of contact can be employed to get a hearing and sort out problems through the various networks that operate. This is widely used when dealing with Mexican authorities and has proved to be very effective. These multiple options facilitate the conduct of business and help generate ideas for further systemic reforms. A very strong sense of "problem-solving" is generated by these processes. The WTO and the multilateral process, in contrast, are too large, diverse and unwieldy to help in these situations. NAFTA systems thus offer a significant advantage to importers, exporters and investors and have been successful in promoting a rolling process of regulatory reform.

As mentioned earlier, NAFTA generally, though not invariably, seems to favour equivalence of regulatory policies and technical standards over harmonization, provided these are open to judicial review and are technically and scientifically founded. In practice, Mexico is tending towards a harmonized system with the United States, largely because it is such an unequal relationship and Mexico is very dependent on the United States for assistance in establishing these standards in the first place. This is further reinforced through the trilateral intergovernmental committees, which are able to focus on specific issues of NAFTA members and consider them in the limited context of a regional agreement. This approach tends to promote the process of harmonization because expert committees and technical subcommittees often come to common agreement on common issues and problems.

Overall, therefore, the impetus is towards a harmonized system of standards and technical regulations built around US practices and procedures, although perhaps not explicitly and also not required under the NAFTA codes. This suggests that the potential for differences between the multilateral approach and the NAFTA approach may be of diminishing importance in terms of these differences operating as a possible barrier to third-party trade.

These features would suggest that NAFTA imparts something of a multiplier effect to the international trading system largely because of the centrality of the United States to both the NAFTA arrangement and the multilateral process. The logic here is that, if the United States flourishes within NAFTA, this increases its demands for goods and services from the multilateral process as well, partly because of higher consumer demand and partly because of the natural effects of more intensive economic activity.

Generally speaking, therefore, this would imply that NAFTA has been a success, measured in economic, institutional and procedural terms. The impact on the multilateral system is, however, harder to estimate. There certainly appears to be evidence of trade diversion from NAFTA's implementation in the merchandise sector. But this could be due to other factors, or could even be seen as broadly supportive of the multilateral process because this shift is part of an overall trade increase, suggesting that improved competition within the NAFTA region may be responsible.

As mentioned earlier, the most striking feature of the NAFTA arrangement and its overall economic performance is the centrality of the United States to the system and the dependence of both Mexico and Canada on US markets, demand, capital and investment. Moreover, since 1994, this dependence has if anything increased. It is not really surprising therefore that any evaluation of NAFTA as a trading arrangement, even in its regulatory aspect, and its impact on the multilateral process would depend largely on an evaluation of the role played by the United States at both these levels, and US attitudes towards them.

Strong domestic demand within the United States, which also started at about the time of NAFTA's entry into force, created major opportunities for both Canada and Mexico to exploit, particularly in Mexico's case with the sharp fall in the value of the peso during the crisis of 1994–5. The United States thus became the engine for economic growth for the region. Indeed, with persistent recession in Japan and economic restructuring in Europe following the reunification of Germany and the European Union's single internal market project, the United States in effect became the engine for global economic demand. East Asia, Europe, Canada and Mexico all benefited.

The point at issue here, therefore, is whether the strength and dynamism of the US economy, regardless of NAFTA, could or would have achieved as much as it did for Canada and Mexico without a formal agreement. Obviously there is no easy answer to this, but it is fairly certain that investment flows were definitely influenced by NAFTA. This in itself would suggest that the regulatory element of this policy must have been of considerable importance in support of this process, particularly where the Mexican market was concerned.

Is NAFTA WTO-plus?

Looking at the NAFTA and GATT/WTO agreements – and standing back from the detail – they are, as mentioned earlier, clearly very similar and indeed evolved in close parallel. They have the same philosophy and principles, they have the same broad structure and many of the same core features, and they apply the same (or very similar) methods and approaches. They also share much of the definitional work, which at a technical and regulatory level becomes very important as it concerns implementation. Both agreements are based on much of the same thinking, arising largely from work done in the OECD (1972), and were driven politically by the United States, which was the principal *demandeur* in both negotiations. This suggests that a lot of the thinking that went into NAFTA coincided with developments taking place within the Uruguay Round.

One feature of the NAFTA process that is significantly different from the Uruguay Round pertains to the structure of the agreement and the use of side agreements. NAFTA as an agreement is a single document (unlike the various agreements in the Uruguay Round) and this ties the application of the underlying principles more closely to the provisions and gives less scope for alternative interpretations or ambiguity. At the same time, NAFTA's side agreements on labour and the environment – quite apart from reflecting the complexity and interconnectedness of issues, and also their extreme political sensitivity – succeeded in isolating them from the body of the main text, thus relieving the trade policy process of associated policy problems. Although this does not mean that labour and environmental issues can be ignored in the NAFTA negotiating context, there is at least a mechanism that can deal with them in parallel and without burdening the main text with too many operating principles. The institutional arrangement created to monitor and supervise these side agreements also offers parallel systems that can be effective in an operational sense without overburdening the trade policy agenda.

The important point about these side agreements is that they represented a political risk for the US president, which he was willing to take in the interests of seeing the main agreement concluded. This political vote of confidence in Mexico's membership of NAFTA was again demonstrated during the peso crisis of 1994–5, when the US government went to extreme and unprecedented lengths to support the Mexican economy.

However, although these measures may indeed appear to be in advance of the current level of agreement in the multilateral process, the question remains of whether these (and other) features of NAFTA, as supported by their regulatory systems and its implementation, may actually create a barrier to the access of other countries' goods and services in this market. In other words, could the regulatory institutions and systems of one system hinder the market access of third countries in these markets, even though these systems are premised on a more accentuated set of free trade principles?

Technical barriers to trade

A number of international agreements have sought to address the plethora of issues relating largely to the use of technical standards and certification procedures for non-tariff barriers.[6] Much of the basic conceptual work relating to this issue was undertaken by the OECD in the early 1970s in the context of environmental regulations (OECD, 1972). This study recognized that harmonization, although ideal in some ways, was difficult to achieve in reality because valid reasons existed for divergent standards to be applied. The OECD accordingly identified three basic approaches, which have shaped most agreements on technical barriers to trade (TBTs) and on sanitary and phytosanitary (SPS) measures in some form or the other (as summarized in Trebilcock and Howse, 1999, pp. 138–9):

1. The first was to suggest harmonization where valid reasons did not exist for distinct national standards.
2. The second was that these standards should not constitute barriers to trade – in other words, this should not be their purpose.
3. The third was to define procedures for checking conformity to product standards that should be mutually agreed.

Although the OECD may have set out in general terms the manner in which TBTs and SPS measures should ideally be applied, the reality in their design and actual application around the world suggested that they were indeed being designed to operate as barriers to trade. This complicated the task of negotiators at both the NAFTA and multilateral levels. There were several reasons for this. In the first place, TBTs (and SPS measures) tended to be more prevalent in developed countries, which of course had the largest markets. Secondly, the issues they dealt with were often politically sensitive. Thirdly, they covered an increasing range of products and could easily become barriers to market access. Fourthly, they could be drawn up and applied at sub-federal or local levels, thus further complicating market access issues. And, finally, they were often set or recommended by private trade or professional associations largely outside the control of governments in these countries.

Building a multilateral or regional agreement capable of systemically addressing issues arising out of this complex situation was a major achievement in itself. The question here is whether the agreement reached at the NAFTA level is compatible with the agreements reached at the multilateral level; if not, we need to assess whether the two approaches could actually be working at cross-purposes.

Broadly speaking, both NAFTA and the Uruguay Round built upon the work done during the Tokyo Round in developing a Standards Code, and divided the issue into two streams: those relating to the protection of human, animal and plant life, and health (sanitary and phytosanitary measures), and those relating to technical barriers to trade, which covered other technical standards and measures *not* covered by SPS agreements. Both agreements are also broadly similar in the application of general principles and in respect of general rights and obligations. There is, therefore, a basic compatibility between what the regional and multilateral systems sought to achieve through these agreements.

The key substantive differences are to be found in their coverage.

Given that the two agreements differ structurally, it is not surprising that the application of NAFTA's TBT provisions should reflect these differences. NAFTA's provisions relating to TBTs are contained in Chapter 6. These provisions are to be applied to trade in goods *and* services, which means that on grounds of coverage alone NAFTA's TBT provisions are broader than the TBT Agreement of the Uruguay Round in two senses: first, services as a sector are covered; secondly, NAFTA's coverage of services is more comprehensive than the General Agreement on Trade in Services (GATS) of the Uruguay Round. This confers a major WTO-plus on the NAFTA accord. There are, in addition, essentially four features of the NAFTA code that distinguish it from the multilateral process. Two of these concern the balance of the agreement in terms of national and international standards, one has to do with the federal reality of NAFTA member states, and the fourth pertains to the institutional support given to the process.

The reasons for this are to be found in the political context in which the NAFTA negotiations took place. The political sensitivity of TBTs and SPS measures was illustrated in the extensive efforts of environmental, consumer and labour lobbies, in the United States in particular, to retain the power to set such standards at the national, state and local levels (both within the government and through trade and professional associations). In the context of the trilateral process that NAFTA represented, the leverage and power of the United States prevailed, whereas in the context of the multilateral process being pursued in the Uruguay Round this was not quite so easy. Hence the balance of the agreement reached in NAFTA on TBTs and SPS measures provided greater authority to the parties to set health and safety standards at levels they considered appropriate than occurred at the multilateral level, in spite of their possible trade-restricting effects.

This would suggest that NAFTA's provisions in this regard were actually WTO-minus, but this was not particularly significant, for two reasons. First, the policies of transparency and due process embedded in the overall system ensured that such measures would need to be justified on explicit health, safety or other regulatory grounds, thus limiting the scope for their deployment as explicit trade barriers. Secondly, the largest regulatory player in the NAFTA context – the United States – retained a high level of market access relative to many other developed countries and was not one of the major offenders in misusing TBTs as barriers to trade. On balance therefore, and taken together with the broader coverage of NAFTA's TBT provisions, the conclusion that NAFTA was WTO-plus in this area would still remain valid.

As regards the differences, first of all NAFTA members have the right to establish measures relating to standards of safety and protection (Art. 904). They are free to establish standards deemed "appropriate" (by them) and are not required to harmonize. This means that countries can decide their own levels of risk for each situation. They are not, however, permitted to use these standards to create an unnecessary obstacle to trade (Art. 904(4)), and such would be deemed not to be the case if the country is in pursuit of a legitimate objective, defined to include protection of human and animal life and health, or in support of policies of sustainable development.

Second, NAFTA's TBT provisions differ from the Uruguay Round TBT in that they do not require standards to be "the least trade restrictive" (Trebilcock and Howse, 1999, p. 148). In other words, they do not set a standard for regulatory or technical standards to aim at. At the same time, NAFTA's provisions relating to standard-setting are constrained by the cornerstone principles of most favoured nation (MFN) and national treatment for "like" products, which paradoxically suggests that harmonization *would* eventually result around technical standards set in the United States because of the relatively dominant size of the US market in the regional context. So, although it would appear at one level that NAFTA provides greater policy autonomy and greater national latitude in standard-setting, the operational reality is that this probably would not result in divergent standards given the pre-eminence and centrality of the US market.

Third, at the sub-federal, regional and local levels, there are lighter obligations to conform to TBT codes. This was in deference to the federal structures of the three members, though it is really only Canada and the United States that were prickly about this. This position also mirrors the approach taken to private and autonomous standard-setting bodies, again largely prevalent in the North American context, and referred to in the first point above.

Finally, with respect to the institutional or procedural arrangements set out for TBTs in NAFTA, these are significantly stronger than those of the WTO, though perhaps weaker than those of the European Union. NAFTA's trilateral intergovernmental consultative structure is meant to support and facilitate the application of the TBT provisions, and involves a number of committees, subcommittees and working groups going into the various issues involved. The impediments faced by these committees are similar to those faced by the negotiators themselves; namely that many standards are set by sub-federal and private trade and professional associations (particularly in the United States) and these cannot be ignored in the discussions. Nevertheless, the work done by these bodies has been effective in resolving some issues.

NAFTA also requires its members to "make compatible their respective standards-related measures" (Art. 906(2)), and "to promote the compatibility of a specific standard or conformity assessment procedure that is maintained in its territory with the standards or conformity assessment procedures maintained in the territory of the other Party" (Art. 906(3)). Read together with the provisions relating to non-discrimination (Art. 904(3)) and to the acceptance of international standards (Art. 905), these provisions suggest that standards will harmonize around US standards even though, as noted before, this is not the stated objective. This is borne out in the actual application of TBT provisions. Problems have arisen mainly between the United States and Mexico, and, on the US–Canada side, only really with respect to subnational authorities.[7]

The (largely US) concern with Mexico has to do with its Metrology and Standards Law, which requires that products subject to technical regulations (normas oficiales Mexicanas, or NOMs) be certified by the government agency that set the standards or by an authorized and independent certification body. At the same time, under NAFTA Mexico was required from 1998 to recognize conformity assessment bodies in the United States and Canada on non-discriminatory terms. The problem (from a US perspective) is that each Mexican government agency has its own process to assess compliance with its NOMs, and there is usually only one authorized agency to issue certificates of compliance, thus slowing down and complicating a process that was to be simplified.

From the Mexican perspective, the problem is organizational and financial. It is expensive and administratively complex to establish procedures for regulatory standards that are transparent and to provide conformance testing that is up to the expectations of its more developed partners. In this respect, procedural provisions in NAFTA in the shape of the trilateral committees are offering technical and financial support to the Mexican authorities.

The outcome is likely to be that Mexico will administer a TBT regime that is modelled largely on the US system, suggesting that a harmonized regime will eventually develop within NAFTA. This must again be seen as significantly WTO-plus (if the OECD's preferred option is to be the appropriate measure). At the same time, and as a result of this process, Mexico will be better placed to meet its obligations under the WTO's TBT provisions and in dealing with third-country imports. The practical effect of this NAFTA process is therefore definitely WTO-plus, for the effect it has both on facilitating regional trade and on reducing levels of regulatory discretion.

Food safety

The Uruguay Round Agreement on Sanitary and Phytosanitary Measures (the SPS Agreement) is broadly similar to NAFTA's SPS agreement in terms of coverage, objectives, application and methods. Nevertheless, because NAFTA provisions in agriculture are more comprehensive and foresee the elimination of barriers at the border, through their replacement with tariffs (Chapter 7 of NAFTA) and subsequent phasing out over a period of 10 years (though with some exceptions), the role and application of SPS measures become more important to the actual conduct of cross-border trade in agriculture. They become, in fact, one of the few legitimate policy instruments to protect consumers and domestic markets, and are thus particularly vulnerable to misuse and distortion.

For the same broad reasons set out in the section on technical barriers to trade, NAFTA's SPS agreement can also be adjudged to be significantly WTO-plus. By virtue of a "deeper" agreement on agriculture, coverage is simultaneously more comprehensive. The greater flexibility provided to national governments to choose appropriate policy measures is again off-set by the pre-eminence and centrality of the US market in the regional context.

NAFTA does not attempt to harmonize standards in this important sector, but in Article 712 establishes the positive right of a party to adopt any measure it thinks fit for the health and protection of human, animal or plant life – even if it is more stringent than international standards – provided it does not operate as a disguised form of trade restriction and is based upon scientific principles and a risk assessment (Chapter 7, section B). This suggests that NAFTA members can adopt policies that may even result in trade restrictions, provided that this is not their intention.

In reality, however, the dominance of the United States in all areas of research, science and testing, together with the size of its market, puts it in the unique position of being able to lay down the scientific standards that others have to follow if they wish to operate in the US market. This is apparent from the abortive attempt by the Mexican government to enforce the domestic verification of meat and poultry imports through its own laboratory facilities by June 2001. Implementation of this law (the Animal Health Law of 2000) had to be postponed twice, because only one facility in Mexico was qualified to carry out the testing procedure. Reliance on US-based health and certification procedures for imports worth US$1.2 billion in this sector alone had to continue (USTR, 2002b, p. 293). Although harmonization is not the stated goal of NAFTA's SPS codes, except with respect to grade and quality standards (Trebilcock and Howse, 1999, p. 40), a form of de facto harmonization is taking place, particularly with respect to Mexico.

If the reality within NAFTA is one of "imperial or hegemonic harmonization", the hegemon appears to be willing to show some flexibility. For example, Mexico and the United States have recently agreed to declare certain regions close to their border "disease free" in respect of wheat, citrus and pork products, and to allow trade in these products to proceed. Prior to this agreement, US health standards required the whole country of supply to be declared disease free, a policy that was fully in line with NAFTA and WTO rules.[8] This agreement suggests that a willingness to find solutions – even if only partial and not entirely balanced – constitutes an important element in NAFTA's success.

NAFTA countries also commit themselves to using relevant international standards and to working towards equivalent SPS measures without compromising their chosen levels of protection. These provisions reflect the US approach regarding the use of scientific risk assessment and suggests that a form of regulatory regionalism relating to this issue could be emerging. However, the NAFTA approach, though at variance with the approach of the European Union, appears to operate comfortably within the ambit of the WTO SPS definition of "sound science" and it is doubtful whether it can be construed to pose a threat to the multilateral process or to third-party interests (see chapter 9 for a more extensive discussion of these points).

NAFTA's institutional arrangement with regard to SPS issues perhaps provides the most positive mechanism for the creation of an impartial regulatory system that applies certain principles and limits regulatory discretion. An SPS Committee, along with nine technical working groups, a Committee on Agricultural Trade and a Committee on Standards Related Measures, with associated subcommittees, meet regularly to discuss issues that emerge from the actual implementation of NAFTA (Trebilcock and Howse, 1999, p. 149). This mechanism, which has a strong problem-solving ethos, works systematically in support of improving the application of SPS provisions and in reducing regulatory discretion. It also works in coordination with similar committees looking at environmental protection issues, thus generating a certain policy consistency across policy sectors. This institutional arrangement imparts a significant WTO-plus dimension to the application of NAFTA's SPS measures.

In assessing whether the regulatory systems of the NAFTA agreement function as a barrier to third-party market access, there should be clear signs that the market shares of third-party suppliers in the NAFTA region have fallen. Even if some trade diversion has occurred, both intra-NAFTA agricultural trade and multilateral agricultural trade expanded rapidly during the period 1994–2000, which would suggest that the NAFTA codes have in fact helped "settle" the regulatory regimes of North America (and particularly Mexico), and have improved their transparency and the integrity of their internal processes. This in turn has improved the regulatory framework, and predictability, for suppliers into the region, whether regional or international.

Services

The NAFTA chapter on services (Chapters 12) scores significantly over the GATS agreements in three important respects relating to coverage.

First, it extends to the whole of the services sector unless specified. This "negative-list" approach to defining coverage is the reverse of the principle applied in GATS, where a "positive-list" approach is employed, and the national treatment principle applied only through mutual, bilateral or regional negotiation. On this ground alone, NAFTA's service provisions are substantially WTO-plus. Furthermore, the NAFTA agreements apply an automatic right of establishment where investment takes place, and this again provides a major WTO-plus feature. NAFTA also applies the MFN principle to both parties and non-parties (in addition to the national treatment principle to NAFTA members) for a larger number of services subsectors, and the scope for regulatory discretion in creating barriers to services trade automatically diminishes to that extent.

Nevertheless, the NAFTA picture is complicated by a combination of additional features that make assessment of its regulatory features quite difficult. In the first place, regulatory impediments to market access in services, particularly in the United States, are often the product of recognition procedures set by private or professional bodies, sometimes at the state or local level. Developing acceptable and recognized standards for the region as a whole therefore depends a great deal on the willingness on the part of these bodies to cooperate with the process. The low levels of actual take-up of traded services would suggest that this remains a problem.

Second, assessment of the economic effects of the provisions on services is difficult, and estimates are invariably hedged with disclaimers about statistical accuracy.[9] US estimates suggest that the United States runs a services trade surplus with Mexico of US$3 billion and with Canada of US$7 billion (Canada–Mexico services trade is minimal). Relative to the total cross-border trading volumes in the NAFTA region (of over US$600 billion during 2001), trade in services in the NAFTA region is still quite low, which may disguise the fact that many services are being delivered from other (i.e. US) NAFTA countries through local subsidiaries.

Third, the services component of NAFTA was obviously to the advantage of the United States and Canada relative to Mexico because of the associated agreement on investment. Because many services require the provider to be established in the target market, liberal investment rules facilitate the provision of services in the "export" market. In a sense this was the trade-off between giving Mexico better market access in merchandise products in return for better services access for US and Canadian products in the Mexican market. The greatest policy movement in this case had to come from Mexico, which had in effect to renounce national control of many major sectors of its economy and to establish regulatory systems from scratch in order to comply with NAFTA. This imbalance in rights and obligations has also generated a series of political problems (for example with truck regulations) that have had a negative knock-on effect on compliance.

The answer to the question of whether regulatory systems and procedures relating to services could act as obstacles to the operation of multilateral principles would appear to be no. The NAFTA services agreement is significantly WTO-plus on the basis of sector coverage alone. On actual implementation, however, it is harder to reach a clear determination because of the low volumes of traded services in the NAFTA region.

The role of NAFTA institutions in fostering agreements on the recognition of qualifications has had some impact, though the process is slow because of the complexity and sensitivity of the issues. NAFTA encourages the licensing of officials in member states to develop procedures to recognize certification and licensing provisions for professional service providers. Representatives of engineering professions, it is reported, have recently reached agreement on the trilateral recognition of licensed engineers.[10]

At the same time, problems have been reported by the USTR in the telecommunications sector in Mexico. Instructions from Mexico's telecom regulators (Cofetel) are, it is claimed by the United States, not being honoured by the state telecom monopoly (Telmex), nor will the government impose penalties on Telmex for its refusal to comply.[11] This raises questions about the political management of Mexico's regulatory regime and its ultimate impact on a rules-based services sector.

The slow and difficult progress made in the integration of service markets in the NAFTA region would suggest that much hinges on the capacity of Mexico to address its regulatory problems in this and the investment sector. Given the political commitment behind much that drives the NAFTA process, however, it is apparent that this is indeed happening, as reflected in growing investment figures. Third-party interests are hoping to use Mexico as a base for commercial operations in the NAFTA region more generally, as witnessed by the European Union's interest in a bilateral trade agreement with Mexico. This all suggests that NAFTA's regulatory requirements, as played out in the Mexican case, are in fact broadly supportive of multilateral objectives.

Public procurement

Public procurement is another area in which NAFTA's provisions are clearly in advance of the multilateral system. This is primarily because public procurement is part of the main NAFTA agreement but is only a plurilateral agreement under the Uruguay Round (the 1994 Government Procurement Agreement, GPA), in spite of the efforts to multilateralize it. Mexico, though a signatory to NAFTA's procurement provisions, is not a signatory to the WTO's GPA.

There are few differences in terms of objectives, scope and approach between the NAFTA provisions and those incorporated in the GPA, with each agreement in a sense matching the progress made by the other. With the OECD providing the intellectual justification for liberalization in public procurement policies, and with agreements confined to the regional and the plurilateral, it is no surprise that it was Europe and North America that forged ahead in developing rules that would establish the principles of non-discrimination in public procurement policies. In the GPA it was possible for a group of like-minded countries (generally OECD members) to enter into an agreement without introducing too many ambiguities or compromises, which are often the hallmark of the multilateral process. Regional agreements have therefore been of pioneering importance to the multilateral process and have clearly helped demonstrate how a rules-based system applying certain basic GATT principles can be applied to such a politically sensitive area. In this sense also, NAFTA's public procurement agreement is WTO-plus.

Another difficulty with accommodating Mexico was that Mexico had no national, legislative provisions on public procurement setting down common requirements for contract award procedures. These are needed to ensure transparent and non-discriminatory purchasing. NAFTA builds on the CUSFTA and the previous GATT/GPA practice, whose core minimum requirements with regard to standard, transparent contract award procedures and since the 1994 GPA are "bid challenge" provisions, which provide private parties with access to the independent reviews that are also required under these rules. Mexico had no overall policy framework in operation and each purchasing entity (both government and public sector) could followed its own procurement procedures. Apart from issues relating to the integrity of this process, public scrutiny and judicial review were in effect impossible in this environment simply because there was no "system" to review. As such, the system as a whole functioned as a barrier not only to international interests but also to many domestic commercial interests. Mexico has had to introduce most of the measures, which it did in 2000 with two new laws on procurement procedures, although the detailed regulations have yet to be issued. It is therefore really too early to take stock of how these arrangements will play out in terms of contracts secured by NAFTA partners as against those secured by third-party interests. As the USTR's National Trade Estimates for Mexico for 2001 put it: "the administration will continue to follow the situation closely to ensure that Mexico implements the new laws in a manner that is fully consistent with NAFTA requirements" (USTR, 2001).

The overall (potential) economic effect of NAFTA is significant in the sense that it could open up a new market ranging from an estimated 5 per cent to 12 per cent of GDP in most signatory countries, which is huge by any standards. Under NAFTA, this market now includes construction and service contracts, and also covers a number of federal agencies, including commercial public sector entities, that had earlier been exempt from the rules. It now covers the supply of both goods *and* services at the federal and sub-federal levels (though the latter is optional). Having said this, many state or sub-federal units within signatory countries are unwilling or unhappy to comply with the codes (Canadian provinces are a good example, to which the US response is to suspend reciprocity with the 37 states that have accepted the codes) and hold out against pressure to do so. This constitutes an internal political rather than regional or multilateral implementational challenge to the agreement.

In conclusion, therefore, NAFTA is broadly in conformity with the plurilateral GPA but WTO-plus in the sense that there is no multilateral regime for public procurement. The main impact of NAFTA's procurement provisions has been on Mexico (the United States and Canada being signatories of the GPA), where they have required quite profound regulatory reform. The overall direction of these regulatory reforms has been towards the institutionalization of the various standards (transparency, etc.). To this extent the contribution of NAFTA to making the Mexican system "multilateral and regional compatible" is significant, and NAFTA can be said to have acted as a building block for the multilateral process, especially in an area of domestic regulatory policy such as public procurement. In terms of actual results, however, there has been little progress, mainly because the detailed codes have yet to be notified although the enabling laws were passed in 2000. Judgement regarding the practical implications of these regulatory measures will therefore have to wait a few more years.

Investment

NAFTA's agreement on investment (contained in Chapter 11) reflects the influence of the OECD's thinking on this matter, together with the practical realities of the North American situation. The dominance of the US economy and its relatively free and open investment regime (except in areas of national security) were perceived by its neighbours to be both a threat and an opportunity. The United States' partners thus systematically excluded a number of sensitive sectors from NAFTA that they thought would be vulnerable to US take-over, and subjected much of the rest to a process of review within a broadly liberalizing framework that went further and deeper than the Agreement on Trade-Related Investment Measures (TRIMs).

TRIMs represents a compromise between the interests of the OECD membership (generally) and the concerns of developing countries about the consequences to their economies and political and social policies. It is therefore far less of a model for countries interested in an investment regime than are the OECD codes, the European Union's single market project and the investment regime sought to be established under NAFTA. (And, of course, it is far weaker than the abortive Multilateral Agreement on Investment.) To this extent, NAFTA's regulatory provisions in the area of services (included in the wider ambit defined through the process of negative listing), and the fact that they are subject to judicial review and dispute settlement challenge, make them strongly WTO-plus.

With respect to sensitive sectors, for Canada it was cultural investments (publishing, broadcasting, and so on) together with some critical economic sectors (uranium, fisheries, logging, oil exploration) that were excluded, while for Mexico it was a much wider range of economic sectors (oil and oil exploration, petrochemicals, telecommunications, transportation, the postal service, professional services, social services, and various categories of land).

At a more general level, Canada and Mexico established bodies to examine take-over or investment proposals above a threshold level, which was to be raised over the period of implementation, suggesting a growing confidence in the NAFTA process. For Canada these were the Department of Cultural Heritage with respect to cultural items and the Department of Industry with respect to the rest. For Mexico it was the National Investment Commission. In their actual functioning, these review bodies have generally tended to allow investments wherever possible as part of a broader policy to attract as much foreign investment as possible.

A similar approach has been followed even more assertively with third-party investment proposals, precisely because *not* being American means being less of a threat to "national interests". The work of these committees does not therefore militate against multilateral principles, but in fact facilitates third-party investments.

At the same time, the United States was able to persuade its NAFTA partners that national treatment and MFN principles should apply (Arts. 1102 and 1103), and that the phase-out of restrictions on ownership, performance requirements, the repatriation of profits and so on in a large number of remaining sectors that were not sensitive or did not relate to national security should take place over a 10-year period. The processes in all member countries, together with other features of the NAFTA agreement on investment, such as the provisions relating to expropriation or near-expropriation, were subject to judicial review through dispute settlement.

In this context, NAFTA's provisions allow for private investors directly to challenge national governments in defence of their property rights. In this sense, the approach adopted by NAFTA in the area of investments requires all national authorities to justify, on grounds that are open to challenge by private investors, investment regulations that in effect nullify the operation of national treatment or MFN principles. As with other sectors dealt with under NAFTA, this underlying structure has compelled national governments to improve and open decision-making processes to scrutiny, although the provision for private investor challenge takes the system of dispute settlement to a new WTO-plus level. This provision has been used on only a couple of occasions (it is thought because companies do not like to enter into legal confrontation with host governments), but it has had a very sobering effect on the willingness of states to legislate on matters that *might* be challenged.

The impact of these measures is reflected in a surge of investment activity within the region, which has if anything increased the influence of the United States in the economies of its neighbours. However, this has to be seen more as an integral part of the process of regional integration of the three economies. US investments in Canada and Mexico appear to underpin much of the manufacturing and services activity in these countries that is meant to feed the requirements of the US economy. Hence both Canada and Mexico run a substantial trade surplus (in goods, though not in services) with the United States, much of it based on plants set up through foreign direct investment. From the perspective of these two countries, this was the trade-off: enhanced access to US investments (which implies enhanced US influence in their domestic situation) in return for the creation of jobs and enhanced economic activity in their countries and access to the US markets.

Conclusions

Table 6.1 sets out in schematic form the broad findings of this chapter. It is apparent that NAFTA's provisions and the way in which the system functions in reality are decidedly WTO-plus in all the "new" regulatory areas examined by this chapter. The table indicates whether they are "minus", "similar", "just plus" or "significantly plus". It is revealing that there appear to be *no* provisions that are WTO-minus.

Although these finding are to an extent subjective, they are based on an evaluation of the criteria developed by Woolcock and Sampson, which

Table 6.1. Areas of potential impact of regional trade agreements relative to WTO provisions

	NAFTA provisions overall	Technical barriers to trade	Food safety	Public procurement (GPA)	Services (cross-border)	Investment (incl. right of establishment)
Coverage	Significantly plus	Similar	Similar	Just plus	Significantly plus	Significantly plus
Procedural elements	Significantly plus	Significantly plus	Significantly plus	Just plus	Significantly plus	Significantly plus
Harmonization/policy approximation	Just plus	Just plus	Just plus	Just plus	Just plus	Just plus
Mutual recognition	Just plus	Just plus	Just plus	Not applicable	Just plus	Just plus
Reduced discretion	Significantly plus	Just plus	Just plus	Significantly plus	Significantly plus	Significantly plus
Remedies and reviews	Significantly plus	Significantly plus	Significantly plus	Just plus	Significantly plus	Significantly plus
Promotion of competition	Just plus	Just plus	Just plus	Significantly plus	Just plus	Just plus

are set out in the substantive sections of this chapter dealing with each of the new regulatory areas. They are merely summarized here for ease of reference. In some cases a finding is apparent from the provisions of the agreement (as with coverage in the services or investment sectors); in other cases it is based on experience with actual implementation of regulatory policies over the past few years. The latter case has additional implications for all other sectors reviewed, because the constructive process of implementation may impart a WTO-plus approach to other issues as well. Another important point that was taken into consideration was an assessment of the broad direction of regulatory policies in the NAFTA region. Where these were felt to tend towards becoming even more "plus" then the finding overall has been given as "significantly plus". This last category thus reflects not only reality but also the potential of the situation.

Some general features of the NAFTA agreements that would appear to account for these findings are summarized here.

- The extended application of NAFTA principles to additional sectors (coverage) would seem to be more important to the multilateral process than questions of "deeper integration". The more sectors that can be covered, the more that TBT and SPS codes apply; the more that procedural and redress processes apply, the more the system functions as a building block to the multilateral process. Deeper integration arrangements could, paradoxically, create the sort of regulatory regionalism that is seen as a threat to the multilateral process.
- The contractual nature of international trade agreements helps build a rules-based system in sectors where none perhaps existed before. The extended coverage of NAFTA codes, particularly in services, investment and government procurement, provides a platform for this to happen.
- US traditions of jurisprudence, especially in the areas of due process and judicial review, are significantly influencing and shaping the regulatory reform process in the NAFTA region – more so in the case of Mexico but even to an extent in Canada.[12] Because these directly address all phases of the regulatory process in terms of transparency, institution-building and rule-making, this translates into the creation of a regional regime that is essentially rules based and, to a growing extent, harmonized around US standards and practices.
- There seems to be little evidence to suggest that the US dominance of NAFTA is creating a form of "regulatory regionalism" that is hostile to the multilateral process.
- With the intensification of trade and investment activity in the NAFTA region, the points of contact between importers, exporters and investors and government regulatory systems have increased. The

problem-solving ethos of NAFTA institutions has consequently led to a process of rolling regulatory reform.

- Although NAFTA is proceeding down the route more of equivalence and conformity assessment of standards than of harmonization, this implies that standards capable of withstanding scientific and procedural scrutiny, in terms of both procedures and outcomes, would at the very least be created where none existed earlier.
- The dramatic improvements in trade and investment flows, even during periods of economic crisis, have been most pronounced in the case of Mexico, where the most substantial changes in the regulatory environment have also taken place. This would *suggest* that there is a clear link between the regulatory capacity of the Mexican state, which has been going through an intense period of reform, and the confidence of investors in the Mexican economy.[13] Mexico's capacity to engage with the rest of the world, and indeed its interest in entering into a host of other trade agreements, would suggest that regulatory capacity and regulatory integrity improve the ability of a country to deal with the rest of the world, whether through the multilateral or the bilateral process.
- The NAFTA process has demonstrated – though by no means conclusively – that a developing country (Mexico) and developed countries can coexist within an asymmetrical regional agreement that sets fairly high standards of liberalization, transparency and compliance. This would suggest two things: first, a rules-based system actually helps developing countries in this sort of situation; and, secondly, it becomes the business of the partner countries in the agreement to make it work. Thus the United States was willing to assist Mexico during the financial crisis of 1994–5 (on a scale unheard of in the past), which indicated the importance of Mexico to the United States politically and economically. Similarly, the various technical assistance programmes provided to the Mexican authorities to help restructure their regulatory systems went well beyond anything that would have been attempted before NAFTA.

The reason these findings would appear to be so decisively WTO-plus also has a lot to do with some of the broader contextual issues that have been touched on in the chapter. These are now brought together and summarized here:

- The basic philosophy, approach, structure and methodology of the NAFTA and Uruguay Round agreements, though not identical and though with some important differences, are so substantially alike that the differences appear marginal to any observer who stands back from the detail. This is reflected in the operational consequences.
- Sustained political support for NAFTA – and increasingly for a Free

Trade Area of the Americas – imparts a very positive problem-solving element to the activities of the Free Trade Commission and the various trilateral committees that operate under its auspices. Evidence can be found for this in the tariff acceleration agreements, dating from July 1997 (Trebilcock and Howse, 1999, p. 40), and in the various agreements reached in the trilateral committees with respect to a variety of implementational issues.[14] This in turn serves to expand and deepen the application of rules-based solutions.

- Political and institutional support for Mexico's transitional requirements has been crucially important. Commitment of two types – of Mexico's leadership to the reform process generally, and of Canada and the United States to Mexico's leadership – substantially accounts for this. The relationship between the United States and Canada, though also in need of the occasional political pump-priming, is more stable and durable.

- The use of side agreements has kept the basic NAFTA process relatively free of the complications facing the WTO. At the same time, the NAFTA approach would probably not be operationally practical at the multilateral level, which suggests that in this area at least RTAs score significantly over the multilateral system.

- The danger that NAFTA would harm third-party interests in the region is again something that has been addressed politically. Both Mexico and Canada, perhaps conscious of their overdependence on the United States and aware of the access opportunities that NAFTA membership offers, have sought a range of bilateral trade agreements to achieve precisely these objectives. These economies now offer a bridgehead for third-party products and services while also diversifying their economic links and promoting competition.

Two qualifications are, however, required. The first is that it may still be too early to make a judgement about the impact of regional regulatory regimes on the multilateral process. Mexico's regulatory systems still have a long way to go and may yet prove to contain insurmountable obstacles, particularly in the enforcement of land and property rights, in the relationship between the federal and state governments, and in judicial reforms. Indeed, many important regulatory reform measures in Mexico are enacted by presidential decree (as in financial sector reforms), and the laws, regulations and codes are worked out later. Law-making is obviously a very complex process involving widespread political consultation, the cooperation of several federal ministries and agencies, the consent of state governments, and so on. Reconciling inconsistencies across this complex set of systems is one of the challenges that the Mexican authorities are currently wrestling with. Although this would pose an equal difficulty for the implementation of multilateral agreements, it is really because NAFTA requires a higher degree of compliance in investor and property rights that real operational difficulties could emerge. These could have adverse consequences for the implementation of both agreements. So the process of regulatory reform generally is fraught with difficulties and cannot be taken for granted.

Second, the economies of the NAFTA region are being pulled along by high consumer demand in the United States (as indeed is the world's economy). Regulatory systems tend to be quite relaxed in times of plenty, but can turn very protective in times of hardship. It therefore remains to be seen how NAFTA countries will react to adverse economic developments in the United States and elsewhere, should these arise.

Within a broad framework that is generally and specifically supportive of the multilateral process and its principles and methods, it is really possible to identify only one feature that could restrict third-party market access: rules of origin. However, this is an inherent feature of all regional agreements and will become a barrier in the case of NAFTA only if the application of GATT principles falls generally behind the levels mandated in the multilateral process. As this is not likely to happen, both the United States and Canada being keen on further liberalization of the multilateral trading system, the danger of rules of origin becoming a barrier to trade is not likely to be of significance for the time being.

Notes

1. This terminology comes from the WTO; see WTO (1995).
2. During his visit to Canada in 1961, President Kennedy said that "geography has made us neighbours, and history has made us friends", a sentiment never expressed either to or by the Mexicans.
3. The famous "triple play" – an expression that Europeans find meaningless.
4. A glance at the websites for the three countries (www.ustr.gov; www.dfait.ca; www.cofemer.gob.mx) would confirm this assessment.
5. Parties generally opt for WTO procedures except in cases of anti-dumping and investor–state disputes. This is because the anti-dumping codes are better under NAFTA, in that they restrict the use of anti-dumping as barriers to trade, and because investor–state disputes are unique to the NAFTA system.
6. This chapter uses terminology current in NAFTA and thus refers to standards, standards-related issues and conformance/testing. The terminology differs from that of the European Union, and for that matter the WTO, which both make a distinction between (mandatory) technical regulations, (voluntary) standards and conformance assessment (testing and accreditation). The terminology is important because it reflects the more carefully structured, institutional approach of Europe, compared with the more market-driven US approach to "standards".
7. USTR's NTE report for Canada in 2002 (USTR, 2002a) grumbles about the provincial-level film certification procedures that in effect exclude US films from Canadian markets in seven provinces.

8. From USTR report on NAFTA at http://www.ustr.gov/regions/whemisphere/ organizations.shtml, paragraph on "Agriculture".
9. USTR NTEs for both Canada and Mexico provide estimates, but simultaneously caution against their accuracy.
10. From USTR report on NAFTA at http://www.ustr.gov/regions/whemisphere/ organizations.shtml, paragraph on "Services".
11. In fact the United States has initiated a dispute settlement complaint in the WTO on this issue (USTR, 2001).
12. Canadian judicial authorities tend to defer to the judgement of government agencies more than their US counterparts do for issues involving the "public interest". Complaints about this tend to promote another development – the gradual harmonization of standards.
13. This is the line that the OECD takes on Mexico's regulatory reform. The OECD is also deeply involved in advising the Mexican government on the reform process, which adds to the sense of security amongst investors.
14. From USTR report on NAFTA at http://www.ustr.gov/regions/whemisphere/ organizations.shtml.

REFERENCES

COFEMER (Comisión Federal de Mejora Regulatoria) (2001), *Mexico's Federal Regulatory Improvement Programme: Towards a New Form of Governance*, at http://www.cofemer.gob.mx/tmp/programa/status1.htm.

NAFTA (North American Free Trade Agreement) Free Trade Commission (2002), *NAFTA at Eight: A Foundation for Economic Growth*, May, at http://www.ustr.gov/naftareport/nafta8_brochure-eng.pdf.

OECD (Organisation for Economic Co-operation and Development) (1972), *Guiding Principles Concerning the International Aspects of Environmental Policies*, Paris: OECD.

Trebilcock, Michael J., and Robert Howse (1999), *The Regulation of International Trade*, 2nd edn., London: Routledge.

USTR (United States Trade Representative) (1995–2001), "Mexico", in *National Trade Estimate Report on Foreign Trade Barriers*, at http:/www.ustr.gov/reports/.

——— (2001), "Mexico", in *2001 National Trade Estimate Report on Foreign Trade Barriers*, at http://www.ustr.gov/reports/nte/2001/Mexico.pdf.

——— (2002a), "Canada", in *2002 National Trade Estimate Report on Foreign Trade Barriers*, at http://www.ustr.gov/reports/nte/2002/Canada.pdf.

——— (2002b), "Mexico", in *2002 National Trade Estimate Report on Foreign Trade Barriers*, at http://www.ustr.gov/reports/nte/2002/Mexico.pdf.

——— (n.d.), *Study on the Operation and Effect of the North American Free Trade Agreement: Executive Summary*, at http://www.ustr.gov/pdf/execsumm.pdf.

WTO (World Trade Organization) Secretariat (1995), *Regionalism and the World Trading System*, Geneva: WTO.

7

The Chile–Canada Free Trade Agreement

Sebastián Herreros

Introduction

This chapter describes how the Chile–Canada Free Trade Agreement (CCFTA) deals with what are potentially regulatory barriers to trade in three main policy areas, namely trade in services, investment and the environment. The last area is covered by the Chile–Canada Agreement on Environmental Cooperation (CCAEC). The chapter assesses the degree to which the Chilean general regulatory regime in these three areas is affected by its commitments in the CCFTA and CCAEC. The provisions of both agreements are also compared with the relevant multilateral agreements of the World Trade Organization (WTO), where applicable, as well as with the North American Free Trade Agreement (NAFTA) and its "side agreement" on environmental cooperation, in terms of scope and disciplines. The purpose of this comparative exercise is three-fold: first, to determine whether the CCFTA and CCAEC go beyond or fall short of the provisions of the World Trade Organization (are "WTO-plus" or "WTO-minus") in the areas under examination, and if so in which aspects; second, to detect and try to explain any deviations in the CCFTA and/or CCAEC from the NAFTA model on which both agreements are largely based; third, to examine whether the CCFTA and/or CCAEC might contain elements of "regulatory regionalism".

In order to address these questions, the CCFTA and CCAEC will be assessed using the analytical framework set out in chapter 2. This consists of assessing:

- whether the scope or coverage of commitments undertaken in the CCFTA, in terms of national treatment and most favoured nation (MFN) treatment, exceed those undertaken by Chile and Canada in the WTO;
- how well both agreements satisfy a number of procedural elements, such as transparency, due process or open decision-making, and the promotion of institutional infrastructure;
- whether the CCFTA and the CCAEC promote the approximation or compatibility of national regulations, standards or conformance assessment provisions; and/or
- whether they promote mutual recognition or equivalence of national regulations, standards or conformance assessment provisions;
- whether the agreements reduce the scope for regulatory discretion by national authorities;
- whether they provide for effective remedies to disputes in the areas covered by the study; and, finally,
- whether they contain provisions aimed at ensuring that anti-competitive practices do not limit trade.

Three of the regulatory policy areas discussed in other chapters of this book are not covered by the CCFTA and therefore are not fully covered here. These are technical barriers to trade, food safety and public procurement.[1] In these three cases, a brief explanation is provided as to why Chile and Canada decided not to include these topics in their bilateral agreement. There is also a general description of how Chile intends to deal with these three issues in the context of its current negotiations with the United States towards a bilateral free trade agreement. For that purpose, the relevant draft Chapters proposed by Chile to the United States at the start of the negotiations in January 2001 are analysed. The FTA negotiations were successfully concluded in December 2002, but at the time this book went to press the agreement had not yet been signed and the negotiated text was not yet public. Moreover, the final shape of the Chapters depended to a significant extent on the mandate the US negotiators got from the US Congress under the Trade Promotion Authority legislation, which was still being discussed at the time of writing (May 2002).

General overview of the Chile–Canada Free Trade Agreement

The Chile–Canada Free Trade Agreement (henceforth the agreement or the CCFTA) was signed on 18 November 1996, and entered into force on

5 July 1997 after ratification by both countries' parliaments. Although negotiations started only in January 1996, the story of the agreement goes back to 11 December 1994, when the prime minister of Canada and the presidents of the United States, Mexico and Chile announced their intention to pursue Chile's accession to the North American Free Trade Agreement (NAFTA). When it became apparent that the Clinton administration would not obtain fast-track negotiating authority from Congress, Chile and Canada decided to negotiate a bilateral agreement, in order, among other objectives, to facilitate and promote Chile's accession to NAFTA.

Because of its "interim" nature, the agreement closely follows the NAFTA model in terms of structure, scope and coverage. Two side agreements also entered into force at the same time as the CCFTA. These are the Chile–Canada Agreement on Environmental Cooperation (CCAEC) and the Chile–Canada Agreement on Labour Cooperation (CCALC). Both are modelled on NAFTA's side agreements on labour and environment. There are, however, some important differences between CCFTA and NAFTA. On the one hand, the CCFTA does not include Chapters on sanitary and phytosanitary measures, technical standards, government procurement, intellectual property and financial services – all matters that are covered by NAFTA. On the other hand, the CCFTA goes beyond NAFTA (and the WTO) in the very important area of anti-dumping. Chile and Canada agreed to phase out the use of anti-dumping measures on trade between them over a period of six years. This commitment is consistent with both countries' broader objectives in the area of trade remedies. Whereas Canada seeks ultimately to eliminate anti-dumping duties within NAFTA, Chile aims to do the same within its own network of agreements in Latin America, and has been very vocal in calling for stricter disciplines on anti-dumping to be negotiated in the WTO.

Horizontal provisions under the CCFTA

The analysis of the CCFTA will focus on the areas of investment and trade in services. However, it is necessary to start with a brief review of some Chapters whose provisions apply horizontally across all areas covered by the agreement. These horizontal Chapters have a bearing on whether there are competitive markets (Chapter J covers competition policy, monopolies and state enterprises), what the procedural requirements are under the CCFTA (Chapter L covers publication, notification and administration of laws), and what institutional arrangements and dispute settlement procedures there are in the agreement (Chapter N).

Competition policy, monopolies and state enterprises

Chapter J commits both parties to adopt or maintain measures to proscribe anti-competitive business conduct and to take appropriate enforcement action. There is an additional "soft" commitment for the parties to
consult "from time to time" on the effectiveness of the measures undertaken by them in this field. This is also a call for the parties to cooperate
on issues of competition law enforcement policy, including mutual legal
assistance, notification, consultation and exchange of information. However, these commitments are not subject to dispute settlement (either
state-to-state or investor–state arbitration).

The CCFTA affirms the right of the parties to "designate" monopolies
and state enterprises (i.e. establish new monopolies and state enterprises
in the future). The designation of monopolies is subject to a requirement
to provide prior written notification where possible and to establish the
monopoly in a manner that minimizes or eliminates any nullification or
impairment of benefits under the agreement.

There are also specific obligations with regard to monopolies and state
enterprises that complement the provisions on investment and cross-
border trade in services. There are obligations with respect to the behaviour of privately owned and government monopolies to the effect that
such entities must:

- act in a manner that is not inconsistent with each party's obligations
  under the agreement wherever a monopoly exercises any regulatory,
  administrative or other governmental authority that the party has delegated to it in connection with the monopoly good or service;
- act solely in accordance with commercial considerations in their purchase or sale of the monopoly good or service;
- provide non-discriminatory treatment to investments of investors, to
  goods and to service providers of the other party in their purchase or
  sale of the monopoly good or service;
- not use their monopoly position to engage, either directly or indirectly,
  including through their dealings with their parent, their subsidiary or
  other enterprise with common ownership, in anti-competitive practices
  in a non-monopolized market in their territory that adversely affect an
  investment of an investor of the other party.

The governments must ensure, through regulatory control, administrative
supervision or the application of other measures, that state enterprises
act in a manner that is consistent with the countries' obligations on investment (under Chapter G). This is important when state enterprises
exercise regulatory or other delegated authority to expropriate assets,
grant licences, or approve commercial transactions or import quotas,
fees or other charges. The governments must also ensure that state

enterprises are non-discriminatory in their dealings with undertakings established in their territory by investors from the other party to the agreement.

The provisions on competition (Chapter J) are identical to those of NAFTA's Chapter 15, except that the latter provides for the establishment of a Working Group on trade and competition. This group had the mandate to make recommendations to the parties on further work as appropriate, within five years of the date of entry into force of the agreement, on relevant issues concerning the relationship between competition laws and policies and trade in the free trade area. The creation of this group seems to point to the willingness of Canada, Mexico and the United States to explore the possibility of moving from the relatively "soft" commitments undertaken in Chapter 15 to more binding obligations in this field. This seems very natural, because the three countries are neighbours, trade intensively with each other and invest significantly in each other's territories. As NAFTA is creating an integrated economic region comprising a number of different competition authorities, this emphasis on competition law and policies may be appropriate as other barriers to trade and investment are lowered. But Canada and Chile are distant countries for which bilateral trade and investment flows are much less important, making strengthened disciplines on competition policy less urgent.

Soft as they are, the CCFTA's provisions on competition policy exceed any commitment undertaken by either Chile or Canada in the WTO, where this subject has, to date, not got beyond a matter of study in a Working Group. It remains to be seen how the CCFTA provisions will compare with those of any future WTO agreement on competition policy. The first step towards that goal was taken at the Doha Ministerial Meeting with a mandate to launch negotiations after the WTO's Fifth Ministerial Meeting to be held in Mexico in September 2003. However, the solid resistance from many WTO members to engage in negotiations on competition at the WTO makes it unlikely that any future agreement will go much further than transparency and cooperation.

Publication, notification and administration of laws

The Chapter on procedural commitments in the CCFTA (Chapter L) is identical to Chapter 18 of the NAFTA. It sets out obligations for the parties concerning transparency and due process.

Transparency

The main commitments undertaken by the parties are: designation of a contact point, publication and notification. First, they must designate a contact point to facilitate communications between them on any matter covered by the agreement. Second, each party must ensure that its laws, regulations, procedures and administrative rulings of general application respecting any matter covered by the agreement are promptly published or otherwise made available in such a manner as to enable interested persons and the other party to become acquainted with them. To this effect, and to the extent possible, each party must: (a) publish in advance any such measure that it proposes to adopt; and (b) provide interested persons and the other party a reasonable opportunity to comment on such proposed measures. Third, and to the maximum extent possible, each party must notify the other of any proposed or actual measure that the party considers might materially affect the operation of the agreement or otherwise substantially affect the other party's interests under it.

Due process

The CCFTA (Chapter L) commits each party to ensure that, in its administrative proceedings applying laws, regulations, procedures and administrative rulings of general application respecting any matter covered by the agreement to particular persons, goods or services of the other party in specific cases: wherever possible, persons of the other party that are directly affected by a proceeding are provided reasonable notice, in accordance with domestic procedures, when a proceeding is initiated, including description of the nature of the proceeding, a statement of the legal authority under which the proceeding is initiated and a general description of any issues in controversy; such persons are afforded a reasonable opportunity to present facts and arguments in support of their positions prior to any final administrative action, when time, the nature of the proceeding and the public interest permit; and its procedures are in accordance with domestic law.

Each party shall also establish or maintain judicial, quasi-judicial or administrative tribunals or procedures for the purpose of the prompt review and, where warranted, correction of final administrative actions regarding matters covered by the agreement. Such tribunals shall be impartial and independent of the office or authority entrusted with administrative enforcement and shall not have any substantial interest in the outcome of the matter.

The parties shall also ensure that, in any such tribunals or procedures, the parties to the proceeding have the right to: a reasonable opportunity to support or defend their respective positions; and a decision based on the evidence and submissions of record or, where required by domestic law, the record compiled by the administrative authority. Finally, each party shall ensure, subject to appeal or further review as provided in its domestic law, that such decisions shall be implemented by, and shall govern the practice of, the offices or authorities with respect to the administrative action at issue.

Institutional arrangements and dispute settlement procedures

Again the CCFTA provisions (Section II of Chapter N) on dispute settlement are essentially identical to Section B of NAFTA's Chapter 20. Permanent cooperation and consultation between the parties on the interpretation of the agreement's provisions are encouraged as a means of arriving at mutually satisfactory resolutions to any possible controversy. Arbitration and other means of private dispute resolution are also encouraged. Failing this, the CCFTA has a dispute settlement mechanism covering all areas included in the agreement, except for competition law and cultural industries.

There are various options available before considering the establishment of a panel. First, the affected party may request consultations with the other regarding any actual or proposed measure or any other matter that it considers might affect the operation of the agreement. The parties must make every attempt to reach a mutually satisfactory resolution at the consultations stage. If they fail to do so within 30 days of delivery of a request for consultations (15 days in matters regarding perishable agricultural goods, or any other period agreed by the parties), either party may request a meeting of the agreement's Free Trade Commission (comprising cabinet-level representatives of the parties), stating the measure or other matter complained of and the agreement's provisions that it considers relevant. The Commission "shall endeavour to resolve the dispute promptly", including through good offices, conciliation, mediation or other procedures. None of these procedures has actually been invoked so far, because all controversies between Chile and Canada since the entry into force of the agreement have been solved through cooperation and consultation at the Commission or lower level.

If the Commission fails to solve the dispute within 30 days after it is convened, a party may request the establishment of an arbitral panel. To this effect, the parties must maintain a roster of up to 20 well-qualified individuals, 4 of whom must not be citizens of either of the parties. The panel shall comprise five members, four of them selected by the parties (two each) and a mutually agreed chair. As in the NAFTA, a party can ask the panel to make findings on the level of adverse trade effects of any measure at issue. This constitutes a significant departure from the WTO model, in that a panel mandated to determine the WTO compatibility of a given measure cannot make any quantitative determination of the adverse trade effects of that measure. In the WTO this assessment is made only at a later stage to determine the authorized level of retaliation if and when the WTO member that should have put the said measure in conformity with its multilateral obligations has failed to do so.

The panel's rules of procedure resemble those of the WTO's Dispute Settlement Understanding (DSU), with initial and rebuttal written submissions and at least one hearing before the panel. As in NAFTA, the panel process has two stages: the Initial Report and the Final Report. This also resembles the WTO process, with its Panel and Appeal stages, although the CCFTA has a shorter total time-frame. Again as in the WTO, the panel may seek information and technical advice from any person or body that it deems appropriate, including a scientific review board if so needed.

Once the panel has delivered its Final Report, the resolution of the dispute should conform to the panel's determinations and recommendations. Wherever possible the dispute should be resolved through the removal of the non-conforming measure or, failing this, compensation. As in the WTO, full compliance with a panel's ruling is seen as the preferred outcome over compensation. However, if neither full compliance nor compensation takes place within a specified time, the complaining party may suspend benefits for an amount equivalent to the damage suffered. This retaliation may last until both parties reach agreement on a resolution of the dispute.

On the whole, the CCFTA and NAFTA dispute settlement mechanisms present two important advantages over the WTO mechanism. There is a faster adjudication of any matter referred to a panel and no grey area of ambiguity as in the WTO's Dispute Settlement Understanding on the issue of sequencing (Arts. 21 and 22). Under the WTO, if there is disagreement about whether a party has implemented the recommendations of a panel or the Appellate Body, there are two different – and contradictory – possibilities. Either a panel determines if the party has in effect complied (Art. 21.5), or the complaining party withdraws concessions for an amount equivalent to the damage suffered (Art. 22.2). The current wording of the DSU does not provide clarity about what course of action should be explored first, as has become evident in several high-profile cases involving the United States and the European Union. For many WTO members, addressing the issue of sequencing is a priority for the current negotiations on improvements and clarifications of the DSU. In comparison, both the CCFTA and NAFTA provide for a clearer sequence. Once the Final Report is issued, the parties to a dispute must reach an agreement on the resolution of it within a short time (30 days). If the party complained against fails to reach an agreement with the complaining party, the latter may suspend benefits for an amount equivalent to the damage suffered until agreement is reached.

Services and investment

In the CCFTA, investment is covered by a separate chapter (Chapter G), whereas trade in services is dealt with in four chapters: G (on investment), H (on cross-border trade in services), I (on telecommunications) and K (on temporary entry for business persons). The provisions on investment and cross-border trade in services share a similar structure. Both establish a core of general, horizontal obligations, among which are national treatment and MFN. Only a limited number of measures, sectors or activities are excluded from these general obligations. Reservations and exceptions for both investment and cross-border trade in services are listed together in Annex I of the agreement (for existing measures) and Annex II (for future measures). This is because many of the reservations listed regarding investment, which restrict the provision of a service through commercial presence, also imply restrictions on the cross-border provision of services.

Investment

Chapter G has three Sections with seven Annexes. Section I sets out the scope and coverage of the Chapter, as well as the obligations that each party assumes towards investors of the other party and their investments, and the reservations and exceptions to those obligations; Section II establishes an investor–state dispute settlement mechanism; and Section III deals with the all important definitions.

Coverage

The CCFTA provisions on investment are comprehensive. The only sector explicitly excluded from its provisions is investment in financial institutions.[2] However, some general obligations regarding transfers and expropriation and compensation apply even in the case of investments in financial institutions. Section II of the Chapter, allowing for investor–state dispute settlement (see below), also applies to investments in financial institutions, but only concerning breaches by a party of obligations concerning either transfers or expropriation and compensation. The investment Chapter also does not apply to measures maintained or adopted by both parties regarding cultural industries. These were left out of the scope of the whole agreement, except for the tariff elimination commitment.

Substantive general obligations

Each party must accord national treatment and MFN to investors of the other party with respect to the establishment, acquisition, expansion, management, conduct, operation and sale or other disposition of investments. Since Canada is a federal state, national treatment means, with respect to a province, treatment no less favourable than the most favourable treatment accorded, in like circumstances, by that province to investors and their investments of the party of which it forms a part.

Neither party may impose or enforce a specified list of performance requirements on an investment in its territory of a party or of a non-party. These are: export performance; domestic content; preferential treatment to local suppliers of goods or services; foreign exchange inflows/earnings; transfer of technology, a production process or other proprietary knowledge (except when such transfer is imposed by a court, administrative tribunal or competition authority to remedy an alleged violation of competition laws); or exclusive supply to a specific region or world market. With regard to subsidies, regulators cannot condition the receipt of an advantage (or "subsidy") on compliance with requirements on domestic content, locally produced goods or foreign exchange inflows/earnings. But "subsidies" can be conditional on investment being made in a specific location (regional policy) or on the provision of training or research and development expenditure.

Similarly, there are exceptions to the prohibition of domestic content requirements or preferential treatment to local suppliers when these measures are necessary to protect human, animal or plant life or health, or for the conservation of living or non-living exhaustible natural resources. However, such measures must not be applied in an arbitrary or unjustifiable manner or constitute disguised restrictions on trade or investment. Nationality requirements for senior management positions are prohibited, but there can be nationality or local residence requirements for the majority of the board of directors, provided that those requirements do not impair the ability of the foreign investor to exercise control over its investment. Finally, each party playing host to an investment of an investor of the other party has the obligation to permit all transfers relating to that investment to be made freely, without delay and in a freely usable currency at market rates of exchange.[3] Similarly, neither party may require its investors to transfer, or penalize them for failing to do so, the income, earnings, profits or other amounts derived from, or attributable to, investments in the territory of the other party. Some of the prohibited performance requirements are permitted in public procurement, export promotion programmes and foreign aid programmes. The parties have extended these commitments not to impose performance requirements to third countries on an MFN basis.

The CCFTA sets four conditions that must be satisfied in any case of expropriation:
- expropriation must serve a public purpose;

- it must be applied on a non-discriminatory basis;
- it must be applied in accordance with due process of law (including international law);
- there must be adequate compensation – compensation must be equivalent to the "fair market value" of the expropriated investment immediately before the expropriation took place; it has to be paid without delay, and must be fully realizable; on payment, compensation shall be freely transferable.

These provisions (in Art. G-10) do not apply to the issuance of compulsory licences granted in relation to intellectual property rights or to the revocation, limitation or creation of such rights, to the extent that such issuance, revocation, limitation or creation is consistent with the Agreement on Trade-Related Aspects of Intellectual Property Rights (TRIPS). It is worth noting that the guarantees given to foreign investors by this Article were already enshrined in Chile's general investment legislation by the time the CCFTA was negotiated.

Reservations and exceptions

The coverage of investment by the CCFTA is ultimately determined by the schedules listing exemptions and coverage. As noted above, there are two general exceptions where the core obligations of national treatment, MFN and the non-imposition of performance requirements do not apply. These are public procurement and public subsidies or grants (i.e. only local companies may benefit from subsidies). Annexes to the agreement also list specific reservations and exceptions under a negative-list approach.

An interesting feature of the CCFTA, inherited from NAFTA, is the "ratcheting effect", which requires that any amendment, after the entry into force of the agreement, to the existing discriminatory measures listed in the parties' schedules to Annex I cannot decrease the conformity of such measures with the above-mentioned core obligations. In other words, any future liberalization of remaining discriminatory measures is locked in. In its schedule to Annex I, Canada took a blanket exception for "all existing non-conforming measures of all provinces and territories", without listing those measures. At the federal level, Canada's negative list in the CCFTA is the same as its list in NAFTA.

In their schedules to Annex II, both parties listed their reservations concerning sectors, subsectors or activities for which they could maintain existing measures, or adopt new or more restrictive measures. Here Chile and Canada listed identical reservations concerning aboriginal affairs, ocean-front land, basic telecommunications, social services, minority affairs and government finance. In addition, Canada listed reservations on speciality air services and maritime cabotage. Chile, for its part, listed reservations on fishing-related activities and professional, technical and specialized services. This last reservation provides for reciprocity when Canada maintains, at the federal or provincial level, measures respecting citizenship, permanent residency or local presence in a given sector. Again, Canada's reservations are the same as those it has under NAFTA.

In their schedules to Annex III (exceptions to most favoured nation treatment), both parties listed those sectors where they reserved the right not to accord MFN treatment to the other party. These include, for example, aviation; fisheries; maritime matters, including salvage; and telecommunications transport networks and telecommunications transport services, which correspond to the exceptions listed under NAFTA for Canada and the General Agreement on Trade in Services (GATS) for Chile.

Dispute settlement

The CCFTA allows investors, along NAFTA lines, recourse to investor–state dispute settlement provisions offering access to international arbitration procedures as an alternative to the standard dispute settlement mechanism of the agreement. If a claim by an investor of a party before the authorities of the other party cannot be settled through consultation or negotiation, the disputing investor may submit the claim to arbitration under the Convention on the Settlement of Investment Disputes between States and Nationals of Other States (ICSID Convention),[4] the Additional Facility Rules of the International Center for Settlement of Investment Disputes (ICSID), or the Arbitration Rules of the United Nations Commission on International Trade Law (UNCITRAL).[5] In order to be allowed to submit its claim to international arbitration, the investor must first waive its right to initiate or continue before any administrative tribunal or court under the law of a party, or other dispute settlement procedures, any proceedings with respect to the measure of the disputing party that is alleged to be a breach of that party's obligations. The chosen tribunal may award monetary damages, restitution of property or both. As yet the investor–state provisions have not been invoked.

Reforms required in Chilean regulations

By and large, the CCFTA did not affect the way in which Chile regulates foreign investment, but merely consolidated (or locked in) its general investment regime. One exception concerns the need to phase out several performance requirements in the automotive sector, which Chile must eliminate anyway because of its obligations under the Agreement on Trade-Related Investment Measures (TRIMs).

The CCFTA does, however, limit Chile's autonomy to regulate foreign investment in a number of quite important respects. First, the "ratcheting" provision means that neither Chile nor Canada can make discriminatory ("non-conforming") measures more restrictive. Secondly, Chile must accord national treatment to Canadian investors who are party to an investment contract pursuant to Decree Law 600. This means the amendment of investment contracts if these contracts provide for less favourable treatment than Article G-04 (which in turn provides for the granting of the better of the treatment required under the national treatment and MFN obligations). Thirdly, Chile also "bound" at a maximum 30 per cent its general reserve requirement for such capital flows for Canadian investments (other than foreign direct investments) and related credits.

Comparison with NAFTA and the WTO

The CCFTA provisions on investment are practically identical to NAFTA's Chapter 11. The main difference is that financial services and investments in financial services are for the most part excluded from the disciplines of the CCFTA, whereas they are included and regulated in a separate Chapter of the NAFTA. However, the core disciplines undertaken by Canada and Chile in the CCFTA are the same as in NAFTA. The investor–state dispute settlement mechanism comes from NAFTA, as does the ratchet mechanism for future amendments to non-conforming measures. Performance requirement provisions are identical, as are Canada's schedules defining the coverage.

With respect to the WTO, the CCFTA – like the NAFTA before it – regulates investment in a comprehensive way, whereas there is as yet no equivalent agreement on investment in the WTO. Investment is addressed in a piecemeal fashion in the WTO: the TRIMs Agreement deals exclusively with some performance requirements, the GATS deals with investment only in so far as it relates to the provision of services, and so on. Secondly, the CCFTA gives investors recourse to dispute settlement procedures against a state, whereas the WTO's dispute settlement procedures are strictly intergovernmental.

In terms of non-imposition of performance requirements, the CCFTA disciplines are stricter than those of the WTO's TRIMs Agreement. The CCFTA covers performance requirements concerning both goods and services, whereas the TRIMs Agreement covers only goods. The CCFTA also explicitly prohibits a wider range of performance requirements than the TRIMs Agreement does. Such is the case with technology transfer or geographical exclusivity requirements. On the other hand, the CCFTA allows for permanent exceptions for certain measures, sectors or activities, whereas permanent exceptions are not allowed under the TRIMs

Agreement (not even for least developed countries, which have only a seven-year transition period to phase out prohibited measures).

Overall assessment

Overall, the CCFTA provisions on investment have extensive coverage and strong disciplines, which are certainly WTO-plus and at the same level as NAFTA standards. Some of those disciplines (i.e. non-imposition of performance requirements) are even applied on a most favoured nation basis. Transparency is greatly increased because reservations and exceptions are listed on a negative-list basis, which implies that only the measures or sectors explicitly listed are excluded from certain disciplines. The "no turning back" or "ratcheting effect" commitments further increase predictability for foreign investors. However, the blanket exception taken by Canada for all its existing discriminatory measures at the provincial level goes against transparency and negatively affects the value of the market access commitments undertaken by that country concerning investment.

Trade in services

The CCFTA covers the four modes of supply defined in the GATS. Chapter H provides for comprehensive coverage of cross-border trade in services, including Modes 1, 2 and 4. Chapter I contains specific rules with respect to measures relating to public telecommunications transport networks and services and value-added telecommunications services, providing for disciplines with regard to access to and use of public telecommunications transport networks and services. Chapter K deals with the temporary movement of natural persons (Mode 4), providing access for a broadly defined group of business visitors, traders and investors, intra-company transferees, and a lengthy list of professionals. Finally, Mode 3 (commercial presence) is regulated by Chapter G on investment, which also regulates investments intended not to provide a service but to produce goods. So here, as with investment, the CCFTA closely follows the NAFTA approach, for example in having a separate Chapter for cross-border provision of services and investment. This is probably partly owing to the precedent set by NAFTA (for Canada) and the fact that there are no general investment provisions in the WTO.

Scope and coverage

The concept of cross-border trade in services in the CCFTA is more comprehensive than the "cross-border supply" mode defined in the GATS. It actually encompasses three of the four supply modes defined in the GATS: cross-border supply (Mode 1), consumption abroad (Mode 2), and presence of natural persons (Mode 4).

Among the measures covered by the Chapter are those respecting:

- the production, distribution, marketing, sale and delivery of a service;
- the purchase or use of, or payment for, a service;
- the access to and use of distribution and transportation systems in connection with the provision of a service;
- the presence in a party's territory of a service provider of the other party;
- the provision of a bond or other form of financial security as a condition for the provision of a service.

The CCFTA Chapter on services has a broad sectoral coverage. However, the following sectors or policies are excluded: cultural industries; the provision of cross-border trade in financial services; domestic and international air services;[6] basic telecommunications; public procurement (both by public agencies and by state enterprises); subsidies or grants provided by a party or a state enterprise; controls on natural persons seeking long-term employment; and core public services (law enforcement, correctional services, income security or insurance, social security or insurance, social welfare, public education, public training, health, and child care).

Main general obligations

Each party must accord national treatment to service providers of the other party. As for investment, in the case of Canada this means treatment no less favourable than the most favourable treatment accorded, in like circumstances, by the province to service providers from the rest of Canada.

The CCFTA requires MFN (Art. H-03) and parties cannot oblige service providers to have a local presence (Art. H-05). With regard to procedural obligations, the parties must establish procedures for notification of new quantitative restrictions (other than at the local government level), liberalization commitments and amendments of existing non-conforming measures. The parties must also establish procedures for consultations on reservations, quantitative restrictions or commitments with a view to further liberalization. These requirements are in addition to the general transparency requirements discussed above.

To ensure that any measure adopted or maintained by a party relating to the licensing or certification of nationals of the other party does not constitute an unnecessary barrier to trade, each party shall endeavour to ensure that any such measure is based on objective and transparent criteria, such as competence and the ability to provide a service; is not more burdensome than necessary to ensure the quality of a service; and does not constitute a disguised restriction on the cross-border provision of a service.

However, the MFN obligation does not apply in this area, in the sense that neither party is obliged to accord to the other the recognition it accords to a non-party (unilaterally or by agreement) relating to education, experience, licences or certifications obtained in the territory of the non-party. In other words, mutual recognition agreements within NAFTA are not automatically extended to Chile, as one would expect. However, the parties committed themselves to encourage the relevant bodies in their territories to (a) develop mutually acceptable standards and criteria for licensing and certification of professional service providers, and (b) provide recommendations on mutual recognition to their governments. The parties also committed themselves to eliminate, within two years of the entry into force of the agreement, any citizenship or permanent residency requirement set out in their respective schedules to Annex I (see next section) that they maintain for the licensing or certification of professional service providers of the other party.

As of May 2002 there had been limited progress on the above-mentioned commitments, chiefly owing to the lack of initiative of both countries' relevant bodies (usually professional associations). This situation apparently has to do with the perception by those entities of limited business opportunities in each other's markets, and is compounded by the fact that membership in professional associations is voluntary in Chile. This makes it difficult for Chilean professionals who are not members of an association to gain access to Canadian service markets.[7] However, the mandate of this Article goes clearly in the direction of avoiding unnecessary trade restrictions and follows the general trend in the Organisation for Economic Co-operation and Development (OECD) area. Market access restrictions in professional services based on nationality and citizenship "have been identified as unreliable indicators of local knowledge and more burdensome than necessary to ensure the quality of a service provided" (OECD, 2000b, p. 10).

Reservations and quantitative restrictions

In its schedule to Annex I, Canada took a blanket exception for "all existing non-conforming measures of all provinces and territories", without listing those measures. The existing non-conforming measures at the federal level listed by Canada in the CCFTA and which affect cross-border trade in services are the same as those listed by that country in the NAFTA.

In their schedules to Annex II (reservations for future measures), both parties listed their reservations with respect to specific sectors, subsectors or activities for which they could maintain existing measures, or adopt new or more restrictive measures, not conforming with the core obligations of national treatment, most favoured nation and non-requirement of local presence. Both countries listed practically the same common reservations as they did under Chapter G. Canada, for its part, listed additional reservations on maritime cabotage and maritime activities that Canada may engage in jointly with other countries in waters of mutual interest.

The non-discriminatory quantitative restrictions maintained by both parties at the national or provincial level are listed in their respective schedules to Annex IV (quantitative restrictions and other items). Several of the measures listed are not strictly quantitative restrictions, but establish that a licence, authorization or concession from a competent authority is required to provide a certain service. Again, the quantitative restrictions listed by Canada in its schedule to Annex IV of the CCFTA are the same as those listed in NAFTA, with one addition. This concerns the authority accorded by the Canadian Criminal Code to each provincial government, either alone or in conjunction with the government of another province, to create, operate and grant licences to operate and regulate lottery schemes.

The CCFTA commits both parties to further negotiations, at least every two years, on the liberalization or removal of listed quantitative restrictions. However, as of May 2002, the parties had not engaged in these negotiations. In the same vein, the parties are required to set out future commitments to liberalize quantitative restrictions, licensing requirements, performance requirements or other non-discriminatory measures. As of May 2002, no such commitments had been made by either party.

Reforms required in Chilean regulations

The CCFTA did not significantly affect the way in which Chile regulates services. As in the case of investment, Chile consolidated its general regulatory regime affecting cross-border trade in services. No law or other piece of legislation had to be modified to conform to the agreement nor are there any phase-outs agreed for existing non-conforming measures. The parties retain total freedom to introduce new quantitative restrictions, as long as these are notified. They may also adopt new non-conforming measures, even in sectors not included in the positive exclusions, as long as the service providers of the other party are not negatively affected. The agreement does not provide for prior consultation requirements in any of these cases. The only important qualification to this general conclusion, which applies as well to investment, is that neither Chile nor Canada can make their existing "non-conforming" measures more discriminatory (for service providers of the other party).

Comparison with NAFTA and GATS

Most of what has already been said about the provisions in NAFTA and the CCFTA on investment is applicable when comparing the provisions of both agreements concerning cross-border trade in services. The CCFTA is practically identical to the equivalent measures in NAFTA (Chapter 12). The coverage of both Chapters is the same, with the difference that financial services and government procurement, which are excluded from the CCFTA, are dealt with in separate Chapters of the NAFTA. The core disciplines on substance and procedural measures are essentially the same as in NAFTA.

Compared with the GATS, the CCFTA goes much deeper towards liberalization of trade in services, in terms of both coverage and disciplines. First, non-discrimination is guaranteed through national treatment and most favoured nation clauses. Both are general obligations for cross-border trade in services and commercial presence under the CCFTA. In comparison, under the GATS national treatment is a specific commitment that applies only to the sectors included in each signatory country's Schedule of Specific Commitments.

Secondly, the CCFTA has a broader coverage because there are only a limited number of exceptions and reservations to national treatment and other general disciplines. Under the GATS, liberalization commitments differ widely in terms of the number of sectors included and the degree of liberalization undertaken by each country. For example, in the GATS, Chile committed to grant national treatment in only 64 service activities, a relatively small number compared with the commitments undertaken by developed countries. The listing of discriminatory measures under a negative-list approach in the CCFTA has the additional advantage of enhancing transparency. This is a key element for trade in services, because barriers to it usually stem from a series of domestic regulations, policies and practices (OECD, 2000a, pp. 4–5).

In terms of market access, Chile consolidated in the CCFTA its general regulatory regime at the time it signed the agreement. This compares favourably with the GATS, where Chile made the same commitment but only for the sectors included in its national schedule, and subject to a horizontal limitation applying to all such sectors. Under this limitation, authorization for foreign investment in service industries may take into account the following elements:

- the effect of the commercial presence on economic activity (including employment generation, use of local parts, components and services, and exports of services);

- the effect of the commercial presence on productivity, industrial efficiency, technological development and product innovation in Chile;
- the effect of the commercial presence on competition in the sector and other sectors, consumer protection, smooth functioning, integrity and stability of the market, and the national interest;
- the contribution of the commercial presence to Chile's integration into world markets.

Although so far not a single foreign investment operation in a service sector has been denied authorization on the above grounds, Chile retains the right to do so. According to a recent report by the United States Trade Representative (USTR), "this restriction undermines the commercial value and predictability of Chile's GATS commitments" (USTR, 2002).

In terms of disciplines, the CCFTA is GATS compatible in a range of topics including the lack of coverage of subsidies, government procurement and safeguards (apart from general exceptions such as for national security or balance of payments purposes). Article H-10 on licensing and certification establishes obligations roughly equivalent to those set out in Articles VI (domestic regulation) and VII (recognition) of the GATS. However, under Chapter G a wide range of performance requirements on foreign investment are outlawed, irrespective of whether the investments are made for the production of goods or for the provision of services. This provision not only goes further than the TRIMs Agreement in terms of the variety of prohibited measures, but also extends the non-imposition of performance requirements to investments made in services sectors, something that is not subject to any general disciplines in the GATS.

The commitments on administrative proceedings and review and appeal provide for a higher level of transparency and due process than is required by Article VI of the GATS. As with GATS Article VI, Article L-05 of the CCFTA requires the parties to establish or maintain judicial, quasi-judicial or administrative tribunals or procedures that provide for the prompt review and, where warranted, correction of final administrative actions regarding any matter covered by the agreement. However, the CCFTA requires that tribunals be independent of the office or authority entrusted with administrative enforcement, whereas GATS Article VI does not. Moreover, Article L-04 of the CCFTA requires a party to provide certain "best efforts" guarantees of due process to persons of the other party (including service providers) regarding administrative proceedings (see the section on due process above). Finally, whereas Articles L-04 and L-05 are general obligations concerning all matters covered by the agreement, the requirement of fairness and due process in Article VI.1 of the GATS applies only to sectors where WTO members have undertaken specific commitments.

The provisions on monopolies and state enterprises of the CCFTA also go beyond those of Article VIII of the GATS. Whereas Article VIII establishes disciplines only for monopoly suppliers of services, the CCFTA also contains disciplines on monopolies exercising any regulatory, administrative or other governmental authority in connection with the monopoly good or service (see the section on competition policy above).

The CCFTA satisfies, for the most part, the criteria set out in Article V of the GATS on regional economic integration. First, the CCFTA has substantial sectoral coverage, with only a handful of sectors or activities completely excluded and a limited number of specific reservations. Admittedly the agreement contains limited commitments on Mode 4 and explicitly excludes any obligations on a party concerning nationals of the other party seeking employment or employed on a permanent basis in its territory. Moreover, most of the commitments undertaken by Chile and Canada towards facilitating access of their professional service providers to each other's markets have not so far been implemented. But the GATS commitments also exclude measures affecting natural persons seeking access to the employment market of a WTO member or measures regarding citizenship, residence or employment on a permanent basis. Most WTO members also adopted very limited specific commitments on Mode 4 during the Uruguay Round. Therefore both Canada and especially Chile adopted stronger commitments, and in a broader range of sectors, in the CCFTA than they did under the GATS.

Secondly, exceptions to national treatment in the CCFTA have been kept to a minimum. On the one hand, existing measures that constitute exceptions to national treatment for both investment and cross-border trade in services are relatively few and cannot be made more discriminatory. On the other hand, new discriminatory measures are not prohibited, but the scope for them is limited to the sectors listed in Annex II.

Thirdly, the CCFTA does not "raise the overall level of barriers to trade in services" towards non-parties compared with the situation prior to the agreement (except, of course, in a relative way, through the preferential treatment accorded by Chile and Canada to each other's service providers). Indeed, the obligation not to impose performance requirements on investment, including in services sectors, was adopted by Chile and Canada on a most favoured nation basis, therefore benefiting third countries that are not parties to the CCFTA.

Overall assessment

The CCFTA marks a significant further guarantee of liberalization in the area of services through its substantial sectoral coverage and the prohibition of new or more discriminatory measures. In addition, the ratcheting effect locks in any future liberalization of existing discriminatory measures maintained by a party and listed in Annex I of the agreement. Transparency is greatly enhanced by the listing of discriminatory measures in the Annexes.[8] The CCFTA also includes provisions on temporary entry that provide for expedited entry for investors, business visitors, intra-company transferees and other business professionals of both parties.

Disputes concerning investment can use the investor–state mechanism or the agreement's standard dispute settlement mechanism. The investor–state mechanism is an alternative that is neither currently available nor likely to be in the future in the WTO. As for the agreement's standard dispute settlement mechanism, this is still more expeditious and clearer than that of the WTO (see the section on dispute settlement above).

Trade and the environment

The CCFTA contains some provisions related to environmental protection. It safeguards the right of the parties to adopt, maintain and enforce any measure, consistent with the provisions on investment, that is considered appropriate to ensure that investment in their territories "is undertaken in a manner sensitive to environmental concerns". The same Article states that the parties should not seek to attract foreign investment by relaxing their domestic health, safety or environmental measures. A party may request consultations when it considers that the other party has offered such encouragement. There are no precedents as yet of any party invoking this Article.

Along with the CCFTA, Chile and Canada negotiated – at the request of Canada – the Chile–Canada Agreement on Environmental Cooperation (CCAEC). This is modelled after the North American Agreement on Environmental Cooperation (NAAEC), which was negotiated between Canada, Mexico and the United States along with NAFTA. The CCAEC provides a framework for bilateral cooperation on environmental issues. The agreement commits the parties to enforce their environmental laws effectively and to work cooperatively to protect and enhance the environment and promote sustainable development. Amongst the agreement's objectives (which are the same as those of the NAAEC) are:

- to foster the protection and improvement of the environment in the territories of the parties;
- to promote sustainable development;
- to strengthen cooperation on the development and improvement of environmental legislation, policies and practices;

- to enhance compliance with, and enforcement of, environmental laws and regulations;
- to promote transparency and public participation in the development of environmental legislation;
- to promote pollution prevention policies and practices.

In pursuing all these goals, trade distortions and trade barriers should be avoided, and economically efficient and effective environmental measures should be promoted.

The key principle behind both the CCAEC and NAAEC is that each party has the right to establish its own domestic levels of environmental protection, environmental development policies and environmental laws and regulations, and to modify them according to its own priorities.[9] Neither agreement provides for harmonization of environmental standards. There are substantive provisions requiring the parties to commit themselves to enforce their own environmental laws and regulations effectively through appropriate government action. To this end, both agreements provide several guarantees in terms of transparency, open decision-making and due process:

- Parties shall ensure the prompt publication of their laws, regulations, procedures and administrative rulings. To the extent possible, parties will also publish proposed measures in advance and provide interested persons an opportunity to comment.
- Parties shall effectively enforce their environmental laws and regulations through appropriate government action, and shall ensure that judicial, quasi-judicial or administrative proceedings are available to seek appropriate sanctions or remedies for violations of those laws and regulations.
- Each party shall ensure that interested persons can request the party's competent authorities to investigate alleged violations of environmental laws and that these requests be given due consideration in accordance with law. Private access to remedies includes rights such as to sue for damages; to seek sanctions or remedies; to request the competent authorities to take action to enforce environmental laws and regulations; and to seek injunctions.
- Each party shall ensure that administrative, quasi-judicial and judicial proceedings comply with the law, are open to the public and are not unnecessarily complicated. Each party shall ensure that final decisions are made available, in writing and without undue delay, are based on the evidence, and state the reasons for the decision. Parties will also ensure that the tribunals that conduct such proceedings are impartial and independent and that parties to such proceedings can seek review and, where warranted, correction of decisions.

The CCAEC has its own dispute settlement mechanism, which follows closely that of the NAAEC. In case a party asserts or suspects that there is a persistent "pattern of failure" by the other party to enforce its environmental law effectively, the agreement allows first for consultations, and, if they fail, for mediation, good offices, conciliation and the creation of expert groups. If the matter has not been solved and the alleged pattern of failure is trade related, the agreement allows for the establishment of an arbitral panel. If in its Final Report the panel finds that there has been such a pattern of failure, the agreement calls on parties to agree on a mutually acceptable action plan to remedy that situation. In case the parties cannot agree on such a plan or on whether the party complained against is implementing an agreed plan, the panel may be reconvened. The reconvened panel can either approve the proposed plan or propose a different plan, consistent with the law of the party complained against. At this stage, both the CCAEC and the NAAEC allow, in specific circumstances, for the imposition by a panel of a financial penalty on the party failing to implement the action plan. In the case of the CCAEC, this fine cannot exceed US$10 million.[10] The funds collected must be used to solve the alleged breach of environmental legislation.

Up to this stage the dispute settlement procedures are identical under the CCAEC and NAAEC. However, they diverge substantially concerning further action. The CCAEC sets out procedures for a party to pursue the enforcement of a panel determination in the other party's domestic courts, whereas the NAAEC grants a complaining party the right to suspend benefits under NAFTA if the financial penalties are not paid within 180 days.[11] The amount of the benefits withdrawn must not be greater than is sufficient to collect the financial penalties. The CCAEC, for its part, does not allow for trade sanctions in any circumstances. This important departure of the CCAEC from the NAAEC model reflects the difference between the more cooperative Canadian and the more aggressive US approach.

An institutional framework is created to oversee the implementation and further elaboration of the CCFTA, exchange information on environmental matters and carry on an annual work programme on issues of mutual interest.

The specific issue of environmental labelling is not regulated by the CCAEC. However, this subject has been discussed in the context of a permanent Roundtable on Trade and the Environment set up by the governments of both countries in September 2000 as part of their annual cooperation programme.[12] The creation of the Roundtable aims at facilitating the exchange of information, experiences and points of view on the relationship between trade and environment and at exploring possible areas of bilateral cooperation. Although the Roundtable is an intergovernmental forum, academic, business and NGO (non-governmental organization) representatives may be invited to participate in discussions that are relevant to their areas of expertise and interest. Discussions at the Roundtable are informal and non-binding. Accordingly, there are no negotiations or adoption of agreements or resolutions.

Assessment

The CCAEC recognizes the differences that exist among countries in terms of economic development, institutional capacity and economic and social priorities, as well as the consequences that those differences have on national policies towards the environment. A cooperative approach is privileged towards solving any deficiencies that may exist or arise in either party regarding environmental protection. Actually, as of May 2002 there had been no dispute settlement cases under the CCAEC. This reflects the fact that the emphasis of the CCAEC is essentially coopera-tive not punitive. According to Chilean officials, this also reflects the fact that Canada values and supports the efforts undertaken by Chile in the environmental area, including through institution-building, legislation and effective enforcement of provisions.

For the Chilean government, the CCAEC provides an adequate model (superior to the NAAEC) to address environmental issues in other trade negotiations, be they bilateral, regional or even multilateral. In this re-gard, Chile has expressed to the United States that it is prepared to ad-dress environmental concerns in the current negotiations towards a free trade agreement, along the lines of the CCAEC. This includes the possi-bility of fines imposed by a panel on a country persistently failing to en-force its own national legislation, but rules out both harmonization of environmental standards and trade sanctions.

The CCAEC is a comprehensive environmental agreement with a broader scope than just "trade and environment". Therefore, it is diffi-cult to compare it with any efforts undertaken so far in the WTO. More-over, there are currently almost no WTO disciplines on trade and the environment (General Agreement on Tariffs and Trade Art. XX (b) and (g) being the most important exception). It should be equally difficult to compare the CCAEC with any future outcome of the negotiations on trade and environment launched at the WTO Ministerial Conference in Doha. This is because the CCAEC and the Doha negotiating mandate deal with very different subjects. However, should WTO members de-cide to negotiate a multilateral agreement on trade and environment – currently an unlikely scenario – the basic principle underlying the CCAEC would arguably be both politically attractive and economically correct. The CCAEC recognizes the basic fact that countries at different levels of economic development naturally have different levels of envi-ronmental protection. It also recognizes that no country should try to impose its own levels of environmental protection on others. On the other hand, it imposes on its member countries the obligation to respect their own environmental laws, therefore addressing fears of a "race to the bottom".

Policy areas not covered by the CCFTA

Technical barriers to trade and food safety

Although the CCFTA is modelled after the NAFTA, one important difference is that NAFTA was negotiated during the Uruguay Round, whereas the CCFTA began to be negotiated after the Marrakesh Agreement had entered into force. This had implications in several areas such as technical barriers to trade (TBTs) and sanitary and phytosanitary (SPS) measures. When the Chile–Canada negotiations began, negotiators agreed that the NAFTA objectives regarding these two areas were adequately incorporated into the relevant TBT and SPS Agreements in the WTO. It was decided that both parties would simply confirm their commitments under these multilateral agreements. When the CCFTA was negotiated in 1996, there was also little practical experience of the implementation of the TBT and SPS Agreements, which had entered into force only on 1 January 1995. So any possible reform requirements in those agreements that could be incorporated into the CCFTA had still not become fully evident. With the benefit of six years of implementation of the TBT and SPS Agreements, in January 2001 Chile proposed to the United States some "WTO-plus" provisions in these two areas.

Technical barriers to trade

The draft TBT Chapter proposed by Chile to the United States draws heavily on the TBT Agreement, but also establishes stronger disciplines in several respects, with the aim of limiting the exercise of discretionary power by national authorities and the consequent use of standards-related measures as covert barriers to trade. To this end, a core of basic obligations is set out, affecting all kinds of standards-related measures (standards, technical regulations and conformity assessment procedures). These core disciplines are non-discrimination (through MFN and national treatment) and avoidance of unnecessary trade restrictiveness measures. The proposal also suggests the preferential use of international standards as a basis for national standards, technical regulations and conformity assessment procedures, except when such international standards would be ineffective or inappropriate means for the fulfilment of the legitimate objectives pursued. These obligations are also contained in the TBT Agreement, but in a less systematic way.

Some of the most important new features in the Chilean draft concern the treatment of equivalence, recognition of conformity assessment and risk assessment. In a similar fashion to Article 2.7 of the TBT Agreement, each party must give favourable consideration to the possibility of accepting technical regulations of the other party as equivalent, even when they differ from its own, provided it is satisfied that those regulations appropriately fulfil the objectives of its own regulations. This commitment is taken further in the Chilean proposal by a new provision stating that, if so requested by the exporting party, the importing party must explain in writing the reasons for not accepting as equivalent a regulation of the exporting party. There are also proposals on procedural measures to facilitate these aims.

With respect to recognition of conformity assessment, the provisions in Article 6 of the TBT Agreement are taken further in several ways. If an importing party refuses to authorize the conformity assessment institutions of the exporting party to participate in its conformity assessment procedures, the importing party shall explain in writing the reasons for its objection. Once these reasons have been eliminated, the importing party shall authorize the participation of the other parties' conformity assessment institution. An identical commitment applies when an importing party refuses to accept the results of the conformity assessment procedures of the exporting party. Each party is encouraged to agree, when so requested by the other party, to engage in negotiations on the mutual recognition of the results of their respective conformity assessment procedures. The reasons for refusal by an importing party to engage in or conclude such negotiations must be explained in writing to whomever so requests. Finally, the parties are encouraged to accept, when possible, the suppliers' declaration of conformity.

The obligation of the parties to conduct risk assessments is more explicitly stated than under Article 2.2 of the TBT Agreement. Additional criteria to take into account in such risk assessments are introduced, most importantly the risk assessments conducted by international bodies. There is also an important transparency requirement: when so requested, a party shall provide the other party with relevant documentation on its risk assessment procedures and the factors considered in them.

Sanitary and phytosanitary measures

The subject of sanitary and phytosanitary measures is of strategic importance for Chile. On the one hand, owing to its geographic location (surrounded by the Pacific Ocean, the Atacama Desert, the Andes mountain range and the Antarctic continent), Chile is free of many animal diseases and vegetal pests prevalent in other countries. The country has a strong defensive interest in preserving this asset. This is reflected in the strict animal health and phytosanitary requirements maintained by the Chilean government, which even result in impeding the entry of certain agricultural and fisheries products depending on their country of origin. On the other hand, Chile is also a main exporter of agricultural and fisheries products, and therefore has an equally strong interest in avoiding the abuse of SPS measures to restrict its exports. The United States in particular is a major export market for Chilean fruit.

The coexistence of powerful "defensive" and "offensive" interests in this area probably explains why the draft SPS Chapter proposed by Chile to the United States in January 2001 does not present major departures from the WTO's SPS Agreement (unlike the draft TBT Chapter). In particular, the precautionary principle (Art. 5.7 of the SPS Agreement) is fully preserved in the Chilean draft. However, there are some innovative aspects in it vis-à-vis the SPS Agreement:

- The commitment towards equivalence of sanitary or phytosanitary measures contained in the proposal rephrases Article 4.1 of the WTO SPS Agreement, apparently with the objective of facilitating the determination of equivalence. According to Article 4.1 of the SPS Agreement, the exporting country must "objectively demonstrate" that its measures achieve the importing country's appropriate level of sanitary or phytosanitary protection. In the Chilean draft, the exporting country must furnish "scientific information" to show that its measures achieve an appropriate level of protection in the exporting country. This formulation leaves open, however, the question of what happens when the levels of protection deemed appropriate by the importing and the exporting country differ considerably.
- If an importing party rejects the request for recognition as a pest-free or disease-free area made by an exporting party, the rejecting party shall provide the technical reasons for its decision in writing.
- The parties shall conclude agreements on specific requirements whose fulfilment allows the importation of a good produced in an area of low pest or disease prevalence, provided such good complies with the agreed level of protection.
- The transparency requirements set out in Annex B of the SPS Agreement are tightened and expanded upon. Each party shall notify:
  (a) changes or modifications to sanitary and phytosanitary measures having a significant effect on bilateral trade at least 60 days before the effective date of the new provision, to allow for observations from the other party; this requirement does not apply to emergency situations;
  (b) changes occurring in the animal health field, such as the appear-

ance of exotic diseases and those in List A of the International Office of Epizootics, within 24 hours of the detection of the problem;

(c) changes occurring in the phytosanitary field, such as the appearance of quarantine diseases or spread of a pest under official control, within 72 hours following its verification;

(d) discoveries of epidemiological importance and significant changes related to diseases and pests not included in (b) or (c) that may affect trade between the parties, within a maximum term of 10 days.

- On the specific subject of food safety, the Chilean draft contemplates the establishment of a subcommittee on food safety. Among the functions of this subcommittee are to conclude specific agreements within its field and to establish expeditious information exchange mechanisms to deal with consultations from the parties.

Government procurement

Government procurement is not covered by the CCFTA for a number of reasons. Both countries' approaches to government procurement are very different. Chile, unlike Canada, is not and does not intend to become a signatory of the WTO's plurilateral Agreement on Government Procurement (GPA). Chile regards the application of the GPA as complex, bureaucratic and costly; moreover, it does not guarantee MFN treatment below federal level. On the other hand, Chilean government procurement procedures are based on transparency, non-discrimination, flexibility and decentralization. Government entities and municipalities (local governments) usually do their own procurement in a decentralized way. Chilean law calls for public bids for large purchases, but procurement by negotiation is permitted in certain cases. State enterprises, which are required to be self-financing, determine their own procurement policies and purchase independently, from national or foreign sources, using the same criteria as private enterprises (WTO, 1997, pp. xi, 57; USTR, 2002). Another reason for not including public procurement was the relatively small commercial gains it promised for both countries. Finally, Chilean negotiators perceived that government procurement, as well as financial services and intellectual property, was an area of special interest to the United States. Therefore, it was decided to reserve it for a future negotiation with that country, either towards accession to NAFTA or a bilateral one (which eventually started in January 2001).

Chile has, however, made proposals on public procurement in the negotiations with the United States in January 2002 that go beyond both the GPA and NAFTA in terms of defining the entities covered by a negative- rather than a positive-list approach. Similarly, the Chilean proposal includes in principle all procurement of goods, services and public works, except that conducted by the excluded entities and procurement (a) related to defence or national security, or (b) financed by third states, regional or multilateral organizations or persons, which require conditions inconsistent with the provisions of the Chapter.[13] In comparison, both the GPA (for services and construction services) and NAFTA (for goods, services and construction services) operate on a positive-list basis.

Apart from its more comprehensive scope, the Chilean draft is similar to both the GPA and NAFTA in many respects. As in these agreements, the Chilean proposal contains various provisions intended to guarantee the principles of non-discrimination and transparency. Among those provisions are: national treatment; prohibition of offsets; effective dissemination of business opportunities generated by government procurement processes and of the results of such processes;[14] and establishment of bid challenge procedures. As a general rule, procuring entities should make their purchasing decisions on the basis of the "best value for money" principle.

Conclusions

The general conclusion on the impact of the CCFTA is that – with the qualifications already mentioned above – it had little effect on the way Chile regulates the areas of investment and services. The same can be said about the impact of the CCAEC on the way Chile regulates environmental matters. In the case of investment and services, Chile just consolidated its general regulatory regime, whereas under the CCAEC both parties committed themselves only to enforce their respective national laws.

Compared with WTO provisions on investment and trade in services, it can be concluded that by and large the CCFTA is WTO-plus. This is particularly clear in the area of investment, because there is as yet no WTO agreement regulating investment in a comprehensive way. It remains to be seen, of course, how the CCFTA will compare with any future WTO agreement on investment, the negotiation of which was agreed in a rather ambiguous mandate at the Doha Ministerial Conference. However, given the failure of the negotiations for a Multilateral Agreement on Investment in the OECD, as well as the substantial opposition that any such agreement faces among many WTO members, it seems very unlikely that any WTO negotiation could produce an agreement with broader coverage or stricter disciplines than those of the CCFTA.

The CCFTA is also WTO-plus in the area of trade in services, owing to its wider sectoral coverage and stronger disciplines compared with the GATS. For both investment and trade in services, the CCFTA (like NAFTA) imposes more demanding requirements on the parties in terms of procedure than the GATS or other relevant WTO agreements. These procedural requirements should also – at least in principle – have a significant effect in terms of limiting the scope for regulatory discretion.

Neither policy approximation nor mutual recognition are contemplated in the area of investment, as the CCFTA basically provides for a "standstill" of the parties' investment regimes at the time the agreement was negotiated. Moreover, those concepts are more relevant in areas such as technical or sanitary standards that apply to trade in goods. Concerning trade in services, a limited degree of mutual recognition is envisaged through "soft" commitments applying to professional service providers. For the most part these commitments have not been implemented.

In terms of reviews and remedies, the CCFTA provides recourse to domestic procedures by aggrieved parties, to investor–state dispute settlement in the case of investment and to the agreement's general dispute settlement mechanism. These provisions are clearly WTO-plus in terms of the investor–state option, and even the standard dispute settlement mechanism of the CCFTA seems to be quicker and clearer than the one existing under the WTO. Of course, this assessment remains to be tested in practice because no cases have so far reached the panel stage under the CCFTA.

With regard to tackling anti-competitive practices, the provisions of the CCFTA go beyond the limited provisions of the GATS/WTO. Commitments on monopolies exist that exceed those of Article VIII of the GATS, and the parties committed themselves to adopt or maintain measures to proscribe anti-competitive business conduct and to take appropriate enforcement action. There are also additional commitments for the parties to consult and cooperate in this field. Moreover, the provisions in the CCFTA on competition policy and monopolies apply to all areas covered by the agreement.

The CCFTA is essentially "NAFTA equivalent". This is unsurprising, because the agreement was modelled after NAFTA. As noted in the relevant sections, the Chapters of the CCFTA on investment and cross-border trade in services mirror very closely those of NAFTA, in terms of coverage (with the exception of financial services), core disciplines and exceptions and reservations. Canada, as an important investor in Chile, was interested in strong provisions on investment along NAFTA lines. Chile, for its part, had an open investment regime and therefore did not have to modify that regime in any substantial aspect to make it fit the NAFTA model.

On the whole, the CCFTA does not appear to be a clear case of "regulatory regionalism". Of course, a certain level of regional preference is in the essence of every regional trade agreement. However, in terms of substantive disciplines the commitments undertaken by both Chile and Canada in the CCFTA concerning investment and services are basically of a standstill nature. Both countries essentially agreed to "freeze" their general regimes of the time for investment and services. Moreover, some important commitments (such as the prohibition of several forms of performance requirements for investment) were adopted on a most favoured nation basis. However, some commitments undertaken in the agreement concerning procedures (including transparency, due process and prior notification), access to the agreement's dispute settlement provisions and cooperation in competition-related matters, among others, do imply a certain degree of regional preference that may be important. The only way in which it could be said that the CCFTA represents "regulatory regionalism" is in the sense that, by adopting the NAFTA model, it tends to strengthen the case for NAFTA to be seen as a model for the ongoing negotiations of the Free Trade Area of the Americas.

Concerning environmental regulations, the Chile–Canada Agreement on Environmental Cooperation is clearly WTO-plus. The CCAEC is practically identical to the North American Agreement on Environmental Cooperation in terms of the procedural guarantees provided. There is, however, one important difference between both agreements concerning remedies. Whereas the NAAEC provides for trade sanctions as a last resort in the event that a NAFTA member fails consistently to enforce its own environmental laws or other regulations, the CCAEC rules out trade sanctions and establishes procedures for a party to pursue the enforcement of a panel determination in the other party's domestic courts. This approach, which puts rules over sanctions, makes the CCAEC a more attractive model than the NAAEC, and possibly one that could have wider application.

The CCAEC explicitly recognizes that each party has the right to establish its own domestic levels of environmental protection and to modify them according to its own priorities. The agreement does not require harmonization of environmental standards; nor is policy approximation explicitly required. However, the cooperative emphasis of the CCAEC may produce some modest degree of institutional convergence on the part of Chile towards the high levels of environmental protection prevalent in Canada. This "upward" convergence, which will become apparent only in the medium run, may come both directly, through the relatively demanding commitments Chile assumed in the CCAEC, and indirectly, through the effect of the cooperation programmes that both countries are carrying forward within the context of the agreement. A concrete ex-

Table 7.1. Summary assessment of the Chile–Canada Free Trade Agreement and the Chile–Canada Agreement on Environmental Cooperation

	Investment[a]	Trade in services[a]	Environmental regulations[b]
Non-discrimination	WTO-plus, NAFTA equivalent	WTO-plus, NAFTA equivalent[c]	Not applicable
Procedural elements	WTO-plus, NAFTA equivalent	WTO-plus, NAFTA equivalent	WTO-plus, NAAEC equivalent
Policy approximation	No	No	Not explicit (it may take place to some extent owing to cooperation)
Mutual recognition or equivalence	No	Limited (for professional service providers)	No (except in the sense that the parties recognize the legitimacy of each other's environmental laws and regulations), NAAEC equivalent
Containing regulatory discretion	WTO-plus, NAFTA equivalent	WTO-plus, NAFTA equivalent	WTO-plus, NAAEC equivalent
Effective reviews and remedies	WTO-plus, NAFTA equivalent	WTO-plus, NAFTA equivalent	WTO-plus, NAAEC-plus (no trade sanctions allowed)
Promoting competition	WTO-plus, NAFTA equivalent	WTO-plus, NAFTA equivalent	Not applicable

Notes:
a. Chile–Canada Free Trade Agreement.
b. Chile–Canada Agreement on Environmental Cooperation.
c. With the exception of cross-border trade in financial services, which was excluded from the CCFTA but is dealt with in NAFTA.

ample is the recent creation of an internet database on Chilean environmental law and regulations, as a result of one such cooperation project. Any improvements in matters such as institution- and capacity-building, transparency, due process, best practices and others that may result from the CCAEC and its implementation will likely become part of Chile's general environmental *acquis*.

Table 7.1 summarizes the assessment of the CCFTA (and the CCAEC, for environmental matters) in terms of the seven criteria defined in chapter 2.

Canada did not use its position as a stronger developed country to act as a "regulatory hegemon" in either the CCFTA or the CCAEC. In the medium term, however, there may be some degree of convergence by Chile to Canadian standards in the environmental area. The interesting point, however, is that any such convergence would most likely be based on incentives and cooperation instead of on coercion or explicit harmonization requirements.

On the whole, Canada has been a much less demanding partner for Chile than the United States has proved to be during the ongoing negotiations towards a bilateral free trade agreement. In the CCFTA negotiations, the NAFTA model was followed closely but with enough flexibility on both sides to leave outside those issues that either were not of real interest for the parties (for example, government procurement or sanitary and phytosanitary measures) or were too sensitive for any of them (financial services and intellectual property in the case of Chile). The same applies to the CCAEC vis-à-vis the NAAEC. In contrast, the United States has been inflexible during the current negotiations in trying to achieve all its goals regardless of Chilean sensitivities.

Notes

1. However, at the Third Meeting of the Chile–Canada Free Trade Commission, held in Santiago in May 2001, it was agreed to establish a bilateral Committee on Sanitary and Phytosanitary Measures. This committee, whose terms of reference are still being worked out, is envisaged to serve as a regular forum for consultations and cooperation on SPS matters.
2. Cross-border trade in financial services is also excluded from the provisions of Chapter H (cross-border trade in services). At the time the agreement was negotiated, financial services were perceived by Chile as a priority area for the United States. Because at that time Chilean authorities believed that negotiations towards the country's accession to NAFTA were near, it was decided to "reserve" financial services for then. Nevertheless, both parties agreed in Annex G-01.3(b) that, if Chile had not begun negotiations towards its accession to NAFTA within 15 months of the entry into force of the agreement, Chile and Canada would start negotiations aimed at reaching an agreement based on NAFTA's Chapter 14 (financial services) no later than 30 April 1999. This commitment has not been implemented as of May 2002 though, owing to lack of interest on both sides. Chile, at the request of the United States, has been negotiating since early 2001 a Chapter on financial services in the context of their bilateral FTA negotiations. This Chapter may provide a model for the inclusion of financial services in the CCFTA.
3. Under Annex G-09.1, Chile reserved the right to maintain some restrictions on both inward and outward flows related to foreign investments, aimed at preserving the stability of its currency. The most important among these restrictions are:
   (a) the prohibition to repatriate the original capital for a year since the date of transfer to Chile (this restriction does not apply to profits, which can be repatriated immediately); and
   (b) the imposition of a non-interest-bearing reserve deposit on investments other than foreign direct investments and on foreign credits relating to an investment. At the

time the CCFTA entered into force the reserve requirement was 30 per cent of the amount of the investment or credit. It was lowered to 10 per cent in June 1998 and to zero two months later, in response to the Asian financial crisis. Although the Chilean Central Bank retained the right to reintroduce the reserve at its discretion, up to a maximum of 40 per cent, in the CCFTA Chile "bound" the reserve at a maximum 30 per cent for Canadian investments and related credits. On 16 April 2001, the Chilean Central Bank announced the elimination of the reserve requirement, to be effective from 19 April.

4. The Convention was done at Washington DC, 18 March 1965.

5. UNCITRAL Arbitration Rules were approved by the United Nations General Assembly on 16 December 1976.

6. Since the CCFTA entered into force, the Chilean government has been expressing to Canada its desire to negotiate an agreement on air transportation. Currently there are no direct flights between Chile and Canada. This is perceived by the Chilean authorities as a disincentive to further growth in bilateral business relations. However, there seems to be not enough interest on the part of both Chilean and Canadian airlines in covering any such routes because they are not commercially attractive without taking or leaving passengers in the United States.

7. An exception to this situation is the case of engineers, where some progress is being made.

8. However, the blanket exception taken by Canada for all its existing discriminatory measures at the provincial level goes against transparency and negatively affects the value of the market access commitments undertaken by that country concerning cross-border trade in services.

9. This is qualified by the requirement that each party shall ensure that its laws and regulations provide for high levels of environmental protection and shall strive to improve them.

10. In the case of the NAAEC, the maximum permitted amount is US$20 million for the first year of implementation of the agreement. Thereafter, any monetary enforcement assessment shall be no greater than 0.007 per cent of total trade in goods between the parties during the most recent year for which data are available.

11. This mechanism does not apply, however, when Canada is the party that has failed to pay the monetary enforcement assessment. In such a case, alternative procedures apply (similar to those of the CCAEC) for a complaining party to pursue the enforcement of a panel determination in Canadian courts. This is due to Canadian constitutional restrictions.

12. Other subjects included are, *inter alia*, the precautionary principle, the relation between the WTO and the multilateral environmental agreements, methodologies for environmental assessment of trade agreements, settlement of disputes concerning trade and the environment, and biodiversity.

13. Cross-border financial services and "governmental services or duties" (law enforcement, pension or unemployment insurance, public education, among others) are also excluded from the Chilean draft Chapter.

14. Chile already has implemented an internet-based information system on government procurement.

REFERENCES

OECD (Organisation for Economic Co-operation and Development) (2000a), *Strengthening Regulatory Transparency: Insights for the GATS from the Regulatory Reform Country Reviews*, TD/TC/WP(99)43/FINAL, Paris, April.

———— (2000b), *Trade and Regulatory Reform: Insights from the OECD Country Reviews and Other Analysis*, TD/TC/WP(2000)21/FINAL, Paris, November.

USTR (United States Trade Representative) (2002), "Chile", in *2002 National Trade Estimate Report on Foreign Trade Barriers*, at http://www.ustr.gov/reports/nte/2002/chile.

WTO (World Trade Organization) (1997), *Trade Policy Review: Chile*, WT/TPR/S/28, Geneva, November.

8

The Closer Economic Relations Agreement between Australia and New Zealand

Gary P. Sampson

Introduction

The CER (Closer Economic Relations) Agreement between Australia and New Zealand was built on a series of preferential trade agreements including the 1966 New Zealand Australia Free Trade Agreement (NAFTA). By the late 1970s, NAFTA and its predecessors had resulted in the removal of tariffs and quantitative restrictions on 80 per cent of trans-Tasman trade. Further advances in trade liberalization were limited because there was no mechanism for the compulsory removal of remaining trade restrictions on merchandise trade. The CER Agreement took effect on 1 January 1983 and established the modalities and timetable for removing the remaining restrictions to trade in goods.[1]

The CER Agreement was recently reviewed by members of the World Trade Organization (WTO) in accordance with the biennial review of the requirements of Article XXIV of the General Agreement on Tariffs and Trade (GATT) 1994 (WTO, 2000; Australian Department of Foreign Affairs and Trade, 1997). The review made clear that the CER Agreement has fulfilled entirely its objective of free trade in goods and extended its coverage to provide for close to free trade in services. It has greatly deepened the integration of the economies of the two countries through, *inter alia*, agreements relating to harmonization of standards, mutual recognition and conformity assessment procedures. There can be little doubt that the CER Agreement has led to trading relations between the two countries that go beyond the provisions of the WTO (WTO-plus) on a number of fronts. In fact, the general view seems to be that the "CER is the cleanest regional trading arrangement in the world, with virtually no exceptions to free trade in goods and services and an absence of bureaucracy. Both countries are now a model for members of the WTO in terms of their observance of both its rules and spirit" (Lloyd, 1998, p. 160).

The objectives of the CER Agreement are to strengthen the broader relationship between New Zealand and Australia; to develop closer economic relations through a mutually beneficial expansion of free trade; to eliminate barriers to trade in a gradual and progressive manner under an agreed timetable; and to develop trade between the two countries under conditions of fair competition. Although these are broad goals, the original CER Agreement focused on liberalized trade in goods. It is the main – but not the only – instrument governing economic relations between Australia and New Zealand. It has evolved considerably since its entry into force. Several aspects of the agreement have been amended, refined or simply become redundant. These changes have been introduced via different modalities, so interpretation of the agreement often requires reference to several different source documents.

For example, three general reviews were provided for in the original CER Agreement. These were important in shaping future relations between the two countries. The first review was in 1988 and accelerated the deadline for free trade in goods. Free trade was scheduled for 1995, but was in fact advanced to June 1990. At this stage, all tariffs and quantitative restrictions on trade between the two countries were eliminated.[2] The second review, in 1990, widened the scope of the 1983 Agreement to include trade in services. The third of the reviews, in 1992, deepened the CER Agreement by seeking to harmonize a range of non-tariff measures on trade in goods and services.

At the annual meeting of Australian and New Zealand trade ministers in 1992, it was decided that subsequent reviews would take place as part of the annual meetings. At the 1995 meeting, the services agreement was extended to cover commitments in the areas of postal services and telecommunications (by Australia) and aviation and shipping (by New Zealand). Other meetings served to widen and deepen the CER Agreement further. For example, there was the conclusion of the Trans-Tasman Mutual Recognition Arrangement. In this arrangement, a good that can be sold legally in one country can be sold legally in the other. Similarly, a person who is registered to practise an occupation in one country is entitled to practise an equivalent occupation in the other. There was the signing of an arrangement establishing a Single Aviation Market, and the formal launching of new institutions to deal with the harmonization of standards and conformity inspection.

A "closer economic relationship" requires not only free trade in goods and services but also free flow in the factors of production – labour and capital.[3] The CER does not formally address either the movement of labour or foreign direct investment. However, the free movement of persons, including those moving for the purpose of employment, was agreed to in the 1920s under the Trans-Tasman Travel Arrangements. It was not incorporated into the CER Agreement at the time of its creation, nor has it been incorporated subsequently. In the case of investment, this is dealt with in neither the CER Agreement nor any other formal arrangement. Although no preferences are formally accorded, a number of political and other statements by the governments and business communities recognize the importance of the free flow of investment between the two countries and undertake commitments to facilitate it when possible.

The important point is that the CER Agreement is only one part of the totality of what constitutes the arrangements governing economic relations between Australia and New Zealand. If all relevant arrangements are taken into account, it becomes clear that the economic relations between the two countries are certainly WTO-plus in many areas.

The purpose of this chapter is to describe the CER Agreement and associated arrangements with a view to assessing their impact on regulatory barriers to trade and the extent to which they are WTO-plus or otherwise. The first section looks at both border protection and industry assistance more generally and notes the rapid move to free trade between the two countries in goods. It highlights the fact that both countries – highly protectionist in the post Second World War period – were already aggressively following unilateral policies of trade liberalization and deregulation at the time of the entry into force of the CER Agreement. An important question is how much of this can be attributed to the existence of the free trade area. The second section describes the extension of the CER Agreement to cover trade in services. This is followed by a description of the various instruments and procedures to ensure that standards do not constitute unnecessary barriers to trade in manufactured goods, food and agricultural products, and services trade. In the fourth section, anti-dumping, safeguard and countervailing measures are described, after which the discussion turns to competition policy and the unique manner in which it is addressed in the CER Agreement. This is followed by a discussion of factor mobility and a description of the dispute settlement procedures. The next section looks at government procurement, intellectual property rights and environmental considerations.

The final section addresses the important question of what is the likely future regional cooperation between the CER Agreement and other free trade areas and customs unions. The chapter closes with a conclusion.

Merchandise trade

The CER Agreement is non-exclusive with respect to merchandise trade and covers all goods originating in the free trade area.[4] As with other free trade areas, rules to determine the origin of goods are therefore important. The minimum rules of origin requirements are relatively simple: namely, the last process of manufacture should have occurred in Australia or New Zealand and at least 50 per cent of the cost of the product should be materials, labour or other value added originating in the area. When compared with the complex rules of origin of a number of other free trade areas, the rules of the CER Agreement are relatively simple.

One way to reduce the trade-restrictive effect of rules of origin is to keep the regional content requirement at a low level as well and the procedures simple and transparent. This has been the goal of the CER Agreement. However, other regional agreements have lower content requirements; for example, the ASEAN Free Trade Area has a 40 per cent content rule (see High-Level Task Force on the AFTA–CER Free Trade Area, 2000). In fact, it is the 50 per cent requirement of the CER Agreement rules of origin – not their complexity – that has led to criticism.[5] It has been reasoned that local content will be reduced as a result of greater local efficiency – and therefore lower cost – which is one of the objectives of the CER itself. Similarly, there could be a small price change in bilateral exchange rates outside the control of the manufacturer that would have important implications for the rules of origin content. It has therefore been suggested that the 50 per cent requirement in the CER Agreement should be reduced or the rules of origin changed to reflect a change in tariff heading requirement (see Lloyd, 1997).

One of the remarkable features of the CER Agreement with respect to goods trade has been the advancement of the date set for free trade in goods. All tariffs and quantitative restrictions were definitively eliminated five years in advance of the proposed date (i.e. in 1990). This is impressive for a number of reasons, not the least being that the two countries have had a tradition of high tariffs and quantitative restrictions since the Second World War. Additionally, they were highly protected at the time of the entry into force of the CER Agreement.

An important question in the current context is what has been the contribution of the CER Agreement to trade liberalization in Australia and New Zealand. The answer to this question is not simple. It is important to note, for example, that both countries have taken unilateral measures that have greatly changed both the nature *and* the extent of protection as part of their national trade policies. After the Second World War, for example, both countries made extensive use of quantitative restrictions through import licensing. This continued in Australia until 1962 and until the mid-1980s in New Zealand. Import licensing was reintroduced in Australia under sectoral schemes for the motor vehicle industry, textiles, clothing and footwear sectors, which have all followed their own industry-specific plans for liberalization. Apart from these sectors (in both countries), there was an aggressive pursuit of unilateral liberalization. Perhaps the best example of this was the across the board 25 per cent reduction of tariffs in Australia in 1973 outside of any commitment undertaken in multilateral rounds of negotiations.

Notwithstanding the substantial reduction of tariffs and quantitative restrictions in the 40 years after the Second World War, Australia and New Zealand remained the most highly protected of all countries of the Organisation for Economic Co-operation and Development (OECD) at the time of the entry into force of the CER Agreement. In Australia, the average nominal level of protection was 16 per cent and the average rate of effective protection was 25 per cent; for New Zealand the corresponding figures were 20 per cent and 39 per cent. However, some caveats are in order. Unlike some other OECD countries, neither country had opted for voluntary export restraints or joined other trade-restraining arrangements such as the Multi-Fibre Arrangement. Although in Australia there were quantitative restrictions on textile and clothing products, import licences were auctioned. The publication of the results made clear which interest groups were benefiting from the associated rents.

This approach was certainly well within the Australian tradition of ensuring public awareness of all the forms of industrial assistance available in the country. Assistance afforded to agriculture and industry in the form of licences, tariffs or other support measures has traditionally been evaluated through a system of public inquiries in which the criterion for the acceptability of the assistance was its usefulness in an economy-wide context (see Laird and Sampson, 1987). In this process, it was clear who were the winners and losers from government assistance, greatly adding to the change in public sentiment from one of post-war protectionism to a higher level of acceptability of trade liberalization.

In Australia, this process was facilitated by (or even largely due to) the work of the Tariff Board, later converted to the Industries Assistance Commission (IAC), then the Industries Commission, and now, in its present form, the Productivity Commission. Under the intellectual influence of Max Corden and other Australian trade economists, the Tariff Board and the subsequent institutions calculated and published on an annual basis the effective rates of assistance for all Australian industries. These calculations were made widely available publicly – not only the effective rates of protection for all industries, but also the ad valorem equivalence of all assistance provided to Australian industries and agriculture. To bring comparability across industries, the "subsidy equivalent" (later used by the OECD and the GATT in the agricultural negotiations in the Uruguay Round) was calculated and published. Although New Zealand did not have the same institutional structure as Australia in this respect, staff from the IAC were borrowed by the New Zealand governmental institutions to make similar calculations. The impact of this process in terms of public acceptance of unilateral trade liberalization cannot be underestimated.

A case can be made that the direct role of the CER Agreement in this process of trade liberalization in both Australia and New Zealand has been marginal, but this view has been contested. It has been argued by both governments and a number of researchers that the CER Agreement made an important contribution to the broader process of liberalization in both countries by constituting a trial run for subsequent multilateral trade reforms (see Lloyd, 1998). New Zealand was, in particular, better prepared for accepting broader reforms after coping with the threat of increased competition from the much larger economy of Australia. Both governments have also seen the liberalization undertaken with respect to the CER Agreement as having been highly successful at creating a more competitive domestic environment. If this is the case, it could be argued that the gains from the CER Agreement are much greater than the simple removal of restrictions between Australia and New Zealand.

Since the product coverage of the CER is complete, and liberalization is total in terms of goods trade, the agreement is certainly WTO-plus in this respect. However, it is important to note that goods trade between the two countries is modest when compared with other customs unions and free trade areas. Although Australia is New Zealand's largest trading partner and New Zealand is Australia's third-largest partner, the share of total trade involved is limited. In 2000, Australia's exports to New Zealand accounted for less than 10 per cent of its total merchandise exports, and the corresponding figure for New Zealand's exports to Australia was one-fifth of total trade. Intra-trade accounted for just 10 per cent of the total trade of the CER countries in 2000. By way of comparison, two-thirds of Canadian and Mexican trade is with North American Free Trade Area (NAFTA) partners and over one-quarter of United States trade is with NAFTA countries. For the European Union, two-thirds of the total trade of the member countries is within the European Union. In fact, the vast majority of the trade of both Australia and New Zealand is with other countries on a most favoured nation (MFN) basis (see Sampson, 1997).

As far as the development of trade between the two countries is concerned, in the initial period after the entry into force of the CER Agreement New Zealand benefited much more than Australia and increased its exports to Australia significantly, almost achieving trade parity. In fact, one of the criticisms from an Australian perspective was that New Zealand was benefiting in a disproportionate manner from the CER Agreement. In more recent times, however, there has been an important change. Australia's exports to New Zealand have grown far more strongly than New Zealand's exports. Over the five years to 2000, Australian exports to New Zealand increased by over one-third, whereas those from New Zealand to Australia increased more modestly at less than 10 per cent.

An interesting feature of Australia–New Zealand trade that may well be influenced by the existence of the CER Agreement is its structure. In particular, exports from Australia and New Zealand to the rest of the world are predominantly made up of unprocessed mining and rural products, whereas their imports are manufactured goods. This is not the case for their bilateral trade. For example, in 2000, one-third of Australia's merchandise exports to the rest of the world were agricultural products and 43 per cent were mining products. In bilateral terms, the trade of both countries with East Asia has been largely an exchange of exports of raw materials and semi-processed goods for imports of final consumer and capital goods. In the case of Australia–New Zealand trade, trade in manufactures accounts for over three-quarters of Australia's exports to New Zealand and about 60 per cent of New Zealand's exports to Australia.[6] Nevertheless, the trade between the CER countries remains small and, not surprisingly, discussions are under way for regional trade groupings involving the CER countries and other country groupings including the countries of East Asia.

Services trade

The CER Trade in Services Protocol dates from 1988. It provides for a negative-list (or "top–down") approach to the scheduling of commitments; that is, all services can be freely traded except for those inscribed in the Annex to the protocol. Trans-Tasman services arrangements are certainly WTO-plus when compared with commitments undertaken under the WTO General Agreement on Trade in Services (GATS). Under the GATS, a positive-list (or "bottom–up") approach is adopted for committed sectors, and a negative-list approach for limitations and conditions on national treatment and market access. The CER Protocol also provides for restrictions on national treatment and market access. Although both approaches can in theory be equally liberalizing, practice reveals that the negative list is more liberal in terms of coverage and commitments.

The core concepts, principles and rules in the CER Protocol are similar to those in the GATS: the basic provisions are national treatment, market access, commercial presence and MFN treatment. For both countries, possibilities exist for horizontal restrictions across all sectors and, as noted, for conditions and reservations to be applied within the services sectors where commitments have been undertaken. Because the Annex to the protocol is closed, all new services are automatically subject to the provisions of the protocol.

In the case of the CER Protocol, the extent of the liberalization of services can be measured by the inscriptions in the Annex and the limitations of a horizontal nature. The inscriptions (exemptions) are modest when compared with the schedules of many GATS members. They are reviewed periodically and have been substantially reduced over time. New Zealand now has only two inscriptions and Australia six. These are for measures applied to activities within sectors rather than to the sector as a whole, and in some instances the liberalization is provided for under a separate agreement (for example, air transport services and maritime services). Australia currently has inscribed telecommunications, airport services, domestic air services, international aviation (passenger and freight services), coastal shipping, broadcasting and television (limits on foreign ownership), broadcasting and television (short-wave and satellite broadcasting), basic health insurance services, third party insurance, workers' compensation insurance and postal services. New Zealand has inscribed airways services, international carriers flying cabotage, telecommunications, postal services and coastal shipping.

As noted, some sectors are liberalized under other arrangements. For example, the CER Protocol does not provide for national treatment of aviation services, but aviation relations between Australia and New Zealand are governed by a bilateral agreement and related understandings. An arrangement establishing a Single Aviation Market entered into force in 1996 and allows the airline of each country to operate domestic services in the other country and to fly without restrictions across the Tasman (subject to safety and other operational regulatory requirements). The movement of labour and the mutual acceptance of professional qualifications are provided for elsewhere and discussed below.

Standards

Following the entry into force of the WTO Technical Barriers to Trade (TBT) Agreement and Sanitary and Phytosanitary (SPS) Agreement, the relations relating to standards have been governed by these WTO agreements. Both New Zealand and Australia were obliged to join the TBT Agreement as members of the WTO – neither had been members of the earlier GATT Standards Code. However, the CER Agreement is WTO-plus because it provides for deeper integration in terms of the harmonization and mutual recognition of standards as well as conformity assessment and other procedures. Although the two governments undertook to "examine the scope for taking action to harmonise requirements relating to such matters as standards, technical specifications and testing procedures, domestic labeling and restrictive trade practices", a number of agreements and arrangements have been negotiated pursuant to this Article that serve to enforce its WTO-plus character. This is in fact a major feature of the CER Agreement (Australian Department of Foreign Affairs and Trade, 1997).

For example, as part of the 1988 review of the CER Agreement, a Memorandum of Understanding on Technical Barriers to Trade reaffirmed the commitment of both governments to work towards the harmonization of standards, technical specifications and testing procedures, and to ensure that the relevant authorities of both countries cooperated in the determination and revision of standards. The memorandum provided for exporters having reasonable access to information regarding such matters as standards, technical specifications, testing procedures, certification requirements and domestic labelling standards. It was agreed that the test results and conformity certification from one country would be accepted by the other, and that the test requirements would be transparent and non-discriminatory. In addition, the Agreement on Standards, Accreditation and Quality (ASAQ) entered into force in October 1990 and tied the two countries firmly to the principles of standards harmonization and mutual acceptance of certification and accreditation. Like the WTO agreements, the ASAQ encourages Australian and New Zealand standards, accreditation, product certification and quality practices to be as far as possible aligned with international standards, and it also provides for a monitoring committee which acts as a forum where representatives of both countries can address areas of non-conformity.

A further development was the formation in October 1991 of the Trans-Tasman Joint Accreditation System (JAS-ANZ), providing for a harmonized approach to auditing and certification of quality management systems in accordance with international standards. The responsibilities of the JAS-ANZ Council include the harmonization of conformity assessment structures (quality management systems certification, product certification, laboratory accreditation, personnel certification, etc.). The JAS-ANZ also provides for uniform criteria, procedures and practices for carrying out and accepting conformity assessments.

As far as food standards are concerned, the 1996 Agreement on Establishing a System for the Development of Joint Food Standards creates a single regulatory agency to develop joint food standards for Australia and New Zealand in a transparent manner. The agency maintains offices in both Australia and New Zealand. The goal of the agreement is to secure lower compliance costs for industry, fewer regulatory barriers and more consumer choice.

Australia and New Zealand also reached agreement in June 1996 on revised inspection arrangements for imported food originating from either country. Under the revised arrangements, foods other than "risk-classified" foods can be exported without import and export certification and inspection requirements. Only risk-classified foods are inspected, with all other foods being subject only to the domestic surveillance arrangements that apply to locally produced foods. A food is "risk classified" if the scientific literature or experience identifies a particular risk for that food, such as the potential for contamination by micro-organisms leading to food poisoning.

Mutual recognition

Under the 1996 Trans-Tasman Mutual Recognition Arrangement (TTMRA), a good that can be legally sold in one country can be legally sold in the other. Further, a person who is registered to practise an occupation in one country is entitled to practise an equivalent occupation in the other. Goods need comply only with the standards or regulations for the sale of goods applying in the jurisdiction in which they are produced or through which they are imported. Mutual recognition is intended to remove technical barriers to trade and impediments to the movement of skilled personnel between jurisdictions without the need for complete harmonization of standards and professional qualifications. The agreement was signed by the Australian prime minister, the state premiers and territory chief ministers and the New Zealand prime minister, thus extending mutual recognition to the sub-federal level.[7]

Through implementing mutual recognition principles, the TTMRA aims progressively to remove regulatory barriers to the movement of goods and service providers between Australia and New Zealand, thereby facilitating trade between the two countries. Its stated objectives are to enhance the international competitiveness of Australian and New Zealand enterprises, increase the level of transparency in trading arrangements, encourage innovation and reduce compliance costs for business. In this sense it is certainly WTO-plus in its application. Mutual recognition is an objective of the TBT Agreement of the WTO, and the CER Agreement puts it into operation.

Quarantine harmonization

As with the WTO SPS Agreement, the CER Agreement specifically allows New Zealand and Australia to adopt measures necessary to protect human, animal or plant life or health. Similarly, although each country may impose quarantine requirements on imports, these must not be used as a means of arbitrary or unjustified discrimination or a disguised restriction on trade. Under the 1988 Protocol on the Harmonisation of Quarantine Administrative Procedures, both countries reaffirmed their commitment that quarantine requirements should not be deliberately used as a means of creating a technical barrier to trade. As with the SPS Agreement, the measures must be scientifically justified. In addition, under the protocol, quarantine restrictions are applied on the basis of individual regions rather than nationwide. The governments also restated their agreement to use relevant international codes and standards where appropriate and to work towards the harmonization of quarantine standards and procedures.

Although the arrangements follow the WTO rules, they are WTO-plus in that they have been operationalized through the adoption of common inspection standards and procedures for both countries. For example, a Quarantine Consultative Group has been established to resolve outstanding technical differences and provide overall impetus and direction for harmonization. The relationship between the two countries with respect to quarantine matters has developed significantly through regular contact between officials.

Customs harmonization

The CER Agreement recognizes that the objectives of the agreement may be promoted by harmonization of customs policies and procedures. The Joint Understanding on Harmonisation of Customs Policies and Procedures, agreed to during the 1988 review, recognizes that some elements of customs policies and procedures, such as rules of origin, are central to the operation of the CER Agreement; it recognizes the benefits to be derived from the adoption of a common approach in meeting the trade promotion objectives of the CER Agreement. The customs agencies of both countries have undertaken to pursue harmonization opportunities and maintain common approaches to the greatest extent possible, and endorsed as a primary objective the closest possible working relationship.

Rules on competition

Following the 1988 general review of the CER Agreement, Australia and New Zealand agreed to rationalize their respective industry policies. This meant an agreement not to provide export subsidies or industry-specific measures that have adverse effects on competition between industries in the two countries. Countervailing measures can be taken to remove injury to an industry caused by importing goods benefiting from government subsidies, but only in accordance with the WTO Agreement on Subsidies and Countervailing Duties and when no other mutually acceptable alternative solution has been found. For a countervailing action to be taken, it is necessary to prove that there is subsidization; material injury, threat of material injury, or material retardation of the establishment of an industry; and a causal link between the two. In the course of investigating a countervailing complaint, the country taking the action is required to keep the other country fully informed about the progress of the complaint and offer full access to all relevant non-confidential evidence and full opportunity for consultations. Each country, likewise, is required to cooperate to expedite procedures, to give access to relevant non-confidential information to the fullest extent possible and to facilitate investigations.[8]

With respect to safeguards, it was agreed in the original CER Agreement that no goods would be excluded from the free trade objectives of the agreement in terms of the removal of tariffs and other barriers. However, slower tariff and quantitative restriction phase-down regimes were permitted for some sensitive industries. With the review of the agreement in 1988, and the decision to advance the implementation of free trade from 1995 to 1990, tariffs and quantitative import restrictions were removed for both non-sensitive and sensitive industries.[9] Thus, no safeguard measures were invoked for the sensitive industries identified for slower liberalization.

As of 1 July 1990, anti-dumping actions were eliminated and folded into the domestic competition law of the two countries (see below). Third-country anti-dumping actions can be taken where dumped imports from a third country are causing or threatening to cause material injury to industry in the other country. As with domestic anti-dumping cases, before third-country anti-dumping measures can be implemented it is necessary to prove dumping, material injury or threat of material injury, and causation. The process is to conform to the requirements of the WTO Anti Dumping Agreement, under which it is necessary for the importing country to seek approval from WTO members if it wishes to impose third-country anti-dumping measures.

Competition policy

One novel feature of the competition policy under the CER Agreement is that anti-dumping provisions were considered an anomaly in a free trade area and anti-competitive business practices were treated as subject to the competition laws of each country. Consequently, Australia and New Zealand have eliminated the possibility of anti-dumping actions on goods originating in each other's markets. In parallel, the countries extended the application of their competition law prohibitions on the misuse of market power. These provisions prohibit the use of substantial market power (Australian law) and dominant position (New Zealand law) in the "trans-Tasman market" for certain anti-competitive purposes. They extend the prohibitions on the abuse of a dominant or powerful market position in the national legislation by redefining the relevant markets as the combined markets of the two countries. They do not, however, cover other horizontal restraints (such as price fixing or collusion) or vertical restraints (such as resale price maintenance) or mergers (see Lloyd, 1997); nor do they cover service markets. As with other institutional arrangements relating to the CER agreements and protocols, this is very much a decentralized approach. There is no joint secretariat and there is no common enforcement institution. In fact, to date, neither of the national bodies (the Australian Competition and Consumer Commission and the New Zealand Commerce Commission) has taken a prosecution action under their respective competition laws. However, the enforcement powers go well beyond those incorporated in any bilateral cooperation agreement or regional trade agreement. And, although they apply to only one form of business conduct and do not apply to services, the competition authorities agreed to cooperate and extend the existing competition cooperation agreement to cover services and all competition law.[10]

The 1988 CER Memorandum of Understanding on Business Law Harmonisation requires a joint examination of the scope for harmonization and removal of business laws and regulatory practices that are impediments to business. An interesting feature of this process of business law harmonization is that it is directed to identifying differences that increase the transaction and compliance costs faced by companies operating in both markets, and areas where harmonization would significantly reduce those transaction costs. The objective has not been to produce identical Australian and New Zealand business laws.

A Memorandum of Understanding on Business Law Coordination between New Zealand and Australia was signed in 2000. It reflects a common understanding of coordination in business law and provides a framework for future cooperation on business law integration. A work programme has been agreed to, and its objectives include reducing business costs through removing differences in laws and administrative systems, improving the effectiveness of the law and reducing the cost of capital to business.

Regulation and factor mobility

Free movement of persons, including those moving for the purpose of employment, is provided under the Trans-Tasman Travel Arrangements. This guarantees the unrestricted movement of citizens of each country. The only requirement is for a passport. Not only is there free movement of labour, there is the provision of national treatment in order that the citizens of one country are treated equally in the labour markets of the other. As noted above, the 1997 Trans-Tasman Mutual Recognition Arrangement provides that a good that is legally sold in one country can be legally sold in the other. Further, a person who is registered to practise an occupation in one country is entitled to practise an equivalent occupation in the other. This arrangement was modelled on mutual recognition in the European Union, and it is the only regional trading arrangement outside the European Union with mutual recognition of standards and labour qualifications. It goes far beyond the WTO GATS agreement and is certainly WTO-plus.

The treatment of capital movements is, however, quite different from that of labour. There is no provision of any form relating to foreign investment in the 1983 CER Agreement or any other subsequent agreement or arrangement. Thus, when the Protocol on Trade in Services was agreed to in 1988, it recognized the two primary aspects of trade in services – market access and national treatment – but it made the application of market access subject to the foreign investment policies of member countries.

The foreign investment policies of the two countries are, however, non-discriminatory, and their bilateral investment agreements provide that investment by all treaty partners shall be accorded MFN treatment. Consequently, the benefits of any special investment agreement between Australia and New Zealand under CER arrangements would necessarily extend to all those countries with which Australia and New Zealand have entered into a bilateral investment arrangement. The national foreign investment review agencies (for Australia, the Foreign Investment Review Board; for New Zealand, the Overseas Investment Commission) are apparently well aware of the bilateral importance of trans-Tasman investment and of their governments' commitment to ensuring that investment review procedures remain at least as liberal as existing practice.

The respective review bodies of each country are committed to streamlining procedures to reduce compliance costs. Thus, through an exchange of letters, Australia and New Zealand have agreed "to avoid to the fullest possible extent, further restrictions on investors and confirm that trans-Tasman investment should be subject to minimum constraint, both now and in the future".[11] Further bilateral liberalization of investment is supported by business organizations in both countries, and has been ranked by them as the highest priority for future work on the CER Agreement.[12]

Settling disputes

There are no specific dispute settlement procedures under the CER Agreement. However, it does set out a consultation and review mechanism aimed at ensuring that both New Zealand and Australia are satisfied with the functioning of the agreement. If either country has a grievance concerning adherence to any part of the agreement, the other country is obliged to enter into consultations to seek an equitable and mutually satisfactory solution. According to the CER Agreement, a grievance may arise if an obligation has not been fulfilled, a benefit under the agreement denied or an objective frustrated. Because consultations are non-binding, successful settlement relies on the goodwill of both parties to work out amicable and practicable solutions. The 1988 Protocol on Trade in Services (Art. 19 and 20) also contains provisions for review and consultation; these essentially mirror those in Article 22 in the 1983 CER Agreement.

Government procurement, intellectual property rights and environmental considerations

According to the CER Agreement, the granting of preferences in the area of government purchasing is inconsistent with the objectives of the agreement. Accordingly, agreement was reached in relation to purchasing undertaken by departments, authorities and other bodies of each of the governments. The Australian and New Zealand governments undertook to treat any content in offers received from Australian or New Zealand tenderers as equivalent to their local content. Thus, given the limited coverage of the plurilateral government procurement arrangements of the WTO, the CER Agreement is again WTO-plus in this respect.

The outstanding issue of the purchasing preferences maintained by

Australian state governments for Australian suppliers was addressed in the 1988 general review of the CER Agreement. The outcome was that New Zealand could join the (Australian) National Preference Agreement (NPA) under which the states had earlier agreed not to apply their preferences against each other. New Zealand became a signatory to the NPA in June 1989, thus securing non-application of the state preferences as against New Zealand content. In return, New Zealand made a commitment to continue its existing policy of not applying a preference margin to any purchases. The NPA was re-titled the Government Procurement Agreement in 1991, reflecting a wider focus on equality of opportunity for Australian and New Zealand suppliers, as well as ending inter-state or trans-Tasman preference margins on Australian and New Zealand content in government purchasing.

Intellectual property rights are not covered formally within the CER family of agreements. In fact, domestic legislation relating to intellectual property is explicitly excluded from the operation of the Trans-Tasman Mutual Recognition Arrangement. Instead, Australia and New Zealand rely for protection of their intellectual property rights on the World Intellectual Property Organization and the WTO Agreement on Trade-Related Aspects of Intellectual Property Rights. The CER Agreement is not WTO-plus in this area.

Although the CER Agreement does not contain any specific provisions on environmental protection, Australia and New Zealand cooperate closely in this field bilaterally and at the multilateral level. The agreement recognizes, however, the importance of the preservation of a favourable regional environment (on land, in the atmosphere, in the oceans and with regard to plant and animal life as well as fisheries) to the economic and trading future of both countries, as well as to their social well-being. Both countries have ratified or acceded to a wide range of international environmental agreements.

Expanded regional cooperation

The CER Agreement provides for the association of any other state. To date, Australia and New Zealand are the only acceding parties and no other state has sought association to the agreement. In the biennial review at the WTO, both countries made clear they were willing to consider free trade agreements with other countries or regional groupings if they would deliver faster and deeper liberalization than the multilateral process. The stated objective of an expanded membership would be to gain better market access for exporters, faster economic growth and stronger employment growth. It was noted in the review that such arrangements would need to demonstrate comprehensive sectoral coverage and reflect the principles underpinning the CER, including WTO consistency (see WTO, 2000; see also Australian Department of Foreign Affairs and Trade, 1997).

In a broader regional context it is noteworthy that none of the larger East Asian countries – Japan, Korea, China, Hong Kong and Taiwan – is a member of any regional trading arrangement. In fact, Japan, Korea and Hong Kong are the only three WTO members that are not parties to a regional trading arrangement. But this situation may be about to change. In recent years, a number of new proposals have emerged for regional trading arrangements involving East Asian countries.

In Asia, the ASEAN Free Trade Area (AFTA) was formed in 1993 and has added four more to its original six members (Brunei, Indonesia, Malaysia, the Philippines, Singapore and Thailand) with the inclusion of the transition economies Cambodia, Lao PDR, Myanmar and Vietnam. Asia-Pacific Economic Cooperation involves 21 economies from four continents: Asia, Oceania and the North and South Americas. In the meantime, hub-and-spoke arrangements have recently been completed (Singapore–New Zealand, Mexico–EU), as well as bilateral arrangements between individual countries from across continents (Chile–South Korea, Chile–Singapore). Australia is currently pursuing free trade arrangements with Singapore and Thailand, and has for some time had a US–Australia free trade area under serious consideration. Discussions are also taking place on the possibility of a free trade area between Japan and South Korea (and perhaps China). Regular consultations between ASEAN and China, Japan and South Korea (ASEAN plus three) may well evolve into some form of regional arrangement in the future.

AFTA provides for the phased reduction of tariffs on manufactured imports from ASEAN countries through the Common Effective Preferential Tariff scheme. Countries are committed to reducing these import tariffs on most products to 0–5 per cent by 2002 (with later implementation dates for Cambodia, Vietnam, Myanmar and Lao PDR). Protocols concluded after 1993 have extended the coverage of AFTA to areas such as services and investment.

An AFTA–CER link was established in September 1995 during informal consultations between ASEAN economics ministers and ministers from Australia and New Zealand, with the aim of facilitating trade and investment flows between the two regions. The two regions undertook a range of practical, business-oriented activities, such as exchange of information, human resource development, trade and investment facilitation and promotion, industrial cooperation and activities relating to customs matters, standards and conformance and competition policy.

At the ministerial talks in October 1999, ASEAN and CER ministers agreed to establish a High-Level Task Force. The Task Force had as its objective to explore the feasibility of an AFTA–CER free trade area by 2010. The mandate covered exploring options for a possible architecture of an FTA (including scope and coverage), the requirements for consistency with WTO obligations, and flexibility for developing countries. The report identified a wide range of benefits that would flow from an AFTA–CER free trade area, including welfare gains to consumers, increasing the region's competitiveness and attractiveness to investment and strengthening its bargaining power in multilateral negotiations (see High-Level Task Force on the AFTA–CER Free Trade Area, 2000).

AFTA–CER ministers considered the report of the High-Level Task Force in 2000 and agreed to work towards a Closer Economic Partnership (CEP). The decision to establish a CEP is particularly significant because it will be the first time that the 12 regional governments will be involved in officials-level talks to promote regional economic integration. The CEP envisages including other more contemporary elements, such as e-commerce, competition policy and non-tariff barriers in regional discussions. The gains from forming an AFTA–CER free trade area have been estimated to be US$48.1 billion of GDP, in net present value terms over the period 2000 to 2020 (see Davis et al., 2000). The gains are US$25.6 billion for AFTA and US$22.5 billion for CER, of which New Zealand gains US$3.4 billion. The gains rise over time, reaching around 0.3 per cent of additional GDP by 2010 for both AFTA and CER. For the newer ASEAN members, the gains in GDP range between 0.1 and 0.4 per cent of GDP per annum.

Australia and New Zealand have also commenced a dialogue with the members of Mercosur (Argentina, Brazil, Uruguay and Paraguay). At a first meeting in Auckland in April 1996, senior officials agreed to a work programme consisting of a number of joint activities to facilitate trade and investment (including the compilation of a customs compendium and the exchange of information on the recognition of standards).

The Trade and Economic Cooperation (TEC) bilateral agreement between Canada and New Zealand entered into effect in 1982 and formalized tariff preferences previously maintained in accordance with the British Commonwealth preference scheme. The TEC provided an umbrella for trade and economic cooperation between the two countries. The agreement aimed to limit increases in tariffs and maintain minimum margins of preference. Under the TEC, Canada enjoyed concessions in the New Zealand tariff for some 3,000 tariff items. During regular consultations held under the TEC in 1995, the parties agreed to maintain existing preference margins on a point-for-point basis for at least a further three years. When combined with the New Zealand policy of unilateral tariff reductions, imports from Canada would be substantially duty free by 1998. The TEC has not been amended and there are no current plans to revise it. The anti-dumping provisions of the TEC have been overtaken by the Uruguay Round outcome.

Apart from the CER, there are other preferential schemes that involve Australia, New Zealand or both. In the case of Australia, other preferential arrangements include the Canada Australia Trade Agreement, the Papua New Guinea Australia Trade and Commercial Relations Agreement and the South Pacific Regional Trade and Economic Cooperation Agreement. Australia also provides preferential access to goods from developing countries on a unilateral basis under the Australian System of Tariff Preferences for Developing Countries.

Although the Asia Pacific region has lagged behind other regions (such as Europe) in negotiating preferential free trade areas, the above discussion as well as that in chapter 1 makes clear that it is fast catching up. There is a great deal of activity in the Asia Pacific area. If only a fraction of the agreements currently under negotiation come into being, the nature of trade in the region could change, with significant commercial implications both locally and for the rest of the world. Suffice it to cite by way of example that, in June 2002, South-East Asian economics ministers met in Kuala Lumpur, Malaysia, to take further steps towards establishing a free trade area between ASEAN countries and China. This would create an integrated market of 1.7 billion consumers, making it the largest free trade area in the world. There can be little doubt that Australia and New Zealand will be watching closely the implications for their own trade with this region – as will the rest of the world.

Conclusions

Apart from this traditional liberalization in traded goods and services that should come with a free trade area, there has been a considerable broadening and deepening in the economic relationship between Australia and New Zealand in terms of their domestic regulations. The end result is that the CER family of arrangements constitutes one of the – if not the – most comprehensive free trade areas operating at present. The regulatory arrangements between the two countries are certainly WTO-plus overall, and although some may be WTO-neutral there is no evidence of their being WTO-minus.

Although both countries have unilaterally and aggressively pursued a policy of eliminating trade distortions, restrictions and other barriers to trade, this process has been facilitated through the bilateral agreements established under the CER Agreement. That there is free trade in goods and liberalized trade in services (including the free movement of natural persons) is certainly WTO-plus. Further, trade under the agreement has undoubtedly provided a learning process for the removal of regulatory measures more generally. Liberalization of trade in services between Australia and New Zealand, for example, pre-dates the entry into force of the WTO GATS Agreement. Similarly, the objectives of harmonization through the adoption of international standards, procedures to permit mutual recognition of standards and other similar objectives pre-date the WTO TBT Agreement. The associated arrangements relating to mutual recognition and conformity assessment are also WTO-plus.

The CER family of arrangements is also WTO-plus in the sense that the coverage is far broader than that of the WTO trade agreements. For example, the arrangements provide for the free movement of labour and mutual recognition of qualifications. Other areas, such as competition policy, are not subject to WTO disciplines but are covered by the CER arrangements. They too are WTO-plus. On the other hand, investment and dispute settlement provide examples where the CER arrangements do not provide for formal deeper integration between the two countries, although informal mechanisms and understandings play an important role.

The manner in which the agreement has evolved over time makes clear that there is a CER "approach" to removing regulatory barriers to trade that sets the arrangements between the two countries apart from other regional trade agreements. New Zealand and Australia have, for example, relied on their own institutions for dealing with the substance of the commitments and refrained from creating an institutional infrastructure to service and implement the agreement such as exists in the European Union. The arrangements relating to competition policy provide an example. Also, the agreement has been both broadened and deepened through protocols and understandings that have grown out of a review process rather than major negotiating sessions. In general, deadlines to meet the agreed objectives in a variety of areas have been either met or advanced.

Further, the CER Agreement has most certainly proved to be a building block rather than a stumbling block for wider multilateral regimes when it comes to dealing with regulatory barriers to trade. This is evidenced in a number of ways. The two countries have unilaterally liberalized and passed this liberalization on to other countries through most favoured nation treatment. This has been done largely outside the context of multilateral rounds of negotiations in the WTO and GATT. In fact, the bilateral liberalization has turned out to be the advanced implementation of MFN liberalization. In terms of regulation relating to standards and other measures more generally, the rules and processes that the two countries have adopted or implemented have been constructed in such a way as to reinforce their commitments under the relevant WTO agreements. Trade facilitation is clearly the goal of many arrangements, such as those relating to customs harmonization.

The CER family of arrangements is WTO-plus in many respects, but it should be noted that the cooperation in terms of deeper integration between the two countries is certainly facilitated by their cultural and social similarities as well as their historical backgrounds. This has led to a number of comparatively loose arrangements that operate without a formal institutional framework because of the degree of mutual trust that exists between the countries. In other words, it is not evident that the CER arrangements provide a model for the regional integration schemes of all other countries.

Notes

1. The CER Agreement was notified to the GATT and examined by a Working Party "in the light of the relevant provisions of the General Agreement, and to report to the Council". The Working Party met on 4 and 19 June 1984 (see WTO, 1985).
2. This provision is contained in Articles 4 and 5 of the 1983 CER Agreement and Articles 1 and 2 of the 1988 CER Protocol on the Acceleration of Free Trade in Goods, under which all transitional arrangements and temporary exceptions to the basic free trade rule were eliminated as of 1 July 1990.
3. For a discussion of the extent to which regional trade agreements extend beyond just trade in goods, see Sampson (1996).
4. As is the case with GATT 1994 and most other regional trade agreements, the CER Agreement allows for exceptions. These are, however, quite standard and similar to those of the GATT 1994 (i.e. Art. XX). Measures can be excepted for specified purposes, provided they are not used "as a means of arbitrary or unjustified discrimination or as a disguised restriction on trade".
5. It should be noted, however, that although ad valorem rules of origin are arguably simpler than other methods, it is still necessary to provide documentation to prove the 50 per cent content, with problems arising over what should be included in the valuation (packaging, insurance, etc.). An important issue is whether there is discretion in the application of such provisions, which makes for uncertainty and opens the door to abuse of such discretion for protectionist purposes.
6. The diversity of composition is at least to some extent attributable to CER preferences under arrangements such as the Closer Defence Relations arrangement, which runs in parallel with the CER Agreement.
7. The TTMRA extends to the eight Australian state/territory governments, the Australian commonwealth government and the New Zealand government. The TTMRA is currently operational in 9 of the 10 TTMRA jurisdictions (i.e. they have enacted their domestic enabling legislation), with Western Australia currently the only outstanding jurisdiction.
8. Third-country countervailing actions are also permitted to address cases where subsidized imports in one member state from a third country are causing or threatening material injury in the other member state.
9. Under the 1988 CER Protocol on the Acceleration of Free Trade in Goods, all transi-

tional arrangements and temporary exceptions to the basic free trade rule were eliminated as of 1 July 1990.
10. For more detail on these aspects, see Lloyd and Vautier (2001).
11. For details relating to the exchange of letters, see Lloyd (1997, p. 4).
12. It has been noted that the "area of foreign investment is the most glaring omission from the CER Agreement" (Lloyd, 1997, p. 12).

REFERENCES

Australian Department of Foreign Affairs and Trade (1997), *Closer Economic Relations: Background Guide to the Australia New Zealand Economic Relationship*, Canberra, Australia.

Davis, Lee, Warwick McKibbin and Andrew Stoeckel (2000), *Economic Benefits from an AFTA–CER Free Trade Area Year 2000 Study*, Canberra and Sydney: Centre for International Economics, June.

High-Level Task Force on the AFTA–CER Free Trade Area (2000), *The Angkor Agenda: Report of the High-Level Task Force on the AFTA–CER Free Trade Area*, available at http://www.aseansec.org.

Laird, Samuel, and Gary P. Sampson (1987), "Case for Evaluating Protection in an Economy Wide Perspective", *The World Economy* 10(2), pp. 177–92.

Lloyd, Peter J. (1997), "Completing the CER", Committee for Economic Development of Australia (CEDA) Working Paper, Melbourne, April.

——— (1998), "Unilateral and Regional Trade Policies of the CER Countries", in J. J. Piggott and A. D. Woodlands, *International Trade Policy and the Pacific Rim*, London: Macmillan.

Lloyd, P. J., and K. Vautier (2001), "Regional Approaches to Cross-Border Competition Policies", mimeo.

New Zealand Ministry of Foreign Affairs (2000), "CER and Its Impact on the Trade Liberalization Debate in New Zealand", tabled at the second AFTA–CER meeting, Queenstown, New Zealand, April.

Sampson, Gary P. (1996), "Compatibility of Regional and Multilateral Trading Agreements: Reforming the WTO Process", *American Economic Review* 86(2).

——— (1997), "The WTO and Regional Trading Agreements", *Australian Economic Review* 30(1), pp. 75–89.

WTO (World Trade Organization) (1985), *Australia New Zealand Closer Economic Relations Trade (ANZCERTA) Agreement, Report of the Working Party*, adopted on 2 October 1984 (L/5664), BISD 31S/170-179, Geneva: WTO, March.

——— (2000), *Biennial Report on the Operation of the Agreement, Communication from the Parties to the Agreement*, WT/REG111/R/B/1, G/L/406, Geneva: WTO, 9 November.

Part III

Horizontal case studies

9

Food safety and eco-labelling regulations: A case of transatlantic regulatory regionalism?

Grant E. Isaac

Introduction

The conclusions of the previous case studies tend to suggest that regional trade agreements (RTAs) are generally consistent with the substantive multilateral principles governing regulatory barriers to trade and, hence, are building blocks for multilateral rules dealing with new regulatory policy issues. Yet, although this may be true for RTAs in general, it appears that specific regulatory issues such as food safety and environmental protection measures are congruent with regional arrangements for a much different reason – to protect regional regulatory approaches from either the divergent approaches of other regional arrangements or the divergent regulatory approach adopted by the multilateral system. In this sense, RTAs may be stumbling blocks for multilateral rules, either preventing their establishment or undermining their success. Consequently, they may potentially create an entrenched regulatory regionalism between developed countries with codified regulatory structures – perhaps more importantly between North America and the European Union (transatlantic regulatory regionalism) – and between developed and developing countries (North–South regulatory regionalism); that is, between the former with codified regulatory approaches and the latter where the codified regulatory approaches of developed countries may be inappropriate.

In this chapter, the propensity for food safety and environmental measures to cause transatlantic regulatory regionalism as well as North–South regulatory tension is examined with respect to the concept of WTO-plus (that is, provisions that go beyond those of the World Trade Organization). However, owing to the importance of the transatlantic relationship in the establishment of successful multilateral rules, this chapter focuses more on the impact of transatlantic regulatory regionalism on the international trading system. Particular attention will be paid to the North American and EU regulatory differences in food safety and environmental measures through two timely and illustrative case studies: the regulation of products of modern biotechnology in the food supply (growth hormones in meat and genetically modified crops) and eco-labelling schemes. Several important research questions will guide the analysis:

• Are RTAs associated with food safety and environmental measures a WTO-plus building block for multilateral rules or are they a stumbling block creating regulatory regionalism?
• What is the impact of these RTAs on market opening?
• Is the transatlantic regulatory regionalism converging or diverging?

In the first section I discuss the general policy objectives prompting RTAs and the similar aspects of food safety and environmental measures that make them increasingly congruent with an RTA. In the next two sections, North–South and transatlantic differences in food safety regulations and eco-labelling schemes are examined. The chapter concludes with an assessment of the impact of RTAs on regulatory regionalism across the various WTO-plus concepts.

Food safety, eco-labelling and regional trade agreements

Regulations for food safety and for environmental labelling (eco-labelling) share several important characteristics that are especially relevant for an assessment of the impact of regional trade agreements on the multilateral trading system.

They both represent regulations deeply embedded in political economy factors such as preferences and concerns that may be unique to a particular country or region. In this sense, there is a distinctly "bottom–up" nature to the policy objectives of these regulations. As a result, the regulatory approaches may differ with respect not just to specific regulations, but also to systemic differences in their regulatory frameworks (the meta-principles of the regulatory approach) (see Isaac, 2002a). When countries or regions differ in their regulatory approaches, regulatory market access barriers are created. When the regulatory frameworks are similar and only specific regulations differ, it is easier to deal with regulatory barriers to market access. Yet, when countries or regions differ in their fundamental regulatory frameworks, dealing with regulatory barriers becomes very difficult because, unlike traditional trade barriers, food safety and environmental regulatory barriers represent a distinct kind of protectionism – consumer or environmental protectionism. Whereas traditional industrial protectionism sought to insulate domestic producers from competition with foreign producers, this new protectionism is highly credible and legitimate in the eyes of the general public because it is applied to imported products in order to insulate domestic consumers from foreign products that are not processed or produced according to domestic regulations or do not otherwise achieve domestic regulations.

This last point – that food safety and environmental protection measures are focused on the imported product's methods of process or production – has crucial trade implications. According to the principle of non-discrimination, trade rules can focus only on *like products*. Essentially, this means that, if two products have the same end-use, then market access rules cannot permit preferential market access for one product because of the way it was produced. Consider two cotton shirts where the cotton for one was produced under organic standards, whereas the cotton for the other was produced within an intensive agricultural setting. Under the trade rules, the cotton shirts must be treated equally because they are like products. Yet, with both food safety and environmental protection measures, the focus is often precisely on how a product was processed or produced. Hence, these regulations inherently contravene the like products aspect of the principle of non-discrimination.

Another important similarity between food safety and eco-labelling regulations is that they represent income-elastic regulations; that is, as incomes rise, so too do the demands for more stringent regulations governing food safety and, especially, environmental protection. Indeed, it is not serendipity that the highest regulatory standards in the world exist in the countries with the highest standards of living. The implication of this is that a categorization of countries with similar levels of food safety and environmental measures parallels a categorization of countries with similar levels of income. Of course, this development itself raises concerns because regional agreements associated with food safety and environmental protection regulations essentially exclude those countries without the incomes necessary to achieve the required regulatory levels, perhaps creating a North–South regulatory regionalism.

Therefore, although other policy areas share this bottom–up nature (such as issues of consumer protection in services regulation), food safety and environmental protection measures have emerged as domestically embedded policy areas particularly sensitive to the development of "top–down" international rules. Moreover, the similar aspects of these measures create pressure for RTAs for very different reasons from those seen in the previous case studies. Rather than being a proactive building block for the creation of multilateral trade rules, RTAs represent stumbling blocks protecting the bottom–up policy objectives of countries within the arrangement from divergent regulatory approaches at either the regional or the multilateral level, even if the countries within the regional arrangement agreed to the other regulatory approaches at one time.

What are these RTAs protecting member countries from? Generally, there is a concern that both food safety and environmental protection measures are under threat by a multilateral approach to market access that imposes trade liberalization rules "top–down" according to neo-classical economic principles with little regard for the domestic concerns and preferences that the regulations may be built on. In addition, unlike the national approach, the multilateral approach is considered to lack openness (transparency and participation), resulting in a democratic deficit that further undermines the credibility and legitimacy of the multilateral trade regime in establishing appropriate regulations. The fear is that the non-open approach to multilateral market access rules advocating regulatory competition will produce a regulatory "race to the bottom".

This has been illustrated vividly with respect to the regulation and market access of genetically modified (GM) crops (which will be discussed in greater detail below). From the early 1970s until the late 1980s, all developed countries were essentially on the same trajectory for regulating the products of modern biotechnology. Yet, in 1990 the European Union dramatically shifted its regulatory approach in reaction to domestic political economy factors and has used its regional arrangement to protect this regulatory approach from the North American regulatory approach, which has come to dominate many international organizations such as the World Trade Organization as well as the World Health Organization (WHO), the Food and Agriculture Organization (FAO) and the Organisation for Economic Co-operation and Development (OECD). As a result, the current international trade for GM crops faces a situation of transatlantic regulatory regionalism that has undermined the multilateral rules and created significant trade uncertainty (Isaac, 2002a, p. 7).

Food safety

In this section I examine how food safety regulations have begun significantly to challenge the multilateral system through RTAs, with a particular emphasis on food safety regulations dealing with products of modern biotechnology. This examination begins with a general discussion of food safety regulations and their inclusion in both regional and international agreements. I then examine the "North–South" differences in regulating food safety as well as the transatlantic differences in approach, which have been so controversial recently.

Food safety tends to be considered as the exclusive domain of the national jurisdiction and there is a long history of domestic laws and regulations covering food production, processing, adulteration, packaging and labelling (see Horton, 1997). These food safety laws often reflect normative domestic factors such as cultural preferences and risk perceptions as much as (if not more than) they reflect actual food safety risk. For instance, whereas many in France would not think of eating pasteurized cheese, there is a general perception in North America that unpasteurized cheese is unsafe, or at least very risky. Moreover, whereas many in North America do not entertain the notion of eating horsemeat, the same is not true in Europe, especially in East European countries. According to these cultural preferences and risk perceptions, and sometimes calculations of actual risk, food safety regulations have emerged. As a result of this mix of normative and empirical assessments of risk, within many countries there is a complex web of regulations, guidelines, recommendations and codes of practice administered by several different government agencies (for example, agriculture, health, industry, environment) at all levels of government (local, provincial/state/county/*Länder* and national).

There is also a long history of food trade. It is difficult, if not impossible, to purchase a food consumption bundle from purely domestic sources. Yet this means that domestic consumers are, perhaps unwittingly, subject to the perhaps quite different food safety systems of exporting countries. The growth of food trade has given rise to both regional and multilateral arrangements addressing food safety regulations. However, the success of standardizing food safety regulations within countries such as Australia and Canada involved significant difficulty and challenge, so it should come as no surprise that standardizing food safety regulations bilaterally, regionally and multilaterally has been an enormous challenge (Spriggs and Isaac, 2001). In both Australia and Canada, the commitment to regional and multilateral arrangements emerged from a "bottom–up" effort to reconcile differing regulations within the countries before attempting to reconcile differing regulations between regional partners. Recognizing that many normative risk perceptions were entangled with assessments of actual risk, this process began with an attempt to find the common ground in the regulatory framework between all provincial/state regulations. Consistent with international trends (to be discussed below), science was used as that baseline under the following logic: although provinces/states differ across normative risk perceptions, ultimately they all want safe food, and a scientific assessment of actual food safety risks is the common ground.

Therefore, food safety regulations face a crucial duality problem: the maximization of domestic food safety and the maximization of food trade and international commercial opportunities for domestic food producers. Consequently, the history of food safety trade rules at the multilateral level has been one of an attempt to accommodate both simultaneously by increasingly focusing on *actual* risk, based on a scientific risk assessment, as the determinant of "legitimate" market access barriers, leaving little room for *perceived* risk.

With the conclusion of the Uruguay Round and the creation of the World Trade Organization's Agreement on Sanitary and Phytosanitary Measures (SPS Agreement), it appeared that the multilateral food safety rules based on scientific assessments of actual risk had won the day and a dramatic convergence of regional rules would soon follow (GATT, 1994). However, this has not happened because this conclusion is based on a flawed assumption that a common regulatory framework unified all the member countries. This assumption appears weak for both the North–South and the transatlantic relationships. With respect to the former, many less developed countries lack the market demand (income-elastic food safety regulations are low when income is low), political impetus (food safety is not a priority policy area) and scientific capacity to shift to a rigorous (and expensive) food safety system dominated by scientific risk assessments. With respect to the transatlantic relationship, recent trade disputes and difficulties associated with products of modern biotechnology have revealed significant differences in the foundational regulatory frameworks employed in each region, especially the role of science that each supports. Prior to discussing the North–South and transatlantic differences in food safety regulations, I shall assess the evolution of the multilateral food safety rules.

Although the contemporary assessment of food safety rules tends to suggest that regional arrangements are stumbling blocks to multilateralization, this has not always been the case. The current multilateral system emerged from a regional arrangement. The predecessor to the Codex Alimentarius (to be discussed below) was the Codex Alimentarius Europeaus – or the European food code. The aim was to standardize food safety regulations within Europe in order to ensure the highest levels of consumer protection and easier food trade. Given its success, the Codex Alimentarius Europeaus became the Codex Alimentarius in 1962 – administratively a joint agency of the United Nations Food and Agriculture Organization and the World Heath Organization (FAO, 1998). Two different policy objectives converged to push for multilateral rules over regional rules. The first was a consumer protection argument: because the internationalization of food trade exceeded the regionalization of food safety regulations, it was argued that only a multilateral approach would ensure the maximum food safety for consumers. The second was a similar commercial argument: because the reach of food trade exceeds even regional groupings, only a multilateral approach to market access rules would disentangle legitimate food safety barriers from spurious market access barriers.

With the shift of the regional Codex Alimentarius Europeaus to the multilateral Codex Alimentarius, the objective for the Codex became to establish science-based, internationally accepted standards for food safety and quality in order to address consumer protection and food trade concerns simultaneously. Membership included national delegations of food scientists, who used scientific risk assessments in order to disentangle legitimate food safety barriers based on actual risk from spurious market access barriers based on perceived risk.

Prior to the enactment of the SPS Agreement in 1995, the Codex Alimentarius – as the only international food safety and trade organization – existed outside the international trading system represented by the General Agreement on Tariffs and Trade (GATT) 1948. The GATT 1948 was unclear on the issue of trade rules for food safety measures. According to several of its Articles, signatory countries retained significant discretion to establish their own bottom–up food safety regulations. For instance, Article XI specifically permitted regulations setting out national "standards or regulations for the classification, grading or marketing of commodities in international trade". Under Article XX(b), signatory countries were permitted to adopt and enforce any measures that they deemed necessary to protect human, animal and plant life or health. In an attempt to be consistent with the principle of non-discrimination, the discretionary measures invoked under Articles XI and XX(b) were not to be applied in a manner that would cause arbitrary or unjustified barriers to trade. However, the problem was two-fold. First, this specification did not provide any direction as to what was an arbitrary or unjustified food safety barrier. Second, no discipline was prescribed in the event that a barrier was found to be arbitrary or unjustified. Hence, there was little recourse under the international trading system to deal with instances of market access barriers. Indeed, at this time the Codex standards were simply viewed as non-binding, international recommendations.

For the most part, the work of the Codex in the multilateral standardization of food safety regulations progressed far removed from public scrutiny and it was not considered a threat to national regulatory sovereignty. All of this was to change with the enactment of the SPS Agreement under the auspices of the World Trade Organization, 1 January 1995 (GATT, 1994). The goal was to rectify the problems associated with food safety barriers by clearly distinguishing a legitimate food safety barrier from an arbitrary or unjustified barrier. Given the science focus of the Codex, it emerged as the logical international organization to establish universal food safety standards that were as free (as possible) from the normative preferences and concerns that had driven domestic food safety regulations. Hence, the SPS Agreement states that "Members shall base their sanitary or phyto-sanitary measures on international standards, guidelines or recommendations" (Art. 3:1).

The SPS Agreement sets out rules for the legitimate application of food safety regulations and it defers to the Codex for expert advice on the application of science and science-based standards. The SPS Agreement outlines when a legitimate, scientific justification exists (as determined by either Codex standards or Codex standards-setting guidelines) for a member country to violate the principle of non-discrimination. As a result, the SPS Agreement has in effect replaced the broad Article XX(b) exemptions with a set of exemptions that are trade compliant only if accompanied by a credible scientific justification (see Isaac and Kerr, 2003).

Four permissible violations of the principle of non-discrimination are outlined in the SPS Agreement. First, members may discriminate against imports because of the presence of food safety risks in the exporting country (Art. 2:3). The agreement recognizes that different regions with different geographical and climatic conditions and different industrial capabilities face different incidences of food contamination. As a result, it is not possible to establish uniform SPS measures to apply to all exporters according to the principles of non-discrimination. Instead, trade measures need specifically to target less safe food products, and other imported products may not face the same measures. This provision is an important exemption from the traditional non-discrimination principles. Members are not required to grant either national treatment or most favoured nation status to food exporters whose products risk contaminating the domestic food supply.

Second, according to the agreement, members may also establish domestic SPS measures higher than the accepted international standard if there is scientific justification to do so (Art. 3:3). Generally, international trade agreements commit members to adopt international standards if available; however, the SPS Agreement permits members to establish even higher standards.

Third, the SPS Agreement permits members to establish SPS measures based on scientific risk as well as broader assessments of risk such as relevant economic factors, which include (Art. 5:3):

- potential damage in terms of loss of production or sales in the event of the entry, establishment or spread of the disease or pest;
- the costs of control or eradication in the territory of the importing member;
- the relative cost-effectiveness of alternative approaches to limiting risks.

Trade agreements traditionally avoid such socio-economic assessments because of the subjectivity complications associated with them. Indeed, the WTO approach allegedly attempts to de-politicize trade and make it a function of comparative advantage (WTO, 1995), yet the SPS Agreement recognizes the socio-economic nature of food safety regulations and permits such consideration.

Fourth, and finally, under the SPS Agreement members may establish provisional SPS measures based on precaution in the event that there is insufficient scientific evidence to conduct an appropriate risk assessment. The agreement states: "In cases where the relevant scientific evidence is insufficient, a Member may provisionally adopt sanitary or phytosanitary measures on the basis of available pertinent information, including that from sanitary or phytosanitary measures applied by other Members. In such circumstances, Members shall seek to obtain additional information necessary for a more objective assessment of risk and review the sanitary or phytosanitary measure accordingly within a reasonable amount of time" (Art. 5:7). That is, members are permitted to establish trade barriers based on the precautionary principle. These barriers can remain in place until enough scientific evidence about the risk has been compiled. Indeed, the temporary barrier provision of the agreement is unique in terms of international trade agreements.

In short, the multilateral SPS Agreement permits significant discretion for member countries to impose market access barriers if they have a scientific justification for doing so. In this case, a scientific justification is one that is acceptable under the standards and standards-making procedures of the Codex Alimentarius.

As previously mentioned, with the enactment of the SPS Agreement it appeared that the multilateral food safety rules based on scientific assessments of actual risk had won the day and that a dramatic convergence of regional rules would soon follow. However, what has happened instead is the emergence of regional arrangements that protect members from this top–down "scientification" of the international food safety rules, which is accused of being insensitive to the political economy factors underlying domestic regulatory approaches.

I shall now examine the North–South and the transatlantic differences. Together, these two types of regulatory differences limit support for the multilateral system in favour of a regional approach more in tune with domestic concerns and preferences and capable of fortifying national regulatory autonomy against the imposition of "top–down" rules.

North–South differences in food safety regulations

There are two crucial reasons for the differences in regulatory approaches, in general, between the developed countries and the developing countries. The first is the income-elastic nature of food safety regulations. Domestic expectations on food safety levels and the need for regulations to ensure these levels tend to rise with domestic incomes. Essentially, when the security of a stable and sufficient food supply is the major concern, adding on enhanced food safety and quality assurance systems is not a priority. On the other hand, developed countries have pushed ahead with major changes to their national food safety systems, tying food safety to the overarching goal of food quality and increasing both the scientific basis for these measures and the industry's responsibility for this framework (Spriggs and Isaac, 2001). Hence, as the developed countries constantly raise the bar on minimum essential standards on food safety in reaction to consumer demands, the gap between food safety regulations in developed and developing countries is widening. This encourages regulatory regionalism in both directions. Developed countries may cluster together to ensure that their higher standards become global standards or to protect their domestic consumers from the "regulatory race to the bottom".[1] Developing countries may cluster together in a formal RTA or in a "Southern coalition" to ensure that multilateral rules for food safety regulations do not become legitimate barriers to trade because of the income-elastic concerns and preferences of consumers in developed countries.[2]

The second reason is a consequence of the first: developing countries tend to have a limited capability or capacity to employ the risk analysis framework in their food safety regulations in the same manner that it is applied in the developed countries and in international organizations such as Codex. The scientific risk analysis framework is widely considered by developed countries to be an effective framework for simultaneously addressing both the complexities and the limitations facing regulatory development as a result of sophisticated technologies such as GM crops. The risk analysis framework was first outlined in 1983 by the Redbook of the US National Academy of Sciences (1983). Although first outlined in the United States, the risk analysis framework has become the regulatory framework broadly employed in most developed countries (for example, Australia, Canada, Japan, and the United States) and within most regional arrangements (for example, the European Union, the North American Free Trade Agreement and the Australia–New Zealand Closer Economic Relations Agreement) and supported by many international organizations (for example, the WTO's SPS Agreement, the WHO, the FAO and the OECD).

According to the Redbook, the risk analysis framework is composed of three parts: risk assessment, risk management and risk communication. Risk assessment has the goal of, to the extent possible, developing objective, neutral, transparent and consensual information about the risks without normative influence. Risk assessment involves hazard identification, exposure assessment and risk characterization according to a sound scientific basis using accepted analytical methods and statistical inference techniques. The information gathered in the risk assessment stage is then used to inform the risk management process.

The goal of risk management is risk prevention and risk reduction. This involves incorporating the objective risk information into a regulatory response. Because risk management is where the regulatory position is adopted, this stage must also address the broader economic, political, social, moral and ethical factors beyond a scientific basis. In this sense, risk management explicitly requires compromise and concession as it balances the rights and interests of all stakeholders in order to establish an acceptable regulatory framework.

The Redbook specified that risk assessment techniques should be institutionally separated from risk management procedures. Essentially, it is vital to disentangle the objective, scientific risk assessment from the normative public response to risk.

Risk communication is a two-way flow of information between risk assessment and risk management as well as between regulators, industry and the public. The scientific risk assessment information must flow to the regulatory development process in risk management, but it is also necessary for the social parameters of risk management to flow back into the risk assessment techniques. In this sense, the goals of risk communication would be to reduce the information gap and to increase confidence in the regulatory framework through greater transparency.

A vital contribution of the Redbook's risk analysis framework was the integration of scientific analytical procedures into the regulatory development process. Science matters for two important reasons. First, scientific analysis has long striven to disentangle normative values from scientific discovery. Although a complete separation has never occurred (and will never occur), there is a level of universality to "science" that is not present in social beliefs, morals and ethics. Because regulations apply across a wide range of social beliefs, morals and ethics, they should endeavour to be as normative free as possible. For instance, food safety regulations should be focused on human safety, equally applicable to all citizens, and not on regulations that support the social values of some, while contravening the values of others.

Second, although scientific disagreement can and frequently does occur, the analytical methodology of science permits debate on disagreement subject to relatively accepted rules of evidence, unlike normative disagreements, which, being based on beliefs, have no apparent methodology or process for resolution. The risk analysis framework seeks to establish a sound scientific basis for risk assessment in order to develop, as much as possible, neutral and objective information to advise the risk management process, and risk communication is intended to provide transparency to the entire regulatory development process.

Regional trade agreements can play a vital role in making the risk analysis framework either a building block or a stumbling block in the creation of consistent North–South multilateral rules. As a building block, RTAs may encourage the technocratic implementation of the risk analysis framework, depoliticizing the process through the development of more effective and transparent infrastructure. As was detailed in chapter 6, Canadian and US assistance to Mexico for capacity-building is an important goal of the North American Free Trade Agreement (NAFTA). Indeed, in the previous case studies, this appears to be exactly what is occurring. Yet developing country food processors may find significant market access barriers in their way because the scientific standards are in place now but capacity-building takes time. During the transition, a significant loss of international competitiveness can occur. Moreover, in order to implement and manage the risk analysis framework properly, a national regulatory authority must have the political will to do so. This is not a problem in most developed countries, where food contamination crises have provided the political will to enhance the use of science in the food safety systems (Spriggs and Isaac, 2001). The problems arise in the developing countries. They tend to lack both the scientific capacity and the political will. This creates a significant North–South difference in views – at least in the short to medium term – on the role of the scientific risk analysis framework and the requirement for considerable scientific capacity in the multilateral food safety rules for market access.

The regional agreements that span developed and developing countries provide examples of how developing countries set their regional SPS obligations consistent with or lower than the WTO commitments. Essentially, the developing countries retain more discretion for trade barriers beyond just scientific justification. For example, the EU–Mexico Agreement (see chapter 4) stops short of substantive provisions on mutual recognition owing to the difficulties in negotiating a mutual recognition agreement with a country that has less capacity for conformance assessment provisions. Similarly, NAFTA (see chapter 6) places limits on the harmonization of standards and conformity assessments, although it should be noted that NAFTA's SPS obligations are very consistent with the multilateral rules under the WTO (see also Bredahl and Holleran, 1997). With respect to both the EU–Poland regional agreement (see chapter 3) and the Euro-Med Agreement (see chapter 4) it is clear that, for the developing countries, the SPS obligations must be consistent with the EU regulatory approach to food safety. Yet, as we shall see, the EU regulatory approach to food safety differs from the North American approach and from the multilateral approach under the WTO's SPS Agreement, despite the fact that the European Union agreed to this approach in the Uruguay Round. The implication is that transatlantic regulatory regionalism is being extended through further regional agreements.

Transatlantic differences in food safety regulations

Regulatory regionalism can exist among developed countries even though there tends to be broad agreement that the risk analysis framework is the most appropriate framework for food safety regulations. Countries may cluster into a regional arrangement as a proactive, international competitiveness strategy or as a reactive, regulatory protection strategy. With respect to the former strategy, the introduction of science into the domestic food safety system can be a source of international competitiveness. In the wake of many food contamination crises, food producers within a domestic jurisdiction with a credible, science-based system tend to have fewer market access difficulties. Countries with both the political will and the scientific capacity to bid up the risk analysis framework cluster together because this regionalism protects the national regulatory pursuit of increasingly science-based standards. This type of regionalism is reflected in the mutual recognition agreements signed between various countries in the meat industry. The majority of these agreements are between developed countries, such as Australia, Canada, the European Union, New Zealand and the United States, not between developed and developing countries (Spriggs and Isaac, 2001).

However, regulatory regionalism may emerge among developed countries as a reactive strategy to protect the regulatory approach of like-minded countries from the science-based multilateral rules designed to enhance international competitiveness. Indeed, it appears that the European Union is seeking to return to a regionally – not multilaterally – dominated food safety regulatory system. A White Paper on food safety in the European Union (European Commission, 2000) included a proposal for a European Food Safety Agency (EFSA).

The transatlantic conflict between the North American international competitiveness approach and the EU regulatory approach results from the fact that, even when two countries or regions follow the risk analysis framework in general, there are significant debates associated with how to properly implement it. The differences in approach are caused by differences both in domestic preferences and concerns and in food safety records. Indeed, it is very difficult to disentangle these two reasons because current preferences and concerns are generally the result of past contamination crises. In order to meet varying domestic demands, domestic jurisdictions must implement the framework according to different approaches.

A useful case study of the transatlantic differences is the trade dispute between the European Union and the United States and Canada over the use of growth-promoting hormones in beef production. The use of hormones in the production of beef has been a controversial issue in Europe for well over 20 years. In March 1988, an EU Directive (88/146/EEC) banned the use of six hormones in beef production, three naturally occurring ones – oestradiol-17ß, progesterone and testosterone – and three synthetic ones – trenbolone acetate, zeranol and melengestrol acetate (MGA). The directive applied a zero-tolerance policy to both domestic beef production and foreign (imported) beef products. As a result, North American beef (Canadian and US beef) containing such hormones was in effect prohibited from EU markets, regardless of the fact that hormone use had been approved as safe in North America.

In 1988, the ban was not in violation of GATT 1948 because it was being applied according to the principles of non-discrimination. In 1995, when the WTO came into force, those parties of export that felt that the ban was scientifically unjustified protectionism now had the legitimate opportunity to challenge the ban under the safety-related provisions of the SPS Agreement, specifically the SPS requirement that a trade barrier based on food safety have a "scientific justification". Canada and the United States complained, on behalf of their domestic beef producers, to the WTO that the EU regulations against imports into Europe of beef treated with growth hormones violated the European Union's obligations under the SPS Agreement (WTO, 1998). They argued that the ban was not consistent with Codex standards and that there was insufficient scientific justification for the European Union to impose a standard higher than the Codex standard. The Codex Alimentarius Commission (CAC) ruled, in 1995, on the maximum residue limits for the safe use of these hormones in beef production (CAC, 1995; and McDonald, 1998), essentially meaning that there was not an international standard supporting a zero-tolerance policy. Similarly, in 1995, an EU conference reported that the hormones were safe and within normal physiological ranges (*Europe*

Drug and Device Letter, 5 February 1996). Despite the advice from its own scientists as well as Codex, the European Commission maintained the ban.

The WTO Dispute Panel decision ruled against the EU ban, and the European Union promptly appealed against the decision. In its decision, the Appellate Body of the WTO was careful to argue that its decision was a "procedural ruling" on the basis of the wording of the SPS Agreement and not a decision about the permissible use of health and safety regulations by members. In fact, it has been argued that the Appellate Body does make efforts to uphold the sovereignty rights of members when making decisions about their obligations under the trade agreements (Jackson, 1996).

The Appellate Body ultimately held that the EC Directive did violate the SPS Agreement because the measures were not based on an appropriate risk assessment and were not scientifically justifiable. No risk assessment had been done for the MGA hormone, and scientific evidence from both North America and Europe along with the Codex standard suggested that the other five hormones were safe if properly administered. The evidence presented concerning the carcinogenic potential of increased hormone ingestion was found to be unrelated to the six hormones in question. The panel also found no evidence that any of the six hormones were being improperly administered on a widespread basis.

At this stage, it appeared that the multilateral rules supporting a distinctly North American approach to SPS measures had won the day and EU compliance would soon follow. However, this order has yet to be implemented. The European Union promptly informed the WTO that it must complete a new risk assessment and then implement new SPS measures to continue to ban hormone-treated beef. An arbitrator had ordered that the European Union must comply with the panel ruling within 15 months (that is, by 18 May 1999).

With respect to the risk analysis framework, the transatlantic difference may be summarized as follows: the North American approach is to use the scientific risk assessment information to *make* regulatory risk management decisions, whereas the EU approach is to use the scientific risk assessment only to *inform* the regulatory risk management decision. This interpretation explains why the European Union continued its ban despite the scientific evidence from its own scientists and from Codex on the safe use of these hormones. Essentially, the regulatory decision makers listened to the scientific information but weighed it against other, non-science factors, such as the concerns and preferences of European consumers and the political implications of dropping the ban. In North America, on the other hand, the scientific risk assessment information determines a risk level, and this is the only information used by the regulatory risk managers to make their decision; they do not entertain other, non-science factors.

This distinction also hints at a difference in the interpretation of the term "regulatory independence" as applied to food safety regulations. In North America, regulatory independence under the risk analysis framework means that objective, scientific risk analysis is independent of subjective political influence. This independence is believed to lead to food safety regulations focused on *actual* risk rather than food safety regulations that are political responses to *perceived* risk. In contrast, the equally compelling EU definition of regulatory independence means the regulatory decision maker is independent of the scientific process. That is, the decision maker is not the scientist but a publicly accountable, elected official in tune with domestic concerns and preferences and best able to make food safety decisions.

Therefore, despite the fact that both regions employ the risk analysis framework, there are important differences over how to implement it properly into food safety regulations. In fact, this general difference is exemplified in more recent transatlantic differences over genetically modified foods. No GM crops approved in the United States have not been approved in Canada, and vice versa, yet many varieties of GM crops approved as safe in North America have faced delayed market access to the European Union. With respect to regulatory independence, it is also useful to note that, to date, no GM crop approved as safe in North America has been disapproved of by the scientific risk assessors of the member states; however, the granting of approval has been delayed or denied when the independent political decision makers have become involved. On the one hand, it is easy to be cynical about this interpretation of "independence" because it seems to be congruent with "protectionism"; on the other hand, a food safety decision made according to domestic concerns and preferences (regardless of their basis) is a credible and legitimate regulatory approach.

The cases of beef and GM crops have reinforced transatlantic regulatory regionalism. The regional NAFTA approach, which is consistent with the multilateral approach under the SPS Agreement, limits the discretion of countries to impose regulatory barriers to the instance of a legitimate scientific justification determined through a risk analysis framework. Here the scientific risk assessment makes regulatory risk management decisions independently of the political process. The regional EU approach to food safety regulations grants greater discretion to impose regulatory barriers for reasons beyond just scientific justification. It supports the risk analysis framework where the scientific risk assessment only informs regulatory risk management decisions along with other, non-science information, and the decision is independent of the scientific process. In this sense, added discretion cannot be considered to be WTO-plus because, in fact, the added discretion makes the EU regional approach even more inconsistent with the multilateral framework.

The developed/developing country differences, together with the transatlantic differences, produce strong propensities for regulatory regionalism that undermine the multilateralization of food safety regulations and fragment international markets according to regional blocs, each interpreting and implementing the risk analysis framework in a different manner. Developing countries see the imposition of top–down, science-based food safety regulations as creating an ever-widening gap, whereas developed countries fully support the increasing use of science to both establish and settle multilateral trade rules for food safety regulations. Yet, how precisely this is done has given rise to transatlantic regulatory regionalism as well, which looks set to continue with respect to beef and GM crops. Therefore, in relation to the questions posed at the beginning of this chapter, regional food safety rules tend to reinforce national regulatory autonomy, protecting it from the influence of the multilateral approach to the risk analysis framework and from the divergent interpretations of this framework, and ultimately becoming a stumbling block to the multilateral system.

Eco-labelling

In this section, eco-labelling schemes and their relationship with RTAs are examined as a case study of environmental protection measures.[3] Similar in format to the discussion in the previous section on food safety regulations, this section begins with an identification of eco-labelling schemes, and then examines the "North–South" differences and the transatlantic differences in approach, respectively.

According to the International Organization for Standardization (ISO, 1998), eco-labelling schemes are voluntary, market-based instruments used by manufacturers or retailers to assist consumers in identifying products with a reduced environmental impact.[4] There are three categories of labels to consider (Consumers International, 1999):

- Type I: voluntary programmes, adjudicated by independent third parties, that rank products within a specific product category according to their comparative or relative environmental impact based upon established criteria.
- Type II: voluntary, first-party (producer, distributor or retailer) declaration of a product's environmental sensitivity, such as "biodegradable".

- Type III: voluntary environmental declarations according to quantified life-cycle assessments that are independently verified.

The focus will be on Type I labels because of the involvement of the public sector in their development, implementation and management. Despite the voluntary nature of eco-labelling schemes, the public sector involvement is the reason such schemes are often viewed as a type of environmental regulation. Foreign countries may be concerned that the standards established under the scheme are de facto import standards for foreign products. Hence, any mention of eco-labels will imply Type I labels unless otherwise specified.

As a result of the growing awareness of environmental problems, there has been a rapid development of (mostly public) national eco-labelling schemes. For instance, national schemes have been developed in Brazil (Brazilian Eco-labelling), Canada (Terra Choice), France (NF-Environment), Germany (Blue Angel), Sweden (Good Green Buy), the United States (Green Seal, Energy Star) and Zimbabwe (Environment 2000).[5] However, regional schemes have also emerged such as the Nordic White Swan scheme and the EU Flower scheme, both of which have a significant public role.

Each of these eco-labelling schemes shares the goal of empowering consumers to make environmentally sustainable consumption choices. They also share a distinctly "bottom–up" approach to the development, implementation and management of the schemes. Each scheme is governed by particular principles, which cannot be disentangled from domestic preferences and concerns. Further, the focus of the various national schemes tends to reflect industry capabilities as well. For instance, the US-based Green Seal scheme has tended to focus on paints and thinners. This was an industry sector in the United States that was already a global leader in enhancing environmental sustainability and also a sector that the general public considered to be a large source of pollution. On the other hand, the Nordic White Swan scheme – a regional scheme – has had a focus on pulp and paper manufacturing which, like the US example, was an industry sector that was already a global leader in enhancing environmental sustainability and a concern among the Nordic region population.

As can be seen, the "bottom–up" approach to eco-labelling schemes means that the multinational growth of any one scheme is bounded by shared industry capabilities and domestic concerns. Without this common foundation, the likelihood of developing an effective scheme decreases dramatically. In fact, this may be shown by the difficulties that the EU Flower scheme has faced during its development. The EU scheme was established on 23 March 1992 (Council Regulation EEC No. 880/92) and has yet to be fully developed and implemented in a manner acceptable to the member states. Two primary forces were behind its inception. First was the increase in national eco-labelling schemes within the common market. The concern of the European Commission was that the various schemes would create internal market fragmentation and, hence, barriers to trade. As a result, the EU Flower scheme was proposed in order to integrate the national schemes into a European scheme, consistently implemented and managed in all member states. The second driving force was the fact that the eco-labelling schemes were emerging on both transatlantic and multilateral trade agendas. The concern was that the European Union needed a strong and cohesive scheme in order to ensure both that any multilateral market access rules adequately incorporated the concerns and preferences of the European Union and that national schemes within the European Union did not threaten to fragment the EU market. However, integrating the common market has proven much harder than originally believed because industry capabilities and "bottom–up" domestic environmental concerns are not the same in, say, Sweden and Greece. In this sense, the EU Flower scheme is indeed bounded by the non-homogeneity of environmental concerns within the common market.

Therefore, despite the common goal of empowering consumers to make environmentally sustainable consumption choices, different eco-labelling schemes have been developed according to particular national circumstances and environmental concerns. The concerns of one country may be different from those of other countries, resulting in different approaches to eco-labelling. These differences in approach have also led to conflicts between national regulatory policies and the multilateral trading regime.

Two broad conflicts are most notable: North–South conflicts and transatlantic conflicts. The key point is that these differences decrease the likelihood that multilateral trading rules acceptable to all countries can be established. Instead, they enhance the attractiveness of RTAs to those who support national regulatory autonomy over eco-labelling regulations.

North–South differences in eco-labelling schemes

There are significant differences between developed and developing countries in general on the role for eco-labelling schemes in market access rules. Essentially, the developed countries think that such schemes are legitimate constraints on trade and should be handled within the multilateral trading regime, whereas developing countries think that rules on environmental performance are not legitimate trade-constraining measures and, hence, there is no place for eco-labelling regulations in international trade rules at all.

At the heart of the North–South differences is the fact that eco-labelling regulations are income elastic in nature. As with food safety regulations, domestic expectations on environmental performance tend to rise with domestic incomes. Developing countries, with more fundamental concerns over stable economic development and growth providing for fiscal health, simply do not have the political will to focus on environmental performance. Another key difference – essentially flowing out of the first – is the scientific capability and regulatory capacity to conduct life-cycle assessments and sustainability impact assessments. Even if developing countries were willing to implement more stringent standards on environmental performance, they may not be able to do so. The impact of these differences on the multilateral system is that they result in two very divergent views on how the international trade regime should deal with environmental performance regulations such as eco-labelling. The "North" tends to feel that, in general, tying environmental performance to trade rules is a progressive step as the trade regime increasingly moves into areas of national competence. For instance, during the lead-up to the 1999 Ministerial Meeting of the WTO, the European Commission (1999) developed a comprehensive sustainability impact assessment (SIA) of its trade policy positions proposed for the next round of multilateral negotiations. As a result of this general acceptance that environmental performance is the next phase of the trading regime, there tends to be acceptance that multilateral rules covering this area must be developed. The "North" tends to believe that national regulations such as eco-labelling should be specified within the scope (in-scope) of international trading rules; that is, there should be some scope for member countries to differentiate between products based on their environmental performance, given certain criteria have been met (similar to the way that food safety rules are now codified in the SPS Agreement and food safety bans are legitimate if a scientific justification exists). In the next subsection, I shall reveal that, despite broad agreement among developed countries that environmental standards should be in-scope, there is significant disagreement over how exactly to do this.

Unsurprisingly, the "South" tends to disagree with this position on a fundamental level, and its disagreement mirrors the reasons given in the food safety case. Developing countries argue that, not having the same level of development, they do not have the same level of industrial capability or the same level of domestic concern about environmental performance. Hence, trade rules that on the one hand impose the standards of environmental performance in the developed "North" while on the other hand limiting the ability of the developing "South" to evolve standards are viewed as multilateral rules that cut twice, and cut deep. The "South" believes that rules on environmental performance are not legitimate trade-constraining measures and, hence, there is no place for eco-labelling regulations in international trade rules, even when they are voluntary. They should be out-scope, which means that there should be no legitimate use of environmental performance standards based on process and production methods under international trading rules. Indeed, both the Shrimp–Turtle and the Tuna–Dolphin decisions of the GATT and WTO, respectively, supported this view (WTO, 2001; also see Isaac et al., 2002).

As a result, the North–South differences in approach to eco-labelling regulations result in a systemic case of regulatory regionalism in which the developed countries – linked by a common willingness and ability to increase standards on environmental performance – want eco-labelling regulations in-scope to multilateral rules. This position is set against that of the developing countries – linked by a common unwillingness and inability to increase standards on environmental performance – which want all environmental regulations out-scope of the multilateral trading rules. Regulatory regionalism gains at the expense of the multilateral system, because regulatory regionalism supports the national regulatory autonomy of the various member countries within the region.[6]

Transatlantic differences in eco-labelling schemes

Despite the fact that developed countries in general think that regulations on eco-labels should be in-scope of trade agreements, there is significant transatlantic difference on how they should be incorporated. There are two distinct points of debate. The first is associated with the role of the public sector in the development, implementation, management and enforcement of eco-labelling schemes. The second is that Canada and the United States generally feel that publicly funded eco-labelling regulations should adhere to the principles of non-discrimination, including "like products" and the subsequent dismissal of process and production methods (PPMs), whereas the European Union feels that eco-labelling regulations should be exempted from the traditional non-discrimination principle so that they can focus on PPMs without violating multilateral trade rules.

With respect to the first difference, there is concern about the legitimacy of the role of public bodies in eco-labelling schemes under the multilateral trading system. Canada and the United States, along with some developing countries (which have implemented privately run schemes), are concerned that publicly funded and/or administered eco-labelling schemes in Europe may create de facto barriers to competitive market access because they display national and common EU environmental preferences for particular PPMs. As a result, this group would like to see public schemes – but not privately run schemes – under the discipline of the WTO so that potential barriers to trade are subject to the non-discrimination obligations of the multilateral trade agreements.

On the other hand, the position within Europe, which is shared by consumer and environmental organizations, is that eco-labelling schemes are simply not a trade issue. It is argued that the schemes are voluntary, market access is possible without an eco-label and, to date, there is no evidence of market access restrictions caused by eco-labelling schemes. Further, the public role is considered important for supporting the development of the schemes, and to achieve environmental sustainability it is absolutely crucial to base the award of an eco-label on PPMs. Trade neutrality, combined with the important role of the public sector in the development, implementation and management of eco-labelling schemes, is the basis of the EU argument that eco-labelling regulations should be in-scope but exempted from the hurdle of non-discrimination. Without an exemption, this group fears that environmental sustainability objectives will be subordinated to trade principles, thus preventing the focus on PPMs or the role of the public sector in their success. With an exemption, however, the unique characteristics of the eco-labelling schemes that are not congruent with traditional non-discrimination can be protected so that the schemes can enhance the environmental performance of various industrial sectors.

With respect to the second difference, Canada and the United States generally feel that having eco-labelling regulations in-scope of the multilateral rules means that they should adhere to the principles of non-discrimination, including "like products" and the subsequent dismissal of PPMs. They argue that such PPMs may be inappropriate or unavailable to exporters. Further, they argue that the use of PPMs contravenes trade principles in two ways: first, trade agreements traditionally focus on "like" products, not on processes; second, trade agreements attempt to limit the extra-territorial extension of domestic policy preferences. Unless eco-labels can overcome the traditional hurdle of non-discrimination, they are not considered legitimate and, consequently, are in violation of the obligations of the WTO. The European Union, on the other hand, believes that, although eco-labelling regulations should be in-scope, they should be in-scope with *exemptions* from the traditional application of non-discrimination, much as the SPS Agreement allows for legitimate violation of non-discrimination. This means that eco-labelling regulations should be exempted from non-discrimination so that they can focus on process and production methods without violating multilateral trade rules. Of course, to make this work, there would have to be some kind of legitimacy trigger for such exemptions similar to the scientific justification trigger for SPS measures. It may seem that an appropriate solution is in fact the increased scientification of the environmental measures; member countries can invoke Article XX(b) exemptions if they have a legitimate scientific justification of environmental risk. However, just like the food safety case, such a trigger essentially decreases the discretion that countries have to impose environmental standards, and this limitation is likely not to be supported.

Together, the "North–South" differences and the transatlantic differences in interpretation about how to deal with eco-labelling regulations in-scope of the multilateral system have led to trade friction. The developing countries see the imposition of environmental performance measures, whether voluntary or not, as non-transparent and complex non-tariff barriers set punitively high. In contrast, developed countries see environmental performance measures as the next logical inclusion in the evolution of the multilateral trade system. However, this inclusion itself has been controversial among developed countries, as the transatlantic differences illustrate. Therefore, with respect to the questions posed at the beginning of this chapter, regional rules reinforce national regulatory autonomy, protecting eco-labelling regulations from the different approaches of other regions and ultimately becoming a stumbling block to the multilateral system.

Implications

The three research questions that have guided this analysis form the framework for this concluding section. The first question asked whether RTAs associated with food safety and environmental measures are a WTO-plus building block for multilateral rules or a stumbling block creating regulatory regionalism. The analysis suggests that food safety and environmental measures are congruent with RTAs not as a proactive building block for multilateralism but instead as a reactive stumbling block imposed to protect the countries within the RTA from divergent approaches embodied either in other regional arrangements or in the multilateral system. The reason for this is linked to the inherently bottom–up nature of food safety and environmental protection measures. Both are a function of domestic political economy factors shaped by domestic concerns, preferences and crises and very resistant to compromise in order to meet market liberalization objectives. Regional arrangements building on the strength and legitimacy of this consumer and environmental protectionism generally enjoy a significant level of public support.

Building on this assessment, the second research question focused on the impact of RTAs on market opening. RTAs make market access easier for countries within the arrangement because their shared approaches are more likely to result in mutual recognition. This has been the case for beef and GM crops in NAFTA and for beef in the Closer Economic Relations Agreement. For countries outside the regional arrangement and seeking to penetrate the regional market, access may in fact be more difficult, as indicated by the market access to the European Union for GM crops approved in North America.

Finally, the third research question asked whether or not the apparent transatlantic regulatory regionalism could be expected to converge or diverge over time. Given that the regional arrangements are protecting a different approach to regulations, convergence at the transatlantic level would require a convergence in regulatory approach. This will come about only through a convergence in domestic political economy factors. With very different experiences of food safety crises and with seemingly different attitudes towards the role of government in environmental protection, it appears that such a convergence is at best a long-term prospect. In the short to medium term, RTAs are likely to entrench differences in approach rather than encourage a convergence towards consistent and stable multilateral rules.

The above assessment implies that there are perhaps some bottom–up policy domains with unique and sensitive political characteristics that are incongruent with trade liberalization objectives such that multilateral trade liberalization rules cannot be expected to deal with the international market fragmentation. Indeed, this undermines the notion that RTAs may contribute to the multilateral process by enhancing procedural and technical market access rules by working at a technocratic level. Clearly, food safety and environmental protection measures require too much domestic discretion, in order to meet often unique political economy factors, to be dealt with at a technocratic level. For example, given the EU approach to the risk analysis framework, in which scientific risk assessment only informs the risk management decision, GM crops approved by the various EU scientific committees have faced delayed or denied market access because of discretionary decisions made at the political level of risk management (Isaac, 2002a). Multilateral WTO rules imposing a strict scientific justification criterion on the food safety and environmental protection regulations would essentially be a ruling against the way in which the European Union regulates these policy domains – a result that would at the very least be unpopular and at the most completely undermine EU confidence in and support for the multilateral rules.

Notes

1. Examples of developed countries clustering together include the proposed European Food Safety Authority in the European Commission's White Paper on Food Safety (2000), as well as the food safety initiatives proposed by the Organisation for Economic Co-operation and Development (see www.oecd.org).
2. Examples of developing countries clustering together include the Caribbean Community and Common Market (CARICOM) – Antigua and Barbuda, the Bahamas, Barbados, Belize, Dominica, Grenada, Guyana, Haiti, Jamaica, Montserrat, St. Kitts and Nevis, St. Lucia, Suriname, St. Vincent & the Grenadines and Trinidad and Tobago – and Mercosur – Argentina, Brazil, Paraguay and Uruguay.
3. This discussion of the trade-related aspects of eco-labelling is derived from Isaac (2002b).
4. For a list of various eco-labels see the US-based Consumers Union (http://www.eco-labels.org/home.cfm) or the Global Eco-Labelling Network (http://www.gen.gr.jp/).
5. See Global Eco-Labelling Network at http://www.gen.gr.jp/product_c.html.
6. Examples of a regional cluster approach for developing countries to promote common environmental policies – more broadly than eco-labelling – are included in a working paper by the Third World Network (2001).

REFERENCES

Bredahl, M. E., and E. Holleran (1997), "Technical Regulation and Food Safety in NAFTA", in R. M. A. Loyns, R. D. Knutson, K. Meilke and D. Sumner (eds.), *Harmonization/Convergence/Compatibility in Agriculture and Agri-Food Policy: Canada, United States and Mexico*, Proceedings of the Third Agricultural and Food Policy Systems Information Workshop, University of Manitoba (Canada), University of Guelph (Canada), Texas A & M (United States), University of California, Davis (United States), pp. 71–86.

CAC (Codex Alimentarius Commission) (1995), *Report of the 21st Session*, Rome, 3–7 July, ALINORM 95/37 Appendix 2, Rome: Food and Agriculture Organization of the United Nations.

Consumers International (1999) *Green Labels: Consumer Interests and Transatlantic Trade Tensions in Eco-Labelling*, Report to Consumers International by the International Trade Policy Unit, London School of Economics and Political Science, London: Consumers International.

European Commission (1999), "Pascal Lamy Exchanges Views with NGO's", Brussels, 7 October; available at http://www.europa.eu.int/comm/trade/speeches_articles/spla02en.htm.

——— (2000), *White Paper on Food Safety*, COM(1999) 719 Final, Brussels; available at http://europa.eu.int/comm/dgs/health_consumer/library/pub/pub06_en.pdf/.

FAO (Food and Agriculture Organization) (1998), *Understanding the Codex Alimentarius: Origins of the Codex Alimentarius*, Rome: FAO, available at http://www.fao.org/docrep/w9114e/W9114e01htm/.

GATT (General Agreement on Tariffs and Trade) (1994), *The Results of the Uruguay Round of Multilateral Trade Negotiations: The Legal Texts: Agree-*

ment on Sanitary and Phyto-sanitary Measures (SPS Agreement), Geneva: GATT Secretariat.

Horton, L. (1997), "International Harmonization of Food and Veterinary Medicine Regulation", in R. P. Brady, R. M. Cooper and R. S. Silverman (eds.), *Fundamentals of Law and Regulation*, Washington DC: FDLI, pp. 381–484.

Isaac, G. E. (2002a), *Agricultural Biotechnology and Transatlantic Trade: Regulatory Barriers to GM Crops*, Oxford: CABI Publishing, p. 7.

–––––– (2002b), "Eco-labels and International Trade", Working Paper, August, available from isaac@commerce.usask.ca.

Isaac, G. E. and W. A. Kerr (2003), "Genetically Modified Organisms and Trade Rules: Identifying Important Challenges for the WTO", *The World Economy* 26(1): 29–42.

Isaac, G. E., M. Phillipson and W. A. Kerr (2002), *International Regulation of Trade in the Products of Biotechnology*, Estey Centre Research Papers No. 2, Saskatoon, Canada: Estey Centre for Law and Economics in International Trade; available at http://www.esteycentre.ca/.

ISO (International Organization for Standardization) (1998), *ISO 14000 – Meet the Whole Family*, Geneva: ISO Central Secretariat.

Jackson, J. (1996), "WTO Dispute Settlement Procedures: A Preliminary Assessment", in J. Schott (ed.), *The World Trading System: Challenges Ahead*, Washington DC: Institute for International Economics, pp. 153–65.

McDonald, J. (1998), "Big Beef up or Consumer Health Threat? The WTO Food Safety Agreements, Bovine Growth Hormone and the Precautionary Principle", *Environmental Planning and Law Journal* 15(2), pp. 115–23.

National Academy of Sciences (NAS), Committee on the Institutional Means for Assessment of Risks to Public Health, Commission of Life Sciences (1983), *Risk Assessment in the Federal Government: Managing the Process*, Washington DC: National Research Council, National Academy Press.

Spriggs, J., and G. Isaac (2001), *Food Safety and International Competitiveness: The Case of Beef*. Oxford: CABI Publishing.

Third World Network (2001), "International Environmental Governance: Some Issues from a Developing Country Perspective", available at http://www.twnside.org.sg/title/ieg.htm.

WTO (World Trade Organization) (1995), *Regionalism and the World Trading System*, Geneva: WTO Secretariat.

–––––– (1998), *Appellate Decision: EC – Measures Concerning Meat and Meat Products (Hormones) – Complaint by the United States and Canada*, AB-1997-4, AB WT/DS26/R/USA and WT/DS48/R/Can, Geneva: WTO.

–––––– (2001), *United States – Import Prohibition of Certain Shrimp and Shrimp Products. Recourse to Article 21,5 of the DSU by Malaysia*, Appellate Body Decision WTO/DS58/AB/RW, 22 October.

10

Regulations confronting trade in services

Bertrall Ross

Introduction

An important debate in the study of international political economy is over the issue of multilateralism versus regionalism and, in particular, whether regional trading arrangements (RTAs) work as a building block or a stumbling block to multilateralism.[1] The debate (Lawrence, 1995, among others) revolves around the issue of whether regionalism serves as an alternative to multilateralism, as a useful supplement to multilateralism, or as a means of accelerating the multilateral process. Much of this debate has focused on the goods market and the accompanying welfare effects of regionalism on the global trading structure. In particular it has used the Vinerian approach (see Viner, 1950) of calculating whether RTAs are trade creating or trade diverting in determining whether RTAs are beneficial or detrimental to the multilateral trading system. This emphasis on goods has resulted in a tariff-based examination of the multilateralism versus regionalism debate.

In contrast to the wealth of literature focusing on the goods aspect of this debate, very little attention has been paid to whether RTAs serve as a building block or a stumbling block to the elimination of regulatory barriers to trade. These regulatory barriers are especially prominent in the services market, which by many calculations amounts to 20 per cent of global trade. The negotiation of the General Agreement on Trade in Services (GATS) resulted in the emergence of a multilateral regime dealing with trade in services, which included a set of principles and approaches to the liberalization of trade in services. Unlike the liberalization of goods, the focus of services market liberalization is on domestic laws and regulations that act as impediments to trade in services.

The GATS does not represent the first attempt to eliminate discriminatory regulations and rationalize non-discriminatory regulation in order to liberalize trade in services. Regional initiatives, in particular those established in the European Union, served as a forerunner to the multilateral initiative. Also, at the same time that the GATS regime was being developed, another initiative was taking place in North America with provisions for services included in the North American Free Trade Agreement (NAFTA). The regional initiatives in Europe and North America represent the most influential models for addressing questions of regulatory barriers to trade. They also represent two divergent approaches towards dealing with the liberalization of trade in services. Despite their differences, it will be argued that both initiatives serve as a building block for the multilateral liberalization of the services market.

In important ways these initiatives go further than GATS in achieving the objectives of non-discrimination and increased market access and transparency. They provide a deeper form of integration with their comprehensive coverage of service sectors and innovative mechanisms for greater transparency and market access. The ability of NAFTA to integrate a developing country into an important service regime is a development that has not yet been paralleled by the GATS initiative. At the same time, the EU initiative has resulted in dramatic regulatory reform in the member states that has facilitated market access and produced arguably the most integrated services market in the world. The NAFTA and EU initiatives on services liberalization have had a binding effect in which governments' reforms are " 'locked in' due to regional commitments and help to demonstrate to trading partners that the domestic reforms or policies are 'for real' " (Yeung et al., 1999, p. 21).

At the same time it could be argued that these RTAs are inherently discriminatory towards third countries. Although GATS allows for an exception from its principle of most favoured nation (MFN) in Article V, which makes provisions for the creation and maintenance of regional integration agreements, some would argue that these initiatives have been harmful to the multilateral process. These commentators continue the arguments presented in the multilateralism versus regionalism debate that focused on the goods market. In particular, they argue that these regional agreements are trade diverting in certain areas.[2] But this is a difficult argument to make because there is little empirical evidence to support the claim that the agreements are trade diverting and also because, prior to these regional agreements, there was very little trade in services with third countries outside the regional agreements.[3]

The most credible argument regarding regional agreements as stumbling blocks to multilateralism focuses on the differences in the approaches of NAFTA and the European Union in the liberalization of trade in services. This divergence in approaches could serve as a stumbling block if it makes it difficult or impossible to negotiate increasingly comprehensive multilateral agreements. In this case, regulatory regionalism emerges in which the differences in regulatory systems serve to limit trade. As will be shown in the following pages, the approaches of NAFTA and the European Union are quite distinct. These differences are based in large part on the differences in the levels of integration in the European Union and NAFTA, with the objective in the Union being the creation of a single market whereas that of NAFTA is the creation of a free trade area of three separate markets. But it will be argued that, despite the divergences in approach, the NAFTA and EU initiatives do not result in the development of competing regulatory regionalism, but instead have a certain synergy from which the multilateral process builds.

In the first part of the chapter, I will examine GATS – its goals, principles and approaches towards the liberalization of trade in services. In this examination, I will also look at the limitations of the agreement, and in particular the lack of sectoral coverage and transparency that result from the agreement. Secondly, I will analyse the approach of the European Union, taking into account the distinctive nature of integration in the Union. This analysis will incorporate the history of attempts at service market integration. Other issues that will be discussed are the additional mechanisms of transparency of regulation, the sectoral coverage of the agreement, the binding effect of regulatory reform on participating countries and the institutions created by the European Union to deal with disputes over issues of market access and discrimination. Thirdly, I will examine the NAFTA approach. I will argue that NAFTA represents a GATS-plus agreement with similar strategies to attain market access and non-discrimination. It builds upon GATS through its comprehensive coverage of sectors and the listing of reservations that enhance market access and transparency. Other issues of importance that will be discussed with reference to NAFTA are the ratchet clause, which serves to stimulate regulatory reform and the elimination of barriers, and the institutional mechanisms for dealing with disputes. Finally, through an analysis of trade in financial services, I will show the dynamic gains from trade in services and demonstrate that, despite the differences in approach, a certain synergy has been created between the European Union and NAFTA. Before getting into the heart of this chapter, however, a brief examination of the differences between services and goods will help in developing the framework for the discussion to follow.

The difference between goods and services

In 1993, global trade in services stood at US$930 billion, which was equal to 22.2 per cent of global trade, compared with 18.8 per cent of total trade in 1980. Countries of the Organisation for Economic Co-operation and Development (OECD) accounted for approximately 80 per cent of this trade during both periods (Hoekman and Kostecki, 1995, p. 127). There are a number of differences between services and goods that result in differences in the modes of trade and the barriers that impede trade.

Services are often intangible and cannot be stored. Many services are not tradable, in the cross-border manner that goods are available to be traded. And, in many cases, the temporary physical movement of provider or consumer is not sufficient for a feasible exchange. Another aspect of services is that they tend to be invisible, meaning that governments cannot see services cross their borders. As a result, the imposition of border barriers such as tariffs and duties is ineffective in impeding trade in services, therefore "controls on the sale and consumption of imported services are usually attached to domestic regulatory programs that are aimed at domestic objectives" (Feketekuty, 1998, p. 130).

The major problem with regulatory barriers to trade in services as opposed to border measures placed on goods is that these barriers are usually not transparent, thus making it difficult for the foreign service provider to identify the impediments to trade. The lack of transparency discourages service providers from undertaking major commitments when they do not have very good information about the restrictions that they are likely to face in the foreign market. "Uncertainty about restrictive regulations governments might impose in the future can be as much a barrier to trade as restrictive measures currently in effect" (Feketekuty, 1998, p. 133).

Transparency provides an element of predictability about the conditions for access to and operation of the foreign market to the providers and allows them to assess the costs and benefits of operating in a market. It also makes it possible for service providers to differentiate between established regulations and discretionary decisions that inhibit the functioning of the business. This ability to differentiate must be supplemented by an appellate procedure and dispute settlement institutions that allow the provider to contest the fairness of discretionary regulations that act as impediments to the service provider.

Owing to the intangible and invisible nature of services, trade in services has been difficult to quantify. Very few statistics on services are maintained, and none have proven to be an effective indicator of the amount of services traded. Therefore it has been difficult to assess the gains from trade in services. Policy makers argue that the greatest benefit of services market integration is its dynamic effects on innovation, productivity improvement and investment, and thus on growth. The integration of markets through the liberalization of services trade incorporating the right of establishment increases the size of the market and gives rise to more competition, resulting in a decrease in oligopolistic mark-ups and reduced market segmentation. The increased market size may enable the profitable provision of an increasingly diverse array of services, thus generating welfare gains resulting from increased variety of services. Increased competition will also provide an impetus for innovation and technological improvements that reduce the costs to the consumers and providers of the service.

Therefore, initiatives to facilitate trade in services are important for the economy as a whole. But the liberalization of services trade is very different from that of goods trade. The European Union and NAFTA employed approaches to alleviate these regulatory barriers to services that thus far have served as a building block for the multilateral foundation established in the GATS. And that is where my attention will now turn.

The General Agreement on Trade in Services

The conclusion of the General Agreement on Trade in Services (GATS) during the Uruguay Round marked the first time that internationally agreed rules and commitments were extended to trade in services. The agreement attained during the Uruguay Round represented merely a beginning that was similar to the limited tariff-cutting that was undertaken when the General Agreement on Tariffs and Trade (GATT) was launched in 1947. Thus, the primary function of the initial GATS negotiation was to bind the status quo and establish a foundation for future rounds of negotiation.

To a great extent, the principles established in GATS were modelled after those of GATT, although their applications differed because of the dissimilarities between goods and services. GATS also differs from GATT in that obligations to liberalize depend on what each member has undertaken in its own schedule rather than on obligations based on general rules and principles as established by the GATT. This arrangement in GATS makes it difficult to assess exactly what rights and obligations members of the World Trade Organization (WTO) have assumed under the services packages (WTO Secretariat, 1999). The overall liberalizing modality of GATS is a sectoral, gradual approach to the opening of services markets (Stephenson, 1999).

The basic aim of GATS is to open up trade in services in order to contribute to economic development, while recognizing the need for members to regulate the supply of services to meet domestic policy objectives. The three major goals of GATS are non-discrimination between trade partners through the granting of MFN status, non-discrimination between domestic and foreign firms through the establishment of the principle of national treatment of foreign firms, and transparency of governmental and sub-governmental regulations (Dobson and Jacquet, 1998).

The scope and coverage of GATS are defined in Article I by making the agreement applicable to measures taken by WTO members that affect trade in services. GATS commitments and obligations are binding on central, regional and local governments, and all services are covered except those "supplied in the exercise of governmental authority".[4] GATS establishes MFN as a general obligation on all sectors, with certain exceptions. National treatment and market access are commitment-specific obligations that are based on the schedule of commitments established by member states. The GATS process involved the establishment of a positive list of sectors in which the member is willing to make commitments of national treatment and market access. It also involved a negative list of derogations from these principles. In sectors not scheduled, the member is not required to make a commitment to liberalize beyond the general obligation of MFN and transparency. In scheduled sectors, the broad obligations of market access and national treatment apply, except in subsectors where members have formulated exceptions individually. Members may also pick and choose among the modes of delivery for which their sectoral commitments will be valid (Dobson and Jacquet, 1998). This division of services trade into modes is an important distinction, to which I will now turn.

Article I establishes a comprehensive definition of services, dividing them into four different modes of supply: cross-border, consumption abroad, commercial presence in the consuming territory and presence of natural persons. Cross-border trade in services (Mode 1) is equivalent to the mode by which goods are traded in which the geographical separation between seller and buyer is maintained and the service crosses national frontiers. Mode 2, or consumption abroad, involves the movement of the consumer to the supplying country, as is the case with tourism or the pursuit of educational opportunities abroad. Mode 3 (commercial presence of the foreign supplier in the territory of another state) is the most prevalent mode of supply of services. It was also the most difficult mode to negotiate during the Uruguay Round because it goes directly to internal policy issues such as the right of establishment, which requires a corresponding freedom of capital movement across frontiers. In many cases Mode 3 is bound with Mode 4 (the presence of natural persons) because the establishment of a foreign service provider usually requires the movement of personnel to be employed in this firm.

General obligations and disciplines are established in Part II of GATS. These obligations and disciplines apply to all service sectors regardless of whether or not they are included in the member's schedules of liberalization commitments. The principle of most favoured nation states that, "with respect to any measure covered by this Agreement, each Member shall accord immediately and unconditionally to services and service suppliers of any other Member treatment no less favorable than it accords to like services and service suppliers of any other country" (GATS Art. II:1). But this general obligation is qualified by exemptions that were allowed during the Uruguay Round in order to achieve agreement on the GATS package. As a result, more than 70 members made their scheduled commitments subject to a further list of exemptions from Article II (WTO Secretariat, 1999). These exemptions were governed by conditions set out in an Annex of GATS, which made it clear that no new exemptions could be granted through this process and that they were subject to a time limit of no longer than 10 years.

GATS allowed two other important departures from MFN. Article V sets forth rules on regional integration agreements, and is modelled after Article XXIV in GATT. Article V allows members "to participate in RTAs that discriminate against the services or service providers of other countries" (Stephenson, 2000, p. 89). The rationale behind this derogation from the principle of MFN treatment was the view that regional integration agreements would serve as a building block to the multilateral process by achieving deeper integration and contributing to further liberalization of the multilateral trading system. But, in order to provide constraints on these preferential trading arrangements so that they would not harm the multilateral system, Article V establishes a set of requirements that must be met by all economic integration agreements. These agreements must cover "substantially all trade", result in the removal of "substantially all discrimination" between the parties to an agreement and not raise the overall level of barriers to trade in services to outside countries. These requirements are to ensure that the agreement facilitates trade amongst its members without harming the ability of non-members to trade with the states participating in the agreement.

A second important departure from the MFN treatment established in GATS is the promotion of mutual recognition in Article VII. This article allows "WTO members to enter into Mutual Recognition Agreements

(MRAs) with regards to 'education or experience obtained, requirements met, or licenses or certifications granted' thus deviating from the MFN principle enshrined in Article II" (Zampetti, 1999, p. 296). Members are thus allowed to enter into bilateral agreements that result in the reciprocal granting of a more favoured national treatment, through the recognition of the standards of another state as equivalent to those established domestically, without extending that treatment to other members. Mutual recognition facilitates trade in services by eliminating the need for foreign service providers to abide by a different set of rules that may act as a barrier to commercial establishment. The only major requirement set forth in Article VII is that "members wishing to enter into negotiations for a MRA are required to inform the Council for Trade in Services about their intent so as to 'provide adequate opportunity' to any other Member to indicate their interest in participating in the negotiations before they enter a substantive phase" (Zampetti, 1999, p. 298). These two derogations from MFN treatment established a means by which regional agreements and GATS could be made compatible and deeper integration could be achieved within the context of the NAFTA and the European Union.

Part III of the GATS deals with the principle of national treatment and rules of market access. In contrast to MFN treatment, which applies generally to all sectors, national treatment and market access apply only to the scheduled sectors set out by the member states. Article XVI states that "each member is to give no less favorable treatment to the services and service suppliers of other members than is provided in its schedule of commitments" (WTO Secretariat, 1999). Thus the article stipulates the minimum required treatment of service suppliers allowed to operate in member states. The remainder of the article establishes six forms of measures affecting market access that cannot be applied unless specified in the schedules.[5] The limitation of the national treatment obligation to scheduled sectors allows states to maintain a regulatory advantage for domestic service suppliers in unscheduled sectors.

Transparency issues are dealt with in Articles III and IV of GATS. Article III requires each member "to publish promptly all relevant measures of general application that affect the operation of the agreement" (WTO Secretariat, 1999). Article IV contains requirements on the administration of domestic regulations to ensure their fairness and impartiality. Unlike the national treatment and market access provisions, the transparency obligation applies generally to all service sectors. Each member is required to establish one or more enquiry points, which are "aimed at facilitating responses to requests for information from other Members" on the regulations employed in service sectors (OECD, 2000). Through these enquiry points, members are required to respond to any specific requests for information made by other members with regard to regulations (GATS Art. III:1). Apart from the prompt publication of measures affecting trade in services, members are required to inform the Council for Trade in Services about the introduction of any new regulations or changes to existing regulations (GATS Art. III:3).

GATS aims to fulfil the goals of non-discrimination between members through MFN, and between foreign and domestic service providers through national treatment, and it establishes the mechanism by which non-discrimination can be achieved, in particular through transparency of regulations and appeal procedures to ensure fair and impartial treatment. Despite the recognition of these goals and the establishment of mechanisms to achieve them, GATS has numerous limitations that make it a shallow form of service market integration.

A major limitation imposed on GATS is the positive-list approach, in which sectors in which commitments are to be made with regard to national treatment and market access are listed. Snape and Bosworth argue that "this approach establishes a bias towards the status quo, presenting further opening as a positive and optional undertaking rather than as the default condition, with the result that opening is likely to be undertaken only when and where it hurts them least" (1996, p. 191). This approach makes it difficult to achieve transparency because the list says nothing about the various restrictions at work in other sectors. According to Dobson and Jacquet, this positive-list approach was pursued despite its limitations because developing countries wanted "to deflect the demands put on them and keep their options open" (1998, p. 75).

A second limitation that relates directly to the first is the inability to implement and enforce transparency provisions. As far as notifications under GATS are concerned, up to 1999, 106 notifications had been made to the Council for Trade in Services. The main types include 17 notifications under Article V regarding economic integration agreements, 4 notifications under Article XXVIII regarding national treatment, 28 notifications under Article VII regarding mutual recognition and 55 notifications under Article III regarding transparency involving any new laws or changes made to existing laws, regulations or administrative guidelines (OECD, 2000, p. 16). The problem with the enquiry points is that, as of 1999, only 58 had been established, and some of those that have been established are rarely updated and include telephone and fax numbers that are no longer applicable (OECD, 2000, p. 16). These enquiry points have been ineffective sources of information for GATS members and are rarely used as the primary means by which members gather information.

The shallow liberalization criteria in GATS are established by its wide array of exceptions and limited general obligations. Each specific commitment may be subject to a qualification with regard to MFN, national treatment or market access. Full liberalization is achieved only when "none" is listed in the schedule of reservations. This ability to schedule restrictions means, as Hoekman has pointed out (Hoekman and Kostecki, 1995, p. 127), that members, instead of locking in a liberal situation if it exists, impose restrictions to be used as negotiating chips in future rounds. According to Stephenson, "this possibility, along with the non-generality of national treatment, and the sector-specificity of market access commitments, is felt by many to have reduced the value of the GATS as a liberalizing instrument" (1999, p. 23). Virtually all commitments made in the Uruguay Round were of a standstill nature, meaning that members promised not to establish more restrictive regulations for listed sectors. The sectoral coverage of these conservative standstill commitments in high-income countries was 53.3 per cent of all services; while developing countries established commitments for only 15.1 per cent of their services (Hoekman and Kostecki, 1995, p. 137). Commitments by large developing countries were substantially higher, at 29.6 per cent of the total possible, but this represents a rather small liberalizing step. The cases where no restrictions were made accounted for 30.5 per cent of the total in high-income countries, 6.7 per cent in developing countries as a whole, and 10.9 per cent in large developing countries. These numbers "vividly illustrate how far away GATS Members are from attaining free trade in services, and the magnitude of the task that remains" (Hoekman and Kostecki, 1995, p. 137).

Attempts to deal with these limitations, in particular increased liberalization of the service markets, have made initial steps at the multilateral level with the completion of the Basic Telecommunications Agreement and the Financial Services Agreement, which have added significantly to the national schedules of commitments. But the primary impetus for increased liberalization and transparency to counteract the limitations of GATS is coming from the regional level. Strides made in the European Union and NAFTA have provided a deeper form of integration that complements the foundations established at the multilateral level.

The European Union approach

The Treaty of Rome committed the original six members of the European Economic Community to the objective of creating a common market based on the four freedoms – the free movement of goods, services, labour and capital.[6] The conclusion of the treaty resulted in the elimination of tariffs, which facilitated the freer movement of goods. The harmonization of technical standards during the 1960s and 1970s resulted in the elimination of some of the non-tariff barriers to trade in goods. Progress was made towards the liberalization of capital with the adoption of capital movement directives in 1960 and 1962.

In contrast, the Treaty of Rome was unique in its "virtual absence of details on services liberalization" (Pelkmans, 1997, p. 105). The treaty contained very few details on how services should be liberalized and what sectors should be liberalized. No stages were defined and a timetable was not set. Guidelines were set forth with regard to the rights of establishment, but these were primarily directed to goods providers.

The treaty divided services into four modes of delivery, along the lines followed by GATS in 1994. The treaty established an obligation to abolish restrictions on the free movement of services and a standstill clause stipulating that member states could introduce no new restrictions. It lacked a programme specifically detailing the mechanisms and the process by which services would be liberalized, but did include a non-discrimination clause for remaining restrictions extended to all residents. With regard to the rights of establishment of firms, the provision required that companies receive national treatment.

Initially, the focus of the liberalization of the service market was on the approximation of laws, which required detailed harmonization. This so-called "old" approach entailed policed national treatment by the European Commission and the European Court of Justice to ensure that foreign service providers were receiving national treatment no less favourable until the time when laws were approximated. The problem was that the approximation of laws proved to be administratively impossible because of the diversity of regulations among the members of the European Communities (EC) and their reluctance to change those laws. Governments also felt uncomfortably constrained by the policed national treatment imposed at the EC level. Thus, service market integration stagnated in the 1970s. A certain Eurosclerosis seemed to be plaguing the European economy as it suffered from segmentation in both the services and capital markets (Wallace and Young, 2000). The poor competitiveness of European firms relative to their main trading partners in the United States and Japan in the early 1980s, which contributed to large trading deficits, provided an impetus for further progress towards a single market. This progress would require a new approach towards the liberalization of the services market.

The main components of the new approach were mutual recognition and minimal harmonization. Provisions for mutual recognition were established in the Treaty of Rome with regard to professional qualifications but were not extended to goods and services until two landmark cases decided by the European Court of Justice. The *Cassis de Dijon* (1979) ruling extended mutual recognition to goods, and the *Dassonville* case extended it to services. The principle of mutual recognition basically required that "if a standard or qualification meets one member's criteria it should be deemed acceptable by the other members" (Winters, 1993, p. 220). Thus a member cannot prohibit the provision in its own territory of a service lawfully provided in another member state, "even if the conditions in which it is provided are different in the country where the service provider is established" (Pelkmans, 1997, p. 108). Mutual recognition implies home country supervisory control, meaning that the regulator in the country of origin of the service provider is responsible for the supervision of its conduct in a foreign territory. In reality, mutual recognition is more managed in nature – supervisory control is split between home and host country supervisors, with many host country supervisors taking control over issues related to prudential regulation. To avoid a regulatory race to the bottom, in which members would lower their regulatory barriers to levels that would be damaging to consumers or the system as a whole, a harmonization of minimum standards was established among the members. The establishment of minimum standards allowed the European Communities to harmonize measures that were non-discriminatory in nature and protect the general interests of EC members.

The objective of the new approach is to create competition among rules, whereby member states "retaining rules which are unfavorable to their firms or consumers come under pressure to reform them, thus inducing a convergence within the Community around relatively attractive rules" (Winters, 1993, p. 220). Thus, the objective of approximation of laws remains an important aim of the new approach and the creation of a single market.

The approach of the European Union is very different from that of GATS but it builds upon it in important ways. Despite the fact that the EU approach does not include provisions in relation to third countries, the notably contagious effect of mutual recognition has resulted in its extension to many third countries. By the mid-1990s the European Union had initiated bilateral talks with the United States, Australia, New Zealand, Canada, Switzerland and Japan (Nicolaidis, 2000). Mutual recognition agreements figure in the Union's approach to several of the Mediterranean countries and to the associate members in Eastern Europe. The agreements with the associate members in Eastern Europe have services provisions that extend far beyond GATS and stimulate and bind regulatory reform in these countries. The European Union does not abide by the major requirement of the GATS provision for mutual recognition agreements, in particular its stipulation that all "members who grant recognition must 'afford adequate opportunity' for other interested members 'to negotiate their accession' to existing or future bilateral or plurilateral MRAs". This lack of automaticity in accession implies a "lack of predictability and remaining room for arbitrary behavior on the part of the host country" (Nicolaidis, 2000, p. 279).

Despite this inadequacy, mutual recognition agreements enhance transparency by establishing standardized criteria for building bridges across service supervisory systems and professional licensing systems. A consolidated supervision mechanism established by mutual recognition agreements allows the supervisory authorities of both states to identify the regulatory barriers that exist between them. This information can be passed on to domestic service providers and result in the elimination of some of the uncertainty that results from a lack of transparency. The benefits of mutual recognition are also based on the fact that an agreement has the potential of opening trade up in all sectors. In theory this is what is supposed to have happened in Europe, but problems with implementation have prevented this from becoming a reality as of yet. Despite the shortcomings in implementation, it has resulted in regulatory reform among the EU countries. Many of the unnecessarily discriminatory regulations are being replaced by competition-inducing regulations that help firms from both EU and non-EU states. These reforms have the effect of increasing market access in these countries.

The NAFTA approach

The approach employed by the North American Free Trade Agreement towards the liberalization of services has often been described as a GATS-plus initiative. The NAFTA approach incorporates the GATS principles of MFN and national treatment, but it also includes innovations that increase transparency and establishes a unique appeals procedure. In addition, it includes a ratchet clause to guarantee future liberalization and provisions on capital movements that go beyond the GATS stipulations. Whereas the liberalizing modality of GATS is a sectoral, gradual approach to the opening of services markets, the NAFTA model is a "comprehensive liberalization of services and investment" (Stephenson, 2000, p. 1).

The principles of national treatment and MFN apply to all modes of supply and cover all service sectors where there are no previous reservations. The MFN and national treatment principles are similar in content to those in GATS. An innovation in the NAFTA approach is the negative-list approach to reservations. NAFTA allows each member to establish reservations with regard to regulations or other measures in force that do not conform to the principles established in the agreement. This approach requires members to incorporate a description of all existing regulations that result in the violation of MFN, national treatment and the local presence principles in each sector and subsector. It also requires members to identify the laws and regulations that support the reservation. This approach provides a mechanism of transparency that is self-executing in that it does not require an additional notification procedure, which has proven ineffective in both GATS and the European Union. The information provided in these reservations allows service providers to develop a clear picture of outstanding restrictions that affect their ability to trade in services and can be referred to in the event of a dispute between the parties.

A party is allowed to appeal to the dispute settlement mechanism established in NAFTA if it believes it has been improperly injured by regulations listed in the reservations or discriminated against by regulations and measures not listed. The NAFTA dispute settlement mechanism is unique in that it gives investors a right to present a case against a state (the mechanism established by GATS allows only state-to-state cases). This is an important guarantee for providers establishing a commercial presence in a foreign territory to ensure their protection against unlawful discrimination.

A third innovation that does not exist in any previous agreement is a ratchet clause, which commits parties to maintain and increase the liberalization of their services sector within specific time-frames, depending on the sector (Stephenson, 2000).

NAFTA differs from GATS in listing non-discriminatory provisions separately from discriminatory provisions in the national schedules. In the agreement, "each NAFTA member was obliged to provide a list of nondiscriminatory provisions in force that limit the number of service providers, or limit their operations in a given sector" (Stephenson, 2000, p. 143). The separate listing of non-discriminatory measures makes it easier for service providers to identify them, which can result in a request for consultation on these provisions in order to negotiate their liberalization or elimination if they prove to be unnecessarily burdensome.

In order to facilitate the commercial presence of service providers in the territory of another member, NAFTA guarantees the right of foreign direct investment for all service sectors included in the agreement, without limits to the form, size or equity of the investment, unless specified (Stephenson, 2000, p. 140). Provisions in the investment Chapter of NAFTA also serve to protect investment in services. These provisions "specify freedom for investment decisions and establish important investor guarantees" (Stephenson, 1999, p. 31).

The NAFTA provisions identified in its Chapter on services apply to all sectors except basic telecommunications and financial services, which are dealt with in separate Chapters. They also do not cover most air services, social services provided by governments and the maritime industry.

The synergy between the NAFTA, EU and GATS approaches is seen in NAFTA's promotion of transparency through its negative-list approach to reservations. This helps service providers globally recognize the regulations that hinder market access. The ratchet clause is a mechanism that ensures regulatory reform within a specified time-frame. This guarantee is also established in GATS but with weaker mechanisms of enforcement. Whereas NAFTA members will be able to appeal directly to a binding dispute settlement mechanism to ensure the elimination of these regulatory barriers, GATS requires only a further round of negotiation within the specified time-frame.

The reform promoted by the ratchet clause can enhance market access only as a result of the requirement that no new regulation should be introduced that acts as a greater obstacle to trade in services. Unlike GATS, which allows for the modification of schedules and the withdrawal of commitments, any exclusion of a sector would require modification, and the withdrawal of commitments would require a listing of additional regulations, which is not allowed for in the agreement.

This NAFTA approach has been extended to countries throughout the Western hemisphere. The Group of Three Treaty, between Mexico, Colombia and Venezuela, employs a strikingly similar approach to services liberalization. This approach is also the basis of liberalization for Mexico in bilateral agreements signed with Bolivia and Costa Rica in 1995 and with Chile and Nicaragua in 1999. Chile and Canada brought into effect a similar agreement in 1997 (see chapter 7) (Stephenson, 1999). Many commentators see this approach being followed in the Free Trade Area of the Americas, if it is ever established.

At a superficial level, the NAFTA and EU approaches seem to build upon the multilateral initiative established in GATS. However, evidence of synergy in the approaches towards liberalization in specific sectors would provide additional support for the argument that the regional approaches serve as a building block for multilateral liberalization. The following section considers the case of the financial services sector.

Financial services

The Financial Services Agreement (FSA) under GATS was concluded in the WTO in December 1997, with implementation set for early 1999.[7] The FSA places over 95 per cent of world trade in banking, insurance, securities and financial information under the jurisdiction of the WTO, on the basis of MFN and under the auspices of the dispute settlement mechanism (Dobson and Jacquet, 1998, p. 89). However, as for services as a whole, Dobson and Jacquet argue that the FSA barely goes beyond the status quo. The agreement makes a modest contribution to financial services liberalization by "enabling most of the main players to bind existing practices in an international agreement and by providing a mechanism for settling disputes" (1998, p. ix). Although the FSA includes market-opening commitments by 102 WTO members, these commitments entail little new liberalization. OECD countries do not do much to open their markets further, and the main emerging market economies offer little new access to their banking sectors.

The FSA provides a legal framework to reassure foreign institutions with long-term investments and provides some external pressure for changes that promote efficiency, but it does little to increase market access for foreign financial institutions. Many standard policy interventions employed by regulators remain out of the reach of commitments made in the FSA, and the prudential carve-out provision in GATS protects the regulators' right to intervene.

The FSA also does little to increase transparency in the financial services sector. Transparency measures in GATS have yielded no notifications of existing or new regulations. Therefore, in order to attain an increase in transparency, GATS has depended increasingly on the development of international standards and codes of good practice, like those established in the OECD and the G-10. On the other hand, regional cooperation in the European Union and NAFTA has been instrumental in promoting greater liberalization and regulatory reform of the financial services sector, which has resulted in increased market access and transparency.

Liberalization in the European Union under the single market programme was based on the harmonization of essential rules combined with the principle of home country control. The principle of home country control means "that the responsibility for prudential control and supervision of all domestic and foreign branches of banks rest with the regulatory authorities of the country of origin" (Tsoukalis, 1991, p. 123). This principle was adopted in the First Banking Directive of 1977, which created the conditions for limited integration of the financial services market. The three directives adopted in 1989 build on the foundations established in the 1977 directive. The Directive on Own Funds established general principles and definitions regarding bank capital and contained an agreement on weighted risk assessment of bank assets and off-balance-sheet items. The Directive on Solvency Ratios harmonized minimum solvency ratios at the level of 8 per cent for all credit institutions. These two directives therefore served the function of harmonizing minimum standards. The harmonization of minimum standards meant that liberalization was based on a few transparent and generally accepted rules rather than on the discretionary powers of different national regulatory authorities. Finally, sector-specific directives, such as the Second Banking Directive, resulted in the creation of the single banking licence, which enabled "any bank which has received authorization by the competent authorities of a member country of the EC to provide services across the border and to open branches in any other member country without the need for further authorization" (Tsoukalis, 1991, p. 124). Banks were thus allowed to provide universal banking services in other EU member states under home country control.

The regulatory framework also establishes a Banking Supervision Committee, which "coordinates information flows generated by the regulatory authorities of each country and the Euro system, as well as co-operation agreements between regulatory authorities of EU member countries" (Inzerillo et al., 2000, p. 306). The transparency mechanism established by the Banking Supervision Committee reduces some of the uncertainty concerning the divergent regulatory environments of the member states.

The empirical effect of this reform reveals dynamic gains such as increases in the efficiency and performance of banks as a result of regulatory reform and increased competition. Before the single market initiative, regulated financial services markets were characterized by high monopoly rents incurred by the consumer and high non-wage operating expenses, which indicated sectoral inefficiency. The evidence suggests there has been increased competition. It could be argued that there was little actual increase in the number of foreign banks operating in other member states, but the threat of increased competition had a knock-on effect. The threat resulted in a dramatic restructuring of, for example, the banking industry through mergers and acquisitions. These consolidations allowed firms to exploit economies of scale and increase their scope of activities to cover banking, investment and insurance, as well as to defend the market power of banks in the domestic market. The concentration of banks in the domestic market, the entrance of a rising number of foreign banks into the market and the elimination of monopoly rents at the national level resulted in a decline in profit margins. This reality, combined with the concern about takeovers, motivated firms to maximize their value. As a result, banks reduced operating and staff costs and became more efficient in their activities. This drive for efficiency brought about technological innovations that reduced costs and had a positive effect on the productivity of labour and the sector as a whole. Mergers and acquisitions also resulted in the reabsorption of excess capacity in the financial sector, resulting in increased efficiency without incurring the costs of bankruptcy.

Empirical evidence also shows that the biggest European banks showed the highest level of productivity and the lowest unit costs (Inzerillo et al., 2000, p. 290). These larger banks are able to attain efficiency gains through the increased diversification of risks, better evaluation of risk and the offering of a more diversified mix of services to its consumers. Efficiency gains then enable the bigger banks profitably to use technology that allows the prevention and control of risk (Inzerillo et al., 2000, p. 291). Consolidation of banks into larger entities accelerates the use of innovative technology, including electronic means of payment, which result in lower costs. These lower costs lead to lower prices for consumers.

The single market programme of the European Union builds upon the Financial Services Agreement established in the WTO in important ways. The initiative goes beyond the binding of the status quo and stimulates regulatory reform that is vital for market access. It establishes a distinction between prudential regulations deemed necessary for the effective functioning of the economy and regulations that affect the conduct of firms. It then establishes harmonization of prudential mechanisms, facilitating a convergence in national banking structures that enables trade and the establishment of branches in the territory of other member states. Although the single market programme does not extend the single banking licence to third countries, this convergence of banking structures and requirements makes it easier for foreign banks outside the European Union to establish a commercial presence within it.

The NAFTA initiative is less ambitious than that of the European Union. However, it is important in its integration of the Mexican financial sector because this is the first integration of a developing country's financial sector with that of developed countries and can serve as an important laboratory for future developments in GATS. The NAFTA principles for financial services liberalization apply to measures that affect the delivery of services by financial institutions. The agreement requires that each country define its liberalization commitments, the timetable for adherence to the agreed principles and any reservations regarding the principles of MFN, national treatment and local presence. Each country is "to permit its residents to acquire financial services in the territory of another party and is not to impose new curbs on cross-border operations in any financial sector unless the country has specifically exempted a particular sector from this obligation" (Gonzalez, 2000, p. 144). Governments are allowed to reserve the right to issue "reasonable" regulations that are necessary to ensure the integrity and stability of the financial system. In certain circumstances, the state can adopt measures to defend itself from balance of payments problems. NAFTA is based on policed national treatment, which requires the maintenance of host country control over the supervision of banks. Thus foreign banks must adopt the regulatory standards of the host country. There is no attempt to harmonize prudential regulations or to integrate the financial markets according to similar and mutually recognizable standards.

Integration in NAFTA is much shallower than integration in the European Union. The regulations among NAFTA countries continue to differ widely, given minimal convergence of regulations and banking structures. The negative-list approach provides transparency by allowing external countries to recognize the regulations of each member state, but the NAFTA approach does not go much beyond that established in the FSA. Most importantly, it does not derogate from any of the provisions in the FSA.

NAFTA has had greatest impact on the Mexican banking sector. The financial institutions in Mexico were weak and inefficient as a result of a restrictive regulatory framework that impeded competition. NAFTA, through its ratchet clause, required the elimination of restrictions on the operation of foreign financial firms in Mexico. However, it allowed Mexico to adopt a phase-in mechanism in which it would be given time to abide by the principles established in NAFTA. This mechanism limits the participation of foreign firms during the initial six years after the agreement (Trigueros, 1994). The threat of impending competition generated incentives for the modernization of the Mexican banking structure and for regulatory reform that would increase competitiveness in the market.

Although many of the provisions of NAFTA with regard to financial services have a neutral effect on the multilateral liberalization of this sector, a few of the mechanisms serve as an important building block for multilateralism. The negative list of reservations increases the transparency of the regulations of the member states. In addition, the effectiveness of NAFTA in stimulating reform and increasing the efficiency and competitiveness of the Mexican financial system could serve as a valuable model for the multilateral framework. At the same time as acting as an important building block, NAFTA has not acted as an impediment to the provision of financial services from providers originating in countries outside NAFTA. For example, since the adoption of NAFTA, the number of European firms operating in the NAFTA markets has grown, which reveals an important synergy that was discussed earlier. The integration of markets in Europe led to a consolidation of small European firms through mergers and acquisitions that made them more competitive internationally. As a result, these larger firms were able to compete more effectively in the NAFTA markets, in particular the US market. This has caused an inadvertent competition among rules, because the United States has been forced to adjust or at least ease its statutory restrictions on the functioning of financial services to maintain the competitiveness of its firms. This transatlantic convergence represents an important element in wider international convergence.

Conclusion

The service trade regimes developed in the European Union and NAFTA represent deeper integration than does GATS – in the shape of substantive measures such as home country control and mutual recognition in the European Union and negative listing in NAFTA. In addition, procedural mechanisms such as independent review and dispute settlement measures have helped in the development of a more rules-based, less discretionary approach to regulation.

Despite the differences in approach between the European Union, which has focused on partial harmonization and mutual recognition, and NAFTA, which calls for no detailed harmonization and relies on policed national treatment, an important synergy has developed between the two regulatory regimes. Instead of a system of competing regulatory regionalism that limits trade, the competition between approaches is having a liberalizing impact on the regulatory barriers to trade, as both agreements introduce innovative procedural devices to facilitate trade and promote transparency.

Finally, the EU and NAFTA approaches serve as a building block for the multilateral system. Both approaches provide models for dealing with regulatory barriers to trade that can be applied multilaterally. It is likely that these innovative mechanisms would not be applied internationally without experimentation at the regional level.

The substantive impact of this deeper form of integration has been dynamic gains from increased trade in services within and between the two trading blocs. These dynamic gains can be seen in the case of financial services, where the potential for increased competition has led to lower costs and greater efficiency in the banking sector. This is important evidence that the regional approaches serve as a building block to the multilateral system.

Notes

1. The phraseology defining this debate is taken from Lawrence (1995).
2. Pelkmans and Winters (1988) illuminate the trade-diverting effects that mutual recognition agreements can have as they impose a regulatory rent on countries that are not a part of these agreements. Although trade creation and trade diversion issues will not be the primary focus of this chapter, it is still interesting to take this argument into account.

3. A major exception being trade in services between the United States and Europe, which was prevalent both before and after the EU initiative to eliminate barriers to trade in services amongst the participating countries. There is no conclusive evidence on the effect of this single market initiative on US trade in services.
4. Examples of such services include central banking and social security, which are not supplied on a commercial basis.
5. Limitations set out in Article XVI include limitations on: the number of service suppliers, the total value of services transactions or assets, the total number of service operations, the number of persons who may be employed in a particular sector or by a particular supplier, percentage limitations on the participation of foreign capital or measures that restrict or require supply of the service through specified types of legal entity or joint venture.
6. The original six members were France, Germany, Italy, Belgium, the Netherlands and Luxembourg.
7. Financial services encompass banking, investment and insurance but, owing to a lack of space, the focus of this case study will be on the initiatives made in the banking sector.

REFERENCES

Dobson, Wendy, and Pierre Jacquet (1998), *Financial Services Liberalization in the WTO*, Washington DC: Institute for International Economics.

Feketekuty, Geza (1988), *International Trade in Services: An Overview and Blueprint for Negotiations*, Cambridge, MA: Ballinger.

Gonzalez, Carlos (2000), "Mexico's FTAs: Extending NAFTA's Approach", in *Services Trade in the Western Hemisphere: Liberalization, Integration and Reform*, Washington DC: Brookings Institution Press.

Hoekman, Bernard, and Michel Kostecki (1995), *The Political Economy of the World Trading System: From GATT to WTO*, Oxford: Oxford University Press.

Inzerillo, Ugo, Morelli Pierluigi and Giovanni Pittaluga (2000), "Deregulation and Changes in the European Banking Industry", in Giampaolo Galli and Jacques Pelkmans (eds.), *Regulatory Reform and Competitiveness in Europe, Vol. 2*, Cheltenham: Edward Elgar.

Lawrence, Robert Z. (1995), *Regionalism, Multilateralism and Deeper Integration*, Washington DC: Brookings Institution.

Nicolaidis, Kalypso (2000), "Non-Discriminatory Mutual Recognition: An Oxymoron in the New WTO Lexicon", in Thomas Cottier and Petros C. Mavroidis (eds.), *Regulatory Barriers and the Principle of Non-Discrimination in World Trade Law*, Ann Arbor: University of Michigan Press.

OECD (Organisation for Economic Co-operation and Development) (2000), *Strengthening Regulatory Transparency: Insights for the GATS from the Regulatory Reform Country Reviews*, Paris: OECD.

Pelkmans, Jacques (1997), *European Integration: Methods and Economic Analysis*, London: Longman.

Pelkmans, Jacques, and Alan Winters (1988), *Europe's Domestic Market*, London: Routledge, for the Royal Institute of International Affairs.

Snape, R. H., and M. Bosworth (1996), "Advancing Services Negotiations", in J.

Schott (ed.), *The World Trading System: Challenges Ahead*, Washington DC: Institute for International Economics.

Stephenson, Sherry (1999), *Approaches to Liberalizing Services*, Policy Research Working Paper 2107, Washington DC: World Bank, Development Research Group, Trade.

—— (2000), "Regional Agreements on Services in Multilateral Discipline: Interpreting and Applying GATS Article V", in *Services Trade in the Western Hemisphere: Liberalization, Integration and Reform*, Washington DC: Brookings Institution Press.

Trigueros, Ignacio (1994), "The Mexican Financial System and the North American Free Trade Agreement", in Victor Bulmer-Thomas, Nikki Craske and Monica Serrano (eds.), *Mexico and the North American Free Trade Agreement: Who Will Benefit?*, London: Macmillan.

Tsoukalis, Loukas (1991), *The New European Economy: The Politics and Economics of Integration*, Oxford: Oxford University Press.

Viner, Jacob (1950), *The Customs Union Issue*, New York: Carnegie Endowment for Peace.

Wallace, Helen, and Alasdair Young (2000), "The Single Market: A New Approach to Policy", in William Wallace and Helen Wallace (eds.), *Policymaking in the European Union*, Oxford: Oxford University Press.

Winters, L. Alan (1993), "The EC: A Case of Successful Integration?", in Jaime De Melo and Arvind Panayariya (eds.), *New Dimensions in Regional Integration*, Cambridge: Cambridge University Press.

WTO (World Trade Organization) Secretariat (1999), *An Introduction to the GATS*, Geneva: WTO, Trade in Services Division, available at http://www.wto.org/english/tratop_e/serv_e/gsintr_e.doc.

Yeung, May T., Nicholas Perdikis and William Kerr (1999), *Regional Trading Blocs in the Global Economy: The EU and ASEAN*, Cheltenham, UK: Edward Elgar.

Zampetti, Americo (1999), "Market Access through Mutual Recognition: The Promise and Limits of GATS Article VII", in Pierre Sauve and Robert Stern (eds.), *GATS 2000: New Directions in Services Trade Liberalization*, Washington DC: Brookings Institution Press.

Part IV
Conclusions

11

Trade in a world of regions

Brigid Gavin and Luk Van Langenhove

Introduction

The past decade has seen a renaissance of regional trade agreements (RTAs) world-wide. The "new regionalism" of the 1990s, which compares with the "old regionalism" of the 1960s, took place against a background of significant structural changes in the global political and economic order. The collapse of the Soviet empire ended the bipolar world of rivalry between democracy and market economics at one end of the spectrum and communism and planned economies at the other. The "end of history" thesis predicted a generalized move towards democracy and free market economies on a global scale. The general trend has been in this direction, which undoubtedly has accelerated economic globalization over the past decade.

Growing regionalism in a world of globalization? Is it just a co-incidence or the emergence of something new? Economic integration in Europe since the fall of the Berlin Wall has taken on a new dimension – "projecting collective power" to defend Europe's values in the world. The new approach sees Europe as a cornerstone of a multipolar world order. Regions must organize themselves and develop as a counterweight to any one single pole of power in the global economy. In this worldview, regionalism is about pooling sovereignty to enhance sovereignty. The more regions can unite, the more they can determine their own destiny in the global order. Because sovereign states feel that their sovereignty is being undermined by globalization, they are "racing to regionalise" (Thomas and Tétreault, 1999).

But regionalism just as much as globalization has been characterized by the Polanyian "double movement".[1] Deepening economic integration driven by business and political élites has provoked a popular social backlash. Civil society has spearheaded the backlash, countering that basic rights of citizens are being trampled on by the new-found economic liberties of corporations. Many of the new economic rights of business resulting from trade liberalization have reduced corporations' responsibilities to labour, to the environment and to communities and governments that provided the infrastructure necessary for those corporations to be profitable. So the trade policy debate has widened. Efficiency is a necessary but no longer a sufficient condition to which governments can appeal in order to justify trade liberalization. They have to balance efficiency considerations with democratic legitimacy, and they have to take into consideration transparency and accountability in the process of policy-making. Consequently, the institutional arrangements of regional organizations and global multilateral institutions have moved up the agenda as an important factor in determining the effectiveness of trade negotiations.

This chapter will analyse the changing relations between regionalism and global trade governance as economic integration between countries deepens. Up until the 1990s, trade policy was typically analysed as a "two-level game" determined by the interaction of special interest groups in the domestic economy with governments negotiating at the international level. In the contemporary world, trade governance has become a more complex three-level game determined by the interaction of networks of stakeholders, including private industry and non-governmental organizations (NGOs), with governments operating at the regional and global levels. So the macro governance framework impacts on the strategies and instruments to achieve micro-level liberalization. The first section will discuss the concept of regionalism, which is a dynamic, evolving process for which there is no one-size-fits-all definition. The second section will review economic theories of the "old" and the "new" regionalism. The third section will focus on institutional questions and ask whether problems accumulated in the global multilateral institutions are making governments turn to regionalism. The fourth section will analyse the European Union as a "laboratory" for institutional reform for future trade governance.

What is regionalism?

The definition of regionalism accepted by the World Trade Organization (WTO) is "actions by governments to liberalize or facilitate trade on a

Table 11.1. Stages of deepening regional integration

Depth of integration	Trade liberalization	Common commercial policy	Free movement of factors	Common monetary and fiscal policy	Common government
Free trade agreement	Yes				
Customs union	Yes	Yes			
Common market	Yes	Yes	Yes		
Economic union	Yes	Yes	Yes	Yes	
Political union	Yes	Yes	Yes	Yes	Yes

regional basis, sometimes through free trade areas or customs unions".[2] In practice, however, regional schemes of integration may have a more general or specific meaning.[3] Regionalism is generally understood as a sequenced process of deepening economic integration, as shown in table 11.1.

1. In the first stage, member countries agree to liberalize their internal trade, but each country maintains autonomy in deciding its external level of protection.
2. One stage further, a customs union implies not only internal free trade but also a common external tariff, which is usually an average of all members' tariffs prior to the formation of the union.
3. A common market calls for considerably deeper integration because it leads to free flows of capital, investment and labour in addition to free flows of goods and services.
4. Economic and monetary integration involves the unification of macroeconomic fiscal and monetary polices and the creation of an independent regional central bank with control over exchange rate policy, inflation rates and fiscal deficits.
5. Political union requires the pooling of sovereignty and the creation of democratic institutions beyond the national level.

This model, which implies an orderly sequence of microeconomic and macroeconomic integration, requires some form of supranational institutions. Political union, which is concerned with regional peace and security, is increasingly linked with regional economic integration because, without political stability, there is little hope of economic growth.

Recently, new and more fluid concepts of regional economic integration have been advanced. Breslin and Higgott (2001) distinguish between "regionalisation", which is a process mainly driven by market forces of trade and investment flows, and "regionalism", which emerges from state-led projects of cooperation, intergovernmental dialogues and treaties. According to Hettne (1997), the "new regionalism" since the end of the Cold War has developed in such a way that it may become a possible structural pattern of a new world order. This wave of new regionalism, which has been triggered by deepening European integration, is a multidimensional regionalism that goes far beyond the common market concept and includes, among other things, an autonomous capacity for conflict resolution (Schulz et al., 2001).

Regional versus global trade

It is now common to speak of regionalism as a worldwide phenomenon (see appendix table 11A.1 for a review of all RTAs notified to the GATT/WTO as of 30 June 2002). Upon closer inspection, however, regionalism is like many other aspects of globalization – strongly concentrated in the North. Not surprisingly, regionalism is most widespread in Europe, where regional trade agreements are an essential element of the European Union's external relations. Nearly 60 per cent of the notified RTAs in force at the end of 2000 had been concluded by European countries; RTAs concluded among developing countries accounted for only 15 per cent of the total.

The thesis that the growth of regionalism is heralding the death of the General Agreement on Tariffs and Trade (GATT) is not supported by the trade figures. Despite the growth of RTAs, there has not been a significant increase in intraregional trade. The WTO regularly reports on the trade of the major RTAs. Looking at intraregional trade defined by geographical region – North America, South America, Western Europe, transition economies, Africa, Middle East and Asia – the share of intraregional trade in overall global trade was 46.7 per cent in 2000, 52.0 per cent in 1990 and 43.3 per cent in 1980. The rise between 1980 and 1990 was largely linked to the fall in oil prices, which boosted trade among developed regions by 6.3 per cent (WTO, 1992, Table III; 2000, Table III.3). The WTO also reports on intraregional trade according to the major RTAs, including the European Union, the North American Free Trade Agreement (NAFTA), the Association of South East Asian Nations, the Central European Free Trade Agreement, the Southern Common Market (Mercosur) and the Andean Community. Their combined intraregional trade accounted for 36 per cent of world merchandise trade in 2000. Between 1990 and 2000 this ratio was always in the range between 35 and 40 per cent (WTO, 2001, Table 1.9).

RTAs were accepted by GATT from the start. It would have been an aberration to prevent a group of countries moving to complete free trade among themselves – the ultimate goal that GATT itself aspires to. Since the original Article XXIV, which set out the general conditions for the compatibility of RTAs with GATT rules, provisions for regional economic integration have been extended. Developing countries may have recourse to preferential agreements under the so-called "Enabling Clause" of the 1979 decision, which permits differential and more favourable treatment for developing countries in the global trade system. Article V of the General Agreement on Trade in Services (GATS) sets out the rules for RTAs covering trade in services in the 1994 Agreement setting up the WTO.

Is regionalism a game for big players such as the European Union and the United States? It looked that way in the 1990s, but the international trade environment has changed profoundly over recent years. Developing countries have begun to claim more "ownership" over multilateral institutions and they too are investing more in capacity-building for regionalism. In Africa, where the 1990s was a lost decade for development, a radical new departure for continental-wide integration on the basis of the European model has been initiated.

The New Economic Partnership for Development in Africa (NEPAD), launched in 2001 by the founding states of South Africa, Nigeria, Egypt, Senegal and Algeria, plans to rebuild the African continent through attracting foreign direct investment (FDI) from industrial countries. It received the support of the G-8 countries at their summit meeting in Canada in June 2002. When NEPAD was unveiled, Africa's economic decline was reflected in the fact that 34 African countries ranked among the world's least developed countries, compared with 27 in 1996. Overseas development aid to Africa had fallen from US$24.2 billion in 1989 to US$14.2 billion in 1999, and, according to the United Nations, FDI was set to fall by 40 per cent in 2001, even before the terrorist events of September 11 in the United States.

In return for economic help, NEPAD offers "good governance", peace and security. In parallel to NEPAD, a new vision of African Union has emerged based on the EU model of peace and economic prosperity. The old Organization of African Unity (OAU), which adhered rigidly to the old principle of non-interference in the domestic affairs of a country, has become discredited in the face of genocide, crimes against humanity and other horrendous aggressions perpetrated by governments against their citizens. Consequently, the OAU failed to provide the framework for either political stability or economic growth. Many African countries now recognize the need for collective decisions to ensure peace and security.

With the collapse of states in Somalia and elsewhere, the spread of the AIDs epidemic and the slashing of public sector spending on health and education, there is a sense of urgency to act. The major constraint on

African countries' development is the size of national markets. Africa needs to regionalize its markets to attract FDI. Trade liberalization would give African countries the capacity to diversify their economies. African countries need to break down internal barriers to trade and investment, which will allow African farmers to market their products in neighbouring countries and to develop South–South trade.

Old and new theories of regional integration

Why do countries regionalize? Neo-classical trade economists have always considered that regionalism was politically motivated. The goal of European economic integration was to achieve peace in Europe. The European Economic Community (EEC) was a child of the Cold War in much the same way that the Council for Mutual Economic Assistance was in Eastern Europe. Although the EEC had a very narrow economic mandate, its ultimate mission was political. The quantum leap from the internal market to monetary union was in response to the fall of the Berlin Wall and to integrate a reunited Germany into Europe.

The growth of RTAs in developing countries was also influenced by the Cold War. Some economists encouraged developing countries to create RTAs as the only viable means of economic development – to diversify their economy, to develop intra-industry trade and to develop South–South trade. However, many schemes of regional economic integration in Africa and Latin America were built on closed economy principles and insulation against outside competition.

The dual nature of RTAs implies the simultaneous existence of both liberalization and protectionism. Hence the recurring question: are RTAs "building blocks" or "stumbling blocks" to global trade liberalization? As long as the external protection of the new trade bloc does not exceed that which existed prior to its formation, and internal liberalization covers substantially all trade, then RTAs will be welfare increasing and, thus, building blocks towards global liberalization.[4]

Old regionalism

The old regionalism theory was based on the concepts of trade creation and trade diversion derived from a partial equilibrium analysis of the welfare effects of tariff elimination.[5] The theory can give no definitive answer as to which effect will predominate. That depends on whether RTAs encourage or discourage protection of internal industries. To the extent that industries inside the RTA are protected there is trade diversion; therefore those preferential trade arrangements are definitely "second best" to multilateral trade liberalization. The opposite is true in the case of trade creation.

The customs union theory fails to take into account the dynamic effects of RTAs – arguably the most important in the long run. A larger regional market offers opportunities for economies of scale, stimulates competition and provides incentives for investment. Achieving economies of scale is very important for firms in small countries, and especially in developing countries. Economies of scale may occur through product specialization enabling firms in two countries to specialize in particular product lines instead of producing the full product line (to rationalize production and to internationalize production).

Perhaps the most important effect of an RTA is the stimulus to competition and investment that it brings. Large firms in small countries protected by tariffs will lose their monopolistic quiet life as border protection falls, forcing them to compete in the larger market. The investment stimulus will include foreign direct investment, which brings added competition. Further competition comes from foreign multinational enterprises (MNEs), which bring new technology, finance and managerial know-how. As MNEs jump over the external tariff wall of the RTA and switch to direct production inside, the growing dynamic market will attract more foreign investors. Firms "follow the leader" for fear of missing out on lucrative new markets.

Customs union theory ignores transport costs, which can ultimately decide the fate of an RTA. Transport costs between countries geographically far apart will prevent the equalization of goods' prices after the formation of an RTA. For an historical example, compare the original six countries of the EEC (EEC-6) with the seven countries of the European Free Trade Area (EFTA-7). The original EEC-6 (France, Germany, Belgium, Holland, Luxembourg and Italy) all share borders, so that transport costs after the removal of trade barriers were zero. The EFTA-7 (the United Kingdom, Denmark, Norway, Sweden, Switzerland, Austria and Portugal) were geographically spread out – consider the huge distance between Portugal and Sweden.

New regionalism

New regionalism theory integrates the dynamic effects of economic integration, the interaction between trade and investment, and the role of institutional arrangements as incentives for regional integration.[6]

The new regionalism is determined by the structural changes in the global economy of the 1990s brought about by globalization. Following successive rounds of trade liberalization in the GATT/WTO, FDI has become much more important in the global economy; investment flows are now growing faster than trade flows. Firms have an incentive to switch from trade to FDI when trading costs (transport costs and government regulatory barriers) are high and investment costs (including communications costs) are rapidly declining. The size of the market is another factor that encourages FDI. Experience shows that, as countries converge in their factor endowments, technical efficiency and market size, there will be a move from intra-industry trade to intra-industry investment, provided that transport costs remain significant.[7] The new regionalism differs from the old regionalism in a number of important ways.

- Typically, the new regionalism involves a number of small countries that are willing to link up with a large neighbouring country, which plays the role of regional hegemon.
- The small countries are involved in a process of unilateral liberalization and they want to consolidate it by linking up with a large anchor country.
- The new regionalism is about deep integration – it goes beyond liberalization of trade in goods and deals with services and investment issues.
- There is no big bang trade liberalization but rather a slow gradualist approach.
- The new regionalism occurs between countries that are geographically close to each other.
- Small countries consider RTAs a means to strengthen their bargaining position in international trade negotiations.

Are the political economy dynamics of the new regionalism fundamentally different from those of multilateral trade liberalization? In practice, multilateral trade liberalization is a mercantilist exercise in which governments weigh up the "benefits" of foreign market access for their exporters against the "costs" of increased import competition for their home industries.

The larger the reduction in multilateral trade barriers, the greater the costs in terms of adverse effects on special interests at home, a factor that has to be reckoned with in national elections. Governments turn to regionalism because, by negotiating with a small number of countries, they will reduce the number of special interests affected. There is a trade-off here: with a smaller number of partners, a country can reach agreement on regulatory barriers to deeper integration.

How does the trade-off translate into benefits? Multilateral trade liberalization fosters global trade but it increases transport costs relative to regional trade. At the same time, the dramatic fall in communications costs is driving the shift from exporting to FDI. So regional integration that fosters investment creation is preferable to further multilateral trade liberalization.

Since the size of the market is crucial in attracting FDI, small countries compete to attract foreign investment by "regionalizing" their market. Small countries may be willing to pay a premium for this by undertaking considerable economic reforms. By linking up with a large country, small countries gain credibility in the eyes of foreign investors based on the belief that the large country will play the role of hegemon in the club and will enforce the rules. Take the example of Ireland as a gateway to the European internal market and its commitment to European monetary union (EMU). In contrast, some foreign investors have expressed doubts about their continued presence in the United Kingdom if it stays outside of EMU.

International trade arrangements can be analysed from a club theory perspective (Fratianni and Pattison, 2001). Clubs are institutions in which members are willing to pay for the "costs" of belonging in order to enjoy the "benefits". The benefit to a member country of a club is considered to be roughly equal to its share of global real gross domestic product. The cost will be calculated in terms of the costs of decision-making, which are determined by the institutional arrangements. Each country will evaluate its membership of the club in terms of overall costs and benefits.

The cost–benefit analysis of club membership is used to explain US hegemony in GATT after the Second World War. At that time the United States produced approximately 60 per cent of global industrial output and it needed open markets for its exports. It was therefore willing to play the hegemon in the club and to bear more than its share of costs by underwriting international economic reconstruction such as the Marshall Plan. It was also the locomotive of trade liberalization in GATT and tolerated developing countries acting as free-riders for a long time.

Today, with the rise of competing powers (notably the European Union and Japan and, increasingly, the emerging market economies of South-East Asia), the share of US global industrial output has fallen to 30 per cent. As the benefits of global leadership have declined, the costs have increased. The most costly form of decision-making is unanimity, which prevails in global multilateral institutions; and, as the number of GATT members has increased from the original 23 to some 142 countries, the difficulty of arriving at decisions has become accordingly more costly. Under these conditions, the United States no longer has an incentive to play the leadership role.

Regional trade arrangements are also clubs based on countries' evaluation of the costs and benefits of membership. There is usually a leader that is willing to pay more than its share of costs in order to reap the corresponding benefits. Take the example of Germany, which was the largest financial contributor to the EU budget but was also the largest producer and exporter in the Union. The benefits of guaranteed access to the large EU market have increased as the costs have declined through greater use of majority voting.

Regionalism and global economic governance

Regional trade agreements are more manageable than multilateral negotiations because they involve smaller numbers, and, because the members are more homogeneous, decision-making is more efficient. International cooperation is easier among a more limited number of countries with one or two large players, so RTAs create conditions favourable to leadership at the regional level and are therefore growing.

However, it needs to be reiterated that trade liberalization at the global level will bring the greatest efficiency gains. This is as true of the liberalization of regulatory barriers in the new trade areas as of the liberalization of tariffs in merchandise trade. So far, only a very small proportion of services have been liberalized by the majority of WTO members, although the "inbuilt negotiations" that started in 2000 are intended to speed up the process of liberalization and to make it irreversible. Yet the GATS negotiations are headed for trouble, which is symptomatic of the more generalized problem of the WTO's "democratic deficit".

The GATS negotiations are more about domestic regulation in its member countries than about liberalization of border measures. The GATS provision that domestic legislation should not constitute an unnecessary barrier to trade could affect a wide range of national regulations relating to environmental and consumer protection, public health, education and culture – all of which could be challenged as a technical barrier to trade. In the event of a dispute, the powerful Dispute Settlement Body (DSB) could judge that the national regulation constitutes an infringement of GATS. Because the WTO will decide what the "least trade restrictive" measure should be, the WTO could indirectly act as a force for deregulation and "privatization by the back door".[8] Thus the WTO could overturn domestic legislation enacted by sovereign parliaments without any responsibility for transparency (public debate with citizens) or accountability to citizens. A similar approach to the negotiation of a multilateral agreement on investment sealed its fate in the Organisation for Economic Co-operation and Development in 1999. So global trade negotiations can no longer be left to economics; politics is now as important as economics.

The politics debate is about various aspects of the democratic deficit. Civil society groups are concerned about the impairment of sovereignty in the only locus in which it resides – in nation-states – and the ever greater intrusion into sovereignty of multilateral institutions in which democratic control is almost completely lacking. These groups have demanded institutional reforms to allow for "internal transparency", which would allow all countries, especially developing countries, to participate equally and effectively in decision-making. They have called for greater "external transparency", which would allow NGOs to participate more actively, in other words to achieve participative democracy. And, thirdly, they have called for reform of the DSB mechanism to prevent the emergence of a hierarchy of laws that places WTO law above other systems of public international law, notably international environmental law.

The dilemmas of global economic governance

Any country that wants to have an open economy must sacrifice sovereignty to some degree. Openness to international flows of trade, technology, investment and capital leads to economic growth. Countries have accepted increasing interdependence for the past 50 years in order to achieve greater efficiency gains. But global economic governance calls for a system that satisfies the criteria of equity and legitimacy as well as efficiency.

Figure 11.1 shows the dilemmas inherent in global economic governance.[9] In international monetary relations, a country cannot simultaneously have all three policies of monetary autonomy, capital mobility and an international monetary system of fixed exchange rates, for example the Bretton Woods system. If it has monetary autonomy and capital mobility, it must have flexible exchange rates. If it wants to have fixed exchange rates and monetary autonomy, it must restrict capital mobility.

In international trade relations, a country cannot have trade autonomy (in the sense of unilaterally deciding its own trade policy), multilateral trade liberalization and international free trade. If it wants to pursue a unilateral trade policy (decide its own level of protection and discriminate between trading partners) and have international trade, it will be excluded from the multilateral trade system. If a country becomes a member of the multilateral trade system and practises international trade, it has to give up its own trade autonomy.

We can view the political dilemma of democratic governance in the same framework. Globalization means enhanced trade and financial integration in the global economy. Economic globalization would ideally require global government. Either we have nation-states managing economic globalization, without global government, or we create a global government to manage economic globalization, which would imply the end of national sovereignty. How can we resolve the dilemma? Since global government is not realistic in the immediate future, we need to design a system of global governance based on the principles of efficiency, equity and legitimacy.

It is necessary to satisfy the criterion of efficiency so that countries will

International monetary relations

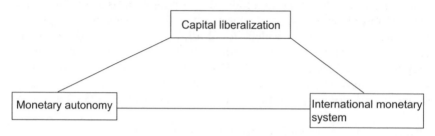

International trade relations

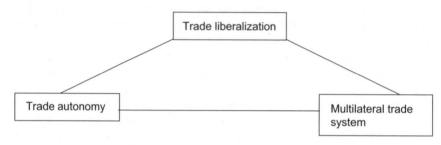

International political relations

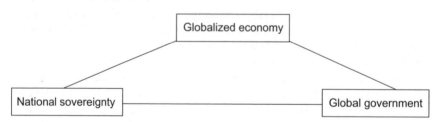

Figure 11.1 The dilemmas of global governance

reap the gains from trade. Equity requires the benefits accruing from international trade liberalization to be fairly distributed. Trade liberalization is sold to the general public on the promise of increased economic welfare and lower prices for consumers. But where special interest groups have access to the political system they can succeed in creaming off a disproportionate share of the benefits. Sovereignty and legitimacy are closely connected. A national government of a sovereign state gets its legitimacy from the "will of the people" who have voted it into power. International organizations that are run by technocrats cannot have this legitimacy; but they can be made more transparent and accountable (Esty, 2002).

The WTO and global trade governance

The success of GATT in the first 50 years of its existence was measured by an unprecedented expansion in international trade, which led to increased living standards in many parts of the world. As rich and poor countries flocked to join, it became the only trade game in town. But the Uruguay Round, which was the eighth round of trade negotiations in the GATT, marked a watershed in the history of trade liberalization. The final outcome, which was accepted as a single undertaking, was very different from the previous GATT model of exchange concessions based on reciprocity. The undemocratic nature of the decision-making led to skewed results favouring rich over poor countries and corporate profits over citizens' well-being.

Asymmetric North–South benefits

The net balance of the Uruguay Round was more favourable to industrial than to developing countries. The agenda attempted to strike the right balance between opening up new areas of special interest to industrial countries, such as services and intellectual property rights, and reducing the entrenched protectionism in sectors of particular interest to developing countries, notably in agriculture and textiles/clothing. But the final outcome resulted in developing countries making far greater concessions than industrial countries on market access (Finger and Nogues, 2002).

The developing countries took the whole Uruguay Round package without realizing what the high cost and the profound significance would be. The concessions granted by the developing countries in new areas such as customs valuation and Trade-Related Aspects of Intellectual Property Rights (TRIPS) imposed high costs of implementation. In many of the poorest countries, institutional capacity and human resources were not adequate. Industrial countries, in contrast, already had such an infrastructure in place.

Industrial countries preserve hard-core protectionism

From the early days of GATT, agricultural trade was kept outside of standard international trade rules. The Uruguay Round aimed to subject agriculture to market disciplines through a tariffication of the numerous non-tariff barriers and then engaging in significant tariff reductions. The complexity of the agricultural negotiations was such that no significant liberalization was achieved. Despite the Uruguay Round, aggregate public support for agriculture in industrial countries has even increased.

The integration of textiles trade into standard GATT law was also a goal of the Uruguay Round. Here, too, complexity and obfuscation resulted from the fact that much of the market liberalization in industrial countries was put off until 2005. The textiles/clothing sector is of major importance to developing countries.

Unequal access for stakeholders

The Uruguay Round raised the profile of multinational corporations (MNCs) in multilateral trade negotiations. They were highly visible and played an intensely active role on the periphery of the negotiations. This was particularly true of the pharmaceutical industry, which lobbied hard for TRIPS; it was at its behest that the US industry pushed it through. The fact that the MNCs were successful in influencing the negotiations and getting an outcome that was in their favour made them an obvious target for their critics and for those who said that the Uruguay Round was conducted primarily in the interests of MNCs.

Democratic deficit writ large

The new institutional structure created an organization with very strong judicial powers, which could enforce WTO rules on its members through the use of sanctions, but with very weak executive powers and an almost complete absence of parliamentary involvement. Such unbalanced constitutional powers would in effect impair the ability of national parliaments to exercise their sovereign right to legislate.

The links between global trade and financial governance

Since the 1990s, financial liberalization has been fostered through the Financial Services Agreement in the WTO and an activist policy on capital liberalization by the International Monetary Fund (IMF).[10] The undemocratic character of decision-making in the IMF has become the focus of debate recently. Research at Warwick University in the United Kingdom shows that the present system of weighted voting leads to an over-concentration of power in the hands of the United States and a corresponding underrepresentation of voting power for developing countries (for example India).

Financial liberalization is more destabilizing in developing countries than in industrialized countries. This is shown by the magnitude of the "GDP gaps" that have occurred following financial liberalization, especially after external liberalization. Financial liberalization usually creates a boom–bust cycle. The bust is longer than the boom and this can have a major negative effect economically, politically and socially. The bust effect is much harsher in developing countries, and affects the poorest people worst where there is no safety net in the form of social welfare.

The evidence seems to show that financial liberalization contributes to banking and currency crises. Through which channels does this occur? Internal liberalization may lead to excessive risk-taking in the absence of adequate supervision and regulation. External liberalization leads to volatile flows of "hot money", which may destabilize the currency. Wyplosz (2001) provides a survey of the new thinking about the causal link between financial liberalization and financial or currency crisis.

If financial liberalization often leads to a crisis, and that crisis is typically followed by a sharp recession, the major policy question is: is it worth it? Financial liberalization is dangerous in the medium term but it has positive long-term effects. Therefore the following factors should be taken into consideration in order to minimize the risks in the short and medium term. Financial liberalization should be conducted in a gradualist manner and not before the proper economic and institutional framework is in place. The sequencing of liberalization is all important. The first steps are free trade and internal liberalization, with accompanying prudential regulation of banks, before moving to external liberalization. It is increasingly recognized that there are market failures in financial markets. The appropriate model of capital liberalization is the European one of slow and gradual financial liberalization.

The European model of regional governance

The European Union, which was established to integrate neighbouring markets into one single internal market, provides an advanced model of regulation in multiple jurisdiction systems. With widening, as it grew from 6 to 15 members, and deepening, as it evolved from a customs union to an internal market and monetary union, the Union gradually took on a more federalist character. Although undergoing dynamic development, the European Union is not moving inevitably towards a "European superstate" but rather has a system of multi-level governance[11] based on the organizing principle of subsidiarity. The institutional structure for decision-making has solved the structural dilemma of sovereignty-sharing through the creation of supranational institutions, which provide for qualified majority voting (see figure 11.2).

The EU regulatory model also suffers from a democratic deficit and it does not satisfy the principles of efficiency, equity and legitimacy (Karlsson, 2001). To date, it has been unable to reconcile these three principles in an acceptable balanced manner. The major achievement of the European Union has been the creation of a comprehensive system of economic governance. But that has not satisfied the citizens of Europe, whose loyalty remains anchored in their nation-states. A positive analysis of the evolution of the EU regulatory model is given in the following subsection.

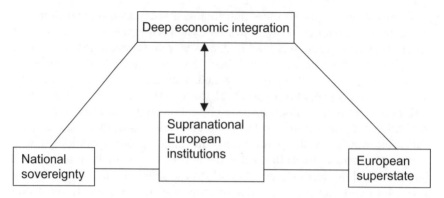

Figure 11.2 The European model of governance

A positive analysis of the EU model of governance

Trade

The single market programme of 1992, which is the centrepiece of the European Union's internal governance, included a number of measures that improved market access for traders and investors from third countries:

- the removal of a vast array of quantitative restrictions including quotas, voluntary export restraints and orderly marketing arrangements in a number of sectors;
- the removal of physical barriers, notably the elimination of customs controls at national borders;
- technical barriers to trade, such as national regulations and standards, either harmonized or subjected to mutual recognition;
- the liberalization of barriers to trade in services, including the right of establishment;
- the harmonization or streamlining of barriers to business operations, including company law and taxation, to facilitate cross-border business practice;
- the deregulation and liberalization of state-controlled monopolies, for example telecommunications;
- the liberalization of public procurement.

Finance

The European Union has created a zone of financial and monetary stability. Financial governance is a horizontal model that includes liberalization, competition and prudential regulation. Central to the approach is the recognition of interdependence between these three elements:

- financial liberalization was introduced in an appropriate sequenced manner;

- capital liberalization was implemented gradually and with clearly defined exceptions;
- standards for prudential regulation and supervision of all financial institutions were harmonized at EU level;
- responsibility for banking supervision was shared between the member states and the European Commission.

Monetary union

Since the currency crisis in 1992–3, the European Union has been a zone of monetary stability. The path to monetary union, which was mapped out in the Maastricht Treaty, called for convergence of members' macroeconomic policies. Between 1992 and 2002 the European Union moved gradually away from the adjustable peg model of the exchange rate mechanism, to institutionally fixed exchange rates, to a single currency.

Environment and social policy

Sustainable development has been adopted as a Treaty goal since the Amsterdam Treaty (1999) and environmental considerations must be incorporated into all EU policies. The social market model, which provided a safety network against shocks from openness to global trade, has been Europeanized to a growing extent. Labour market standards governing health and safety in the workplace have been set at EU level and the Commission is responsible for promoting a social dialogue between management and labour at the EU level. Redistribution of income to the poorest regions of the Union has been achieved through the structural funds.

Normative analysis of the EU regulatory model

The EU system of multi-level governance, based on the organizing principle of subsidiarity, implies that decision-making should operate at different levels, including local/regional, national and European level. Decision-making should be as close as possible to EU citizens. Subsidiarity was included in the Maastricht Treaty of 1993 as a safeguard mechanism against any major shift of power to the centre.

However, subsidiarity did not satisfy EU citizens – far from it. Since Maastricht there has been a backlash against the European Union and citizens have become much more openly critical. Many of the new economic rights acquired by corporations in the internal market reduced their responsibilities to labour, to the environment and to communities and governments that provided the infrastructure necessary for those corporations to be profitable. Monetary union has prevented national governments from Keynesian deficit-spending to create jobs even when unemployment is very high.

Citizens fear that their governments can no longer protect their basic rights against the European Union, which is acting as a Trojan horse for economic globalization. The new economic policies are being made by EU institutions, which are not subject to the normal democratic control prevailing in sovereign states. Democracy is defined as "government by the people" – citizens can exercise control over the government by holding it accountable for its actions and by voting it out of office if they are not satisfied. In the European Union there is bureaucratic but not democratic control over its institutions.

The future drivers of European integration will not just be institutional reforms. The main challenges will be how to achieve legitimacy for EU institutions and to win the loyalty of European citizens. How can a common European identity be created? Institutional reforms, from the top down and forced upon citizens, when there is no feeling of common values, will not create a community of solidarity. The EU leaders need to define more clearly the mission of the European Union and its future role in world affairs. European citizens now consider that "the future of Europe is Europe in the world".[12] The central focus is now on developing democratic governance.

The future of Europe: Democratic governance

The European Convention, which was set up in February 2002, has been mandated to prepare for major constitutional reform of the European Union. Europe's ultimate political destiny is still undefined, as expressed in the oxymoron "Federation of Nation-States". Whatever the outcome of the Convention process, the EU form of governance must be reformed to achieve a proper separation and balance of constitutional powers among the institutions and a stronger role for Europe in the world:

- The Commission, which has a monopoly on proposing legislation, must become a democratically legitimate executive.
- The European Parliament, which is the only directly elected institution, should be given appropriate legislative powers in co-decision with the Council of Ministers.
- The Council of Ministers must operate transparently, with qualified majority voting in place of the "horse-trading" package deal method that currently prevails.
- The European Union must improve its relations with civil society. The Charter of Fundamental Rights should be incorporated into a future constitutional treaty. This Charter covers individual and collective rights and their recognition would lead to public involvement in policy-making.
- The European Union must become a community of common values. It

must be built from the bottom up and provide for participatory democracy to complement representative democracy.

- The European Union must become a more effective global actor. It must accept responsibilities in the world commensurate with its economic power. It therefore needs a coherent common external policy for trade, finance, development, environment, peace-keeping and peace enforcement, and it must contribute to the reform of global multilateral institutions. Policy coherence matters.

Conclusions

This chapter has focused on the amazing growth of RTAs in the global economy since the 1990s. According to the WTO, there is now a complex network of over 160 regional trade agreements in force and almost all WTO members participate in one or more of these. Despite the rapid growth of RTAs, there has not been a significant increase in the share of intraregional trade as a proportion of overall global trade.

So what is driving the new regionalism? Paradoxically, globalization is a major driver. Globalization has fundamentally changed the structural conditions of the international economy and FDI now plays a much more important role than in the past. This has made the old customs union theory obsolete. The new theory, based on investment creation and regionalization of markets, provides a more robust explanation of why countries are "racing to regionalize".

Institutional arrangements matter. Regional organizations are more manageable than global institutions because they have fewer and more homogeneous members. This makes for more efficient decision-making and, in addition, provides incentives for a regional leader to emerge as hegemon. Regionalism is still largely concentrated in the North, but that may now be set to change. Developing countries have become increasingly disillusioned with the global multilateral institutions, which are seen to operate more in the interests of the industrial countries and delivered very unbalanced outcomes in the 1990s. Recent developments in Africa, Latin America and Asia point to a bigger role for regionalism in the future.

The European Union pioneered the old regionalism of the 1960s and the deep integration of the new regionalism. European integration has always been a few steps ahead of global integration. Now the EU debate has shifted to resolving the democratic legitimacy of its governance system. Will the future constitutional treaty of Europe reconcile efficiency, legitimacy and effective participation of civil society in policy-making? If it does, it will be a laboratory for the rest of the world and quite possibly a role model.

Appendix

Table 11A.1. Regional trade agreements notified to the GATT/WTO and in force, by date of entry into force, as of 30 June 2002

Agreement	Date of entry into force	GATT/WTO notification			WT/ document series	Examination process	
		Date	Related provisions	Type of agreement		Status	Ref.
EC (Treaty of Rome)	1-Jan-58	10-Nov-95	GATS Art. V	Services agreement	REG39	Under factual examination	…
EC (Treaty of Rome)	1-Jan-58	24-Apr-57	GATT Art. XXIV	Customs union	…	Report adopted	6S/70 & 109 29.11.57
EFTA (Stockholm Convention)	3-May-60	14-Nov-59	GATT Art. XXIV	Free trade agreement	REG85	Report adopted	9S/70 04.06.60
CACM	12-Oct-61	24-Feb-61	GATT Art. XXIV	Customs union	REG93	Report adopted	10S/98 23.11.61
TRIPARTITE	1-Apr-68	23-Feb-68	Enabling Clause	Other	…	Report adopted	16S/83 14.11.68
EFTA accession of Iceland	1-Mar-70	30-Jan-70	GATT Art. XXIV	Accession to free trade agreement	…	Report adopted	18S/174 29.09.70
EC–OCTs	1-Jan-71	14-Dec-70	GATT Art. XXIV	Free trade agreement	REG106	Report adopted	18S/143 09.11.71
EC–Malta	1-Apr-71	24-Mar-71	GATT Art. XXIV	Customs union	REG102	Report adopted	19S/90 29.05.72
EC–Switzerland and Liechtenstein	1-Jan-73	27-Oct-72	GATT Art. XXIV	Free trade agreement	REG94	Report adopted	20S/196 19.10.73
EC accession of Denmark, Ireland and United Kingdom	1-Jan-73	7-Mar-72	GATT Art. XXIV	Accession to customs union	…	Report adopted	C/M/107 11.07.75

Name	Date	Date	Legal basis	Other	REG	Status	Reference
PTN	11-Feb-73	9-Nov-71	Enabling Clause	Other	...	Examination not requested	...
EC–Iceland	1-Apr-73	24-Nov-72	GATT Art. XXIV	Free trade agreement	REG95	Report adopted	20S/158 19.10.73
EC–Cyprus	1-Jun-73	13-Jun-73	GATT Art. XXIV	Customs union	REG97	Report adopted	21S/94 21.06.74
EC–Norway	1-Jul-73	13-Jul-73	GATT Art. XXIV	Free trade agreement	...	Report adopted	21S/83 28.03.74
CARICOM	1-Aug-73	14-Oct-74	GATT Art. XXIV	Customs union	REG92	Report adopted	24S/68 02.03.77
Bangkok Agreement	17-Jun-76	2-Nov-76	Enabling Clause	Other	...	Report adopted	25S/109 14.03.78
EC–Algeria	1-Jul-76	28-Jul-76	GATT Art. XXIV	Free trade agreement	REG105	Report adopted	24S/80 11.11.77
PATCRA	1-Feb-77	20-Dec-76	GATT Art. XXIV	Free trade agreement	...	Report adopted	24S/63 11.11.77
EC–Egypt	1-Jul-77	15-Jul-77	GATT Art. XXIV	Free trade agreement	REG98	Report adopted	25S/114 17.05.78
EC–Jordan	1-Jul-77	15-Jul-77	GATT Art. XXIV	Free trade agreement	REG100	Report adopted	25S/133 17.05.78
EC–Lebanon	1-Jul-77	15-Jul-77	GATT Art. XXIV	Free trade agreement	REG100	Report adopted	25S/142 17.05.78
EC–Syria	1-Jul-77	15-Jul-77	GATT Art. XXIV	Free trade agreement	REG104	Report adopted	25S/123 17.05.78
ASEAN	31-Aug-77	1-Nov-77	Enabling Clause	Other	...	Report adopted	26S/321 29.01.79
SPARTECA	1-Jan-81	20-Feb-81	Enabling Clause	Other	...	Examination not requested	...
EC accession of Greece	1-Jan-81	24-Oct-79	GATT Art. XXIV	Accession to customs union	...	Report adopted	30S/168 09.03.83
LAIA	18-Mar-81	1-Jul-82	Enabling Clause	Other	...	Examination not requested	...

Table 11A.1. (cont.)

Agreement	Date of entry into force	GATT/WTO notification			WT/ document series	Examination process	
		Date	Related provisions	Type of agreement		Status	Ref.
CER	1-Jan-83	14-Apr-83	GATT Art. XXIV	Free trade agreement	REG111	Report adopted	31S/170 02.10.84
United States–Israel	19-Aug-85	13-Sep-85	GATT Art. XXIV	Free trade agreement	...	Report adopted	34S/58 14.05.87
EC accession of Portugal and Spain	1-Jan-86	11-Dec-85	GATT Art. XXIV	Accession to customs union	...	Report adopted	35S/293 19.10.88
CAN	25-May-88	12-Oct-92	Enabling Clause	Other	...	Examination not requested	...
CER	1-Jan-89	22-Nov-95	GATS Art. V	Services agreement	REG40	Consultations on draft report	...
GSTP	19-Apr-89	25-Sep-89	Enabling Clause	Other	...	Examination not requested	...
Laos–Thailand	20-Jun-91	29-Nov-91	Enabling Clause	Other	...	Examination not requested	...
EC–Andorra	1-Jul-91	25-Feb-98	GATT Art. XXIV	Customs union	REG53	Factual examination concluded	...
MERCOSUR	29-Nov-91	5-Mar-92	Enabling Clause	Customs union	COMTD/1	Under factual examination	...
AFTA	28-Jan-92	30-Oct-92	Enabling Clause	Other	...	Examination not requested	...
EC–Czech Republic	1-Mar-92	13-May-96	GATT Art. XXIV	Free trade agreement	REG18	Factual examination concluded	...

Agreement	Entry into force	Notification	Provision	Type	Reg.	Status	Reference
EC–Slovak Republic	1-Mar-92	13-May-96	GATT Art. XXIV	Free trade agreement	REG18	Factual examination concluded	...
EC–Hungary	1-Mar-92	3-Apr-92	GATT Art. XXIV	Free trade agreement	REG18	Consultations on draft report	...
EC–Poland	1-Mar-92	3-Apr-92	GATT Art. XXIV	Free trade agreement	REG18	Factual examination concluded	...
EFTA–Turkey	1-Apr-92	6-Mar-92	GATT Art. XXIV	Free trade agreement	REG86	Report adopted	40S/48 17.12.93
EFTA–Czech Republic	1-Jul-92	3-Jul-92	GATT Art. XXIV	Free trade agreement	REG87	Report adopted	41S/116 08.12.94
EFTA–Slovak Republic	1-Jul-92	3-Jul-92	GATT Art. XXIV	Free trade agreement	REG88	Report adopted	41S/116 08.12.94
Czech Republic–Slovak Republic	1-Jan-93	30-Apr-93	GATT Art. XXIV	Customs union	REG89	Report adopted	41S/112 04.10.94
EFTA–Israel	1-Jan-93	1-Dec-92	GATT Art. XXIV	Free trade agreement	REG14	Factual examination concluded	...
CEFTA	1-Mar-93	30-Jun-94	GATT Art. XXIV	Free trade agreement	REG11	Consultations on draft report	...
Kyrgyz Republic–Russian Federation	24-Apr-93	15-Jun-99	GATT Art. XXIV	Free trade agreement	REG73	Under factual examination	...
EC–Romania	1-May-93	23-Dec-94	GATT Art. XXIV	Free trade agreement	REG2	Factual examination concluded	...
EFTA–Romania	1-May-93	24-May-93	GATT Art. XXIV	Free trade agreement	REG16	Factual examination concluded	...

Table 11A.1. (cont.)

Agreement	Date of entry into force	GATT/WTO notification Date	Related provisions	Type of agreement	WT/ document series	Examination process Status	Ref.
Faroe Islands–Norway	1-Jul-93	13-Mar-96	GATT Art. XXIV	Free trade agreement	REG25	Factual examination concluded	...
Faroe Islands–Iceland	1-Jul-93	23-Jan-96	GATT Art. XXIV	Free trade agreement	REG23	Factual examination concluded	...
EFTA–Bulgaria	1-Jul-93	30-Jun-93	GATT Art. XXIV	Free trade agreement	REG12	Factual examination concluded	...
MSG	22-Jul-93	7-Oct-99	Enabling Clause	Other	...	Examination not requested	...
EFTA–Hungary	1-Oct-93	23-Dec-93	GATT Art. XXIV	Free trade agreement	REG13	Consultations on draft report	...
EFTA–Poland	15-Nov-93	20-Oct-93	GATT Art. XXIV	Free trade agreement	REG15	Factual examination concluded	...
EC–Bulgaria	31-Dec-93	23-Dec-94	GATT Art. XXIV	Free trade agreement	REG1	Factual examination concluded	...
EEA	1-Jan-94	10-Oct-96	GATS Art. V	Services agreement	...	Factual examination not started	...
NAFTA	1-Jan-94	1-Feb-93	GATT Art. XXIV	Free trade agreement	REG4	Consultations on draft report	...

Agreement	Date 1	Date 2	Provision	Type	REG	Status	
EC–Hungary	1-Feb-94	27-Aug-96	GATS Art. V	Services agreement	REG50	Consultations on draft report	…
EC–Poland	1-Feb-94	27-Aug-96	GATS Art. V	Services agreement	REG51	Factual examination concluded	…
BAFTA	1-Apr-94	15-Jun-99	GATT Art. XXIV	Free trade agreement	REG77	Factual examination concluded	…
NAFTA	1-Apr-94	1-Mar-95	GATS Art. V	Services agreement	REG4	Consultations on draft report	…
Georgia–Russian Federation	10-May-94	21-Feb-01	GATT Art. XXIV	Free trade agreement	REG118	Under factual examination	…
COMESA	8-Dec-94	29-Jun-95	Enabling Clause	Other	…	Examination not requested	…
CIS	30-Dec-94	1-Oct-99	GATT Art. XXIV	Free trade agreement	REG82	Under factual examination	…
Romania–Moldova	1-Jan-95	24-Sep-97	GATT Art. XXIV	Free trade agreement	REG44	Factual examination concluded	…
EC–Lithuania	1-Jan-95	26-Sep-95	GATT Art. XXIV	Free trade agreement	REG9	Factual examination concluded	…
EC–Estonia	1-Jan-95	30-Jun-95	GATT Art. XXIV	Free trade agreement	REG8	Factual examination concluded	…
EC–Latvia	1-Jan-95	30-Jun-95	GATT Art. XXIV	Free trade agreement	REG7	Factual examination concluded	…
EC accession of Austria, Finland and Sweden	1-Jan-95	20-Jan-95	GATT Art. XXIV	Accession to customs union	REG3	Consultations on draft report	…

Table 11A.1. (cont.)

Agreement	Date of entry into force	GATT/WTO notification		Type of agreement	WT/ document series	Examination process	
		Date	Related provisions			Status	Ref.
EC accession of Austria, Finland and Sweden	1-Jan-95	20-Jan-95	GATS Art. V	Accession to services agreement	REG3	Consultations on draft report	...
EC–Bulgaria	1-Feb-95	25-Apr-97	GATS Art. V	Services agreement	...	Factual examination not started	...
EC–Czech Republic	1-Feb-95	9-Oct-96	GATS Art. V	Services agreement	...	Factual examination not started	...
EC–Romania	1-Feb-95	9-Oct-96	GATS Art. V	Services agreement	...	Factual examination not started	...
EC–Slovak Republic	1-Feb-95	27-Aug-96	GATS Art. V	Services agreement	REG52	Factual examination concluded	...
Faroe Islands–Switzerland	1-Mar-95	8-Mar-96	GATT Art. XXIV	Free trade agreement	REG24	Factual examination concluded	...
EFTA–Slovenia	1-Jul-95	18-Oct-95	GATT Art. XXIV	Free trade agreement	REG20	Factual examination concluded	...
Kyrgyz Republic–Armenia	27-Oct-95	4-Jan-01	GATT Art. XXIV	Free trade agreement	REG114	Under factual examination	...
Kyrgyz Republic–Kazakhstan	11-Nov-95	29-Sep-99	GATT Art. XXIV	Free trade agreement	REG81	Under factual examination	...

			Enabling Clause	Other			...
SAPTA	7-Dec-95	22-Sep-93			...	Examination not requested	...
CEFTA accession of Slovenia	1-Jan-96	8-Jan-98	GATT Art. XXIV	Accession to free trade agreement	REG11	Consultations on draft report	...
EC–Turkey	1-Jan-96	22-Dec-95	GATT Art. XXIV	Customs union	REG22	Under factual examination	...
Estonia–Ukraine	14-Mar-96	25-Jul-00	GATT Art. XXIV	Free trade agreement	REG108	Factual examination concluded	...
EFTA–Estonia	1-Jun-96	25-Jul-96	GATT Art. XXIV	Free trade agreement	REG28	Factual examination concluded	...
EFTA–Latvia	1-Jun-96	25-Jul-96	GATT Art. XXIV	Free trade agreement	REG29	Factual examination concluded	...
Georgia–Ukraine	4-Jun-96	21-Feb-01	GATT Art. XXIV	Free trade agreement	REG121	Under factual examination	...
Georgia–Azerbaijan	10-Jul-96	21-Feb-01	GATT Art. XXIV	Free trade agreement	REG120	Under factual examination	...
Slovenia–Latvia	1-Aug-96	20-Feb-97	GATT Art. XXIV	Free trade agreement	REG34	Factual examination concluded	...
EFTA–Lithuania	1-Aug-96	25-Jul-96	GATT Art. XXIV	Free trade agreement	REG30	Factual examination concluded	...
Slovenia–Former Yugoslav Republic of Macedonia	1-Sep-96	20-Feb-97	GATT Art. XXIV	Free trade agreement	REG36	Factual examination concluded	...

Table 11A.1. (cont.)

Agreement	Date of entry into force	GATT/WTO notification			WT/document series	Examination process	
		Date	Related provisions	Type of agreement		Status	Ref.
Kyrgyz Republic–Moldova	21-Nov-96	15-Jun-99	GATT Art. XXIV	Free trade agreement	REG76	Factual examination concluded	…
Slovak Republic–Israel	1-Jan-97	30-Mar-98	GATT Art. XXIV	Free trade agreement	REG57	Factual examination concluded	…
Poland–Lithuania	1-Jan-97	30-Dec-97	GATT Art. XXIV	Free trade agreement	REG49	Factual examination concluded	…
Slovenia–Estonia	1-Jan-97	20-Feb-97	GATT Art. XXIV	Free trade agreement	REG37	Factual examination concluded	…
EC–Faroe Islands	1-Jan-97	19-Feb-97	GATT Art. XXIV	Free trade agreement	REG21	Under factual examination	…
Canada–Israel	1-Jan-97	23-Jan-97	GATT Art. XXIV	Free trade agreement	REG31	Factual examination concluded	…
EC–Slovenia	1-Jan-97	11-Nov-96	GATT Art. XXIV	Free trade agreement	REG32	Factual examination concluded	…
Slovenia–Lithuania	1-Mar-97	20-Feb-97	GATT Art. XXIV	Free trade agreement	REG35	Factual examination concluded	…
Israel–Turkey	1-May-97	18-May-98	GATT Art. XXIV	Free trade agreement	REG60	Factual examination concluded	…

Agreement			GATT/GATS	Type	REG	Status	
CEFTA accession of Romania	1-Jul-97	8-Jan-98	GATT Art. XXIV	Accession to free trade agreement	REG11	Consultations on draft report	...
Slovak Republic–Latvia	1-Jul-97	14-Nov-97	GATT Art. XXIV	Free trade agreement	REG47	Factual examination concluded	...
Slovak Republic–Lithuania	1-Jul-97	14-Nov-97	GATT Art. XXIV	Free trade agreement	REG48	Factual examination concluded	...
Czech Republic–Latvia	1-Jul-97	13-Nov-97	GATT Art. XXIV	Free trade agreement	REG45	Factual examination concluded	...
EC–Palestinian Authority	1-Jul-97	30-Jun-97	GATT Art. XXIV	Free trade agreement	REG43	Factual examination not started	...
Canada–Chile	5-Jul-97	13-Nov-97	GATS Art. V	Services agreement	REG38	Under factual examination	...
Canada–Chile	5-Jul-97	26-Aug-97	GATT Art. XXIV	Free trade agreement	REG38	Factual examination concluded	...
Czech Republic–Lithuania	1-Sep-97	13-Nov-97	GATT Art. XXIV	Free trade agreement	REG46	Factual examination concluded	...
EAEC	8-Oct-97	6-Apr-99	GATT Art. XXIV	Customs union	REG71	Under factual examination	...
Czech Republic–Israel	1-Dec-97	30-Mar-98	GATT Art. XXIV	Free trade agreement	REG56	Factual examination concluded	...
Slovenia–Croatia	1-Jan-98	25-Mar-98	GATT Art. XXIV	Free trade agreement	REG55	Factual examination concluded	...

Table 11A.1. (cont.)

| Agreement | Date of entry into force | GATT/WTO notification | | | WT/ document series | Examination process | |
		Date	Related provisions	Type of agreement		Status	Ref.
Kyrgyz Republic–Ukraine	19-Jan-98	15-Jun-99	GATT Art. XXIV	Free trade agreement	REG74	Under factual examination	…
EC–Lithuania	1-Feb-98	11-Feb-02	GATS Art. V	Services agreement	…	Factual examination not started	…
EC–Estonia	1-Feb-98	11-Feb-02	GATS Art. V	Services agreement	…	Factual examination not started	…
Romania–Turkey	1-Feb-98	18-May-98	GATT Art. XXIV	Free trade agreement	REG59	Factual examination concluded	…
Hungary–Israel	1-Feb-98	24-Mar-98	GATT Art. XXIV	Free trade agreement	REG54	Factual examination concluded	…
Czech Republic–Estonia	12-Feb-98	3-Aug-98	GATT Art. XXIV	Free trade agreement	REG62	Factual examination concluded	…
Slovak Republic–Estonia	12-Feb-98	3-Aug-98	GATT Art. XXIV	Free trade agreement	REG63	Factual examination concluded	…
EC–Tunisia	1-Mar-98	23-Mar-99	GATT Art. XXIV	Free trade agreement	REG69	Factual examination concluded	…
Poland–Israel	1-Mar-98	25-Feb-99	GATT Art. XXIV	Free trade agreement	REG65	Factual examination concluded	…

Name					REG No.	Status	
Lithuania–Turkey	1-Mar-98	8-Jun-98	GATT Art. XXIV	Free trade agreement	REG61	Factual examination concluded	...
Kyrgyz Republic–Uzbekistan	20-Mar-98	15-Jun-99	GATT Art. XXIV	Free trade agreement	REG75	Under factual examination	...
Hungary–Turkey	1-Apr-98	12-May-98	GATT Art. XXIV	Free trade agreement	REG58	Factual examination concluded	...
Estonia–Turkey	1-Jun-98	23-Mar-99	GATT Art. XXIV	Free trade agreement	REG70	Factual examination concluded	...
Czech Republic–Turkey	1-Sep-98	24-Apr-99	GATT Art. XXIV	Free trade agreement	REG67	Factual examination concluded	...
Slovak Republic–Turkey	1-Sep-98	24-Mar-99	GATT Art. XXIV	Free trade agreement	REG68	Factual examination concluded	...
Slovenia–Israel	1-Sep-98	8-Mar-99	GATT Art. XXIV	Free trade agreement	REG66	Factual examination concluded	...
Georgia–Armenia	11-Nov-98	21-Feb-01	GATT Art. XXIV	Free trade agreement	REG119	Under factual examination	...
Estonia–Faroe Islands	1-Dec-98	26-Jan-99	GATT Art. XXIV	Free trade agreement	REG64	Under factual examination	...
Bulgaria–Turkey	1-Jan-99	4-May-99	GATT Art. XXIV	Free trade agreement	REG72	Factual examination concluded	...
CEFTA accession of Bulgaria	1-Jan-99	24-Mar-99	GATT Art. XXIV	Accession to free trade agreement	REG11	Consultations on draft report	...
EC–Slovenia	1-Feb-99	11-Feb-02	GATS Art. V	Services agreement	...	Factual examination not started	...

Table 11A.1. (cont.)

| Agreement | Date of entry into force | GATT/WTO notification | | | WT/document series | Examination process | |
		Date	Related provisions	Type of agreement		Status	Ref.
EC–Latvia	1-Feb-99	11-Feb-02	GATS Art. V	Services agreement	...	Factual examination not started	...
Poland–Latvia	1-Jun-99	29-Sep-99	GATT Art. XXIV	Free trade agreement	REG80	Factual examination concluded	...
Poland–Faroe Islands	1-Jun-99	18-Aug-99	GATT Art. XXIV	Free trade agreement	REG78	Under factual examination	...
CEMAC	24-Jun-99	28-Sep-00	Enabling Clause	Other	...	Examination not requested	...
EFTA–Palestinian Authority	1-Jul-99	21-Sep-99	GATT Art. XXIV	Free trade agreement	REG79	Factual examination not started	...
Georgia–Kazakhstan	16-Jul-99	21-Feb-01	GATT Art. XXIV	Free trade agreement	REG123	Under factual examination	...
Chile–Mexico	1-Aug-99	14-Mar-01	GATS Art. V	Services agreement	REG125	Factual examination not started	...
Chile–Mexico	1-Aug-99	27-Feb-01	GATT Art. XXIV	Free trade agreement	REG125	Factual examination not started	...
EFTA–Morocco	1-Dec-99	20-Feb-00	GATT Art. XXIV	Free trade agreement	REG91	Factual examination concluded	...
Georgia–Turkmenistan	1-Jan-00	21-Feb-01	GATT Art. XXIV	Free trade agreement	REG122	Under factual examination	...

EC–South Africa	1-Jan-00	14-Nov-00	GATT Art. XXIV	Free trade agreement	REG113	Factual examination not started	...
WAEMU/UEMOA	1-Jan-00	3-Feb-00	Enabling Clause	Other	...	Examination not requested	...
Bulgaria–Former Yugoslav Republic of Macedonia	1-Jan-00	21-Jan-00	GATT Art. XXIV	Free trade agreement	REG90	Factual examination concluded	...
Hungary–Latvia	1-Jan-00	20-Dec-99	GATT Art. XXIV	Free trade agreement	REG84	Factual examination concluded	...
EC–Morocco	1-Mar-00	8-Nov-00	GATT Art. XXIV	Free trade agreement	REG112	Under factual examination	...
Hungary–Lithuania	1-Mar-00	20-Dec-99	GATT Art. XXIV	Free trade agreement	REG83	Factual examination concluded	...

Source: http://www.wto.org/english/tratop_e/region_e/region_e.htm

Notes:

AFTA — ASEAN Free Trade Area — Brunei, Darussalam, Cambodia, Indonesia, Laos, Malaysia, Myanmar, Philippines, Singapore, Thailand, Vietnam

ASEAN — Association of South East Asian Nations — Brunei, Darussalam, Cambodia, Indonesia, Laos, Malaysia, Myanmar, Philippines, Singapore, Thailand, Vietnam

BAFTA — Baltic Free-Trade Area — Estonia, Latvia, Lithuania

BANGKOK — Bangkok Agreement — Bangladesh, China, India, Republic of Korea, Laos, Sri Lanka

CAN — Andean Community — Bolivia, Colombia, Ecuador, Peru, Venezuela

CARICOM — Caribbean Community and Common Market — Antigua & Barbuda, Bahamas, Barbados, Belize, Dominica, Grenada, Guyana, Haiti, Jamaica, Montserrat, Trinidad & Tobago, St. Kitts & Nevis, St. Lucia, St. Vincent & the Grenadines, Suriname

CACM — Central American Common Market — Costa Rica, El Salvador, Guatemala, Honduras, Nicaragua

CEFTA — Central European Free Trade Agreement — Bulgaria, Czech Republic, Hungary, Poland, Romania, Slovak Republic, Slovenia

309

Table 11A.1. (cont.)

Notes:

CEMAC	Economic and Monetary Community of Central Africa	Cameroon, Central African Republic, Chad, Congo, Equatorial Guinea, Gabon
CER	Closer Economic Relations Trade Agreement	Australia, New Zealand
CIS	Commonwealth of Independent States	Azerbaijan, Armenia, Belarus, Georgia, Moldova, Kazakhstan, Russian Federation, Ukraine, Uzbekistan, Tajikistan, Kyrgyz Republic
COMESA	Common Market for Eastern and Southern Africa	Angola, Burundi, Comoros, Democratic Republic of Congo, Djibouti, Egypt, Eritrea, Ethiopia, Kenya, Madagascar, Malawi, Mauritius, Namibia, Rwanda, Seychelles, Sudan, Swaziland, Uganda, Zambia, Zimbabwe
EAC	East African Cooperation	Kenya, Tanzania, Uganda
EAEC	Eurasian Economic Community	Belarus, Kazakhstan, Kyrgyz Republic, Russian Federation, Tajikistan
EC	European Communities	Austria, Belgium, Denmark, Finland, France, Germany, Greece, Ireland, Italy, Luxembourg, Netherlands, Portugal, Spain, Sweden, United Kingdom
ECO	Economic Cooperation Organization	Afghanistan, Azerbaijan, Iran, Kazakhstan, Kyrgyz Republic, Pakistan, Tajikistan, Turkey, Turkmenistan, Uzbekistan
EEA	European Economic Area	EC, Iceland, Liechtenstein, Norway
EFTA	European Free Trade Association	Iceland, Liechtenstein, Norway, Switzerland
GCC	Gulf Cooperation Council	Bahrain, Kuwait, Oman, Qatar, Saudi Arabia, United Arab Emirates
GSTP	General System of Trade Preferences among Developing Countries	Algeria, Angola, Argentina, Bangladesh, Benin, Bolivia, Brazil, Cameroon, Chile, Colombia, Cuba, Democratic People's Republic of Korea, Ecuador, Egypt, Ghana, Guinea, Guyana, Haiti, India, Indonesia, Islamic Republic of Iran, Iraq, Libya, Malaysia, Mexico, Morocco, Mozambique, Nicaragua, Nigeria, Pakistan, Peru, Philippines, Qatar, Republic of Korea, Romania, Singapore, Sri Lanka, Sudan, Thailand, Trinidad and Tobago, Tunisia, United Republic of Tanzania, Uruguay, Venezuela, Vietnam, Yugoslavia, Zaire, Zimbabwe

LAIA	Latin American Integration Association	Argentina, Bolivia, Brazil, Chile, Colombia, Cuba, Ecuador, Mexico, Paraguay, Peru, Uruguay, Venezuela
MERCOSUR	Southern Common Market	Argentina, Brazil, Paraguay, Uruguay
MSG	Melanesian Spearhead Group	Fiji, Papua New Guinea, Solomon Islands, Vanuatu
NAFTA	North American Free Trade Agreement	Canada, Mexico, United States
OCT	Overseas Countries and Territories	Greenland, New Caledonia, French Polynesia, French Southern and Antarctic Territories, Wallis and Futuna Islands, Mayotte, Saint Pierre and Miquelon, Aruba, Netherlands Antilles, Anguilla, Cayman Islands, Falkland Islands, South Georgia and South Sandwich Islands, Montserrat, Pitcairn, Saint Helena, Ascension Island, Tristan da Cunha, Turks and Caicos Islands, British Antarctic Territory, British Indian Ocean Territory, British Virgin Islands
PTN	Protocol relating to Trade Negotiations among Developing Countries	Bangladesh, Brazil, Chile, Egypt, Israel, Mexico, Pakistan, Paraguay, Peru, Philippines, Republic of Korea, Romania, Tunisia, Turkey, Uruguay, Yugoslavia
SAPTA	South Asian Preferential Trade Arrangement	Bangladesh, Bhutan, India, Maldives, Nepal, Pakistan, Sri Lanka
SPARTECA	South Pacific Regional Trade and Economic Cooperation Agreement	Australia, New Zealand, Cook Islands, Fiji, Kiribati, Marshall Islands, Micronesia, Nauru, Niue, Papua New Guinea, Solomon Islands, Tonga, Tuvalu, Vanuatu, Western Samoa
TRIPARTITE	Tripartite Agreement	Egypt, India, Yugoslavia
UEMOA/ WAEMU	West African Economic and Monetary Union	Benin, Burkina Faso, Côte d'Ivoire, Guinea Bissau, Mali, Niger, Senegal, Togo

311

Notes

1. The "double movement" thesis was originally developed by Karl Polanyi (1945); he argues that, because economic liberalization aggravates economic inequalities and destroys many social and cultural patterns of life, it will lead to a social backlash.
2. The WTO website provides comprehensive information and analysis on regionalism world-wide. In 1996 the WTO General Council created the Committee on Regional Trade Agreements, which examines RTAs to assess whether they are consistent with WTO rules and how they affect the multilateral trade system; see http://www.wto.org/regionalism/.
3. For a comprehensive analysis of different economic integration schemes, see El-Agraa (1997).
4. There is a voluminous literature on the relation between RTAs and multilateralism which cannot be cited here. A good flavour of the debate is given in Bhagwati and Pangariya (1996); see also Winters (1999).
5. The old regionalism is built upon the seminal work of customs union theory by Jacob Viner (1950).
6. For the essentials of new regionalism theory, see Lawrence (1995) and Ethier (2001).
7. For an analysis of the relation between trade and investment in the globalizing economy, see Gavin (2001a).
8. See *Trading Health Care Away?* (2001).
9. This model is derived from Rodrik (2000). The principles of the international economic order that underpin the model of governance are discussed by Valaskakis (2001).
10. The links between trade and financial liberalization are analysed in Gavin (2001b).
11. For a discussion of the original concept of multi-level governance, see Wessels (1997). For a more recent analysis, see Hooghe and Marks (2001). The European Commission published its White Paper on Governance in July 2001 as a basis for consultation with the major stakeholders.
12. The fusion of internal and external governance is discussed by Telo (2002).

References

Bhagwati, J. N., and A. Pangariya (1996), "Preferential Trading Areas and Multilateralism: Strangers, Friends or Foes?" in J. N. Bhagwati and A. Pangariya (eds.), *Free Trade Areas or Free Trade? The Economics of Preferential Trade Agreements*, Washington DC: American Enterprise Institute.

Breslin, S., and R. Higgott (2001). "Studying Regions: Learning from the Old, Constructing the New", *New Political Economy* 5(3), pp. 333–52.

El-Agraa, A. M. (1997), *Economic Integration Worldwide*. London: Macmillan.

Esty, D. C. (2002), "The World Trade Organization's Legitimacy Crisis", *World Trade Review* 1(1), pp. 7–22.

Ethier, W. J. (2001), "Regional Regionalism", in S. Lahiri (ed.), *Regionalism and Globalization*, London: Routledge.

Finger, J. M., and J. J. Nogues (2002), "The Unbalanced Uruguay Round Outcome: The New Areas in Future WTO Negotiations", *The World Economy* 25(3), pp. 321–39.

Fratianni, M., and J. Pattison (2001), "International Organisations in a World of

Regional Trade Agreements: Lessons from Club Theory", *The World Economy* 24(3), pp. 333–58.

Gavin, B. (2001a), "Trade and Investment", in *The European Union and Globalization: Towards Global Democratic Governance*, Cheltenham, UK: Edward Elgar.

―――― (2001b), "Trade and Finance", in *The European Union and Globalization: Towards Global Democratic Governance*, Cheltenham, UK: Edward Elgar.

Hettne, B. (1997). "Europe in a World of Regions", in R. Falk and T. Szneter (eds.), *A New Europe in the Changing Global System*, Tokyo: United Nations University Press.

Hooghe, L., and G. Marks (2001), *Multilevel Governance and European Integration*, Lanham, MD: Rowman & Littlefield.

Karlsson, C. (2001), "Democracy, Legitimacy and the European Union", Ph.D. thesis, Uppsala University.

Lawrence, R. (1995), *Regionalism, Multilateralism and Deeper Integration*, Washington DC: Brookings Institution.

Polanyi, K. (1945), "Universal Capitalism or Regional Planning?", *London Quarterly of World Affairs*, January.

Rodrik, D. (2000), "Governance of Economic Globalization", in J. S. Nye and J. S. Donahue, *Governance in a Globalizing World*, Washington DC: Brookings Institution.

Schulz, M., F. Söderbaum and J. Ojendal (2001), *Regionalization in a Globalizing World. A Comparative Perspective on Actors, Forms and Processes*. London: Zed.

Telo, M. (2002), "L'Interdependence entre la gouvernance européenne et la gouvernance globale", *European Union Review*, no. 1, pp. 7–27.

Thomas, K. P., and M. A. Tétreault, eds. (1999), *Racing to Regionalize*, London: Lynne Rienner.

Trading Health Care Away? GATS, Public Services and Privatisation (2001), London: The Corner House Briefing 23, Trade and Health Care.

Valaskakis, K. (2001), "Long-Term Trends in Global Governance: From 'Westphalia' to 'Seattle'", in *Governance in the 21st Century*, Paris: OECD.

Viner, J. (1950), *The Customs Union Issue*, New York: Carnegie Endowment for Peace.

Wessels, W. (1997), "An Ever Closer Fusion? A Dynamic Macropolitical View on Integration Processes", *Journal of Common Market Studies* 35(2), pp. 267–99.

Winters, L. A. (1999), "Regionalism vs. Multilateralism", in R. Baldwin, D. Cohen, A. Sapir, and A. Venables (eds.), *Market Integration, Regionalism and the Global Economy*, Cambridge: Cambridge University Press.

WTO (World Trade Organization) (1992), *International Trade 1990–91*, Geneva: WTO.

―――― (2000), *International Trade Statistics*, Geneva: WTO.

―――― (2001), *International Trade Statistics*, Geneva: WTO.

Wyplosz, C. (2001), *How Risky Is Financial Liberalisation in Developing Countries?*, G-24 Discussion Paper No. 14, New York and Geneva: United Nations.

12

Conclusions

Stephen Woolcock

Introduction

By way of conclusions this chapter covers the three main questions posed in chapter 1:

1. What is the impact of regional agreements in the area of regulatory policy?
2. Do the approaches to regulatory barriers differ from region to region, and if so does this represent a risk of "regulatory regionalism"?
3. Are regional approaches competing with or complementing multi-lateral attempts to remove regulatory barriers to trade?

The first of these questions will be dealt with in a fairly comprehensive fashion in the following section, which summarizes the evidence from the case studies. This reveals a diverse picture, but one in which regional agreements tend to go beyond the provisions of the World Trade Organization (i.e. are WTO-plus) either in coverage or in terms of procedural provisions rather than substantive rule-making.

This leads to a discussion of differences in the approaches adopted by the various regional agreements. This shows that there are some quite significant differences, for example between the greater use of policy approximation/harmonization in agreements concluded by the European Union compared with the preference for a "policed national treatment" approach that tends to characterize the agreements centred on the United States. This section also shows that differences in how regions approach detailed aspects of regulatory policy can be as likely, if not more likely, to result in "regulatory regionalism" when they become politicized, as in the case of the use of precaution in the regulation of risk in food safety rules.

The final section addresses the building versus stumbling block issue. This section argues that what characterizes policy development in dealing with the regulatory issues in trade and investment regimes is a multi-level process rather than a choice between regional and multilateral approaches. Regional agreements represent one aspect of this multi-level process. The question should therefore be about what role regional agreements play in this multi-level process.

Are regional trade agreements WTO-plus?

In the absence of comprehensive economic evaluations of the impact of regional trade agreements (RTAs) in the areas described above, it is necessary to assess their impact in qualitative terms. The qualitative assessment used here is essentially to determine to what extent and in which areas the RTAs are WTO-plus. This section provides some illustrations of the findings of the case studies. Tables 12A.1 to 12A.4 in the appendix to this chapter summarize the findings for each of the case studies and each of the four main policy areas covered by the study.

The EU–Poland Agreement

The case of the EU–Poland Europe Agreement of 1991 was taken as an example of a preferential agreement with potential accession states. This approach will clearly apply to other Central and East European countries (CEECs) seeking membership and for that matter to the countries in the Mediterranean region seeking accession, such as Malta, Cyprus and ultimately Turkey.

Articles 68 and 69 of the Europe Agreement (EA) require Poland (and other CEECs) to adopt the *acquis communautaire*. Compliance with at least important parts of the *acquis* is a precondition for accession and progress is monitored by the European Commission in regular reports. In other words, a process of regulatory approximation/harmonization is under way across a wide range of issues, including those covered by the study. This provides the incentive and momentum for regulatory reform in the accession states. It is a process facilitated by the multidimensional interaction between the European Union and Poland, involving ministerial-level engagement and Association Councils and Committees on aspects of the *acquis*, as well as lower-level working groups, cooperation and exchanges between regulators in EU member states and Polish regulators. Finally, there is technical assistance in the form of funding via such schemes as the EU Phare programme. In other words, there are not only detailed substantive provisions that are WTO-plus but also extensive procedural measures that are clearly WTO-plus, and the whole process draws its momentum from the accession objective.

In investment, the Europe Agreement provided a standstill on any new restrictions. There was asymmetric access for Polish investors in the sense that the European Union offered immediate national treatment for Polish firms in the European Union and delayed national treatment for EU firms in Poland in some sensitive sectors, such as mining, pharmaceuticals and some power sectors. In all sectors there is also a safeguard provision that can suspend national treatment for investment (right of establishment) in the event of adjustment problems. Natural resources, agricultural land and forests were excluded from the EA's coverage, although this and other provisions in the EA are, of course, subject to renegotiation in the actual accession negotiations. The investment regime in Poland is therefore fairly liberal, although there is reason to believe that this would have been the case even without the EA. Nevertheless, the EA codifies investment and sets out a clear programme for liberalization.

In services, Poland is committed to the provisions of the General Agreement on Trade in Services (GATS), which lock in existing liberalization. Article 55.1 of the EA calls for the progressive liberalization of services in Poland, which is likely to go hand in hand with EU GATS commitments. The accession negotiations with the European Union will therefore be GATS-plus in coverage by including a further series of sectors including tourism. There is provision for temporary movement of key workers in the sensitive Mode 4 area.

Technical barriers to trade (TBTs) are one of the priority areas for regulatory harmonization mentioned in the 1991 Agreement. Not only is Poland required to adopt EU technical regulations and standards, which means, for example, adopting 80 per cent of EU standards before the relevant Polish standards institutions can be admitted to the European standards bodies (the European Standardization Committee and the European Electrotechnical Standardization Committee); it is also required to establish a wholly new set of institutional arrangements. Prior to a change in the law in 1994, technical regulations and standards were mandatory in Poland and determined unilaterally by various government ministries. Most of these standards were not compatible with Western standards and until recently there had been no effort to check the growth of national regulatory standards. Information on new regulations was often hard to get and when it was available it was generally only in

Polish. Institutional change was also needed in conformance assessment (including accreditation) to make it more effective and objective. These conditions were the antithesis of what would classify as regulatory best practice as defined by the Organisation for Economic Co-operation and Development (OECD). So it is clear that major institutional change was needed. Requiring national treatment and most favoured nation treatment (MFN) would have clearly not resulted in much market opening. The adoption of EU standards and conformance assessment procedures, which are in line with international standards, together with procedural measures that enhance transparency and openness in decision-making, will however result in a significant market opening, which will benefit third parties as well as the EU suppliers. In this sense, the EU–Poland Agreement is WTO-plus and market opening in the TBT field.

The position in food safety is very similar to that in TBTs. Because agriculture is an important sector for Poland, there has been pressure for longer transition periods before the adoption of some standards. As with industrial standards, the adoption of EU standards and more transparent procedures will tend to benefit third-country suppliers as well as EU suppliers. On risk assessment in food safety, the Polish approach appears to be closer to the current EU approach than to the North American approach (see below) and has tended to adopt a restrictive line on the use of hormones in beef and the application of biotechnology in agriculture.

Public procurement, like TBT, is an important issue in Poland because of the lack of experience with open procedures under central planning. Poland, like other CEECs, has observer status in the Government Procurement Agreement (GPA). Bulgaria, Estonia and Latvia are, in fact, negotiating accession to the GPA. Membership of the GPA is a condition for accession to the European Union. So regional agreements with the CEECs will provide an incentive for some increase in membership of the GPA and thus arguably contribute to the credibility of – in this case plurilateral – rules in the WTO.[1] Again, there is asymmetric access in favour of Polish firms, which were granted national treatment with EU firms when bidding for contracts in the Union from day one, whereas EU firms in Poland would be granted this only after a transition period. EU firms established in Poland do, however, benefit from national treatment. The EA provided the incentive for Poland to revamp its laws on public procurement in line with the EU *acquis* and thus bring them into line with international practice. So the institutional infrastructure is being put into place that will facilitate more open markets. As with TBTs and sanitary and phytosanitary (SPS) measures, this will benefit third-country suppliers as well as EU suppliers. Progress is likely to be slow, however. A new law that was to be implemented in 2001 will bring Polish practice closer to the EU *acquis* and thus set out detailed procedures to be followed when contracts are awarded. But open markets will be some time coming, as they have been in this sector in the European Union itself. For example, Poland still retains a 20 per cent price preference for Polish suppliers and uses a 50 per cent value-added test for the origin rule.

In procurement, the Europe Agreement, and the EU accession process in general, has been a very important factor in moving Poland towards more liberal policies. The European Union has also provided technical assistance in terms of funding and training of Polish officials working on procurement and has thus helped to build the requisite institutional infrastructure. It is unlikely that liberalization in procurement would have occurred as a result of domestic push without this external pull. Public procurement in Poland therefore provides a good example of how RTAs can promote more transparent, open procedures, best practice and the effective implementation of these procedures,[2] which are the essence of market opening in many sectors characterized by regulatory barriers to trade.

In general, therefore, the adoption of EU regulatory standards has facilitated market access by bringing Polish regulations in line with harmonized EU standards. Improved regulatory procedures set out in the EU *acquis* also promote transparency and predictability where the previous regime was opaque and open to the abuse of discretionary powers. Secondly, institutional deficits are a characteristic of transition economies and the cooperation and institution-building under the EA have helped speed the move towards regulatory best practice in Poland. However, this process has been driven by the incentive of membership of the European Union. It is doubtful that this model would work for countries not eligible or likely to join the European Union.

The EU–Mexico Agreement

The EU–Mexico Agreement is a very useful case in that it allows an assessment, albeit of a very tentative nature, of the potential clash between EU-centred and US-centred regional agreements. With regard to substantive provisions, the EU–Mexico Agreement is WTO-plus in services and government procurement. In services, the standstill provisions in the EU–Mexico Agreement ensure that the European Union has access at least as favourable as members of the North American Free Trade Agreement (NAFTA) to the Mexican market. But this is as much a result of the Mexican practice of transposing international agreements into national law as it is of the EU–Mexico Agreement itself. All four modes of supply are included, as are all sectors, except for audio-visual, air transport and maritime cabotage. There are also provisions for further negotiations in three years to "eliminate substantially all the remaining discrimination" in services after a maximum 10-year transition period and to negotiate a mutual recognition agreement on Mode 4 (natural persons). Finally, a Committee on Financial Services is established, which will review market access and will, in particular, negotiate further opening should either the European Union or Mexico agree to further liberalization with another party. In other words, if NAFTA's coverage of financial services is increased, the European Union has the right to seek equivalent access. One difficulty in services was that the structure of NAFTA, with separate Chapters for establishment/ investment and cross-border service provision and no modes as such, differed from GATS, with its four modes including right of establishment.

In public procurement, the EU–Mexico Agreement, which entered into force in March 2001, is broadly in line with the GPA and could therefore be said to be WTO-plus, in the sense that there is no multilateral agreement yet on public procurement. There is a framework text that sets out requirements concerning non-discrimination in the application of procurement practices but, more importantly, the agreement includes detailed provisions concerning contract award procedures, transparency (information on calls for tender and applications for contracts awarded by restricted tendering), and so on. As in services, the European Union and Mexico agree to renegotiate the procurement provisions if either negotiates more favourable treatment for third parties. The framework agreement covers procurement in most sectors including utilities. The coverage in terms of sector schedules and thresholds is based on NAFTA for Mexico and the GPA for the European Union. This means that sub-federal purchasers are excluded because NAFTA does not include these, or does so only on a voluntary basis. Indeed, the procedural rules for awarding contracts, which are central to the agreement, use the NAFTA rules for Mexico and GPA rules for the European Union. In practice, this does not represent a major difficulty because NAFTA and GPA procedures are more or less the same. But such parallel provisions in cross-regional agreements could cause problems in policy areas where there is greater substantive divergence in the rules.

The TBT and SPS provisions in the EU–Mexico Agreement are not WTO-plus but WTO-consistent. Indeed, they confirm the parties' obligations under the WTO. Product labelling, which has been a major problem for the European Union in the Mexican market, was not covered, except that a Special Committee on TBTs was established to work towards approximation of standards and simplification of labelling requirements, including voluntary schemes, which appears to include eco-labelling. The EU–Mexico Agreement also stops short of substantive provisions on mutual recognition. Given the central role of mutual recognition agreements (MRAs) in the EU *acquis* and its policy of promoting MRAs in relations with third countries, this is surprising, especially given the fact that Mexico was apparently willing to negotiate. It is probably because of the complexities of negotiating MRAs, which suggests that MRAs are unlikely to be the instrument of choice in dealing with TBTs, at least when countries with less developed conformance assessment provisions, such as Mexico, are included. The provisions on SPS are essentially the same. These confirm WTO commitments but go WTO-plus in establishing a Special Committee to provide a "forum to identify and address problems that may arise from the application of specific sanitary and phyto-sanitary provisions" as well as to consider provisions for the application of equivalence.

In the field of investment, the EU–Mexico Agreement is some way short of existing OECD and TRIMs (Trade-Related Investment Measures) provisions. The parties to the agreement simply "recall their international commitments with regard to investment". This may be owing, among other things, to the timing of the negotiations, coming as they did after the experience of the Multilateral Agreement on Investment (MAI), which made national governments wary of potential opposition to liberalization.

Finally, the EU–Mexico Agreement includes a bilateral dispute settlement provision, but its application is likely to be fairly limited given that reference to WTO rules means that there will be little in the form of bilateral rules to be covered.

The Euro-Med Agreements

The case study of Euro-Mediterranean Agreements, which uses EU–Tunisia as an example, shows that the content of the European Union's RTAs can vary from case to case. The priorities in the EU–Tunisia Agreement are TBTs and competition. Whereas TBTs have generally been the first regulatory issue to be covered in any trade agreement, the choice of competition is not at first sight obvious. Article 40 of the EU–Tunisia Agreement seeks to promote the use (by Tunisia) of EU standards and conformance assessment provisions and food safety standards. The ultimate aim is to negotiate an MRA. So here the European Union is at least holding up an MRA as the ultimate aim. In the meantime, the agreement sets out the means by which closer collaboration can help ensure the use of EU standards and the updating of Tunisian laboratories. So the Euro-Med provisions on TBTs and SPS are WTO-conform on substance and again WTO-plus on procedures, in the sense that the European Union will presumably be more willing to cooperate with and help its Euro-Med partners and other WTO members in the field of TBT and SPS issues.

The Euro-Med Agreement with Tunisia includes provisions on competition. Article 36 calls for action against restrictive practices, the abuse of market dominance and controls on state aid. The agreement refers to the principles set out in European law on this issue in Articles 81, 82 and 87 (ex Arts. 85, 86 and 92 of the Treaty) and appears to provide for the inclusion of EU secondary legislation and principles established in EU jurisprudence. The implementation of these principles is to be decided by the Association Council within five years. In the sense that the WTO contains no such competition principles, as yet, this is WTO-plus.

The services provisions in the Euro-Med Agreements reaffirm the obligations of the parties under GATS, including, in particular, those providing for MFN in service sectors covered by the schedules. The Mediterranean partners of the European Union have made GATS commitments in only 6 per cent of their service sectors. The aim of extending commitments on services is included, especially with regard to right of establishment. For Mediterranean countries that are not members of the WTO and thus not signatories to GATS, a basic framework agreement similar to that of GATS is established, as in the case of Jordan. The parties will then consider, after five years, whether to negotiate an agreement under Article V of GATS covering services. The modalities of these further efforts will be decided by the Association Council(s). On investment there are no substantive provisions and, as with the EU–Mexico Agreement, the Euro-Med Agreements envisage the continued use of bilateral investment treaties between the individual member states of the European Union and the Mediterranean partners. In services, therefore, the Euro-Med Agreements appear to be no more than WTO-conform, although they have the aim of being more, and in investment they are clearly OECD/WTO-minus.

NAFTA

The NAFTA provisions on services and investment adopt a somewhat different approach from GATS, in that there are separate Chapters on the cross-border provision of services and investment (or right of establishment). This difference in approach reflects the fact that NAFTA was negotiated before the GATS agreement was concluded and expresses the preferences of the major actors, in this case the United States. On balance, the difference in structure of the agreement does not seem to have had any impact on the compatibility of NAFTA provisions with the WTO rules.[3]

NAFTA is WTO-plus in services and investment. The services provisions under NAFTA go further and deeper than GATS, with respect to both substantive measures and sectoral coverage. Sector coverage of services is based on a negative-list approach rather than the positive-list approach of GATS. NAFTA includes services and investment in a coherent fashion within a single agreement. This is in contrast to the position in the WTO, where services and goods are in separate agreements and investment is covered only in the form of fragmentary elements. This more extensive coverage appears to have contributed to the growth of investment and trade within the NAFTA region, although US growth has clearly been a key factor behind regional, and for that matter global, growth during the period since NAFTA was ratified, as it has within the global economy.

The implementation of services provisions has also probably been pushed further than in the wider GATS by procedural provisions that facilitate continuous consultation and review in various trilateral commissions and technical working groups. Together with the NAFTA provisions on judicial review, both within the bilateral dispute settlement system and within local jurisdiction, such procedural aspects of NAFTA have helped to establish the integrity of the regulatory process in the countries concerned and in Mexico in particular. Although US influence has been profound in shaping the institutional structures in Mexico, so that one could speak of the extension of the dominant US norms to Mexico, this does not detract from the point that the new system is more open, impartial and accessible. Here, as in the case of the extension of the EU *acquis* to Poland, one must conclude that, if the United States is a hegemon in the region, it has been a benign hegemon.

The separate NAFTA provisions on investment can be found in Chapter 11 and are clearly WTO-plus. Once again, the US norms tend to prevail, but one should not forget that these reflect the norms developed in the OECD. So the regional norms applied are generally compatible with established international norms. NAFTA requires parties to comply with national treatment and MFN in their treatment of foreign investment (Arts. 1102 and 1103) and thus remove or phase out restrictions on ownership, performance requirements, controls on capital flows such as repatriation of profits, and so on. As under the OECD provisions, there are exceptions for sensitive sectors. In the United States these include ownership of broadcasting, airlines and certain strategic sectors such as nuclear energy. In Canada the list is similar but with the addition of publishing and oil, and in Mexico the list is longer (as one would expect) and includes petrochemicals, telecommunications, transport and the postal services. Both Canada and Mexico retain review procedures for investments over a set threshold and thus some regulatory discretion in the hands of national regulators. Such controls tend to be aimed at limiting US dominance in certain sectors and therefore tend to be more liberal vis-à-vis third-country investors than vis-à-vis US investors – although in practice the Canadian and Mexican review procedures have not been used to stop US foreign direct investment.

In one area NAFTA is clearly OECD-plus and this is in the provision of rights for private investors to challenge decisions of national governments or regulators. This takes remedies and redress into new realms for a free trade agreement, although there has been direct effect in the European Union for many years of course. It is clearly beyond existing WTO and OECD rules; indeed, the failure of the MAI was in part due to opposition to efforts to extend this aspect of the NAFTA model to a "multilateral" agreement on investment. The inclusion of investor–state redress also clearly reflects the predominant US approach to dealing with regulatory barriers based on transparency, open decision-making and judicial redress. As with services in general, however, US influence could be seen as benign in the sense that NAFTA appears to have contributed to a significant increase in investment within the NAFTA region, which has clearly benefited the Mexican economy as a whole. From Mexico's point of view, the benign effects of this US influence were strengthened by the US support for Mexico during the peso crisis of 1994.

With regard to technical barriers to trade, NAFTA is probably not WTO-plus and could be said to be WTO-minus in some detailed but potentially important respects. NAFTA, like the TBT Agreement, requires national treatment and MFN with regard to technical regulations, standards and conformance assessment for products within the region. In contrast to the EU approach to TBTs, NAFTA does not place great emphasis on harmonization of standards. Indeed, compatibility rather than harmonization is the term used in the agreement. Nor does NAFTA say much about harmonization of conformance assessment, which means that mutual recognition or market access for products based on equivalence are likely to be problematic. If anything, NAFTA places the right to establish higher standards than those pertaining in other NAFTA countries first, and then creates a system of transparency and due process to ensure that this right is not abused. However, the "softer" nature of the provisions on TBTs may mean that national treatment may be harder to police. Although this is similar to the EU (Art. 30, former/Art. 36 EEC) and WTO (Art. XX) provisions, NAFTA's codification of what is a legitimate policy objective justifying exceptions to non-discrimination includes explicit reference to sustainable development and the protection of consumer rights. The WTO TBT Agreement does not make specific reference to these "legitimate objectives", so there may be scope for a greater degree of national regulatory policy autonomy under NAFTA than under the WTO. Furthermore, in NAFTA the norm for testing whether a technical regulation is proportionate does not include the "least trade restrictive" test as the WTO (and the EU) provisions do.[4] NAFTA could therefore be said to be WTO-minus in the sense that it provides less of a constraint on the use of discretionary regulatory powers. This approach appears to be due to the jurisprudence within the United States on the interpretation of the dormant commerce clause and the political opposition to trade rules that restrict national regulatory autonomy on the part of environmental and consumer lobbies in the United States (see Woolcock, 2001).

As with other regional agreements, NAFTA's procedural provisions on TBTs appear to be WTO-plus, as in the more immediate nature of the transparency requirements and the scope of reviews and dispute settlement provisions. It remains to be seen whether these procedural rules and the system of due process they safeguard will be enough to ensure that TBTs do not continue to be used as a means of restrictive barriers to access.

The regulation of food safety within NAFTA is covered by Chapter 7 of the agreement. This is compatible with the substantive provisions of the WTO's SPS Agreement. As with TBTs, the NAFTA rules provide a positive right for members of NAFTA to retain more stringent standards than the prevailing international standards (Art. 712). The SPS Agreement has a different emphasis in that it calls upon parties to defer to international standards where they exist and allows higher standards only if backed by sound science. In practice, there may be little difference between the effect of the two systems because the NAFTA approach to risk assessment – and thus to decisions concerning the legitimacy of higher standards of safety – is based on science as the final arbiter. In other words, risk management is determined by scientific committees. The United States and Canada, which have both championed the NAFTA approach to risk assessment and management, do not envisage any threats to their agri-food exports from SPS regulations and standards within NAFTA; the threats come from the competing EU approach.[5] Agricultural and food exports and imports have grown for Mexico as well as the United States and Canada since NAFTA entered into force, which suggests that the greater transparency and due process in regulatory policy in the sector have facilitated trade.

In SPS, as in TBT regulations and standards, NAFTA tends to be WTO-plus in terms of the procedures it establishes. The combination of transparency requirements, open decision-making and access to reviews and dispute settlement under national laws and within bilateral dispute settlement helps to ensure that regulation is not used to inhibit trade and investment. Thus the greater scope for regulatory autonomy that appears to be created in the NAFTA agreements on TBT and SPS compared with WTO rules does not mean that regulatory autonomy will or can be abused.

The NAFTA rules on public procurement are probably slightly below the standards of the Government Procurement Agreement of 1994, because NAFTA was concluded before the GPA. The main contribution that NAFTA makes to enhancing market access in public procurement markets is in Mexico, where there were no national laws governing procurement. The NAFTA provisions requiring transparency and open decision-making in contract award procedures therefore make the market potentially open for foreign suppliers where this was simply not the case before. As with other transparency and process measures, the benefits are extended to third-country suppliers, in the sense that national regulatory policy begins to approximate best practice. Having said this, it is still too early to say what impact these obligations on Mexico will have because regulations implementing them have not been put in place, even if legislative measures have been adopted. The bid challenge provisions included in NAFTA should help ensure implementation. Mexico is not alone in having difficulties with implementation; the Canadian provinces continue to oppose inclusion in the regime, with the result that the United States has suspended Canadian access to the 37 US states that voluntarily agreed to be covered by the rules.

NAFTA includes provisions on competition and could therefore be said to be WTO-plus in this regard because the WTO does not yet include any general norms on competition. The NAFTA provisions require each state to have national policies that preclude anti-competitive practices.

The Chile–Canada Agreement

The Chile–Canada Free Trade Agreement (CCFTA) came about when plans for an extension of NAFTA to include Chile in 1994 fell through with the failure of the US Congress to grant negotiating authority. Chile and Canada decided to continue to negotiate the agreement in order to facilitate the promotion of Chile's accession to NAFTA (see chapter 7). NAFTA is the clear model for much of the CCFTA, although in some areas of interest to this study it is NAFTA-minus and in one or two it is NAFTA-plus. The CCFTA does not include TBT or SPS agreements, financial services or government procurement (or intellectual property). The TBT and SPS issues were not included because the parties believed that the WTO provisions adequately covered these issues. In the light of eight years experience with the WTO TBT and SPS provisions agreed during the Uruguay Round, however, there have been proposals in the context of the Chile–US negotiations to go somewhat deeper than the WTO. With regard to TBTs, the Chilean proposals seem to point to a strengthening of the provisions on conformance assessment with a view to promoting the use of mutual recognition. In the SPS field, Chile is proposing measures to facilitate findings of equivalence and to tighten transparency provisions, especially with regard to short-term emergency measures.

Financial services were also excluded from the CCFTA because they were considered to be an issue of central interest to the United States and therefore best left for negotiations that included the United States, in the framework of either a Chilean accession to NAFTA or the bilateral negotiations with the United States, which finally began in early 2001. Public procurement was also excluded from the CCFTA, in part because of important differences between Chile and Canada. Chile had not signed the GPA and was a firm opponent of the kind of detailed "bureaucratic" provisions included in the GPA in an attempt to enhance transparency and thus greater competition in the sector.

The Chile–Canada Agreement therefore covers only investment and services of the issues included in our study. With regard to investment and (cross-border) services, the CCFTA broadly follows the NAFTA model and is therefore WTO-plus, which is not difficult, but also possibly OECD-plus with regard to investment. The CCFTA, like NAFTA, includes a comprehensive set of principles on investment rather than the ad hoc partial approach used in the WTO (GATS and TRIMs). As in NAFTA, investment covering goods and services is contained in one Chapter and cross-border services in a separate Chapter, and the modes of service provision 1, 2 and 4 of GATS are included in the cross-border Chapter. Both the investment and cross-border service trade Chapters require national treatment and MFN and use a negative-list approach, which makes them more comprehensive than the GATS agreement. As noted above, financial services are excluded and will come under a separate Chapter in any future negotiations that include the United States. A comprehensive list of performance requirements is prohibited under the investment provisions, making the CCFTA TRIMs-plus. However, the CCFTA does seem to allow permanent exclusions from this ban on performance requirements, which the TRIMs agreement does not allow.

In line with OECD instruments and NAFTA, certain sensitive sectors are excluded from the investment rules. In the case of Canada these are the same as for NAFTA and the OECD instruments. Chile's exclusions are fairly limited and cover such sectors as nuclear energy and hydrocarbons. Both countries exclude basic telecommunications and social services. As under NAFTA there is both a bilateral dispute settlement procedure as well as investor–state dispute settlement, the latter making the CCFTA significantly WTO-plus.

As discussed in chapter 2, RTAs can be seen as WTO-plus in terms of coverage, substantive provisions or procedural measures. The CCFTA includes horizontal provisions (i.e. covering all substantive policy areas) on procedure. These closely follow the NAFTA model, which in turn implements US administrative practice. The CCFTA requires transparency, including prior notification and the right of interested parties to make submissions. In adopting the "policed national treatment" approach of NAFTA, it also requires the parties to establish independent judicial or administrative review bodies to ensure that regulatory decisions do not discriminate against suppliers or investors from the other party. These general procedural measures are clearly WTO-plus.

With regard to dispute settlement, the CCFTA again uses the NAFTA model, although the dispute settlement provisions are not available for disputes concerning cultural industries or the application of the competition provisions. The CCFTA is therefore also compatible with the WTO dispute settlement procedures, but with a couple of exceptions. First, it is arguably faster because of the deadlines set. It also provides for dispute settlement panels to determine the level of adverse trade effects at the same time that it assesses compliance with the rules. In the WTO Dispute Settlement Understanding (DSU) this is done only later. Under the WTO there remains therefore more ambiguity about when a country can take retaliatory measures. This has been a problem in a number of high-profile cases, such as the *Banana* case. In including these measures the CCFTA is in part reflecting the North American view on this issue but also implementing ideas that were discussed in the review of the DSU by the WTO, but which could not be agreed because they were linked to negotiations on other issues.

One area in which the CCFTA diverges from NAFTA is that it includes provision to phase out anti-dumping actions between the parties over a period of six years. This must also be seen in the context of future negotiations on NAFTA or a Free Trade Area of the Americas. Chile would like to see dumping between parties excluded, although it is likely to have to settle for something less. Canada always saw the Canada–US Free Trade Area and NAFTA as a means of controlling US "administrative protection", i.e. anti-dumping and other fair trade measures. Dispensing with anti-dumping actions is seen as something that countries can do when they have equivalent measures, in the shape of competition policy, to counter the abuse of market power. The CCFTA provisions on competition are, however, very weak. One can say that they are WTO-plus because there are, as yet, no general competition provisions in the

WTO. But the CCFTA competition provisions merely follow the NAFTA precedent in calling for national policies that proscribe anti-competitive practices; they do not set out any standards for policy or even the types of anti-competitive practices that have to be covered by national policies.

The CER Agreement

The Closer Economic Relations Agreement between Australia and New Zealand is WTO-plus in an important number of areas. In terms of non-discrimination, for example, the application of national treatment in the area of services has been extended well beyond what is provided for at the multilateral level in the GATS schedules of the WTO. A negative-list approach has been adopted to coverage, with a limited number of sub-sectors being excluded (those that are typically excluded from services and investment agreements). In some of these, such as civil aviation and maritime transport, separate agreements liberalizing markets have been undertaken outside the context of the CER Agreement. In terms of labour movement, although not provided for in the CER Agreement, there is free movement of labour between the two countries, with mutual recognition of key professional qualifications.

Because of the regional commitments on services, the CER Agreement is WTO-plus with respect to investment in services activities. It is not WTO-plus, however, in the sense of creating preferential investment provisions. Investment is not part of the CER Agreement – or any other agreement between the two countries for that matter.

In terms of industrial standards affecting trade, Australia and New Zealand are both signatories to the TBT Agreement of the WTO, but the CER goes further than the WTO. As noted above, there is full mutual recognition, so that goods and services (such as professional services) that are approved for sale in one country can be marketed and sold in the other country. In the case of SPS, a number of trade facilitation measures have been put in place. There is, for example, a single regulatory agency chartered with developing joint SPS standards for both Australia and New Zealand and measures to facilitate inspection arrangements for imported food originating from either country. In terms of quarantine, there are arrangements to harmonize standards and to adopt common inspection standards and procedures.

Government procurement is WTO-plus, in the sense that public pro-curement is excluded from the GATT/WTO. The CER is, however, GPA-minus; in other words, the provisions on procurement are short, by some margin, of those in the plurilateral GPA. The CER commits gov-ernments and the states not to give explicit preferences to local suppliers. But provisions on rules to be followed in contract award procedures are not provided. Provisions on reviews and bid challenge also fall short of the GPA standard. Neither New Zealand nor Australia is a signatory of the GPA.

With regard to provisions aimed at maintaining competitive markets, the CER is significantly WTO-plus for two reasons. First, the CER does away with the right to take anti-dumping actions against imports that are dumped on the local market. Second, in so doing, it replaces anti-dumping with competition provisions, which serve the purpose of holding in check the abuse of market dominance. The scope of the competition provisions stops well short of the EU policy, which covers areas such as cartels and mergers that the CER does not.

In terms of institutional arrangements, there have been remarkably few arrangements (compared with other agreements) put in place to service the CER Agreement. Each country has relied on its own institutional infrastructure and a continuing exchange of information at the level of officials as well as at the political level. An example is in the area of competition policy, where the two countries have adopted common competition regulations but without any accompanying institutional infrastructure. Existing national institutions deal with the implementation of the policies. It is these existing institutions that have also led to a highly transparent approach to the public availability of regulations relating to the CER Agreement. In fact, no new institutions were created to promote transparency.

Summing up on WTO-plus

From the complex picture set out above it is possible to identify a few general points. First of all, in so far as the regional agreements are WTO-plus, they tend to be so in terms of either coverage or procedural measures. In the case of coverage, WTO-plus generally means that the existing multilateral provisions are extended to cover new sectors. This clearly represents perhaps the main preferential nature of regional agreements in regulatory issues. Whether or not the RTAs are complementary to the multilateral process then depends on whether these further commitments are extended on an MFN basis, and if so when.

The WTO-plus procedural provisions can generally not form the basis of preferences for local producers. These tend to provide improved transparency measures, over and above those of the multilateral rules, because of the more immediate nature of links within the regional level. The related improvements in decision-making, which make the regulatory process more open, contribute to better regulatory practices and also cannot generally be used to grant preferences to local suppliers. Measures that contribute to institution-building, for example through technical assistance for partner countries, financial support or cooperation between regulatory authorities, will contribute to best practices in regulatory policy, from which all can be expected to benefit. In the case of RTAs between developed Northern countries and developing Southern countries, procedural provisions will be particularly important.

The tables in the appendix also show that RTAs may also be WTO-plus in terms of implementing and enforcing agreements. Generally speaking, conciliation and reviews are likely to be more effective in resolving disputes at the regional level than at the multilateral level. Regional agreements are also contributing to the general trend towards introducing independent administrative or judicial bodies to deal with complaints about regulatory decisions made by foreign suppliers. In this respect one could also say there is a form of institution-building taking place that will facilitate best practice in regulatory policy in the sense that regulators are forced to justify decisions. This will tend to reduce the likelihood of regulators abusing discretionary judgements to discriminate in regulatory decisions. WTO-plus dispute settlement provisions, such as the investor–state provisions in NAFTA and the CCFTA, should also contribute to more effective implementation of the rules. However, these are at the expense of a loss of national policy autonomy and are unlikely to be accepted at a multilateral level.

The broad conclusion is therefore that the RTAs tend to complement rather than undermine multilateral rules. However, there are some important qualifications to this conclusion. In the horizontal case studies considered, food safety and environmental labelling show signs of differences between the major actors being consolidated in the respective regional agreements. Chapter 9 argues that regional agreements are being used to defend policy autonomy against liberalization in the form of multilateral rules. This case may illustrate what can happen when "bottom–up" forces, in this case in the form of consumer and environmental interests, prevail over "top–down" liberalizing factors. If one looks at the structure of the regional and multilateral agreements, in the shape of the WTO SPS and regional agreements on SPS, the multilateral norms appear to prevail. When it comes to implementing these agreements, however, consumer interests in Europe have opposed the WTO and associated Codex norms. In other words, institutional compatibility between regional and multilateral agreements does not guarantee that there will not be disputes and potential divergences between regional approaches.

It may be that the difficulties with food safety and the environment are the result of the nature of these policy areas, in the sense that they are very close to the interests of consumers and the now large number of voters interested in environmental issues and therefore more likely to be susceptible to bottom–up pressures. If so, then the general conclusions reached here need not be revised. On the other hand, the difficulties may represent what can happen when bottom–up forces are more important than top–down forces. Some of the other policy areas also involve important choices concerning consumer interests, such as the protection of consumer rights, and interests in the regulation of services. Some consumer lobbies already see GATS as a threat to these interests and to policy autonomy in the provision of core public services, such as health and education. So the scope for bottom–up pressures shaping developments in other policy areas cannot be excluded. In other words, the complementarity between the "new regionalism" and the multilateral rules-based system depends on continuing support for the liberal paradigm which shaped policies throughout the 1990s. Without this support, the trade aspects of regulatory policies could well become more politicized. Domestic interests might then seek to use the regional level to help defend their policy preferences, with the result that what otherwise have seemed to be relatively minor differences may become the source of "regulatory regionalism".

Another general qualification to the conclusion that regional agreements complement rather than undermine multilateral agreements is that the case studies covered here, although representing regulatory issues, do not cover all aspects of regional trade and integration agreements. In particular, the volume has not looked at the important area of rules of origin. In addition, many of the regional agreements between developing countries, and to some extent those between developed and developing countries, still deal with important tariffs issues, which are likewise not the subject of this volume.

A comparison of regional approaches and cross-regional linkages

"Regulatory regionalism" or the development of competing approaches to dealing with regulatory barriers to trade could result if there is a divergence between different models or approaches to regional agreements. Such a divergence would create difficulties in cross-regional agreements and make it harder to reach agreement in the future on multilateral rules. This section looks at the major models, namely the EU-centred model (*acquis communautaire*) and the US-centred model (NAFTA). It also discusses how these models might find wider application in negotiations between the RTAs concerned and third countries.

The case studies included in this project reveal a broad measure of similarity between the approaches adopted by the EU-centred and US-centred models. This is not surprising because the principles on which these models are based generally have a common origin in the OECD. The Organisation for European Economic Co-operation and the OECD developed concepts and methods for addressing investment (from the 1960s onwards), TBTs (in the 1960s), public procurement (in the 1970s), services, investment and competition (in the 1980s), and are currently working on regulatory reform.

Notwithstanding the similarities between the EU- and US-centred approaches, there are a number of differences of both a detailed and a general nature. The detailed differences have already been addressed in this chapter and summarized in Tables 12A.1–12A.4 in the appendix. This section will consider whether there are some more general differences between the NAFTA and EU models for dealing with regulatory policies in integrating markets.

The European Union as a single market and monetary union is comprehensive in coverage because of the aim of creating a single market, whereas NAFTA is more limited in coverage. The EU model has seen all regulations as potential barriers to trade, although the European Court of Justice has stepped back from the *Dassonville* judgment in recent years. This argued that all regulatory measures are potential barriers to trade. Nevertheless, the EU model still tends to see all national regulatory policies as potential barriers. It also aims to include all levels of government, and even private companies when these are granted special and exclusive rights. Finally, private restraints on trade are included through European norms on competition. This EU *acquis* finds application in agreements with potential members of the European Union and in the European Economic Area, but RTAs between the European Union and non-applicant countries have been more limited in their coverage, as the vertical case studies have shown. For example, the EU–Mexico Agreement does not provide for mutual recognition and leaves investment out altogether. Interestingly, the recently negotiated text of an agreement between the European Union and Chile goes further than the EU–Mexico Agreement and may suggest that the European Union will seek to apply more of the *acquis* in future generations of RTAs.

The US-centred model of RTAs as reflected in NAFTA falls between the EU *acquis* and the coverage of the EU RTAs. NAFTA coverage is generally WTO-plus in the sense that it is based on negative listing in schedules. The coverage of sub-federal government is more restrictive than the EU *acquis* however, because US states and Canadian provinces have sought to retain a higher degree of policy autonomy than has been the case with sub-central government in Europe. This issue of including subnational levels of government brings out the fact that the multi-level process of forming regimes covering regulatory policy issues goes below the level of the nation-state. NAFTA is still more based on the coverage of trade-related regulatory issues, rather than the more comprehensive approach of the European Union.

The EU model also places considerable importance on policy approximation and mutual recognition as means of overcoming regulatory barriers to trade. Although there are resource constraints and limits to approximation, the EU model generally sees approximation and mutual recognition as the ultimate means of removing regulatory barriers to trade. This is reflected in the *acquis* but also in agreements with accession countries and in the Euro-Med Agreements. In this respect the European Union represents a form of regional hegemon, in that smaller neighbouring countries are obliged to adopt the prevailing European regulatory norms and technical standards. In RTAs between the European Union and other non-accession states, approximation and mutual recognition are seen as much longer-term aims. The difficulties in negotiating mutual recognition agreements, even with developed countries, have also dampened the European Union's earlier enthusiasm for mutual recognition.

The US-centred model places less importance on approximation or policy harmonization, as is reflected in the limited standards-harmonization working groups established under NAFTA. However, efforts to harmonize have been made, albeit on a more selective basis. The compatibility of standards is held up as the aim of NAFTA but, compared with the European approach, there is no great emphasis on creating institutions to promote conformance. For example, there are few joint bodies developing common norms and no efforts to promote common conformance assessment/accreditation capabilities that would facilitate the mutual recognition of test results. The US-centred model appears to assume that market factors will bring about equivalence and compatibility. As the NAFTA case study suggests, this may simply mean de facto approximation to US regulatory norms or standards.

Dealing with regulatory issues raises the important question of regulatory jurisdiction. Regulatory authority remains with national (or in some cases subnational, state and provincial) regulatory authorities, except in a few cases such as competition in the European Union where there is a supranational regulatory authority. But markets are regional or global in nature, with investors and companies operating across borders. A central question, therefore, is how to delineate the jurisdiction of regulators. This is less of a problem when regulatory policies are harmonized or there is at least a degree of policy approximation, because each national regulator is applying the same or similar norms. But harmonization has generally proved difficult. The approach developed in the EU *acquis* (and in the CER) has been to base regulatory jurisdiction on home country control; in other words, goods or services approved for sale in one country can be sold in other jurisdictions. This is reflected in the mutual recognition and home control of service providers. The NAFTA approach has been based on host state control, in which the local regulatory jurisdiction prevails and (policed) national treatment remains the basis of ensuring non-discrimination and open markets. In practice there are difficulties with each approach when it comes to implementation, and there remains some doubt that home country control is an option for agreements outside of Europe.

With regard to discipline over regulatory discretion, the EU model appears to have more substantive provisions limiting discretion in the application of regulatory policies, because rules and criteria are set out in a more detailed fashion in the EU *acquis*. For example, the European Union applies the "least trade restrictive" test in order to check regulatory discretion. NAFTA does not apply this test and also has broader criteria (including sustainable development and consumer protection) for assessing what are "legitimate policy objectives" in the application of exceptions to non-discrimination.

If the US-centred model is less stringent in its substantive constraints on regulatory discretion, it compensates with procedural provisions aimed at ensuring that regulators follow due process. In other words, transparency, rights for all parties to make their views known and legally binding procedures analogous to those used in the US Administrative Procedures Act provide an equivalent check on the abuse of regulatory discretion. Many of the procedural measures in NAFTA are designed to ensure that private actors potentially affected by the decisions of regulatory authorities in other countries have both a means of seeking to influence these decisions and a means of redress or review when they are not happy with the decision. Although the EU model also places great importance on transparency and has scope for reviews, it does not follow the due process approach of the United States.

In sum, one can characterize the NAFTA approach as "policed national treatment" (see chapter 10) and the EU *acquis* as being more based on approximation. In RTAs between the European Union and countries that are not its near neighbours seeking ultimate accession to the Union, the European Union will probably also have to use a form of agreement closer to that of NAFTA, but one that reflects the precedents and experience gained with the EU *acquis*.

In terms of the application of the respective approaches, the NAFTA approach appears to have influenced other regional agreements in the Western hemisphere. Thus Mexico's agreements with other countries in the region are based on NAFTA. The Chile–Canada Agreement also follows the NAFTA approach closely, at least in those policy areas covered. On the other hand, it does deviate from NAFTA in dispensing with anti-dumping duties between parties, which seems quite a significant difference. A key question will be the extent to which NAFTA provides the model for the Free Trade Area of the Americas (FTAA). Although the parties to NAFTA, led by the United States, will clearly want to see NAFTA as the model, it remains to be seen how the members of Mercosur, which in some respects is closer to the EU model, will respond to this. Much will depend on the balance of interests in the US position on the FTAA. On the one hand, if the aim is to provide a "pathfinder role" for broader multilateral negotiations, the NAFTA model is likely to find wide application. On the other hand, NAFTA has been selective in its approach and specific interests in the United States may push certain elements of the NAFTA model and not others. Some elements of the NAFTA model seem problematic, such as extending the investor–state dispute settlement system. This suggests that, just as the EU *acquis* has limited application outside of Europe, NAFTA may have limited application outside of North America. This tends to be confirmed by the selective approach to the application of the NAFTA model in the bilateral agreements negotiated by the United States. The US–Jordan Agreement is perhaps a classic example of selective use of the NAFTA model. The US–Chile negotiations can be expected to be much more inclusive of other elements of the model.

The EU model finds full application in relations between the European Union and states in the process of seeking accession to the European Union. In these cases, as shown by chapter 3 on the EU–Poland Agreement, the EU *acquis* is adopted in its entirety. The same, of course, applies to the countries in the European Economic Area. When it comes to the more recent bilateral agreements concluded by the European Union, one finds a more partial application of the *acquis*. This is illustrated in the Euro-Med Agreements and the EU–Mexico Agreement. The structure of the EU agreements with developing or middle-income countries (like those of the United States) must, of course, be expected to be different from those with relatively developed countries seeking accession. The nature of agreements will also be shaped by the circumstances in any bilateral relations. However, the European Union, like the United States, does not seem to follow a consistent approach in its bilateral agreements. A consistent application of the EU *acquis*, even of those parts that are difficult for developing countries, would be preferable to a set of ad hoc bilateral agreements. As in the case of the United States, the EU bilaterals seem to be shaped as much by domestic political factors as by a coherent, if staggered, application of the EU model.

Finally, there is the question of compatibility between the agreement the European Union is negotiating with Mercosur/Chile and the FTAA agreement. Our case study of the EU–Mexico Agreement suggests that the EU approach could be reconciled with the NAFTA approach without too many difficulties. But it is still too early to say whether this will be the case with the FTAA and the EU–Mercosur negotiations. Here is an area where further work is needed.

Regional agreements in a multi-level process

The broad conclusion of this report is that the conventional debate on whether regional agreements are building blocks or stumbling blocks for the multilateral system may have detracted from more detailed work on how the various levels that are involved in establishing international regimes interact.

Regional agreements can contribute to the development of rule-based trade and investment regimes in a number of ways. Regional agreements have provided models for wider multilateral agreements. Thus the European Union has provided the model of mutual recognition as a means of overcoming regulatory barriers to trade without extensive and unduly intrusive harmonization, and NAFTA offers policed national treatment based on ensuring due process in regulatory policy-making. These models are important in that the WTO framework is unlikely to provide detailed provisions on how to deal with many regulatory policy issues, because of the difficulties of adopting harmonized regulatory norms at the multilateral level. In the field of regulatory policy, therefore, it may be more appropriate to consider "competition among rules", but within the WTO principles of non-discrimination, as the way forward. In other words, RTAs provide scope for experimentation in different regions, which may have varying traditions, levels of development and existing structures. Trying to force all regions into one set of regulatory norms is likely to be difficult and counter-productive, just as trying to force all national approaches into one set of multilateral rules has faced opposition. However, as the case studies in this volume have shown, models developed in the European Union, NAFTA or the CER may well have limited application in other regions.

The procedural provisions in RTAs also tend to promote regulatory best practice among national regulators. The essence of "liberalization" in the new areas characterized by regulatory barriers is, as the OECD has pointed out, the use of regulatory best practices (OECD, 2000). Regional agreements can contribute to this because they are much more immediate than WTO or other multilateral rules. Thus, provisions to promote transparency, open decision-making and institution-building tend to be more effective at the regional level. Regional enforcement provisions then help to ensure that these provisions are effectively implemented. Such promotion of regulatory best practice through regional agreements is almost certainly positive because it does not lend itself to preference-building. This contrasts with RTA measures that extend substantive measures such as national treatment and MFN to a wider number of sectors. Here, regional preferences can be created and with them comes a potential for diversion.

RTAs provide a pathfinder and a learning function. This is especially important for developing countries, where RTAs can provide the time and space to make the domestic changes needed to engage more fully in the global trading system. If RTAs illustrate that market opening or liberalization are beneficial in the regional setting, this can help reduce opposition to wider multilateral liberalization. When liberalization is resisted for political or psychological reasons, such as fear of a neighbouring power in the case of Mexico, or Brazil and Argentina before the mid-1980s, regional initiatives remove one of the important blocks on autonomous economic development.

Because the RTAs are generally compatible with the substantive provisions of the WTO, increased membership of regional agreements will also strengthen the multilateral system, in the sense that more countries are signing up to the principles set out in the WTO. Examples of this would be increased membership of the Government Procurement Agreement as a result of EU enlargement or the de facto extension of the GPA provisions to countries in Latin America via NAFTA-based agreements, for example between the United States and Chile.

RTAs also bring about a degree of policy approximation, which helps to reduce the costs of market access for all suppliers, whether within or outside the region. The economic weight of the European Union and the United States tends to result in the regulatory norms of these two actors becoming the de facto or, as in the case of EU accession states, de jure requirement for their trading partners. This tendency could have negative implications if the smaller trading partners of the European Union and the United States are forced to adopt regulatory norms and practices or standards that are inappropriate for their level of development or that do not reflect their national policy preferences. The background case studies carried out for this project suggest that both the European Union and the United States tend to export their regulatory norms and standards. In the long run, the application of such norms should be beneficial to the developing countries concerned. The enhanced regulatory and institutional capacity they often imply may well also help improve market access to other markets. For example, the establishment of local conformance-testing facilities can be used to show conformance of goods with the standards in other countries. In the short term, however, the adoption of such regulatory norms imposes costs.

In a few instances the major actors appear to have sought to use regional agreements as a means of shaping future trade agendas to fit their policy preferences by setting precedents. This appears to be the case with the US–Jordan Agreement covering environment, labour standards and intellectual property. It also appears to be the case with the central role of competition in the Euro-Med Agreements, not to mention the attempt by Chile and Canada to establish a precedent of dispensing with anti-dumping actions for negotiations within the FTAA.

A multi-level process

The development of regimes and rules for dealing with regulatory barriers (in the cases considered here) suggests that a multi-level process is in operation in which there is considerable interaction between national (and subnational), regional, plurilateral and multilateral levels. There is also the level of private regimes, such as the work on international standards.[6] If this is the case, the relevant question to ask is not whether regional agreements are building or stumbling blocks, but what role regional agreements play in the multi-level process. Given the difficulties of developing multilateral rules for all policy issues, at least in the short term, regional and plurilateral agreements may have to play an important role. This is particularly the case in the "new" regulatory policy issues, where many developing countries may not yet be willing to accept inclusion in any single undertaking. If this is the case, then it becomes important to identify and apply best practice in regional and other levels of agreement. Such "best practice" would include a means of ensuring that regional agreements do not preclude future multilateral norms. In this respect, and drawing on the case studies considered, it would seem that the regional level (at least in terms of the European Union and NAFTA) has to date both implemented existing principles and concepts developed in the OECD or within GATT and provided models for how to improve wider multilateral liberalization.

Towards a model of "best practice" in regional agreements

It follows from the above that one aim in developing RTAs would be to ensure that regional agreements contribute to the multilateral process of tackling regulatory barriers to trade, on the one hand, and avoid precipitating regulatory regionalism, on the other. This raises the question of whether there is such a thing as "best practice" when negotiating regional agreements.

This leads to the further question of how best to structure regional agreements so that they contribute most effectively to this multi-level process. From the agreements analysed in the chapters in this volume, the following elements seem suitable for consideration when fleshing out what a model of best practice for regional agreements should look like:

- Regional agreements should concentrate on procedural measures, such as improved transparency, the use of clear predictable criteria for regulatory policy and open decision-making. These measures should promote regulatory reform and best practice and contribute to market opening. In this sense there is little likelihood that WTO-plus provisions of this kind in RTAs will create difficulties for future multilateral negotiations.
- Procedural measures should consist of effective transparency measures, including prior notification of major changes to regulatory law or practice.
- Regulatory/technical cooperation aimed at enhancing or building expertise and institutional infrastructure should be created for the adoption of regulatory best practice.
- Regional agreements should eschew detailed regulatory harmonization whenever possible. In so far as RTAs are WTO-plus (or go beyond other international standards), detailed harmonization of regulatory norms or standards retains the potential for creating regulatory regionalism. Harmonization may also not be suitable for all countries, given their level of development or national preferences.
- Regional agreements should have extension clauses that enable renegotiation when either party agrees to more favourable treatment with a third party.
- Mutual recognition offers a suitable long-term means of overcoming regulatory barriers to trade within RTAs, but the case studies discussed above suggest that such agreements require considerable effort and support in order to build the regulatory infrastructure needed in many countries. MRAs should be open to third parties that meet the qualifications laid down in the RTA on equivalence of objectives and conformity assessment.
- Ideally, regional agreements should ensure that independent review procedures exist for the regulatory policy areas covered by the RTA, and that legal persons have access to such review procedures.
- An effective regional agreement should include provision to ensure that anti-competitive practices do not develop following regulatory reform or deregulation.

Appendix

Table 12A.1. Investment (including establishment under services provisions)

		WTO	EU–Poland	EU–Mexico
Coverage	Sectoral coverage of NT and MFN provisions	Positive-list coverage of Mode 3 in GATS and TRIMs	Significantly WTO-plus Phased introduction of nearly full liberalization	In effect not covered
Procedural elements	Transparency	Limited owing to complex scheduling	Association Council to monitor implementation	Not covered
	Due process	Not applicable	Not applicable	Not applicable
	Institution-building	Not applicable	Not applicable	Not applicable
Substantive measures	Policy approximation	Prohibition of some performance requirements under TRIMS Sector-specific in GATS financial services and telecommunications	Significantly WTO-plus Application of the EU *acquis* across goods and services	None relating to investment
	Mutual recognition	Not applicable	Not applicable	Not applicable
	Reduced discretion	Only selective limitations on policy autonomy	WTO-plus, but safeguard measures for Poland provide some discretion	WTO-conform
Implementation and enforcement	Remedies and reviews	None	WTO-conform	WTO-conform
	Dispute settlement	Government to government under DSU	WTO-conform	WTO-conform
	Promotion and maintenance of competition		Significantly WTO-plus Fully fledged common policies	

Euro-Med	NAFTA	CCFTA	CER
No provisions	Significantly WTO-plus Negative-list schedules Goods and services covered	Significantly WTO-plus, as for NAFTA	WTO-conform No general investment measures
No provisions	WTO-plus owing to negative-list approach	WTO-plus owing to negative-list approach	No provisions
Not applicable Not applicable	Not applicable Not applicable	Not applicable Not applicable	Not applicable Not applicable
None	Slightly WTO-plus Some performance requirements prohibited, others allowed Some selective harmonization of provisions in services	As for NAFTA	No provisions
Not applicable	Not applicable	Not applicable	Not applicable
WTO-conform, i.e. limits on some performance requirements	Significantly WTO-plus	Significantly WTO-plus	WTO-conform
WTO-conform	WTO-conform	General horizontal measures	WTO-conform
WTO-conform	Significantly WTO-plus Investor–state dispute settlement	Significantly WTO-plus Investor–state dispute settlement	WTO-conform
WTO-plus Eventual adoption of EU policies	Slightly WTO-plus Requirement to have a national competition policy	Slightly WTO-plus as for NAFTA, but anti-dumping to be phased out	Significantly WTO-plus Positive comity and mutual recognition of national regulatory policies

Table 12A.2. Services (cross-border)

		WTO/GATS	EU–Poland
Coverage	Sectors	Combination of positive and negative listing	Slightly WTO/GATS-plus
Procedural elements	Transparency	Basic notification measures	GATS-compatible
	Due process		
	Institution-building		Technical assistance and support
Substantive provisions	Degree of policy approximation	NT and MFN with only selective approximation in financial services and tele-communications	GATS-plus with alignment to EU *acquis*
	Mutual recognition	Provided for under additional commitments	GATS-compatible
	Limits on discretion	Article VI wording provides considerable scope for discretion (outside sectors covered by the Annexes)	GATS-compatible
Implementation and enforcement	Reviews and remedies	None	None
	Dispute settlement	DSU	Association Council
	Promotion of competition	As in table 12A.1	

EU–Mexico	Euro-Med	NAFTA	CCFTA
Slightly GATS-plus in sector coverage Use of negative listing approach Review with view to increased coverage	GATS-compatible for WTO members (which means limited commitments for the Mediterranean Partner Countries; for others best endeavours only)	GATS-plus through use of negative-list approach	
GATS-compatible	GATS-compatible	GATS-compatible	
		GATS-plus Horizontal measures apply	
	Working Group on Services created		
GATS-conform	Basic GATS framework for countries not members of the WTO	NT and MFN with selected policy approximation in specific Chapters	
Commitment to negotiate after three years	No provisions	GATS-plus provision, including efforts to promote mutual recognition	
	GATS-conform	Possibly slightly GATS-plus owing to "policed national treatment" approach	
	None	WTO-plus Horizontal measures apply	
Bilateral dispute settlement	Association Council	Bilateral dispute settlement	

Table 12A.3. Technical barriers to trade and sanitary and phytosanitary measures

		WTO	EU–Poland	EU–Mexico
Coverage		Regulations and conformance covered by NT and MFN	WTO-plus Coverage of standards-making and subnational bodies	WTO-compatible (i.e. reaffir-mation of WTO)
Procedural elements	Transparency	Modest Notification of new technical regulations	WTO-plus Prior notification for technical regulations and standards	WTO-consistent
	Due process	Modest Other govern-ments have opportunity to comment	Significantly WTO-plus for other RTA members	WTO-consistent
	Institutional infrastructure	In effect very little	Significantly WTO-plus Cooperation, funding and twinning	Slightly WTO-plus
Substantive measures	Policy approximation	National treatment	Significantly WTO-plus Based on EU *acquis*	WTO-compatible
	Mutual recognition	Encouraged but no provisions	WTO-plus Ultimate objec-tive is mutual recognition of national regu-latory mea-sures	WTO-compatible Not provided for
	Containing discretion	Exceptions from NT for TBTs and SPS, lat-ter limited by requirement to use inter-national stan-dards	WTO-plus Tighter criteria for exceptions	WTO-consistent
Implementation and enforce-ment	Reviews and remedies	No concrete provisions	Significantly WTO-plus in the sense of central moni-toring by EU	WTO-consistent
	Dispute settlement	Government to government DSU	Slightly WTO-plus Conciliation in Association Council	WTO-plus Bilateral dispute settlement

Euro-Med	NAFTA	CCFTA	CER
WTO-compatible	WTO-compatible	Not covered	WTO-compatible
WTO-consistent	WTO-consistent	WTO-minus Covered only by horizontal provisions	WTO-plus Plus effective prior notification
WTO-consistent	Significantly WTO-plus Prior notification, access to regulatory process for interested parties		Significantly WTO-plus for other RTA partners
Moderately WTO-plus Technical assistance	Significantly WTO-plus Joint committee and technical assistance		WTO-compatible Regulatory cooperation
WTO-compatible Ultimate aim is approximation based on EU *acquis*	Slightly WTO-plus Approximation is an aim in selected sectors; others seek "compatibility"	Not covered	Significantly WTO-plus Approximation across the board Joint measures
WTO-compatible Aim of mutual recognition of conformance testing	Slightly WTO-plus Provisions for mutual recognition of test results	Not covered	Significantly WTO-plus Mutual recognition of national regulatory policies
WTO-consistent	WTO-consistent, with some areas possibly slipping below WTO level		WTO-consistent System based on mutual trust
WTO-consistent	Significantly WTO-plus Reviews and remedies for legal persons and government through consultations	Horizontal measures apply	WTO-consistent Government to government consultations
WTO-consistent and conciliation	WTO-plus Bilateral dispute settlement	WTO-plus Bilateral dispute settlement applies to horizontal measures	WTO-consistent

Table 12A.4. Government procurement

		WTO/GPA	EU–Poland	EU–Mexico
Coverage	Sectors	Limited Positive list	GPA-plus All sectors covered except defence	GPA-consistent
	Levels of government	Central government, public enterprises and subnational government on voluntary basis	GPA-plus All levels of government	GPA-consistent
	Signatories	Limited number of signatories to GPA	Poland required to sign GPA before accession to the EU	Mexico a non-signatory of GPA, locked in to GPA norms
Procedural provisions	Transparency	Detailed provisions	GPA-consistent provisions	GPA-consistent provisions, possibly to be enhanced through use of information technology
	Due process	Detailed procedural measures	GPA-consistent	GPA-consistent
	Institution-building	In effect none	Significantly GPA-plus for Poland	Slightly GPA-plus Cooperation through Special Committee
Substantive provisions	Policy approximation	GPA requires common procedures	GPA-consistent plus use of European/ international standards	GPA-consistent
	Mutual recognition	Not applicable	Not applicable	Not applicable
	Containing discretion	Limited GPA provides considerable flexibility	Perhaps GPA-plus	GPA-consistent
Implementation and enforcement	Remedies and reviews	Bid challenge provides access for aggrieved parties	GPA-consistent EU compliance provisions	GPA-consistent
	Dispute settlement	DSU available for signatories	Association Council	Bilateral dispute settlement
	Promoting competition	As for table 12A.1		

Euro-Med	NAFTA	CCFTA	CER
Potential for GPA-plus on selective basis (e.g. bilateral with Israel)	GPA-consistent, but with Mexican commitments below the GPA level	Not covered	GPA-plus Covers all sectors
GPA-minus Only objective of liberalization, but no provisions	GPA-consistent, but Canada not applying at sub-federal level	Not covered	GPA-plus Covers all levels of government
Only Israel signatory of GPA among EU partners	Mexico non-signatory; bound to effective GPA norms		Neither Australia nor New Zealand is a GPA signatory
Non-specified	GPA-consistent Provisions enhanced through use of information technology	Not covered	Broadly GPA-consistent in provision of information
Non-specified	GPA-consistent	Horizontal measures apply but too general to have any bearing	GPA-minus No standard procedures for contract award processing
Potential through Association Council	Significantly GPA-plus for Mexico	Not covered	None except through cooperation
None	GPA-consistent	Not covered	GPA-minus No common procedures
Not applicable	Not applicable		Not applicable
Not covered	GPA-consistent, but possibly more actions brought by companies	Not covered	GPA-minus Based on trust
Not covered	GPA-consistent	Not covered	GPA-minus
None	Bilateral NAFTA significant	Not covered	General consultation provisions

Notes

1. This strengthening of the GPA comes, however, at a time when there is dwindling support for the multilateralization of the GPA disciplines, which could be confirmed by developments in other regions, such as the Free Trade Area of the Americas.
2. The EU–Poland Europe Agreement includes provision for "bid challenge" by companies if they feel they have not been treated fairly in contract award procedures.
3. See chapter 6 on NAFTA, but also parts of chapters 4 and especially 7, which discuss some detailed provisions on NAFTA in the policy areas under consideration.
4. OECD guidelines on good regulatory practice and open international markets also place some emphasis on the "least trade restrictive measure" test (OECD, 1998).
5. See chapter 9, which argues that here is a case of regulatory regionalism.
6. The case studies in this volume do not cover such private regimes in any depth, but these are likely to play a growing role in regulatory responses to globalization.

REFERENCES

OECD (Organisation for Economic Co-operation and Development) (1998), *Regulatory Reform. Volume II: Thematic Studies*, Paris: OECD.

———— (2000), *Trade and Regulatory Reform: Insights from OECD Country Reviews and Other Analysis*, Working Party of the Trade Committee, TD/TC/WP(2000)21/Final 3, Paris, November.

Woolcock, Stephen (2001), "A Synthesis of the Results of Horizontal Case Studies in Technical Barriers to Trade, Public Procurement, Services and Investment", background paper for the European Commission funded project "Looking at Regional Agreements Afresh", April.

Contributors

Tomas Baert is EU and government affairs representative of a large multinational science company of US parentage, based in Brussels. Prior to that, he worked at the Enterprise Directorate-General of the European Commission as a trainee, where he was involved in several bilateral and regional trade negotiations from an industrial/sectoral perspective. He has an M.Sc. in the Politics of the World Economy from the London School of Economics and Political Science.

Magnus Feldmann is a Ph.D. candidate in Political Economy and Government at Harvard University. His research interests are international political economy and trade policy, comparative politics and political economy, and comparative economic systems and post-socialist transition. His recent publications include "The Fast Track from the Soviet Union to the World Economy: External Liberalization in Estonia and Latvia", *Government and Opposition*, 36(4), 2001; "From the Soviet Union to the European Union: Estonian Trade Policy, 1991–2000", *The World Economy*, 25(1), 2002 (with Razeen Sally).

Brigid Gavin is currently Research Fellow at the Comparative Regional Integration Studies Programme of the United Nations University (UNU/CRIS) in Bruges, Belgium. Previously she has been Lecturer in the Economics of European Integration at the Europa Institute, University of Basle, Switzerland, worked for the Permanent Delegation of the European Commission to the International Organizations in Geneva, and has acted as Policy Advisor to the Greenpeace EU Unit in Brussels.

Sebastián Herreros has served since 1996 at the Economic Directorate of the Chilean Ministry of Foreign Affairs, where he has worked in the European Union and WTO Departments. Between October 2001 and September 2002 he was head of the WTO Department. In October 2002 he was posted as a Counsellor to the Chilean Mission at the WTO in Geneva. He holds a B.A. in Business Administration with a Minor in Economics from the Catholic University of Chile and an M.Sc. in the Politics of the World Economy from the London School of Economics and Political Science. He has lectured in International Political Economy at the University of Chile's Institute of International Studies and his research interests are centred on the formulation of trade policy, particularly in developing countries, as well as on the regulation of international economic issues.

Grant Isaac is Associate Professor of Biotechnology Management at the University of Saskatchewan, Canada. His current research centres on (1) examining the efficiency and effectiveness of the Risk Analysis approach to regulating new technologies, with a focus on regulatory principles such as the precautionary principle and the substantial equivalence principle, and (2) examining the implications of these regulatory regimes for international trade policy. His recent publications include two books – *Agricultural Biotechnology and Transatlantic Trade: Regulatory Barriers to GM Crops* (CABI Publishing, 2002) and *Food Safety and International Competitiveness: The Case of Beef* (CABI Publishing, 2001, with John

Spriggs) – as well as articles in academic and professional journals including *The World Economy*, *AgBioForum, ISUMA – Canadian Journal of Policy Research* and *AgBiotech Bulletin*.

Luk Van Langenhove has been Director since 1 October 2001 of the Comparative Regional Integration Studies Programme of the United Nations University (UNU/CRIS) in Bruges, Belgium, and teaches at the Vrije Universiteit Brussel (VUB). He was Deputy Secretary-General of the Belgian Federal Services for Scientific, Technical and Cultural Affairs from May 1995 to September 2001. Between 1992 and 1995, he was Deputy Chief of Cabinet of the Belgian Federal Minister of Science Policy. Before that he worked as a researcher and a lecturer at the VUB. He has published on many different social sciences issues.

Joakim Reiter is Trade Policy Analyst at the Ministry for Foreign Affairs, International Trade Policy Department, in Sweden. During 2000 and 2001, he participated as Swedish delegate in the negotiations between the European Union and Chile, as well as between the European Union and Mercosur. Since 1999, he has also been a Ph.D. candidate at Lund University. His research interests are centred on international political economy, with a focus on "new" trade issues and developing countries. His recent publications include a co-edited book with Christer Jönsson, *Handelspolitik i förändring* (Centre for Business and Policy Studies, 2002) and "Financial Globalization, Corporate Ownership and the End of Swedish Corporatism?", *New*

Political Economy (forthcoming). He has previously worked as Special Advisor on globalization issues to the Trade Minister's Cabinet and Research Officer at the Swedish National Board of Trade.

Bertrall Ross received his M.Sc. in the Politics of the World Economy from the London School of Economics and Political Science in 2001 and is currently pursuing further graduate studies in Economics and Public Policy at the Woodrow Wilson School of Public and International Affairs at Princeton University. His major areas of concentration are trade policy and legal and regulatory policy towards markets. He has worked with the United States Agency for International Development in Manila, the Philippines, where he focused on trade initiatives involving the tuna industry in the Mindanao region. Prior to his studies at Princeton, he worked at the Center for Strategic and International Studies in Washington DC where he analysed the U.S.–African Growth and Opportunity Act and legislation to reduce the debt burden of Highly Indebted Poor Countries (HIPC). He contributed to an article written by Vladimir Kolossov and John O' Loughlin entitled "Pseudo-States as Harbingers of a New Geopolitics: The Example of the Transdniester Moldovan Republic" while serving as a research assistant at the Institute of Behavioral Science in Boulder, Colorado.

Gary P. Sampson worked at UNCTAD between 1975 and 1983. From 1984 to 1986 he was Senior Fellow in Economic Policy at the Reserve Bank of Australia and Professorial Fellow at the Centre of Policy Studies at Monash University. He was appointed Director at the GATT in 1987 and Director at the WTO in 1995. He is presently Professor of International Economic Governance at the Institute of Advanced Studies at the United Nations University and Senior Counsellor at the WTO. He teaches on a regular basis at the Melbourne Business School and at INSEAD in France. He has written extensively on areas relating to international economic governance; his most recent books include *Trade, Environment and the WTO: The Post Seattle Agenda* (Overseas Development Council, Policy Essay No. 27, 2000) and *The Role of the World Trade Organization in Global Governance* (United Nations University Press, 2001).

Julius Sen is a Tutorial Fellow and Ph.D. candidate at the London School of Economics and Political Science, where he is researching into trade policy in India and teaching international political economy. Before joining the LSE he served in the Indian Civil Service. His recent publications include *Negotiating the TRIPS Agreement: India's Experience and Some Domestic Policy Issues* (a Research Report for the CUTS Centre for International Trade, Economics, and the Environment, 2001), and *The WTO and the World Trading System* (with Heidi Ullrich and Thanos Mergoupis; Polity Press, forthcoming).

Stephen Woolcock is a Lecturer in International Relations at the London School of Economics and Political Science, where he teaches international political economy, economic diplomacy and the politics of international trade. He also helps to run the International Trade Policy Unit at the LSE, which conducts research on current trade issues and runs in-service programmes for trade negotiators. His research interests are centred on the regulation of integrating markets, both regionally within regional integration agreements and globally within the international trade and investment regimes. His recent publications include "Investment in the World Trade Organization" in Klaus Deutsch (ed.), *The European Union in the Millennium Round* (Cambridge University Press, 2001), *The Use of the Precautionary Principle in the European Union and Its Impact on Trade Relations* (Centre for European Policy Studies, 2001) and *The New Economic Diplomacy: Decision-making and Negotiations in International Economic Relations* (Ashgate, G8 Global Governance series, 2003). Before joining the LSE in 1994, Woolcock was Senior Research Fellow at the Royal Institute of International Affairs (Chatham House), Deputy Director for International Affairs at the Confederation of British Industry and Paul Henri Spaak Fellow at the Center for International Affairs, Harvard University.

Index

Catalogue Request

Name: _____

Address: _____

Tel: _____

Fax: _____

E-mail: _____

To receive a catalogue of UNU Press publications kindly photocopy this form and send or fax it back to us with your details. You can also e-mail us this information. Please put "Mailing List" in the subject line.

United Nations
University Press

53-70, Jingumae 5-chome
Shibuya-ku, Tokyo 150-8925, Japan
Tel: +81-3-3499-2811 Fax: +81-3-3406-7345
E-mail: sales@hq.unu.edu http://www.unu.edu